ADVANCE PRAISE FOR *RULING EMANCIPATED SLAVES AND INDIGENOUS SUBJECTS*

"Owolabi demonstrates that forced-settlement colonies are a distinctive form of colonial rule, fostering economic and political trajectories that diverge from—and surpass—the trajectories of other formerly extractive colonies. This counter-intuitive finding offers an important corrective to usual understandings of colonialism and development."

—**John Gerring**, University of Texas at Austin

"In this book, Owolabi asks an intriguing question and, through an impressive multimethod analysis of several former empires, offers a compelling answer linked to the institutional legacies of colonialism. *Ruling Emancipated Slaves and Indigenous Subjects* is a must-read for any scholar interested in the long-term impact of colonialism."

—**Matthew Lange**, Professor of Sociology, McGill University

"A bold, provocative, and persuasive account of the lasting effects of colonial rule. *Longue durée* arguments are exceedingly difficult to make yet *Ruling Emancipated Slaves and Indigenous Subjects* delivers on its ambitious goal: to show the importance of emancipation during the colonial era for post-colonial development and democratization."

—**Adria Lawrence**, author of *Imperial Rule and the Politics of Nationalism: Anti-Colonial Protest in the French Empire*

"This excellent book rethinks the consequences of extractive colonial institutions. Analyzing the importance of early legal rights, Owolabi explains the puzzle of why countries in the West Indies have experienced better development outcomes than those in West Africa. This book is a must-read for anyone interested in colonialism, development, and democracy."

—**Jack Paine**, Associate Professor of Political Science, Emory University

D1570141

Ruling Emancipated Slaves and Indigenous Subjects

*The Divergent Legacies of Forced Settlement
and Colonial Occupation in the Global South*

OLUKUNLE P. OWOLABI

OXFORD
UNIVERSITY PRESS

OXFORD
UNIVERSITY PRESS

Oxford University Press is a department of the University of Oxford. It furthers
the University's objective of excellence in research, scholarship, and education
by publishing worldwide. Oxford is a registered trade mark of Oxford University
Press in the UK and certain other countries.

Published in the United States of America by Oxford University Press
198 Madison Avenue, New York, NY 10016, United States of America.

© Oxford University Press 2023

Library of Congress Cataloging-in-Publication Data
Names: Owolabi, Olukunle P. (Olukunle Patrick), author.
Title: Ruling emancipated slaves and indigenous subjects :
the divergent legacies of forced settlement and colonial occupation in
the global south / Olukunle P. Owolabi.
Description: New York, NY : Oxford University Press, [2023] |
Includes bibliographical references and index.
Identifiers: LCCN 2022054523 (print) | LCCN 2022054524 (ebook) |
ISBN 9780197673034 (paperback) | ISBN 9780197673027 (hardback) |
ISBN 9780197673058 (epub)
Subjects: LCSH: Europe—Colonies—Administration. |
Europe—Colonies—Social conditions. | Developing countries—Social
conditions. | Postcolonialism—Developing countries. |
Indigenous peoples—Developing countries—Social conditions. |
Indigenous peoples—Legal status, laws, etc.—Developing countries. |
Children of freed persons—Developing countries—Social conditions. |
Children of freed persons—Legal status, laws, etc.—Developing countries. |
Forced migration—Europe—Colonies—America. |
Forced migration—Europe—Colonies—Africa.
Classification: LCC JV152 .O95 2023 (print) | LCC JV152 (ebook) |
DDC 325/.341—dc23/eng/20230103
LC record available at https://lccn.loc.gov/2022054523

DOI: 10.1093/oso/9780197673027.001.0001

Paperback printed by Marquis Book Printing, Canada
Hardback printed by Bridgeport National Bindery, Inc., United States of America

To my parents, Titus and Paula Owolabi, who worked hard to provide the best education for my siblings and I, and to show us the best aspects of our African and Caribbean heritage. E şe gan ni. Thank you for your enduring love, wisdom, and support. And to my wife, Catalina, whose love and encouragement sustained me through this project. Te amo con todo mi corazón.

Contents

Illustrations

Figures

Maps

Tables

Acknowledgments

This book has been a labor of love that has consumed most of my intellectual energy for the past 15 years. The core ideas of this book were first outlined in graduate seminar papers supervised by Michael Coppedge and the late Guillermo O'Donnell, when I was a doctoral student at the University of Notre Dame. My dissertation research began as an exploration of the long-term consequences of British forced settlement and British colonial occupation for state-building and postcolonial democratization in the Global South. The project expanded into its current form after I encountered Matthew Lange's influential research on the divergent developmental legacies of direct and indirect British rule. One of my dissertation committee members, Naunihal Singh, suggested that I take advantage of my area studies expertise and multilingual proficiency to examine the developmental legacies of forced settlement and colonial occupation across multiple colonial empires. I initially balked at the idea of tackling such a formidable project, but I was touched by the generous support of my professors, friends, and mentors at the University of the Notre Dame. I would like to thank my dissertation adviser, Michael Coppedge, and my committee members Scott Mainwaring, Robert Fishman, and Naunihal Singh, for their expert advice and tireless support during my long years of study at the University of Notre Dame. I would also like to thank Fr. Paulinus Odozor, Fr. Robert Dowd, Anibal Pérez-Liñan, Dianne Pinderhughes, Jaimie Bleck, Paul Ocobock, Guillermo Trejo, Andy Gould, Ted Beatty, Jim McAdams, Frances Hagopian, Carlos Gervasoni, and Michael Driessen for their mentorship and friendship during my PhD years and afterward. I could not have asked for a more supportive group of intellectual mentors, and I am eternally grateful for your encouragement, friendship, and critical feedback that sustained and nourished me throughout this project.

One of the joys of writing this book was the significant archival and library research that has enriched the comparative-historical evidence in the latter chapters. Consequently, I would like to thank the various funding agencies and research institutes that enabled me to conduct library and archival research in the United Kingdom, France, Portugal, Senegal, and Cape Verde. My PhD research was partially funded by a generous doctoral fellowship from the Social Sciences and Humanities Research Council of Canada. The University of Notre Dame's Kellogg Institute for International Studies provided a seed money grant for my first research trip to the British Library and the UK National Archives in the summer of 2007. The Kellogg Institute also provided a dissertation fellowship that funded library and archival research in London and Lisbon in the Fall Semesters of 2008 and 2009. A summer research grant from Notre Dame's Nanovic Institute for European Studies funded my first research trips to the Bibliothèque Nationale de France (Paris) and the French colonial archives in Aix-en-Provence in the summer of 2009. I also benefited from generous research funding from Villanova University, where I expanded my research as an assistant professor. I am very grateful for the faculty development grant that supported additional archival and library research in London, Paris, and Aix-en-Provence during the summer of 2013. Villanova University also provided a Research Support Grant that funded my research trips to London, Paris, Senegal, and Cape Verde in the Summer and Fall Semesters of 2015. I also received a generous Subvention of Publication grant from Villanova University that covered the copyright costs for the book's cover art and other incidental publication expenses. This book would never have been completed without the generous financial and research support that I have received from various sources over the years.

Completing an academic book of this scope can be a lonely endeavor filled with moments of extreme anxiety, self-doubt, and even self-hate. I've had more than my share of these moments over the years, so I am extremely grateful for all the words of encouragement and support that I have received from fellow academics along the way. I would like to thank everyone who offered encouraging words or critical feedback on work that I presented at academic workshops and conferences in the United States, Canada, Spain, and the United Kingdom. Over the years, I have received incredible feedback, both generous and critical, from leading scholars of colonialism and development, including Matthew Lange, James Mahoney, Mahmood Mamdani, Robert Woodberry, Adria Lawrence, Maya Tudor, David Laitin, and Jack Paine. Each of you has inspired me, and at times challenged me, to refine my core concepts, sharpen my arguments, deepen my statistical analyses, and consider alternative theoretical frameworks that have enriched the scope and rigor of my work. John Darwin, Laurence Whitehead, Nancy Bermeo, and Alexandra Scacco provided critical feedback at Nuffield College, Oxford, where I presented earlier drafts of my research in 2009. Matthew Lange encouraged me to push beyond the confines of democratization literature, and to think more broadly about other aspects of development that are shaped by colonial legacies. Robert Woodberry encouraged me to think more critically about the developmental legacies of Protestant missionary evangelization in colonial and postcolonial states. He also nominated one of my earlier working papers for the American Political Science Association's "Best Paper" award in Comparative Democratization in 2012. I would also like to thank the anonymous reviewers that provided critical feedback that facilitated the publication of my earlier work in *Comparative Politics* and the Kellogg Institute for International Studies' Working Paper series. The data analysis in Chapter 4 and the data appendices expand my research from an earlier paper, "Literacy and Democracy Despite Slavery," that was published in *Comparative Politics* in 2015.

Many kind and generous librarians, archivists, and fellow academics helped me to locate important primary documents and secondary literature during my research trips to the UK, France, Portugal, Senegal, and Cape Verde. Mandy Banton was particularly helpful in helping me to find, locate, and navigate the rich collection of historical records at the UK National Archives. I also received advice and support from my former professors and mentors at Oxford University, including Alan Knight, Laurence Whitehead, and the late Abdul Raufu Mustapha. I would also like to thank Tiago Fernandes, Gerhart Seibert, and Antonio Costa Pinto for their advice and insights on Portugal colonialism during my research trips to Lisbon in 2009. Rita Almeida de Carvalho, Pedro Tavares de Almeida, and Isabel Gomes helped me to locate little-known historical records from the colonial elections to the Portuguese National Assembly between 1911 and 1973. These records have significantly enriched the historical evidence in Chapter 6, which highlights the more inclusive nature of colonial citizenship in Cape Verde relative to other Portuguese African colonies. I am also eternally grateful to friendly and professional staff who provided access to electoral data and census records at the National Historical Archives of Cape Verde.

Closer to home, I am very grateful for the support of my faculty colleagues who patiently supported and encouraged the completion of this work at Villanova University. I am especially grateful to the three graduate research assistants that supported me during the seven long years that it took for me to write, edit, and revise three drafts of this book. Thank you, Willis Orlando, Jillian Andres, and Lirona Joshi, for your research support, encouragement, and friendship during these years. I also received generous feedback and encouragement from the graduate students in my seminar course on Colonialism, Institutions, and Development. Teaching and mentoring graduate and undergraduate students has been the most rewarding aspect of my academic career, and I am very grateful for the friendship, encouragement, and critical feedback that I have received from current and former students over the years. I also want to acknowledge the Villanova faculty colleagues, friends, and mentors that have supported and encouraged me over the years. Special thanks to Maghan Keita, Chiji Akoma, Theo Arapis, Eric Lomazoff, David Barrett, Camille Burge, Catherine Warrick, Jennifer Dixon, Cera Murtagh, Mark Schrad, Christine Palus, and Mike and Anna Moreland for your friendship, advice, and support. If I have forgotten to mention any Villanova colleagues here, thank you for your kind words, your support, and your encouragement.

I would also like to thank Jack Paine and Matthew Lange for their extensive feedback on two earlier drafts of my book manuscript. Both reviewers encouraged me to expand my chapter on French colonial legacies, and Matthew

Lange encouraged me to push beyond the "usual suspects" to include some little-known cases like the Comoros Islands. Matthew Lange also encouraged me to write about the legacies of mixed plantation colonization for Afro-descendants in Brazil, Cuba, and the southern United States. His extensive feedback contributed to significant improvements in the third draft of my manuscript, which was submitted to Oxford University Press in 2021. I would like to thank David McBride, and the entire team at Oxford University Press, for your support, encouragement, and professionalism. I was pleasantly surprised by the smoothness of OUP's review process, and I would like to thank the third anonymous reviewer whose generous feedback complimented the earlier reviews of my book manuscript. It has been a joy to work with OUP, and I will be eternally grateful to David McBride for taking a chance on a little-known emerging scholar from an R2 university.

I would also like to thank all the family and friends across the globe whose love, friendship, encouragement, and support sustained me during the lengthy process of researching, writing, and editing this book. I would like to thank Auntie Bose and Uncle Tunde, Auntie Bisi, Gbenga and Yewande Falowo, Luciano Ciravegna, and Sara Roberts, whose friendship, laughter, and hospitality sustained and nourished me during my research trips to London. Thank you, Henri-Michel Yéré and Rachel Kantrowitz, for the lifelong friendships that developed from our research at the French colonial archives. Special thanks to Father Paulinus Odozor, Fabian and Francesca Udoh, Daniele Puccinelli, Carlos Gervasoni, Michael Driessen, Luca and Jen Cottini, Daniel and Suur Ayangeakaa, Ibrahim Garba, Annie Rashidi-Mulumba, Lakwame Anyane-Yeboa, Jonathan Richardson, and Kate Schuenke and Fredo Lucien for the lifelong friendships that began during our shared time at the University of Notre Dame. I also owe an enormous debt of gratitude to the celebrated Cape Verdean singer, Tété Alhino, and her husband, Enrique Aguirre, for hosting me during my 2015 research trip to Cape Verde. I enjoyed meeting your entire family, and I will never forget the enriching conversations, food, music, and laughter that we shared over breakfast and lunch, with Enrique, Diego, and Sara. All of you brought joy, laughter, music, great food, and unforgettable memories into my life when I needed them most.

Last, and most importantly, I would like to thank my parents, Paula and Titus Owolabi; my brother, Kola; my sister, Kemi; my brother-in-law, Lance; my nephew and niece, Mateo and Shiloh; my aunt and uncle, Erica Mapp and Alan Bass; my cousin Chloe Bass and her new husband, James McAnally; my best friend Adrian Brathwaite (and the entire Brathwaite clan); my extended family in Trinidad, London, and Nigeria; my lifelong family friends Ibukun, Jola, and Femi Omole; and my wife Catalina and her entire family in Colombia, Spain, and Canada. My wife Catalina also played an indispensable role in designing and formatting the figures and flowcharts that appear in this book. I am very blessed to have such a loving, supportive, and immensely talented wife, whose strengths make up for my weaknesses. To Catalina, *muchísimas gracias por todo tu amor y apoyo!* To my parents, siblings, in-laws, and extended family in Toronto, New York, South Bend (Indiana), London, Nigeria, Trinidad, and Colombia, I am eternally grateful for your love, laughter, and unconditional support, laughter, and emotional support. Thank you, also for your generous hospitality, music, and nourishing food that have kept me close to my African, Caribbean, and Hispanic cultural heritage. I could not have completed this book without your encouragement and words of wisdom that have sustained me and kept me grounded during the ups and downs of academic research, writing, and publishing. Thank you for everything! *E ṣe gan ni!*

Abbreviations

ANC	African National Congress (South Africa)
APC	All People's Congress (Sierra Leone)
CMS	Christian Missionary Society
CODESRIA	Council for the Development of Social Science Research in Africa
DC	District Commissioner (Sierra Leone)
DOM	French Overseas Departments / Départements d'Outre-Mer
FF	French Francs
FHIP	Freedom House Imputed Polity Scores
FLN	National Liberation Front (Algeria) / Front de Libération Nationale
GDP	Gross Domestic Product
HDI	Human Development Index (United Nations)
JHA	Jamaica House of Assembly
JLP	Jamaica Labour Party
MDRM	Democratic Movement for Malagasy Restoration (Madagascar) / Mouvement Démocratique de la Rénovation Malgache
MpD	Movement for Democracy (Cape Verde) / Movimento para a Democracia
MPLA	People's Movement for the Liberation of Angola / Movimento Popular de Libertação de Angola
NA	Native Authorities (Sierra Leone)
NCSL	National Council of Sierra Leone
PAICV	African Party for the Independence of Cape Verde / Partido Africano para a Independência do Cabo Verde
PAIGC	African Party for the Independence of Guinea-Bissau and Cape Verde / Partido Africano para a Independência da Guiné e Cabo Verde
PNM	People's National Movement (Trinidad and Tobago)
PNP	People's National Party (Jamaica)
PT	Workers' Party (Brazil) / Partido dos Trabalhadores
RUF	Revolutionary United Front (Sierra Leone)
SLPP	Sierra Leone People's Party
TOM	French Overseas Territories / Territoires d'Outre-Mer
UNC	United National Congress (Trinidad and Tobago)
UNECA	United Nations Economic Commission for Africa
V-DEM	Varieties of Democracy
VIF	Variance Inflation Factors

1

Introduction

Forced Settlement, Colonial Occupation, and the Historical Roots of Divergent Development in the Global South

There was a lively and celebratory atmosphere in Port-of-Spain, Trinidad, on August 31, 2012, when the twin-island Caribbean republic celebrated its fiftieth year of independence from British rule. The independence jubilee began with the festive calypso music and rhythms of the national police band and members of the Trinidad and Tobago Defense Forces marching through the crowded streets of the capital city. Trinidad and Tobago's golden jubilee celebration was not only pageantry and festive calypso music: it was also a celebration of the political and development achievements that distinguished the twin-island Caribbean nation from the majority of developing countries that emerged from Western colonial domination after World War II. Prime Minister Kamla Persad-Bissessar publicly acknowledged her country's "steadfast . . . commitment to . . . democracy, . . . the rule of law, and . . . the belief that all men and women are created equal and endowed with inalienable rights," as she addressed the attendees in Queen's Park Savannah (Caribbean Journal 2012). The prime minister also paid homage to the country's independence leaders, who enshrined a political culture of respect and social tolerance that sustained more than five decades of effective democratic governance in a country with significant racial, ethnic, and religious diversity. These are remarkable accomplishments for a country that emerged from an exploitative colonial system that lasted more than four centuries.

The Republic of Trinidad and Tobago is the southernmost nation in the Caribbean, and it consists of two islands where European colonists established sugar plantations with imported African slaves and South Asian indentured laborers. Virtually the entire population of the smaller island, Tobago, are descendants of enslaved Africans who were brought to the island by English, French, and Dutch colonists during the seventeenth and eighteenth centuries.[1] Trinidad's colonial development was somewhat less dependent on imported slave labor, but the island's French Creole planters imported 150,000 South Asian indentured laborers to maintain their agricultural plantations following

Ruling Emancipated Slaves and Indigenous Subjects. Olukunle P. Owolabi, Oxford University Press.
© Oxford University Press 2023. DOI: 10.1093/oso/9780197673027.003.0001

the abolition of slavery in the 1830s (Engerman 2012, 598). Despite this brutal history of coercive labor migration and labor-repressive plantation agriculture, Trinidad and Tobago is one of the most successful developing countries that gained independence after World War II. Today, the twin-island republic boasts a highly educated, multiethnic population that supports a dynamic energy-based economy and a thriving financial sector with close ties to the United States, Latin America, and other Caribbean markets. The islands' diverse population enjoys one of the highest living standards in the developing world, as the country's oil and gas reserves are effectively managed in ways that promote economic growth and human well-being.[2] The country has also experienced several decades of robust parliamentary democracy with regular electoral alternation between competing political parties that represent and mobilize voters from the country's largest ethnic groups.[3]

The Caribbean island of Barbados provides another example of inclusive human development and effective democratic governance in a postcolonial state with a brutal history of forced settlement. Between 1660 and 1810, Barbados' English colonists transported more than half a million enslaved Africans to work, and often die, on the island's sugar plantations. Barbados' surface area is tiny—less than one-tenth the size of Trinidad and smaller than US cities like Houston, New York, or Chicago. Nevertheless, Barbados' English colonists imported more enslaved Africans than the total number of slave shipments to the entire United States during a much longer historical period (Eltis and Richardson 2010, 18).[4] Enslaved African laborers suffered untold abuses on Barbados' colonial plantations in the colony: demographic data suggest that most died from disease, overwork, torture, starvation, or suicide within a few short years of their arrival. The living conditions for enslaved Africans in Barbados were so appalling that the island's entire population barely exceeded 100,000 inhabitants when slavery was abolished in the 1830s (Engerman and Higman 1997, 50). Given Barbados' brutal history of forced settlement and plantation slavery, one could reasonably expect to find the kind of impoverishment and underdevelopment that persists in Haiti or in many parts of sub-Saharan Africa. Instead, Barbados also boasts a strong record of human development, outperforming nearby Trinidad and Tobago on key indicators of human well-being, including educational attainment and life expectancy at birth (United Nations Development Program 2016). Barbados also boasts a thriving parliamentary democracy that has generated seven decades of electoral alternation between competing political parties. Today, Freedom House, a US-based political agency, recognizes Barbados as one of the "freest" countries on the planet.[5]

Directly across the Atlantic from the Eastern Caribbean, the little-known Cape Verdean islands provide another striking example of postcolonial development and democratization in an archipelago nation that was colonized with imported slave labor. These "Creole" African islands were uninhabited when the first Portuguese colonists arrived in the 1460s and populated the region with African slaves from the nearby Guinea Coast. These were the first islands where European colonists established agricultural plantations with enslaved African labor prior to Christopher Columbus' first voyage to the New World in 1492. Nevertheless, the expansion of agricultural plantations in tropical regions of the New World generated an unprecedented demand for enslaved African labor after 1600, and the Cape Verdean islands became an important supply and refueling station for slave ships crossing the Atlantic. Slavery was ultimately abolished in the Cape Verdean islands after 1869, when Portuguese imperialists shifted their attention toward consolidating their political control over indigenous Africans on the mainland. Thereafter, the Cape Verdean islands became a forgotten colonial outpost in the Atlantic Ocean: Portuguese administrative neglect and poor resource management generated a devastating cycle of famines that claimed more than 80,000 Cape Verdean lives between 1860 and 1950. The physical and economic devastation of the Cape Verdean islands compelled tens of thousands of Cape Verdeans to "volunteer" for indentured plantation labor in other Portuguese African colonies during the first half of the twentieth century. Upon gaining independence in 1975, Cape Verde was the second poorest country in Africa, and its government was controlled by a Marxist liberation party that established authoritarian political control and restricted electoral competition. Despite these inauspicious beginnings, the country has experienced several decades of sustained economic growth that generated significant improvements in education, health, and poverty reduction after independence. These improvements in human well-being generated popular demands for democracy, and Cape Verde was one of the first African countries to introduce multiparty elections and consolidate democracy after 1990. By the early 2000s, the Creole archipelago nation was widely regarded as "the most democratic country in Africa" (Baker 2006).

In contrast to the successful record of postcolonial development and democratic consolidation in Cape Verde, Barbados, and Trinidad and Tobago, some of the poorest and most underdeveloped countries on the planet are located at similar tropical latitudes, along the "Guinea Coast" of West Africa. This coastline stretches from Senegal's Cassamance region to present-day Sierra Leone and Liberia, directly adjacent to the nearby Cape Verdean islands. European explorers first arrived in this region during the 1460s, when Portuguese colonists settled the nearby Cape Verdean islands with enslaved Africans whom they kidnapped from the Guinea Coast. The entire coastline and adjacent interior hinterlands were dramatically transformed by the transatlantic slave trade, which transported more than 12 million enslaved Africans to the New World between 1500 and 1860. Following the abolition of slavery in the New World, the Guinea Coast of West Africa was carved up into British, French, and Portuguese colonies that controlled their indigenous African subjects with significant labor coercion and political repression.

Many of these countries maintained repressive forms of political control following their independence from colonial rule. For example, the independence leader of the Republic of Guinea, Ahmed Sekou Touré, established a repressive dictatorship that endured for 26 years after his country's independence from French rule in 1958. Neighboring Sierra Leone experienced three successive military coups within its first decade of independence from British rule in 1961. These military coups ushered in a brutal single-party dictatorship that plundered the country's mineral wealth and devastated its economy during the 1970s and 1980s. The impoverished West African nation was later plunged into a devastating civil war that claimed more than 50,000 lives during the 1990s. Further north, Guinea-Bissau's hard-won independence from Portugal followed a brutal anticolonial war that lasted from 1963 until 1974. Thousands of Cape Verdeans participated in Guinea-Bissau's independence war, and the two countries were initially governed by the same political party. Nevertheless, Guinea-Bissau has been devastated by significant regime instability and persistent underdevelopment after gaining independence from Portugal. Its independence government was toppled in a military coup in 1980, and the country experienced two decades of predatory authoritarian rule that culminated in a civil war that ended with foreign military intervention by French and African Union troops.

The persistent underdevelopment of impoverished West African states like Sierra Leone, Guinea, and Guinea-Bissau provides a stark contrast to the comparatively successful Caribbean islands like Barbados and Trinidad and Tobago and Creole African islands where European colonists established agricultural plantations with imported African slaves. The diverse developmental trajectories of postcolonial states in the black Atlantic world exposes an important empirical puzzle that has not been sufficiently examined in existing empirical studies on the developmental legacies of colonialism. The dominant assumption from existing literature is that coercive labor practices and extractive economic institutions hindered the long-term development and postcolonial democratization of colonial states with limited European settlement (see Sokoloff and Engerman 2000; Acemoglu, Johnson, and Robinson 2001, 2002; Acemoglu and Robinson 2012). Many existing studies also demonstrate favorable developmental outcomes in former British colonies relative to French or Iberian colonies (La Porta et al. 1998, 1999; Grier 1997, 1999; Brown 2000; Lee and Paine 2019a). Nevertheless, these studies overlook an important conceptual distinction between forced settlement and colonial occupation as distinctive modes of imperial control in the Global South. This conceptual distinction is important because of the favorable developmental trajectories of forced settlement colonies, where European colonists established agricultural plantations with imported African slaves, relative to colonies of occupation, where Europeans exploited the labor and natural resources of indigenous colonial subjects. To a surprising degree that is obscured by existing studies, my research demonstrates more inclusive patterns of state-building and human development—specifically, educational attainment, life expectancy at birth, economic development, and postcolonial democratization—in forced settlement colonies relative to continental African states and other Global South countries that emerged from colonial occupation after World War II (see Owolabi 2010, 2014, 2015).

I first experienced the contrasting legacies of forced settlement and colonial occupation as the Canadian-born child of immigrant parents from Trinidad and Tobago and Nigeria. During the early 1980s, my father established a medical hospital in Nigeria with his childhood best friend, and our two families relocated from Toronto, Canada, to the provincial town of Ilesha, in southwestern Nigeria. The 1970s oil boom imploded shortly after our arrival in Nigeria, and the resulting economic crisis exacerbated ethnic, religious, and political tensions within the country. In fact, my first political memory was a military coup that ended Nigeria's short-lived second episode of democratic rule on December 31, 1983. These were challenging years to live in Nigeria: economic and social ills like malaria, electricity power cuts, water shortages, and widespread corruption were routine features of everyday life, even for relatively privileged families with professional middle-class jobs. These developmental challenges were far less prevalent in Trinidad and Tobago, where we spent several weeks visiting my mother's family in August 1985. Even as a seven-year-old child, it was clear to me that economic and social goods were more broadly distributed in Trinidad: the electricity was stable, the roads were paved, and there was no need to take antimalaria medication. These contrasting developmental trajectories of Trinidad and Nigeria are permanently etched in my memory because my family's return to Nigeria was delayed by the sixth military coup in Nigeria's history, on August 27, 1985. These childhood memories generated unanswered questions that motivated my graduate studies and subsequent research on the divergent legacies of forced settlement and colonial occupation in the black Atlantic world and across the Global South.

The Divergent Legacies of Forced Settlement and Colonial Occupation

My research introduces an important conceptual distinction between forced settlement and colonial occupation as distinct modes of imperial domination among Global South countries and territories that emerged from colonial rule after World War II.[6] I define forced settlement as the pattern of imperial domination in which European colonists developed agricultural plantations in newly settled tropical regions using imported African slaves and/or Asian indentured labor (see Owolabi 2010, 2014, 2015). This pattern of colonization was established in Creole African islands like Cape Verde and Mauritius, and in tropical regions of the New World, where the descendants of emancipated slaves and Asian indentured laborers account for more than three-quarters of the population living in these territories today. These New World territories were intensively colonized after their indigenous populations were decimated by imperial conquest, forced labor, and exposure to European diseases during the sixteenth century. Consequently, European colonists turned to continental Africa to provide enslaved labor for their sugar, coffee, and cocoa plantations. By the middle of the eighteenth century, enslaved Africans comprised more than 80% of the population in forced settlement colonies like Barbados, Jamaica, and Haiti. This far exceeded the proportion of enslaved Africans in mixed plantation colonies like Brazil,[7] Cuba,[8] or the mainland British colonies of North America,[9] where enslaved Africans were outnumbered by local white settlers.

Most forced settlement colonies abolished plantation slavery during the nineteenth century, after the British Industrial Revolution and revolutionary violence in the United States, France, Haiti, and Latin America brought abolitionist governments to power in much of the Atlantic world. In response to these upheavals, the British and French parliaments enacted liberal reforms that abolished plantation slavery in British and French forced settlement colonies during the 1830s and 1840s, respectively. Nevertheless, many forced settlement colonies maintained their agricultural plantations by recruiting indentured laborers from the Indian subcontinent. This is why many forced settlement colonies have racially diverse Creole populations of mixed African, European, and South Asian ancestry. Although the political economy of forced settlement generated racialized class structure that persisted into the twentieth century, most forced settlement colonies gained independence with high levels of educational attainment, and they have generally experienced greater postcolonial democratization than postcolonial states with large indigenous populations that predate the onset of colonial rule.

In contrast to forced settlement colonies that established agricultural plantations with foreign nonwhite labor, colonial occupation refers to the more typical pattern of imperial domination in which Europeans exploited the labor and natural resources of indigenous nonwhite populations that predate the onset of colonial rule. Colonial occupation was carried out with minimal European settlement, but the small number of colonists exploited the labor and natural resources of indigenous populations on the Indian subcontinent, continental Africa, and significant portions of the Arab world and Pacific Asia following the abolition of slavery in the New World. The rapacious territorial expansion of colonial occupation is best exemplified by the "Scramble for Africa" between 1880 and 1914, when European colonists expanded from their coastal African settlements and trading posts to control and dominate indigenous populations and territories of the vast African continent. Within a single generation, the entire African continent—apart from Ethiopia and Liberia—was carved up into colonial states that protected European geostrategic and commercial interests.

The political economy of colonial occupation involved significant resource extraction and the exploitation of indigenous African labor. Colonial African states implemented coercive labor recruitment and punitive taxation policies that forced millions of indigenous Africans to work for foreign-owned plantations and commercial mines. There is an extensive body of literature on coercive labor practices and extractive economic institutions in colonial Africa (Young 1994; Ibekwe 1975; Rodney 1981; Ferreira 1974; Acemoglu and Robinson 2010), and the bifurcated legal-administrative frameworks that privileged colonial settlers over indigenous African "subjects" (Mamdani 1996). Scholars have also emphasized the devastating developmental and political consequences of arbitrary borders that divided African ethnicities into illegitimate colonial states (Englebert 2000a; Herbst 2000; Davidson 1992), and the "divide and rule" policies that the privileged certain ethnic and/or religious communities at the expense of others (Mamdani 2002, 2012; Lange and Dawson 2009; Lange 2012; King 2014; Posner 2003, 2004, 2005). These policies have generated ethnic and political grievances with devastating consequences for postcolonial democratization and human well-being in much of continental Africa. These practices may have been more rapacious in sub-Saharan Africa than in other developing regions, but many Asian countries and much of the Arab world also emerged from colonial occupation with poor developmental outcomes that undermined postcolonial democratization efforts.

My research investigates the historical and institutional factors that enabled many forced settlement colonies to advance human well-being and democracy following the abolition of slavery. This trend is clearly evident in Figure 1.1, which demonstrates higher levels of educational attainment and greater postcolonial democratization in forced settlement colonies relative to Global South countries that emerged from colonial occupation after 1945.[10] The scatterplot uses 1960 adult literacy rates to measure educational attainment during the late colonial era, whereas Freedom House Imputed Polity scores assess the extent of postcolonial democratization between 1972 and 2012.[11] Most forced settlement colonies are concentrated in the upper-right corner of Figure 1.1, indicating high adult literacy rates in 1960 and high democracy scores after independence. At first glance, one might assume that British legal and political institutions facilitated favorable development in forced settlement colonies like Barbados (BRB), Jamaica (JAM), Mauritius (MUS), and Trinidad and Tobago

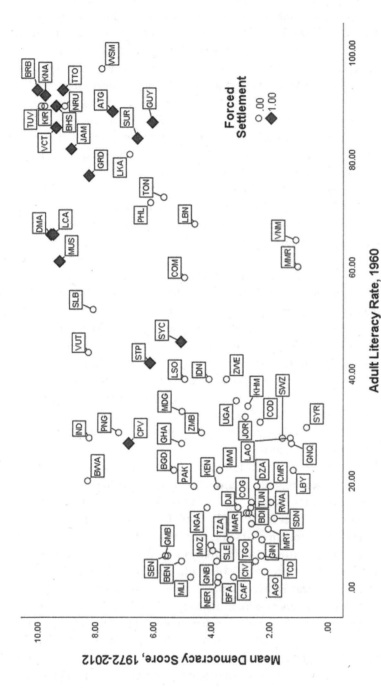

Figure 1.1 The divergent development legacies of forced settlement and colonial occupation in the Global South: Colonial education and postcolonial democracy

(TTO), but British colonial occupation is associated with poor developmental outcomes in postcolonial states like Sierra Leone (SLE), Uganda (UGA), Nigeria (NGA), and Pakistan (PAK). Indeed, nearly all colonies of occupation, regardless of the colonizing power, are concentrated in the lower left quadrant of Figure 1.1, indicating low adult literacy rates in 1960 and limited postcolonial democratization.[12]

The favorable developmental legacies of forced settlement relative to colonial occupation are still evident today. Table 1.1 provides Human Development Index (HDI) scores to evaluate human well-being in postcolonial states in 2015. The United Nations' HDI provides an aggregate measure of human well-being encompassing educational attainment, life expectancy at birth, and per capita income, with higher scores indicating favorable development outcomes. The data in Table 1.1 reveal high or very high HDI scores in most countries or territories that experienced forced settlement colonization.[13] Moreover, the favorable developmental legacies of forced settlement relative to colonial occupation are not unique to the British colonial empire: The Netherlands Antilles (i.e., Aruba, Bonaire, and Curaçao) and the French Antilles (i.e., Guadeloupe, Martinique, and Réunion) boast higher HDI scores than British forced settlement colonies like Barbados, Mauritius, or Trinidad and Tobago.[14] By contrast, most Global South countries that experienced British, French, or Iberian colonial occupation had low, or at best intermediate, HDI scores. It seems entirely plausible that the larger size and diverse population of continental states like Nigeria, Sudan, India, and Vietnam may have hindered their long-term development relative to Caribbean microstates and Creole African islands that were colonized by forced settlement. Nevertheless, the correlation between small island states and favorable development is neither straightforward nor simple. The geographic isolation of island microstates enabled Europeans to control and repress enslaved plantation laborers in forced settlement colonies for more than two centuries. Yet despite the brutality of plantation slavery, most forced settlement colonies show favorable development outcomes relative to Pacific island microstates, as well as continental African, Asian, and Arab states that experienced colonial occupation.[15]

Do We Really Need Another Empirical Study of Colonialism, State-Building, and Postcolonial Development?

My short answer to this question is yes! To the best of my knowledge, this is the first book that systematically explores the long-term developmental consequences of forced settlement and colonial occupation in the Global South. This research is important because the distinctive legacies of forced settlement

Table 1.1 The Divergent Development Legacies of Forced Settlement and Colonial Occupation as Indicated by HDI Scores in 2015

HDI Score, 2015	Forced Settlement	Colonial Occupation
Very High ≥ 0.800	*Guadeloupe 0.842, Martinique 0.859, Reunion 0.822, Netherlands Antilles 0.860*	
High 0.700 to 0.799	Antigua and Barbuda 0.783, Bahamas 0.790, Barbados 0.785, Dominica 0.724, Grenada 0.750, Jamaica 0.719, Mauritius 0.777, Seychelles 0.772, Saint Kitts and Nevis 0.752, St. Lucia 0.729, St. Vincent and the Grenadines 0.720, Suriname 0.714, Trinidad and Tobago 0.772	Algeria 0.736, Jordan 0.748, Lebanon 0.769, Libya 0.724, Samoa 0.702, Sri Lanka 0.757, Tonga 0.717, Tunisia 0.721
Intermediate (0.550 to 0.699)	Cape Verde 0.646, Guyana 0.642, São Tomé and Principe 0.555	Botswana 0.698, Cambodia 0.555, Congo, Rep. 0.591, Equatorial Guinea 0.587, Gabon 0.678, Ghana 0.570, India 0.609, Indonesia 0.684, Kenya 0.548, Kiribati 0.590, Laos 0.579, Morocco 0.628, Nauru 0.652, Philippines 0.668, Swaziland 0.561, Syria 0.594, Tuvalu 0.590, Vanuatu 0.594, Vietnam 0.666, Zambia 0.586
Low (less than 0.550)		Angola 0.532, Bangladesh 0.57, Benin 0.480, Burkina Faso 0.402, Burundi 0.400, Cameroon 0.512, Central African Republic 0.350, Chad 0.392, Comoros 0.503, Congo, Dem. Republic 0.433, Cote d'Ivoire 0.462, Djibouti 0.470, Gambia 0.441, Guinea 0.411, Guinea-Bissau 0.420, Lesotho 0.497, Madagascar 0.511, Malawi 0.445, Mali 0.419, Mauritania 0.506, Mozambique 0.416, Myanmar 0.536, Niger 0.348, Nigeria 0.514, Pakistan 0.538, Papua New Guinea 0.505, Rwanda 0.483, Senegal 0.466, Sierra Leone 0.413, Solomon Islands 0.506, Somalia 0.364, Sudan 0.479, Swaziland 0.531, Tanzania 0.521, Togo 0.484, Uganda 0.483, Zimbabwe 0.509
N	20	63

Note: Dependent territories are listed in italics. HDI scores were obtained from the United Nations Development Programme (2016), http://hdr.undp.org/en/composite/HDI. HDI scores for France's overseas departments (i.e., French Guiana, Guadeloupe, Martinique, and Réunion) were calculated by the Agence Française de Developpement, based on data from 2010. The HDI score for the Netherlands Antilles is calculated using the mean scores for Aruba (0.908) in 2008 and Curaçao (0.811) in 2012. HDI scores for the French and Dutch overseas territories were obtained from https://simple.wikipedia.org/wiki/List_of_countries_by_Human_Development_Index and https://en.wikipedia.org/wiki/Cura%C3%A7ao.

and colonial occupation are not adequately explained by existing theoretical frameworks that highlight the favorable developmental legacies of European settler colonialism relative to "extractive" forms of colonization with limited European settlement (Acemoglu, Johnson, and Robinson 2001, 2002; Easterly and Levine 2016). Moreover, the fact that forced settlement generated favorable long-term development legacies relative to colonial occupation is not adequately explained in empirical studies that emphasize the distinctiveness of British rule relative to French or Iberian colonization (La Porta et al. 1998, 1999; Grier 1997, 1999; Lee and Paine 2019a; Paine 2019b). Many British forced settlement colonies have successfully promoted inclusive human development and postcolonial democratization, but my research demonstrates that forced settlement also generated favorable development outcomes relative to colonial occupation in the French and Portuguese empires.

To better understand the diverse range of colonial experiences beyond the British Empire, this study also examines the developmental trajectories of overseas dependencies that experienced French, Dutch, or Portuguese colonization. Many overseas dependencies experienced longer and more intensive colonization than the countries that gained independence after 1945, yet they are frequently excluded from existing empirical studies of colonialism and postcolonial development. Many overseas dependencies, like the French and Dutch Caribbean territories, are forced settlement colonies with successful development outcomes; their exclusion from existing literature has contributed to the widespread assumption that British colonization resulted in favorable developmental outcomes relative to French or Iberian colonization.

Furthermore, many forced settlement colonies are excluded from existing studies that employ datasets that exclude small countries and/or dependent territories with less than a million inhabitants. To cite one example, only four of the 21 forced settlement colonies in my primary dataset are included in Acemoglu, Johnson, and Robinson's (2001) seminal research paper on colonial settler mortality and postcolonial development. As a result, most forced settlement colonies are also excluded from subsequent research that builds on this work (e.g., Acemoglu, Johnson, and Robinson 2002; Krieckhaus 2006; Fails and Krieckhaus 2010; Albouy 2012). My research addresses these shortcomings by providing evidence from all Global South countries that emerged from colonial domination after 1945, as well as overseas dependencies that were partially decolonized after World War II.

Moreover, existing studies of colonial legacies tend to focus on economic growth as the primary measure of postcolonial development (see Acemoglu, Johnson, and Robinson 2001, 2002; Krieckhaus 2006; Fails and Krieckhaus 2010). By contrast, my research examines the long-term developmental consequences of forced settlement and colonial occupation for various aspects of human well-being and postcolonial democratization. This study embraces Amartya Sen's definition of human development as "the process of expanding the real freedoms that people enjoy" (1999, 3). Sen's concept of human development assumes that democracy and personal freedoms reinforce the economic and social well-being of individuals in society; it also recognizes the extent to which personal freedoms depends on social, economic, and legal arrangements that provide education and healthcare, as well as political and civil rights (Sen 1999, 3). By embracing this broad concept of human development, my research examines how forced settlement and colonial occupation generated very different patterns of state-building, with distinctive consequences for human well-being and postcolonial democratization in the Global South.

My decision to examine human well-being and democratization, instead of economic growth and development, is informed by Matthew Lange's (2004, 2005, 2009) insightful research on the developmental legacies of direct versus indirect British colonization, and James Mahoney's (2010) research on Spanish colonialism and postcolonial development in Latin America. At the same time, the broad historical and geographic scope of my research extends beyond existing studies that demonstrate important developmental variations within a single geographic region (e.g., Mahoney 2001, 2010) or a single colonial empire (Lange 2004, 2009; Lawrence 2013). It also addresses geographic regions and colonial variations that are largely overlooked in Atul Kohli's (2020) recent book on the developmental consequences of British and US imperialist interventions in Latin America, the Middle East, and Pacific Asia. In short, none of the existing books on colonialism or imperialism in the global periphery have examined the divergent legacies of forced settlement and colonial occupation in the black Atlantic world and across the Global South. In doing so, this book fills an important lacuna in the existing canon of scholarly literature on colonialism, state-building, and postcolonial development in the Global South.

The theoretical arguments in this book are informed by previous works that explore the impact of diverse aspects of state-building and institutional development on human well-being and democratization (see Lipset 1959; Dahl 1971; Hadenius 1992; Przeworksi et al. 2000; Kohli 2004; Lange 2009; Mahoney 2010; Acemoglu and Robinson 2012; Gerring, Thacker, and Alfaro 2012). Like other key works in the democratization canon, this work employs a liberal and procedural definition of democracy that emphasizes individual freedoms, voting rights, and the ability of adult citizens to choose their political leaders in free, fair, and competitive multiparty elections that generate turnover in key executive and legislative offices (see Huntington 1991; Linz and Stepan 1996; Collier and Levitsky 1997; Przeworski et al. 2000). Existing studies have long emphasized a positive correlation between democracy and human well-being: inclusive human development reinforces popular support for democracy, which makes democratic political regimes less susceptible to authoritarian reversals during periods of crisis (Przeworski et al. 2000). Moreover, countries that establish and maintain democratic political governance for long periods of time are more effective at improving human well-being and development over the *longue durée* (Gerring, Thacker, and Alfaro 2012).

Given the established relationship between democracy and human development, the data analysis in this book examines the long-term developmental consequences of forced settlement and colonial occupation for diverse indicators of human well-being and postcolonial democratization in the Global South. I also present comparative-historical evidence that documents how forced settlement and colonial occupation generated distinctive legal-administrative institutions and citizenship rights for emancipated Afro-descendants (in forced settlement colonies) versus indigenous nonwhite populations (in colonies of occupation). This contributed to very different patterns of state-building that favored the expansion of state-funded education, political representation, and voting rights in forced settlement colonies relative to colonies of occupation. These case studies highlight the extent to which the historical expansion of state-funded education and political representation was often linked to the formal expansion (or restriction) of individual legal rights and citizenship rights during the colonial era. The case studies and statistical evidence in this book demonstrate the favorable developmental and political legacies of forced settlement relative to colonial occupation across multiple colonial empires.

Argument, Theoretical Claims, and Research Contributions

The central claim of this book is that the divergent developmental legacies of forced settlement and colonial occupation reflect the distinctive legal-administrative frameworks that colonial officials developed to control emancipated Afro-descendants versus indigenous colonial subjects in the Global South. The core argument is outlined in Figure 1.2, which presents a rough historical timeline of forced settlement and colonial occupation in the British and French colonial empires. Figure 1.2 highlights the distinctive patterns of state-building and institutional development associated with forced settlement and colonial occupation. The lengthy duration of forced settlement provides a stark contrast to the shorter duration of colonial occupation, and the significant territorial expansion of colonial occupation during the late nineteenth century. Consequently, the institutional development of forced settlement colonies was more directly impacted by liberal reforms that resulted from the British Industrial Revolution and the recurrent cycles of revolutionary violence that established democracy and republican government in France during the long nineteenth century.[16] The flow chart in Figure 1.2 primarily reflects the contrasting developmental legacies of forced settlement and colonial occupation in the British and French empires, but I also demonstrate similar developmental variations within the Portuguese colonial empire.

Figure 1.2 demonstrates that forced settlement colonies initially established extractive and labor-repressive institutions that enabled white planters to control the lives and livelihoods of their African slaves. From the early 1600s until the mid-nineteenth century, forced settlement colonies maintained repressive slave codes that enforced a rigid racial-caste hierarchy that privileged local white planters at the expense of enslaved Africans and free people of color. These institutions were substantially reformed during the nineteenth century, when the British Industrial Revolution undermined the economic rationale for slave-based sugar production in British forced settlement colonies. France's revolutionary upheavals between 1789 and 1870 also spurred slave revolts against white planter control, and undermined domestic political support for aristocratic landowners in France. The Haitian Revolution of 1791–1804 also dealt a significant blow to French colonial domination and white planter control in the black Atlantic world. Although Guadeloupe, Martinique, and Réunion remained under French control throughout the nineteenth century, they were also impacted by the revolutionary violence that undermined the political dominance of local white planters. Because enslaved Africans and free people of color embraced the republican creed of liberty, freedom, and equality during the revolutionary upheavals of the nineteenth century, French republican leaders ultimately embraced the abolition of slavery and the extension of citizenship rights to emancipated Afro-descendants.

My research highlights the extent to which liberal institutional reforms expanded the legal rights and political agency of emancipated Afro-descendants in British forced settlement colonies and the French Antilles colonies (i.e., Guadeloupe, Martinique, and Réunion) following the abolition of slavery. The middle decades of the nineteenth century brought significant liberal reforms to the United Kingdom, while France experienced recurrent cycles of revolutionary violence that transformed its long history of royal absolutism and Bonapartist dictatorship into a secular republic that expanded parliamentary representation, universal male suffrage, and citizenship rights. The initial attempts to establish a secular and democratic French Republic did not survive Napoleon's rise to power in 1800, and the ill-fated Second Republic lasted only three years after the 1848 French revolution. Nevertheless, the ultimate triumph of republicanism generated sustained democratic reforms following the 1870 Franco-Prussian War. These events generated liberal institutional reforms in forced settlement colonies, where emancipated Afro-descendants gained legal rights as free British subjects or metropolitan French citizens. These colonial

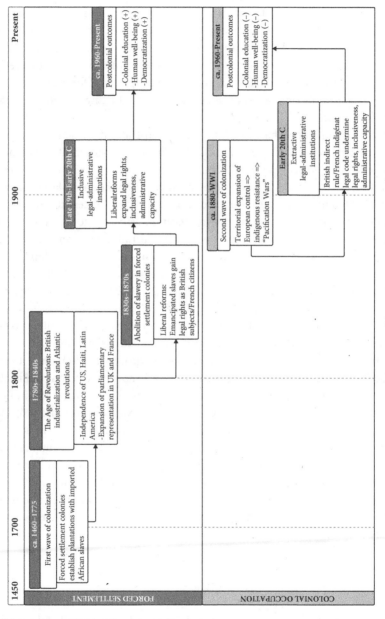

Figure 1.2 Mapping the argument: Divergent legacies of forced settlement and colonial occupation

states implemented liberal reforms that strengthened the rule of law and expanded inclusive citizenship norms following the abolition of slavery. Liberal institutional reforms also strengthened the administrative capacity of forced settlement colonies to distribute public goods like state-funded education, sanitation, and poor relief. Consequently, I argue that liberal institutional reforms expanded the legal rights and political agency of emancipated Afro-descendants in forced settlement colonies following the abolition of slavery. Liberal reforms also expanded the administrative capacity of forced settlement colonies to promote significant advances in human well-being and postcolonial democratization.

In contrast, the flow chart in Figure 1.2 demonstrates that colonial occupation generated extractive legal-administrative institutions that inhibited human well-being and postcolonial democratization. This is because the territorial expansion of colonial occupation occurred after the abolition of slavery in the New World, and indigenous populations often resisted the territorial expansion of European control during the "pacification wars" of the late nineteenth century. Indigenous resistance prompted colonial military commanders and district officials to devise extractive and repressive methods of administrative control at minimal cost to European taxpayers. This is what Jeffrey Herbst (2000) refers to as "administration on the cheap" (73). In the Indian subcontinent and across continental Africa, British colonial administrators relied heavily on indirect rule, which empowered "customary chiefs" to collect taxes, administer "native justice" in "customary courts," and recruit labor for infrastructural projects or European commercial enterprises (see Mamdani 1996; Lange 2009). The French *indigénat* legal code also empowered colonial officials and administrative "chiefs" to enforce collective punishments on entire indigenous communities and recruit forced labor for public infrastructure projects and European commercial enterprises (Merle 2002; Mann 2009). I argue that colonial occupation generated extractive legal-administrative institutions that undermined the rule of law, restricted citizenship rights, and limited the administrative capacity to effectively distribute public goods like state-funded education. Over the long term, these extractive institutions undermined human well-being and postcolonial democratization in countries that experienced colonial occupation.

Theoretical Claims

My research identifies three ways in which liberal reforms expanded the legal-administrative capacity of forced settlement colonies following the abolition of slavery. First, I find that liberal institutional reforms strengthened the rule

of law in ways that empowered emancipated Afro-descendants in forced settlement colonies. This pattern is evident in the British colonial empire, where
British common law protected the core personal freedoms of emancipated
slaves and their descendants. Consequently, British forced settlement colonies developed an inclusive legal system that protected property rights, religious liberty, and, to a lesser extent, freedom of speech and association. The
legal protection of these core personal freedoms enabled many emancipated
Afro-descendants to purchase small plots of land, establish civil society
associations, and join labor unions that expanded their economic and political agency during the late colonial era. This type of inclusive legal system was
rarely implemented in colonies of occupation following the abolition of slavery
in the New World. British common law was not strongly institutionalized in
British-occupied colonies that were established during the nineteenth century.
Research by Matthew Lange (2009) shows that "customary courts" controlled
by indigenous "chiefs" handled half of the legal cases in the Indian subcontinent, and more than three-quarters of the legal cases in British-occupied
African colonies like Nigeria, Sierra Leone, Sudan, and Uganda during the
1950s. Lange's research indicates that indirect British rule undermined human
development and effective postcolonial governance in these countries (Lange
2009, 2004). By contrast, direct British rule institutionalized a uniform and inclusive legal-administrative framework based on common law, which provides
strong protections for property rights and individual civil liberties (La Porta
et al. 1998, 1999). My research demonstrates that British common law was institutionalized as the sole legal system in British forced settlement colonies following the abolition of slavery. Consequently, it is not surprising that liberal
institutional reforms that strengthened the rule of law also helped to facilitate postcolonial democratization and human well-being in forced settlement
colonies.

Second, my research documents the extension of citizenship rights in forced
settlement colonies following the abolition of slavery. This pattern is evident in
the French colonial empire, where citizenship rights were extended to emancipated Afro-descendants during the revolutionary upheavals of the nineteenth
century. Colonial citizenship laws played an important role in determining access to public goods like state-funded education, voting rights, and political
representation (Mamdani 1996; Cooper 2014). Consequently, the extension of
citizenship rights to emancipated Afro-descendants expanded political representation and state-funded education in the French Antilles following the consolidation of republican government in France after 1870. By contrast, French
republican elites did not advance the citizenship rights of indigenous populations
that resisted the territorial expansion of French colonial occupation following
the abolition of slavery in the New World. Consequently, citizenship rights were

largely restricted to local white settlers in Algeria, Indochina, and across continental Africa, where the French *indigénat* legal code undermined the legal rights and political agency of indigenous colonial subjects. The blatant denial of citizenship rights exposed indigenous African, Arab, and Asian populations to forced labor recruitment and the summary "justice" of French district officials and administrative "chiefs" (Merle 2002; Mann 2009). My research demonstrates that the denial of citizenship rights hindered the expansion of state-funded education and voting rights in French-occupied colonies like Algeria, Senegal, Gabon, Madagascar, and the tiny Comoros Islands. By contrast, the extension of citizenship rights to emancipated Afro-descendants contributed to the significant expansion of state-funded education, political representation, and voting rights in the French Antilles colonies. This suggests that the earlier extension of citizenship rights contributed to the favorable long-term development of forced settlement colonies relative to Global South countries that experienced colonial occupation.

Last, my research demonstrates that liberal reforms expanded the administrative capacity of forced settlement colonies to provide public goods that promoted inclusive long-term development. The abolition of slavery eroded the political dominance of local white planters and expanded the political authority of elected representatives and/or colonial administrators who were responsible to elected governments in Europe. These reforms expanded the administrative capacity of forced settlement colonies to provide public goods and services to a broader subset of the population. The historical evidence in this book highlights the extent to which liberal institutional reforms expanded access to state-funded education in postabolition Jamaica and the French Antilles colonies. Reformist colonial governments also promoted infrastructural development and economic diversification to reverse the partial collapse of large-scale sugar production in forced settlement colonies. This historical evidence suggests that liberal institutional reforms promoted greater economic and social inclusiveness in forced settlement colonies following the abolition of slavery. In contrast, most colonies of occupation never developed the administrative capacity to efficiently distribute public goods in their rural indigenous hinterlands. This is particularly evident in continental African states whose larger population and territory proved more difficult for European officials to control (Herbst 2000). It also reflects the more limited political objectives of colonial rulers in these territories (Young 1994; Mamdani 1996). Whereas forced settlement colonies significantly expanded the legal and political rights of emancipated Afro-descendants following the abolition of slavery, colonial rulers tended to prioritize tax collection, forced labor recruitment, and the maintenance of public order in colonial territories with significant indigenous populations.

Research Contributions

The argument outlined above and the empirical evidence that supports it make three important contributions to the field of colonialism, state-building, and postcolonial development. First, this is the first book-length project to systematically examine the developmental legacies of forced settlement and colonial occupation in the Global South. Other prominent analyses assume—either implicitly or explicitly—that the labor-repressive and extractive economic structure of colonial states with predominantly nonwhite populations would limit the long-term development of forced settlement colonies as well as colonies of occupation (see Acemoglu, Johnson, and Robinson 2001, 2002; Acemoglu and Robinson 2012). This assumption is challenged by the favorable developmental legacies of forced settlement relative to colonial occupation in the black Atlantic world and across the Global South. My research explains this puzzle by documenting the distinctive patterns of state-building and institutional development associated with forced settlement and colonial occupation, and the liberal institutional reforms that expanded the legal rights and political agency of emancipated Afro-descendants following the abolition of slavery in the New World. The distinctive legal-administrative frameworks that governed emancipated Afro-descendants and indigenous colonial subjects ultimately favored the long-term development of forced settlement colonies relative to Global South countries that experienced colonial occupation.

Second, this book provides the only mixed-methods analysis of forced settlement and colonial occupation across multiple colonial empires. Previous research has tended to emphasize the distinctive nature of British colonization relative to French or Iberian colonization (La Porta et al. 1998, 1999; Grier 1997, 1999; Lee and Paine 2019a) or developmental variations within a single colonial empire (e.g., Lange 2009; Mahoney 2010; Lawrence 2013). By contrast, my research provides statistical evidence and comparative-historical case studies that trace the favorable developmental legacies of forced settlement relative to colonial occupation across multiple colonial empires. In doing so, this book compiles a new and impressive dataset on colonialism and demonstrates important institutional, developmental, and political variations within and across the British, French, and Portuguese colonial empires.

Last, this project engages with recent studies that highlight the impact of Protestant missionary evangelization on educational attainment, human well-being, and postcolonial democratization in the Global South (Woodberry 2012; Lankina and Getachew 2012, 2013; Okoye and Pongou 2014). The theoretical and empirical claims of these studies are somewhat persuasive for British colonies, but they fail to explain the favorable developmental legacies of forced settlement relative to colonial occupation in French and Iberian colonies, where

Protestant missionary activity was historically limited and often restricted. Nevertheless, my research also examines the impact of colonial missionary activity, but it demonstrates that liberal institutional reforms, rather than Protestant missionary evangelization, account for the favorable developmental legacies of forced settlement relative to colonial occupation in the Global South.

Methodology, Case Selection, and Chapter Organization

The book's core arguments are tested using a mixed methodology that combines statistical data analysis with historical case studies that trace the diverse legacies of forced settlement and colonial occupation under British, French, and Portuguese rule. This mixed methodology harnesses the unique strengths of quantitative and qualitative research while minimizing the limitations of each approach (Coppedge 1999; Brady and Collier 2004; Lieberman 2005; Howard 2017, 113–14). The statistical data models demonstrate the favorable developmental legacies of forced settlement relative to colonial occupation in the Global South. These empirical trends are buttressed by comparative-historical case studies that trace the distinctive patterns of state-building and institutional development associated with forced settlement and colonial occupation in the British, French, and Portuguese empires.

Historical Overview and Theoretical Framework

Chapter 2 presents a historical overview of forced settlement and colonial occupation in the Global South. This chapter highlights the extractive and repressive nature of plantation slavery in forced settlement colonies, and the liberal institutional reforms that expanded the legal rights and political agency of emancipated Afro-descendants in forced settlement colonies. The chapter also outlines the geostrategic and economic factors that contributed to the territorial expansion of colonial occupation following the abolition of slavery in the New World. The historical overview of forced settlement and colonial occupation also highlights the distinctive legal-administrative frameworks that governed emancipated Afro-descendants and indigenous colonial subjects under British, French, and Portuguese rule.

Chapter 3 expands the theoretical framework that explains the favorable developmental legacies of forced settlement relative to colonial occupation. My theory highlights two critical historical junctures that transformed the patterns of state-building and institutional development associated with forced settlement and colonial occupation. The first critical juncture was the abolition of slavery, which undermined the political control of local white planters, and expanded the legal rights and political agency of emancipated Afro-descendants in forced settlement colonies. The second critical juncture was the territorial expansion of colonial occupation, which undermined the legal rights and political agency of indigenous colonial subjects in continental Africa and other developing regions that were colonized after the abolition of slavery in the New World. The theoretical arguments in this chapter incorporate insights from historical-institutionalist scholarship on colonial state-building and institutional development in the Global South (e.g., Acemoglu and Robinson 2012; Mahoney 2010; Lange 2009; Mamdani 1996). My arguments also demonstrate the limits of existing theories that emphasize the importance of European settlers (Acemoglu, Johnson, and Robinson 2001, 2002), British legal and political institutions (La Porta et al. 1998, 1999), Protestant missionary evangelization (Woodberry 2012), ethnic diversity (Horowitz 1985; Easterly and Levine 1997), and geographic determinants of human development and postcolonial democracy (see Sachs and Warner 1997; Herbst 2000; Anckar 2002, 2006).

Statistical Evidence

Chapter 4 presents a global statistical analysis of developmental outcomes in more than 90 Global South countries with nonwhite populations that emerged from colonial rule between 1945 and 1985. The OLS regression models in Chapter 4 demonstrate favorable development outcomes in forced settlement colonies relative to colonies of occupation in terms of education, health, and economic well-being at the end of the colonial era. Forced settlement is also associated with greater exposure to mass electoral competition during the late colonial era and higher mean postcolonial democracy scores after independence. Moreover, both British and continental European forced settlement generated favorable development outcomes relative to colonial occupation in the Global South. These statistical results are robust to different model specifications that control for confounding factors like European settlement, British colonization, ethnic diversity, religious composition, geography, and Protestant missionary evangelization. Although forced settlement predicts favorable development outcomes relative to colonial occupation in most data models, the regression coefficient for forced settlement is insignificant in statistical models that control for the extension of metropolitan (i.e., European) legal rights to nonwhites prior to World War II. This suggests that liberal institutional reforms enabled forced settlement colonies to expand educational access and voting rights following the abolition of slavery.

Despite the consistency of these results, it is important to recognize that cross-sectional data models are not particularly useful for understanding long-term patterns of institutional change within individual countries. The data analysis in Chapter 4 does not explicitly capture the historical and institutional factors that transformed the developmental capacity of forced settlement colonies following the abolition of slavery. Nor does it capture the extent to which colonial occupation subjected indigenous populations to extractive and repressive legal-administrative institutions that undermined effective state-building and postcolonial development. Moreover, regression models are not useful for understanding the experience of countries whose developmental trajectories deviate from the dominant empirical trend. Regression diagnostics reveal that Portugal's forced settlement colonies—i.e., Cape Verde and São Tomé and Príncipe—were important outliers in several models. This likely reflects Portugal's weakness as an imperial power (Newitt 1981) and the perpetuation of coercive labor practices that limited the expansion of state-funded education and democratic political representation in Portuguese forced settlement colonies (Ferreira 1974; Mentel 1984; Seibert 2006). Furthermore, Haiti is the most extreme negative outlier in the expanded sample of countries that gained independence after 1800. Haiti's long-term development outcomes are significantly worse than other forced settlement colonies, despite its historical significance as the only country to establish independence following a successful slave revolt against white planter control and French colonial domination. The historical reasons for Haiti's persistent underdevelopment will be explored separately, and in comparative-historical perspective with other forced settlement colonies.

Comparative-Historical Evidence

To address these concerns, I also provide comparative-historical evidence of the distinctive patterns of state-building and institutional development associated with forced settlement and colonial occupation in the British, French, and Portuguese colonial empires. Britain and Portugal were the two most dissimilar colonial powers in terms of their economic development and democratization trajectories leading up to World War II. The Industrial Revolution expanded Britain's global power and imperial dominance during the nineteenth century (Abernethy 2000; Ferguson 2003), and Britain's parliamentary reforms generated a liberal and increasingly democratic political culture that expanded political representation and electoral competition in many British colonies after World War II (Collier 1982; Rueschemeyer et al. 1992, 236–44; Lee and Paine 2019a). By contrast, Portugal's imperial power declined significantly after Brazil gained independence in 1822. Moreover, Portugal failed to industrialize during the nineteenth century, and its *Estado Novo* dictatorship resisted colonial demands for democratic representation and political self-determination after World War II. Given these differences, it would be reasonable to expect distinctive patterns of state-building and institutional development in the British and Portuguese colonial empires. Nevertheless, my comparative research demonstrates the favorable developmental legacies of forced settlement relative to colonial occupation in both colonial empires. The case studies in Chapters 5, 6, and 7 use process-tracing to examine how colonial rulers and colonized populations responded to critical historical junctures such as the abolition of slavery in forced settlement colonies, and the territorial expansion of colonial occupation at the end of the nineteenth century.

Chapter 5 examines the contrasting developmental legacies of British forced settlement in Jamaica and the British occupation of Sierra Leone, using secondary historical sources and Colonial Office records obtained from the British Library and UK National Archives. Despite Jamaica's long and brutal history of forced settlement, the Caribbean island outperforms Sierra Leone on key indicators of human well-being and postcolonial democratization. This outcome is paradoxical, given Sierra Leone's historical importance as a British haven for "liberated Africans" and emancipated slaves returning from the New World. To explain this paradox, my research documents the liberal institutional reforms that accompanied the British abolition of slavery in Jamaica, and the deterioration of Sierra Leone's legal-administrative institutions following indigenous resistance to the territorial expansion of British colonial occupation during the 1890s. The historical evidence in this chapter documents the liberal institutional reforms that reduced the political dominance of Jamaica's colonial planters following the British abolition of slavery. Liberal reforms also expanded the legal rights and political agency of Jamaica's emancipated Afro-descendants, as British officials established direct political control to curb racial tensions between local whites and free people of color. Direct British rule expanded the administrative capacity of reformist colonial officials to provide public goods and services like education, sanitation, and poor relief. It also institutionalized key civil liberties that empowered nonwhite activists to mobilize for labor reforms and greater political representation after World War II. Over time, Jamaica's institutional reforms facilitated broad-based human development and postcolonial democratization, whereas Sierra Leone followed a very different pattern of state-building and institutional development. Indigenous African resistance to the territorial expansion of British colonial occupation revealed the limits of direct British rule in Sierra Leone, where British officials appointed indigenous elites to collect taxes and recruit labor on their behalf. In exchange for their loyalty to Britain, Sierra Leone's "protectorate chiefs" enforced "customary laws" that enshrined elite privilege and limited the political agency and economic well-being of indigenous

Africans in outlying rural districts. The comparative-historical evidence in this chapter suggests that extractive institutions undermined human well-being and postcolonial democratization in Sierra Leone, whereas Jamaica's liberal reforms established inclusive legal-administrative institutions that advanced human well-being and postcolonial democratization.

Chapter 6 contrasts the distinctive patterns of state-building and institutional development that resulted from Portuguese forced settlement in Cape Verde and Portuguese colonial occupation in Guinea-Bissau. This comparison is ideal because Cape Verde and Guinea-Bissau share extensive historical, cultural, and political ties that result from their geographic proximity. The two countries also participated in a joint revolutionary struggle that enabled the African Party for the Independence of Guinea-Bissau and Cape Verde to establish single-party control over both countries after independence. Despite these similarities, Cape Verde and Guinea-Bissau developed very different legal-administrative institutions that reflect their respective modes of colonization. My research demonstrates that Cape Verde established an inclusive legal-administrative framework that expanded the legal rights and political agency of emancipated Afro-descendants. By contrast, Portuguese colonial occupation in Guinea-Bissau enforced a rigid legal distinction between Creole and indigenous African subjects. Consequently, Guinean Creoles enjoyed the same legal status as Cape Verdeans, whereas indigenous Africans were subject to forced labor recruitment under a repressive legal code that denied their citizenship rights. My research uses Portuguese official records and secondary historical sources that document the extent to which colonial citizenship laws impacted the expansion of state-funded education, political representation, and voting rights across Portuguese Africa. I find that Cape Verde's inclusive citizenship laws expanded educational access and political representation relative to Portuguese-occupied colonies that enforced the repressive *indigenato* legal code. Moreover, the early establishment of inclusive state institutions enabled Cape Verde's postcolonial leaders to promote significant improvements in human well-being that reinforced popular support for democracy. By contrast, Guinea-Bissau's ineffective colonial state was crippled by anticolonial violence, and the institutionalized legal distinctions between its Creole and indigenous African populations undermined its political stability and governmental effectiveness after independence.

Chapter 7 examines the diverse developmental legacies of forced settlement and colonial occupation in the French colonial empire. France's colonial legacy is more complex than that of Britain or Portugal because of the greater extent of neocolonial intervention in former French colonies. For example, the Bank of France controlled the monetary policy of former French colonies in West and Equatorial Africa until 2020, and French military forces maintained authoritarian political stability in many postcolonial African states. France also maintains political authority over former colonies that were legally reconstituted as overseas departments or overseas territories after World War II. Given the greater complexity of the French colonial empire, this chapter covers a broader range of abbreviated case studies: I examine the contrasting legacies of forced settlement in Haiti and the French Antilles (i.e., Guadeloupe, Martinique, and Réunion). I also examine the negative developmental legacies of French colonial occupation in Algeria, Senegal, Gabon, Madagascar, and the Comoros Islands.

The chapter begins with a comparative analysis of the historical and institutional factors that hindered Haiti's long-term development relative to the French Antilles colonies. All of these territories established agricultural plantations with enslaved African labor, but their political trajectories diverged following Haiti's independence in 1804. Today, Haiti remains the most impoverished and underdeveloped country in the Western Hemisphere, despite its glorious past as the only forced settlement colony to establish independence following a successful slave rebellion against French colonial domination and white planter control. My research demonstrates that Haiti's postcolonial development was undermined by French—and later US—neocolonial exploitation, and the political ascendancy of Haitian military elites that exploited the country's agricultural workers after independence. By contrast, French republican governments implemented liberal reforms that expanded the legal rights and political agency of emancipated Afro-descendants in the Antilles colonies following the 1848 French revolution and the establishment of the Third French Republic in 1870. The expansion of citizenship rights and political representation in the French Antilles was intrinsically linked to the revolutionary upheavals that pitted French republicans and abolitionists against aristocratic landowners and local white planters during the nineteenth century. Consequently, emancipated Afro-descendants benefited from the revolutionary upheavals that expanded political representation and established a republican system of government in France. The chapter also examines the extractive and repressive legal-administrative institutions that controlled indigenous Arab Muslims in Algeria, and indigenous African ethnicities in Senegal, Gabon, Madagascar, and the Comoros Islands. These French-occupied colonies maintained a rigid legal distinction between metropolitan citizens and indigenous subjects, despite profound differences in the extent of European settlement, ethnic diversity, religion, geography, and population size. These diverse examples of French colonial occupation highlight the negative developmental legacies of extractive legal-administrative institutions that undermined the legal rights and political agency of indigenous colonial subjects under French rule.

The case studies of British, French, and Portuguese colonization are informed by secondary historical literature, but I also obtained historical data from British Colonial Office records in the UK National Archives and the British Library during five research trips to London between 2007 and 2015. The Colonial

Office *Blue Books* and annual reports provide detailed information on colonial revenues and expenditures, primary school enrollment, and political representation in British colonies dating back to the nineteenth century. These sources were invaluable for tracing the distinctive developmental legacies of British forced settlement and colonial occupation in Jamaica and Sierra Leone, respectively. My research on French colonialism incorporates citizenship and education data from colonial census records and statistical yearbooks that I consulted during three research trips to the Bibliothèque Nationale de France, the Public Information Library in Paris, and the French colonial archives in Aix-en-Provence, France. The National Library of Portugal, the National Archives of Cape Verde, and other Portuguese official sources provided similar data on citizenship, educational access, and political representation in Portuguese African colonies. The National Archives of Senegal were closed during my research trip to West Africa in 2015, but I obtained valuable information from the United Nations' Economic Commission for Africa and the Council for the Development of Social Science Research in Africa's research library in Dakar, Senegal. These data sources enrich my comparative-historical analysis of forced settlement and colonial occupation in three colonial empires.

Chapter 8 outlines the main theoretical and conceptual contributions of this rich empirical analysis. The chapter identifies the conditions that enabled many—but not all—forced settlement colonies to advance human well-being and postcolonial democratization following the abolition of slavery. The chapter also outlines avenues for future research on Global South countries that gained independence during the nineteenth century. For example, the Union of South Africa and most Latin American states gained independence under the control of powerful white minorities that excluded their indigenous and/or Afro-descendant populations from meaningful citizenship rights and political representation. Many of the Global South countries that emerged from colonial rule during the nineteenth century remained heavily exploited by domestic elites that maintained an authoritarian grip on political authority after independence. I briefly examine this dynamic that delayed the abolition of slavery and sustained racial exclusion in Brazil, Cuba, and the southern United States. I also outline the repressive "native laws" that marginalized indigenous black South Africans following that country's independence in 1910, and prior to the establishment of apartheid and single-party authoritarian control in 1948.

The fact that South Africa's long history of racial exclusion was more severe than in the United States, Brazil, Cuba, or any country with a nonindigenous black population only lends further support to my core arguments. The ongoing socioeconomic marginalization and renewed political mobilization of black and indigenous populations in the United States and Canada and across Latin America, South Africa, and Oceania are beyond the scope of this book, but they highlight the importance of revisiting the past to better understand our present. These realities not only highlight the need for more nuanced research on the colonial origins of racialized political exclusion but also call for renewed deliberations on the legacies of colonialism in contemporary societies and institutions. Exploring the divergent legacies of forced settlement and colonial occupation in Global South regions that emerged from colonial domination after World War II, this book retraces the legacies of colonialism through the pages of history to ascertain where and why the paths diverged for different states.

2

A Historical Overview of Forced Settlement and Colonial Occupation in the Global South

This chapter provides a historical overview of forced settlement and colonial occupation as distinctive patterns of "extractive" colonization in Global South countries with limited European settlement. Forced settlement refers to the pattern of imperial domination in which European colonists established agricultural plantations in tropical regions of the New World using imported African slaves. By contrast, colonial occupation refers to the more common pattern of imperial domination in which Europeans exploited the labor and natural resources of indigenous populations in the Indian subcontinent, Southeast Asia, and continental Africa. Both patterns of colonization were "extractive" and labor-repressive, but my research highlights the distinctive patterns of state-building that favored the long-term development of forced settlement colonies relative to the Global South countries that emerged from colonial occupation after 1945. Whereas liberal reforms established relatively inclusive legal-administrative institutions in forced settlement colonies following the abolition of slavery, British- and European-occupied colonies maintained extractive and repressive "native legal codes" that undermined the legal rights and political agency of indigenous colonial subjects. This empirical pattern is consistent across multiple colonial empires, and it challenges the assumptions of existing studies that highlight the favorable developmental legacies of British colonization relative to French or Iberian colonization (Huntington 1984; Weiner 1987; Grier 1997, 1999; La Porta et al. 1998, 1999; Bernhard, Reenock, and Nordstrom 2004; Lee and Paine 2019a). The favorable developmental legacies of forced settlement vis-à-vis colonial occupation, as outlined in the previous chapter, also question the core arguments of previous studies that link labor-repressive and "extractive" colonization to persistent underdevelopment and limited democratization in tropical regions of the Global South (see Acemoglu, Johnson, and Robinson 2001, 2002; Sokoloff and Engerman 2000; Acemoglu and Robinson 2012; Easterly and Levine 2016).

The chapter is organized into three sections that highlight the conceptual distinction between forced settlement and colonial occupation as distinctive

Ruling Emancipated Slaves and Indigenous Subjects. Olukunle P. Owolabi, Oxford University Press.
© Oxford University Press 2023. DOI: 10.1093/oso/9780197673027.003.0002

modes of imperial control. The first section highlights the brutality of plantation slavery in forced settlement colonies, the revolutionary factors that contributed to the abolition of slavery in the nineteenth century, and the liberal reforms that accompanied the abolition of slavery in forced settlement colonies. The second section examines the economic and political factors that contributed to the rapid territorial expansion of colonial occupation, and the repressive legal-administrative institutions that controlled indigenous nonwhite populations in the Indian subcontinent, Southeast Asia, and continental Africa following the abolition of slavery in the New World. The final section situates the conceptual distinction between forced settlement and colonial occupation within existing typologies of colonial domination. This section highlights the limits of existing typologies that emphasize distinctions between settler and extractive colonialism (see Acemoglu and Robinson 2001, 2002; Krieckhaus 2006; Easterly and Levine 2016), direct versus indirect rule (Mamdani 1996; Lange 2004, 2009; Gerring et al. 2011; Naseemullah and Staniland 2016), and formal versus informal empire (Kohli 2020). These older designations are still useful for understanding specific legacies of colonialism and imperial domination, but they obscure the distinctive patterns of state-building and institutional development that resulted from forced settlement and colonial occupation. Consequently, this chapter's overview of forced settlement and colonial occupation generates novel insights that expand upon existing conceptual frameworks of colonial state-building and postcolonial development.

A Historical Overview of Forced Settlement in the Global South

Forced settlement colonization dates back to the late 1400s, when Portuguese colonists established agricultural plantations in the previously uninhabited Cape Verdean islands using enslaved African laborers from the nearby Guinea Coast of West Africa.[1] During the 1600s, however, forced settlement became the dominant mode of colonization in the Caribbean region, where European colonists established large-scale agricultural plantations with enslaved African labor, following the destruction and decimation of the region's precolonial indigenous peoples. The establishment of sugar, coffee, and cocoa plantations in the New World generated an insatiable demand for cheap labor, and more than 5 million enslaved Africans were forcibly settled in English, French, and Dutch Caribbean colonies between 1660 and 1815. By the mid- eighteenth century, the forced settlement colonies in the West Indies had a higher proportion of enslaved African laborers than any other part of the New World.[2] Although forced settlement colonization was primarily concentrated in the British, French, and Dutch Caribbean region (i.e., the West Indies), forced settlement colonies were also established in Creole African islands like Mauritius, Réunion, and the Seychelles islands.

Forced settlement colonization generated enormous profits for the local white planters and metropolitan elites who benefited from the transatlantic slave trade. The economic historian David Eltis (1997) estimates that the per capita income of the largest Caribbean colonies exceeded that of early modern Britain prior to the Industrial Revolution (123). Indeed, the profits from the transatlantic slave trade and Caribbean sugar plantations provided much of the capital that financed the British Industrial Revolution during the first half of the nineteenth century (see Williams 1994; Sokoloff and Engerman 2000, 2006).[3] Yet despite the enormous profitability of forced settlement colonies, the living and working conditions of enslaved African laborers were so brutal that most enslaved Africans died from disease, torture, exhaustion, or suicide within a few years of their arrival in the New World. The death rate for enslaved Africans in the West Indies was so high that the region's planters needed to import at least 20,000 new slaves every year just to maintain their existing labor force (Curtin 1972, 257).[4]

All forced settlement colonies maintained draconian slave codes that gave white plantation owners and managers almost complete control over the lives and livelihoods of enslaved African laborers. Historical sources demonstrate the widespread use of torture and rape to control enslaved Africans on colonial plantations. Indeed, the practice of raping female slaves was so extensive that, over time, it generated a mixed-race population that occupied an intermediate social caste between white planter elites and African slaves. Some light-skinned members of this intermediate class were able to acquire wealth and social status through agriculture, trade, or craftsmanship, but colonial laws severely restricted the civil liberties and political rights of free people of color until the 1830s (Wesley 1934; Murch 1971, 32; McCloy 1966, 15–33).

Many forced settlement colonies maintained coercive labor practices long after the abolition of slavery in the nineteenth century. As emancipated blacks fled the plantations that had once enslaved them, plantation owners recruited hundreds of thousands of indentured laborers from the Indian subcontinent, and to a lesser extent from China, Java, and sub-Saharan Africa. The widespread recruitment of indentured plantation laborers enabled many forced settlement colonies, including Mauritius, British Guiana (present-day Guyana), Suriname, and Trinidad, to expand their agricultural plantations following the abolition of slavery (Carter 1996; Knight 1997; Allen 1999; Engerman 2012). Indentured laborers were legally bound to work on these plantations for a period of five to seven years, and their working conditions differed little from those of the African slaves that preceded them (see Tinker 1974; Kale 1998; Hoefte 1998).[5]

The twin processes of African slave labor and indentured labor migration had profound consequences for the economy and society of forced settlement colonies. The massive influx of African slaves and South Asian indentured laborers generated high levels of ethnocultural and religious diversity in forced settlement colonies like Guyana, Mauritius, Suriname, and Trinidad and Tobago (Brerreton 1979; Carter 1996; Hoefte 1998; Allen 1999; Eriksen 1998; Ledgister 1998). Barbados, Cape Verde, Jamaica, and the Lesser Antilles of the West Indies did not attract many indentured laborers because their agricultural plantations declined significantly following the abolition of slavery. These societies are more homogenous in terms of ethnicity, religion, and culture, but they also developed hybrid Creole populations of predominantly African and European ancestry.

The geographic isolation of these island colonies and the rigidities of plantation life forced African slaves to adopt the language of local whites, and similar religious beliefs and practices. This process is known as creolization, and it results from the admixture of different cultural heritages and ethnic groups in a new space, which develops a shared cultural heritage and collective identity. Emancipated Afro-descendants appropriated hybrid Creole language and cultural practices that blended European and African customs and beliefs. In general, European social and cultural norms are more established in the upper echelons of the economy and society, whereas African social and cultural norms are stronger among the working-class population.[6] Nevertheless, even the poorest and most marginalized Afro-descendants grow up with local creolized versions of European languages rather than indigenous African languages. In this regard, the emancipated Afro-descendants in Creole African islands and the West Indies are culturally distinct from indigenous African ethnicities that experienced colonial occupation following the abolition of slavery in the New World.

Postabolition Reforms in Forced Settlement Colonies

The central claim of this book is that liberal institutional reforms enabled most forced settlement colonies to expand state-funded education and voting rights, and to promote more inclusive human development outcomes following the abolition of slavery in the nineteenth century. Britain was the first colonial power to permanently abolish plantation slavery in its forced settlement colonies. The British 1832 Reform Act and the Emancipation Act of 1833 undermined the economic and political dominance of British landed elites and plantation owners in the British colonial empire. The French revolutionary upheavals of 1789, 1830, and 1848–49 also undermined the political dominance of conservative royalist elites that protected the economic interests of royalist white planters in the

French Antilles. Between 1789 and 1871, France experienced recurrent episodes of revolutionary violence that pitted republican leaders against conservative monarchists and Bonapartists. During these revolutionary upheavals, enslaved Africans and nonwhite political activists supported French republican elites that advanced the promise of liberty, fraternity, and equality. French republican leaders reciprocated by abolishing slavery to weaken the political control of royalist white planters in the Antilles colonies (McCloy 1966; Wright 1976; Knight 1997, 336–39; Blackburn 1988; Beauvois 2017).

Local white planters staunchly opposed the abolition of slavery in forced settlement colonies, but their preferences were ultimately overruled by abolitionists and liberal reformers that controlled the British Parliament during the 1830s. French Republican elites also abolished slavery after gaining control of the French state during the 1848 French Revolution. Consequently, liberal reformers in the British and French parliaments offered generous monetary compensation to colonial planters in exchange for liberating their slaves. This financial assistance—worth £20 million in the British colonial empire (more than $360 billion in 2010) and 126 million francs in the French colonies (around $90 billion in 2010)—was conditional on the successful abolition of slavery and the implementation of liberal reforms in the forced settlement colonies (McCloy 1966, 147–53; Knight 1997, 336–37; Blackburn 1988, 501; Draper 2010, 100–107; Beauvois 2017).[7]

It is important to acknowledge that the abolition of slavery contributed to long-term decline of sugar production in many forced settlement colonies. In Barbados, Jamaica, British Guiana, Suriname, and the French Antilles, for example, sugar production declined by 40%–60% in the three decades following the abolition of slavery (Beauvois 2017, 104; Engerman 2012, 601). The spectacular decline in sugar production prompted British and French officials to implement liberal reforms that spurred modest economic diversification in forced settlement colonies during the late nineteenth century. The historical evidence in subsequent chapters also highlights the extent to which liberal reforms expanded the administrative capacity of forced settlement colonies to provide public goods like education, sanitation, and poor relief. The partial collapse of the plantation economy enabled many Afro-descendant families to acquire modest plots of land following the abolition of slavery. Despite this historical evidence, the dominant view in the existing literature is that "former slaves and generations of descendants remained landless, impoverished, unschooled, and disenfranchised" (Lowenthal 1995, 179–80). This is because most forced settlement colonies did not promote significant economic expansion until after World War II, and existing studies have emphasized their persistent underdevelopment relative to European settler societies in the New World (Beckford 1983; Sokoloff and Engerman 2000).

In contrast to these existing studies, my research emphasizes the liberal reforms that expanded the legal rights and political agency of emancipated Afro-descendants in forced settlement colonies. These reforms enabled most forced settlement colonies to promote favorable development outcomes relative to Global South countries that experienced colonial occupation. As outlined in the previous chapter, the British Industrial Revolution and the French revolutionary upheavals between 1789 and 1848 undermined the economic and political support for plantation slavery among British and French parliamentary elites.

The historical evidence in subsequent chapters highlights the extent to which liberal reforms expanded the legal rights and political agency of emancipated Afro-descendants in forced settlement colonies. The extension of metropolitan legal rights—i.e., British common law or European civil law—to emancipated Afro-descendants generated a uniform and inclusive legal-administrative framework that resembled that of classically liberal European states prior to the suffrage extensions of the late nineteenth century. The economic collapse of large-scale sugar production also promoted colonial officials to enact bureaucratic and administrative reforms that promoted modest economic diversification and expanded the provision of public goods like state-funded education, healthcare, sanitation, and poor relief. Taken together, these liberal reforms enabled most forced settlement colonies to promote more inclusive patterns of human development following the abolition of slavery. It is important to recognize that there were important variations in the extent, timing, and implementation of liberal reforms across different colonial empires. These variations are succinctly outlined here and explored in greater detail in subsequent chapters.

The Industrial Revolution, Abolition, and Liberal Reforms in British Forced Settlement Colonies

Historians have long emphasized the importance of Britain's Industrial Revolution in undermining domestic political support for slave-based sugar production among British political elites and the general British public. The British Industrial Revolution promoted the ascendancy of industrial capitalist elites that opposed the tariffs and duties that protected the economic interests of slave-based sugar production in the British West Indies. In contrast to the preferences of colonial planters, British industrial elites also favored free trade and free wage labor policies that promoted the global expansion of British manufactured exports. These competing economic models were incompatible, and British industrial elites ultimately won out over the conservative aristocratic landowners who supported slave-based sugar production in British forced settlement colonies (Williams 1994, esp. 135–77; Drescher 1987).

The expansion of religious liberty in the United Kingdom also strengthened the political agency of Protestant missionary activists from reformist denominations like the Quakers, Baptists, and Methodists after 1813 (Etherington 2005; Stamatov 2010; Woodberry 2012). Reformist church leaders actively sought to reform the British *ancien régime* that protected the privileges of the established Church of England, and the political dominance of aristocratic landowners, many of whom were slaveholders and plantation owners in the British West Indies (Williams 1994, 178–96). Reformist church leaders and industrial bourgeois capitalists supported the 1832 Reform Act that undermined the political control of aristocratic landowners in Britain and the 1833 Emancipation Act that abolished plantation slavery in British forced settlement colonies. Protestant missionary activists also mobilized British public opinion in favor of abolition and the legal recognition emancipated slaves as free British subjects (Woodberry 2012, 254; Stamatov 2010; Etherington 2005). They successfully lobbied Parliament to establish denominational schools that educated emancipated Afro-descendants in the forced settlement colonies (see Wesley 1932, 1933, 1938; Latimer 1964).

Most British forced settlement colonies experienced a modest expansion in electoral participation and political representation following the abolition of slavery, although income, tax, and property qualifications prevented most Afro-descendants from participating in local elections. These colonial voting restrictions were not initially different from Britain's domestic electoral laws. When slavery was abolished in the British colonial empire, only 4% of British adults were eligible to vote in parliamentary elections.[8] Given the limited extent of voting rights in nineteenth-century Britain, it is not surprising that British forced settlement colonies only permitted a modest expansion of political representation and voting rights following the abolition of slavery. Instead, British colonial officials established direct political control over the forced settlement colonies following the 1865 Morant Bay Rebellion in Jamaica. This system of government is typically referred to as "direct British rule" (see Lange 2009) or "crown colony rule," as it empowered British colonial bureaucrats at the expense of local white planters and emancipated Afro-descendants (see Wrong 1923; Ledgister 1998, 13–19).

British crown colony rule was simultaneously liberal and authoritarian (Ledgister 1998). On the one hand, crown colony rule institutionalized British common law as the sole legal system in British forced settlement colonies. Over time, this enabled emancipated Afro-descendants in the British forced settlement colonies to benefit from the expansion of religious liberty, property rights, and to a lesser extent, freedom of speech and association. The comparatively liberal nature of British common law enabled emancipated slaves to acquire land as independent peasant farmers. It also facilitated the development of civil society organizations—for example, professional associations and labor unions—that enabled nascent political parties to establish deep societal roots prior to independence (see Ledgister 1998). Over the long term, British forced settlement colonies implemented liberal reforms that expanded the administrative capacity of colonial state officials to provide public goods like education, sanitation, and poor relief. Yet direct British control also limited the expansion of voting rights and political representation in British forced settlement colonies (see Ledgister 1998, 13–15, 38–40; Rueschemeyer et al. 1992, 236–44). As late as 1939, fewer than 6% of adults enjoyed voting rights in Barbados, Jamaica, or Trinidad and Tobago (Wallace 1977, 56). Despite the limited extent of voting rights prior to World War II, the historical evidence in Chapter 5 will explore how the expansion the expansion of public goods like state-funded enhanced the legitimacy of the colonial state in ways that facilitated the implementation of democratic reforms after World War II and democratic consolidation after independence.

Revolution, Abolition, and Liberal Reform in the French Antilles Colonies

The French abolition of slavery was driven by revolutionary violence that pitted republican reformers against conservative monarchists and reactionary Bonapartists during the first half of the nineteenth century. The revolutionary upheavals of 1789–1800, 1830, and 1848 generated republican advances that expanded parliamentary representation in France and undermined domestic political support for aristocratic landowners and royalist white planters in the French Antilles colonies. During each revolutionary episode, enslaved Africans and free people of color supported republican demands for liberty, fraternity, and equality. The 1830 French revolution established a liberal constitutional monarchy that expanded parliamentary representation and extended civil and political equality to free people of color in the French Antilles colonies. The 1848 French revolution established a secular and democratic republic that permanently abolished plantation slavery in French colonial territories. The republican government that rose to power in the 1848 French revolution extended parliamentary representation, citizenship rights, and universal male suffrage to emancipated slaves and their descendants in the Antilles colonies (McCloy 1966; Murch 1971; Ledgister 1998, 13; Wright 1976; Girollet 2001). These gains were reversed by the Bonapartist coup that overthrew the Second French Republic in December 1851. The subsequent dictatorship of Louis Napoleon (1852–70) enabled local white planters to regain political control and establish repressive labor laws that severely restricted the civil liberties and economic autonomy of emancipated Afro-descendants in the French Antilles (Heath 2011).

The republicans' egalitarian creed of liberty, fraternity, and equality ultimately prevailed following the establishment of the Third French Republic in the 1870s. Nonwhite Antillean activists organized a republican insurrection against local white planters in French-ruled Martinique during the 1870 Franco-Prussian War (Chivallon and Howard 2017). At the same time, the collapse of Louis Napoleon's dictatorship restored French republicans to power after the Franco-Prussian war. Once again, France's republican elites expanded their electoral coalition by extending political representation and voting rights to emancipated Afro-descendants in the Antilles colonies. The historical evidence in Chapter 7 reveals that the restoration of universal male suffrage and parliamentary representation in the French Antilles colonies was a deliberate political strategy to boost electoral support for republican French governments after 1870. The restored French republic also expanded free, secular, and compulsory primary schooling in the Antilles colonies during the 1880s (McCloy 1966, 153–64; Murch 1971; Wright 1976). French official census records indicate that Guadeloupe, Martinique, and Réunion were the only colonial territories where the overwhelming majority (i.e., more than 98% of the population) enjoyed citizenship rights prior to World War II (France 1944). This enabled the French Antilles colonies to establish compulsory education, parliamentary representation, and universal male suffrage prior to World War II.

The Limited Extent of Liberal Reforms in Portuguese Forced Settlement Colonies

Portugal also experienced a short-lived liberal revolution following the Napoleonic invasion of the Iberian Peninsula between 1808 and 1815. During this period, the Portuguese royal court was evacuated to Rio de Janeiro in Brazil, and the Iberian-American colonies began to agitate for independence from Spanish and Portuguese rule. In response to these events, Portuguese liberal reformers campaigned to extend civil and political equality to "free people of color" in the Portuguese colonial empire. These reforms were intended to secure the political loyalty of Brazilian elites and free people of color following the independence wars in Spanish America (Nogueira da Silva 2011, 106). Brazil ultimately secured its independence from Portuguese rule in 1822, and Cape Verdeans became the primary beneficiaries of the expansion of metropolitan citizenship to emancipated Afro-descendants in the Portuguese colonial empire. Consequently, Cape Verde was the only Portuguese forced settlement colony to recognize universal citizenship rights prior to World War II (Davidson 1989, 43).

Despite the extension of citizenship rights, the legal and political benefits of emancipation were rather limited in Portuguese colonies relative to their British and French counterparts. This is because Portugal failed to democratize (or industrialize) during the nineteenth century. Indeed, Portugal's limited democratization efforts came to an abrupt end following the military coup that overthrew the First Portuguese Republic in 1926. Portuguese conservative elites backed the establishment of a repressive single-party dictatorship, the *Estado Novo* (or New State), that dominated the Portuguese state and its colonial empire from 1930 until 1974 (Davidson 1989; Mentel 1984). The Portuguese dictatorship closed down many of Cape Verde's public schools and prohibited multiparty electoral competition. Despite these setbacks, Cape Verdeans continued to benefit from greater access to state-funded education and electoral participation than indigenous Africans in Portuguese-occupied colonies like Guinea-Bissau, Angola, or Mozambique. Cape Verde has also been far more successful than other Portuguese African colonies in promoting inclusive broad-based development and postcolonial democratization.

This brief historical overview highlights the extent to which liberal reforms were implemented in British, French, and Portuguese forced settlement colonies following the abolition of slavery. Each colonial power introduced liberal reforms that expanded the legal rights and political agency of emancipated Afro-descendants relative to indigenous colonial subjects in their colonies of occupation. The theoretical framework in the next chapter explores the developmental consequences of these reforms for human well-being and postcolonial democratization in forced settlement colonies. The developmental legacies of forced settlement are then contrasted with that of Global South countries that emerged from colonial occupation after 1945.

Colonial Occupation

Rationale and Motivation

Colonial occupation is the more typical mode of imperial domination in which Europeans seized control over indigenous populations and territories that were exploited for their labor and natural resources. The indigenous hinterlands of tropical Asia, Africa, and the Indian subcontinent only came under Western imperial domination after the abolition of slavery in the New World, as Europe's Industrial Revolution fueled rising demand for industrial inputs such as rubber, cotton, and palm oil. The second global wave of imperialist expansion was also fueled by rising nationalism in Europe and the expansion of export markets for European manufactured goods. The territorial expansion of colonial occupation is best exemplified by the "scramble for Africa" at the end of the nineteenth century. Following the 1885 Treaty of Berlin, Europe's dominant imperial powers carved up the entire African continent—apart from Ethiopia and Liberia—into colonial states with little regard for the preexisting social and political considerations of indigenous African ethnicities.[9] In many ways, today's political map of Africa still resembles the colonial map that Europeans established at the Treaty of Berlin.

Colonial occupation lasted less than a century in most African states, but its consequences were profound. European colonists and settlers established agricultural plantations and commercial mines that relied heavily on conscripted labor (Young 1994, 124–38; Ferreira 1974; Cooper 2000). Christian missionaries introduced Western education in ways that favored certain African ethnic groups and subnational regions at the expense of others (Gallego and Woodberry 2010; Frankema 2012; Okoye and Pongou 2014). Several existing studies emphasize the ways in which colonial rulers politicized ethnic differences between indigenous ethnic groups, with negative consequences for postcolonial governance and development (see Posner 2003, 2004, 2005; Mamdani 2002; Ekeh 1975). Colonial administrators also established bifurcated legal-administrative frameworks that privileged colonial settlers and urbanized African elites over rural indigenous African subjects (Mamdani 1996). For these and other reasons, many scholars have argued that colonial occupation hindered the long-term development and democratization of postcolonial African states (see Herbst 2000; Englebert 2000a; Mamdani 1996; Young 1994; Davidson 1992). These studies frame their arguments in a generalized way that is applicable to continental African states with indigenous populations that predate the onset of colonial rule. By contrast, my research highlights important distinctions between forced settlement in Creole African islands like Cape Verde or Mauritius, and the colonial occupation experienced by indigenous African ethnicities in countries like Gabon, Madagascar, Nigeria, Sierra Leone, and Uganda.

Economic Extraction and Compulsory Labor

The political economy of colonial occupation was often as extractive and labor-repressive as that of forced settlement colonies prior to the abolition of slavery. Many African colonies relied on compulsory labor to support infrastructural development. Compulsory labor was also used to develop foreign-owned agricultural plantations and commercial mines. Local chiefs were co-opted to recruit cheap labor for public works, state-owned enterprises, and private commercial enterprises, where they were forced to grow cash crops for export (see Young 1994, 124–38; Ajayi and Crowder 1971; Duignan and Gann 1975, 12–17; Ferreira 1974; Buell 1928). Colonial officials and indigenous intermediaries (i.e., local "chiefs") used extra-economic coercion to recruit African laborers for European-owned enterprises and public works. Compulsory labor laws ensured that African workers were compensated well below the free-market wage rate: indeed, wages were often paid in food or vouchers (Mamdani 1996, 148–65). The forced recruitment of indigenous African laborers remained legal and widespread long after the abolition of plantation slavery and indentured labor migration in forced settlement colonies. Many British-occupied colonies maintained forced labor recruitment into the 1920s or later (Duignan and Gann 1975, 16–17). French- and Belgian-occupied colonies maintained forced labor recruitment until the end of World War II (Cooper 2000; Mann 2009; Cooper 2014, 67–68; Jennings 2015); and Portuguese-occupied colonies maintained forced labor recruitment until the outbreak of anticolonial revolutionary violence in Angola in 1961 (Ferreira 1974; Mamdani 1996, 156).

The Bifurcated Colonial State and Its "Native" Legal Codes

Colonial occupation also resulted in the construction of bifurcated colonial states, with separate legal-administrative frameworks for "colonial settlers" and "indigenous subjects" (see Mamdani 1996; Lange 2009, 4; Mann 2009; Owolabi 2017). A small number of colonial officials controlled Africa's vast indigenous populations and territories using bifurcated legal-administrative institutions that privileged colonial settlers, urban elites, and, in some cases, Western-educated Africans over rural indigenous subjects. The bifurcated colonial state had a thin bureaucratic apparatus that was concentrated in its administrative capital and principal areas of European settlement. Outlying rural areas, by contrast, were governed with decentralized and patrimonial institutions that controlled indigenous colonial subjects under a separate legal code. Metropolitan (i.e., European) legal rights were restricted to colonial settlers, emancipated Creole Africans, and urbanized African elites. Colonial migrant populations, like the South Asian communities in East Africa, or the Lebanese and Syrian migrants in French West Africa, were also governed under European legal institutions. By contrast, rural indigenous Africans were subject to distinctive "native" legal codes that denied basic individual liberties such as freedom of speech, freedom of movement, freedom of association, and trial by jury (Mamdani 1996).[10] Throughout this book, the term *indigenous colonial subjects* refers to indigenous populations that were subject to "native" legal codes that restricted their civil liberties and political rights during the colonial era. All colonies of occupation maintained important legal distinctions between colonial settlers and indigenous subjects, despite the important differences between indirect British rule and the more centralized administrative approach of continental European powers like France and Portugal.

Legal-Administrative Bifurcation and Extractive Institutions in British-Occupied Colonies

British colonial officials favored an indirect approach to colonial occupation that delegated significant local autonomy to traditional indigenous elites (i.e., "chiefs") that controlled important government functions such as tax collection, labor recruitment, and the maintenance of law and order. Indirect British rule was pioneered in colonial India, where British colonial officials devolved local political autonomy to more than 600 Indian "princes" following the 1857 Sepoy rebellion (Lange 2009, 23–24). Indirect rule became the preferred British method for controlling indigenous African populations during the first half of the twentieth century (see Hailey 1957; Crowder 1964; Lange 2009, 170–71). Existing research by Matthew Lange (2009), Mahmood Mamdani (1996), and others have highlighted the extent to which indirect British rule created "bifurcated colonial states" based on two radically different organizational principles: the central government was under the control of a tiny bureaucratic apparatus that was primarily concentrated in the administrative capital and areas of European settlement. In peripheral regions, by contrast, indigenous intermediaries—i.e., African "chiefs," Indian princes, traditional Muslim emirs, or sultans—controlled "customary" legal-administrative institutions that were organized along patrimonial lines. Accordingly, "Patrimonial rulers and bureaucratic officials . . . depended on and collaborated with one another to maintain a decentralized and divided system of colonial domination" (Lange 2009, 4).

British indirect rule empowered traditional African rulers (i.e., "chiefs") to collect taxes, recruit labor for commercial enterprises and infrastructural projects, and enforce "customary laws" in "native courts." In African societies that lacked traditional chiefs, the British simply appointed "administrative chiefs" or "warrant chiefs" to fulfill these roles (Afigbo 1966, 1973). Colonial governments supported local chiefs with monetary stipends and granted them extensive local autonomy over "native administration," including control over local courts, prisons, and "native police." Many British officials genuinely believed that they were preserving the traditional authority structure of African societies (see Crowder 1964; Hailey 1957; Perham 1937), but recent studies suggests that indirect British rule increased the despotic power of traditional "chiefs" by removing traditional checks on their authority (see Migdal 1988; Mamdani 1996, especially 43–48; Lange 2009, 96–100; Acemoglu, Reed, and Robinson 2014; Palagashvili 2018). Control over "customary courts" enabled African chiefs to impose levies and fines and extract resources and labor from their communities, which often encouraged widespread corruption and rent-seeking behavior. So long as African chiefs supported the British by collecting taxes, recruiting labor, and maintaining social control in rural areas, British district officials turned a blind eye to extractive or rent-seeking behaviors that impeded the long-term development of their societies (Lange 2009; Mamdani 1996; Palagashvili 2018).

The legal distinction between metropolitan British subjects in directly ruled urban areas and indigenous subjects in indirectly ruled rural areas was very clear to African populations and foreign observers at the time. In general, rural indigenous populations were subject to indirect rule and "customary law," whereas direct British rule predominated in the administrative capitals and areas of European settlement, where the colonial state maintained a monopoly over law, policy, and administration. In colonial Sierra Leone, for example, the capital city, Freetown, was directly ruled under British law, whereas African chiefs enforced "customary laws" in outlying rural districts (Lange 2009, ch. 5). The same was true of colonial Nigeria, although indirect rule was not particularly effective in southeastern regions of the country that lacked traditional "chiefs" prior to colonization (Falola 1999, 71–72). During the 1930s, the Afro-Trinidadian historian George Padmore wrote that direct British rule conferred "[legal] rights and privileges" on metropolitan British subjects, including the Creole African descendants of liberated slaves in Freetown. In peripheral regions, by contrast, "British-protected natives [i.e., indigenous Africans] had no civil liberties, no freedom of the Press, no freedom of speech," and "no constitutional rights to invoke" (Padmore 1969, 313–14). Perhaps not surprisingly then, existing empirical studies demonstrate poor developmental outcomes and ineffective postcolonial governance in British colonies that relied heavily on indirect rule, such as Nigeria, Sierra Leone, Sudan, and Uganda (see Migdal 1988; Lange 2004, 2009; Acemoglu, Reed, and Robinson 2014). By contrast, existing studies demonstrate favorable development outcomes in directly ruled British colonies such as Barbados, Hong Kong, Jamaica, Mauritius, Singapore, and Trinidad and Tobago (see Lange 2004, 2009).

Legal-Administrative Bifurcation and Extractive Institutions in French-Occupied Colonies

French colonial officials favored more centralized methods of administrative control than their British counterparts (see Perham 1937; Crowder 1964, 1968; Ajayi and Crowder 1973; Grier 1999; Herbst 2000, 81), but they also developed distinct "native codes" to control indigenous colonial subjects. The French *indigénat* legal code was first devised to quell Arab Muslim resistance to French colonial expansion in Algeria. Following their military success in Algeria, French colonial officials extended the repressive *indigénat* legal code to control indigenous populations in Indochina, New Caledonia, and throughout French West and Equatorial Africa (Merle 2002; Mann 2009, 333). The *indigénat* legal code enabled French colonial administrators to impose summary justice on indigenous colonial subjects, including Algerian Muslims, black Africans, Indochinese, and native Pacific Islanders, whose civil liberties were not protected by French civil law.

Historian Gregory Mann describes the *indigénat* legal code as a "regime of exception" that concentrated local authority in the hands of French district officials known as *commandants*. The French *commandant* held administrative, judicial, and, in many cases, military powers over local administrative districts. The *indigénat* legal code empowered French district officials "to accuse, condemn, and sanction [indigenous colonial subjects] in an instant, [and] with little oversight" (Mann 2009, 333). Moreover, French administrative officials served as "both judge and prosecutor" in local courts that operated independently of French civil law (Mann 2009, 339–40). The *indigénat* legal code created a separate series of crimes that only indigenous people could commit, including "witchcraft," insulting a colonial official, disobeying the orders of a colonial official, or carrying firearms in areas inhabited by Europeans (Merle 2002, 87). It also empowered French colonial officials to collect taxes and recruit corvée labor for road construction and other public works. Perhaps most egregiously, the *indigénat* legal code permitted the collective punishment of entire indigenous communities that resisted tax collection or forced labor recruitment. In this way, French colonial administrators could impose sanctions such as fines or forced labor on an entire village or community. This practice of collective punishments completely violated any notion of individual liberty or "rule of law" for indigenous African subjects (Mann 2009, 340–43). Nevertheless, French administrators considered these extraordinary powers as necessary, given the limited administrative capacity of colonial state officials in outlying rural districts.

French colonial occupation also generated ineffective colonial states that resembled the bifurcated legal-administrative structure of British-occupied colonies. The French-occupied colonies in West and Equatorial Africa also had an extremely "thin" bureaucratic apparatus that was heavily concentrated in two administrative capitals, Dakar and Brazzaville. There were very few colonial officials in the rural indigenous hinterlands. As late as 1939, only 3,660 French colonial officials were responsible for 15 million colonial subjects in French West Africa. In French Equatorial Africa, only 887 French colonial officials were responsible for governing 3 million African subjects in a vast and densely forested territory with 2.5 million square kilometers—more than four times the landmass of France (Herbst 2000, 78). To compensate for their limited manpower, French district officers (i.e., *commandants*) appointed "administrative chiefs" (known as *chefs de canton*) to collect taxes, maintain public order, and recruit labor. Because of the limited number of European colonial officials in sub-Saharan Africa, both the French and the British relied heavily on local indigenous intermediaries to carry out basic administrative functions in outlying rural districts of colonial states with significant indigenous populations.

Nevertheless, the French method of colonial administration was more centralized and hierarchical than in indirectly ruled British colonies. Whereas British officials sought to preserve traditional authority structures as much as possible, French colonial officials, were far more distrustful of traditional African elites. Consequently, they tended to recruit French-speaking African soldiers, clerks, and interpreters who had served the colonial administration for at least four years. Given France's preference for centralized administrative control, these "administrative chiefs" were paid state officials who served at the lowest rung of the colonial administration. They were typically posted to distant administrative districts (i.e., *cantons*) where they had no traditional legitimacy. Furthermore, they did not control traditional "customary courts" like their counterparts in the British colonial empire. Instead, they were empowered to collect taxes, recruit labor, and enforce the hated *indigénat* legal code on other African subjects (Crowder 1964, 199–200). Perhaps not surprisingly, the "administrative chiefs" in French West Africa had less legitimacy in rural African communities than their counterparts in British African colonies (see Geschière 1993; Kirk-Greene 1995).

The *indigénat* legal code was the most repressive aspect of French colonial occupation in sub-Saharan Africa (Mann 2009). As a result of the *indigénat* legal code, indigenous colonial populations were subject to heavy taxation and forced labor, and colonial schools primarily catered to the sons of urban elites and administrative chiefs. A small number of indigenous colonial subjects—mostly administrative chiefs, veterans that had served in the French army, and Western-educated Africans that maintained a "European" lifestyle—were exempted from the *indigénat* legal code after World War I (Young 1994, 155), but the *indigénat* legal code was enforced in French-occupied colonies until 1946 (Merle 2002; Mann 2009). Indigenous black Africans only gained limited citizenship rights within the French Union after 1946, but they were never able to secure equal political representation in the French National Assembly. This was one of the political grievances that generated demands for political independence from France after 1958 (Cooper 2014; Chafer 2002).

Legal-Administrative Bifurcation and Extractive Institutions in Portuguese-Occupied Colonies

Portuguese-occupied colonies also established a bifurcated legal-administrative framework that distinguished metropolitan Portuguese citizens (i.e., *civilisados*) from indigenous colonial subjects (i.e., *indigenas*). Portuguese civil laws only applied to metropolitan citizens, while a distinctive legal framework, the *regime do indigenato*, was applied to indigenous colonial subjects. The Portuguese *indigenato* system was even more extractive, repressive, and arbitrary than the French *indigénat* code. In addition to imposing compulsory labor on indigenous African subjects, the Portuguese *indigenato* legal code prevented indigenous Africans from attending state-funded public schools (Duffy 1961). The Portuguese *indigenato* legal code was also used to mobilize labor recruitment for colonial plantations, commercial mines, and public infrastructure projects (Ferreira 1974; Duffy 1959). The *indigenato* legal code was enforced in Portuguese-occupied colonies—i.e., Angola, Guinea-Bissau, Mozambique, and Timor—until the start of Angola's independence war in 1961 (Mamdani 1996, 83–74; O'Laughlin 2000).

Colonial Occupation and Bifurcated Legal-Administrative Institutions beyond Sub-Saharan Africa

Bifurcated legal-administrative institutions were also used to control indigenous colonial populations beyond sub-Saharan Africa. This is clearly evident in the Indian subcontinent, where British officials used both indirect and direct methods of political control. British officials established direct political control over parts of the Indian subcontinent where the British East India company had expanded its territorial control between 1757 and 1857. Nevertheless, Indian army recruits rebelled against the territorial expansion and political control of the British East India Company during the 1857 Sepoy mutiny. It took more than a year for British military forces to suppress this rebellion, which forced Britain to recognize the local autonomy of more than 600 indirectly ruled "princely states" (Lange 2009, 23–24, 176–79; Varghese 2016, 22–23; Naseemullah and Staniland 2016; Lankina and Getachew 2012). These princely states co-existed alongside directly ruled areas of "British India," and they were ultimately integrated into the modern nations of India, Pakistan, and Bangladesh following the independence of these countries. The political autonomy of these "princely states" limited the expansion of British common law in the Indian subcontinent, where 50% of legal cases were handled by "customary" law courts rather than British common-law courts (Lange 2009, 48).[11]

Bifurcated legal-administrative institutions were also established in French-ruled Algeria, where the French *indigénat* code restricted the legal rights of indigenous Arab Muslims (Merle 2002; McDougall 2017). These extractive institutions enabled French colonists and settlers to expropriate indigenous lands and undermine the political agency of Arab Muslims in Algeria. The same type of bifurcation existed in French Indochina, where French civil law protected the rights of colonial settlers, and denied the citizenship rights of indigenous colonial subjects. The *indigénat* legal code also sanctioned the widespread use of forced labor in French Indochina (Merle 2002).

One might argue that the large populations and expansive territory of these colonies necessitated the use of extractive legal-administrative institutions and repressive "native" legal codes to control vast and widely dispersed indigenous populations. After all, the population and territory of most colonies of occupation was significantly larger than the forced settlement colonies that implemented significant liberal reforms following the abolition of slavery. This is why several scholars, including Jeffrey Herbst (2000) and Adria Lawrence (2013), have argued that colonial authorities were less likely to implement reforms in colonial states with large and widely dispersed indigenous populations. Nevertheless, "native" legal codes were also used to control indigenous populations in island microstates like French Polynesia and New Caledonia (Merle 2002), Fiji and the Solomon Islands (Lange 2009, 174–76), and Portuguese Timor (Portugal 1950, 1960). These island microstates have small populations and territories that resemble forced settlement colonies, but their overwhelmingly indigenous populations were nonetheless excluded from European citizenship, and their legal rights were restricted by "native" legal codes. This demonstrates that colonial officials favored the use of "native" legal codes to control indigenous colonial subjects, even in island microstates with tiny populations. Every colonial power used bifurcated legal-administrative institutions to control indigenous colonial subjects, and this practice was not unique to sub-Saharan Africa.

Comparing Forced Settlement and Colonial Occupation

So far, this chapter has outlined an important conceptual distinction between forced settlement and colonial occupation as distinctive modes of imperial domination in the Global South. Both modes of imperial domination established "extractive" colonial economies with limited European settlement, but the important differences between forced settlement and colonial occupation are summarized in Table 2.1. To recap, forced settlement refers to the pattern of colonization in which Europeans established agricultural plantations in newly settled territories using imported African slaves and/or Asian indentured labor. This primarily occurred in Creole African islands that were uninhabited prior to colonization (e.g., Cape Verde, Mauritius) and in Caribbean territories where enslaved Africans replaced indigenous populations that were decimated by European colonization efforts during the sixteenth century. The mass influx of enslaved Africans and South Asian indentured laborers into forced settlement colonies generated hybrid Creole societies that are significantly different from

Table 2.1 Key Differences between Forced Settlement and Colonial Occupation

	Forced Settlement	Colonial Occupation
Definition	European colonists establish agricultural plantations with imported African slaves and/or South Asian indentured laborers. Descendants of "forced settlement" comprise at least 75% of the postcolonial population.	Europeans control indigenous populations and territories to exploit their labor and natural resources. Indigenous ethnic groups comprise at least 75% of the postcolonial population.
Geographic location(s)	Creole African islands + non-Hispanic Caribbean region (i.e., West Indies)	Continental Africa, the Indian subcontinent, parts of Southeast Asia, Middle East, and North Africa
Years of formal colonization	Mostly 1600s–1975	Mostly 1880s–1960s
Cultural differences	Creole societies of mixed African, European, and/or Asian ancestry. Varying levels of ethno-racial and religious diversity.	Indigenous societies with varying levels of ethnic, religious, and linguistic diversity.
Institutional differences (late 19th century):	Abolition of slavery → liberal reforms that expand the legal rights and political agency of emancipated Afro-descendants.	Territorial expansion of European control → indigenous resistance → bifurcated legal-administrative institutions that undermine the legal rights and political agency of indigenous colonial subjects.
Legal-administrative institutions	Colonial powers implement liberal reforms → inclusive legal-administrative institutions following the abolition of slavery. Postabolition reforms generate a centralized colonial state with territory-wide bureaucratic apparatus; uniform and inclusive legal code derived from metropolitan law (e.g., British common law or French civil law).	Bifurcated colonial states establish extractive institutions with distinct legal codes for "colonial settlers" vs. "indigenous subjects." Colonies are governed with a thin bureaucratic apparatus concentrated in the administrative capital; colonial state reinforces patrimonial institutions in outlying rural districts.

(continued)

Table 2.1 Continued

	Forced Settlement	Colonial Occupation
Legal rights / citizenship rights	Inclusive legal rights based on British common law / French civil law. Emancipated Afro-descendants are legally classified as free British subjects or metropolitan European citizens.	Extractive legal-administrative institutions. Indirect British rule/French "native legal codes" limit the institutionalization of British common law / French civil law, undermining the legal rights and political agency of indigenous colonial subjects.
Postcolonial development	Effective, inclusive state-building promotes broad-based human development that facilitates postcolonial democratization.	Bifurcated colonial state limits broad-based human development and hinders postcolonial democratization.

the indigenous cultures and ethnicities that predate the onset of European colonization in these regions. In contrast to forced settlement, colonial occupation refers to the more typical pattern of imperial domination in which Europeans exploited the labor and natural resources of pre-existing indigenous populations that were present in the territory at the time of its colonization. Colonial occupation is primarily associated with the second global wave of imperialist expansion in the late nineteenth century, when Europeans expanded their territorial control over indigenous populations in the Indian subcontinent, Southeast Asia, and continental Africa.

Table 2.1 also highlights the very different legal-administrative institutions associated with forced settlement and colonial occupation following the abolition of slavery in the nineteenth century. In general, forced settlement colonies implemented liberal reforms that expanded the legal rights and political agency of emancipated Afro-descendants following the abolition of slavery in the nineteenth century. By contrast, colonies of occupation developed a bifurcated legal-administrative framework with separate governing institutions for "colonial settlers" and "indigenous subjects." While the institutions varied across different colonizers, the bifurcated legal-administrative frameworks associated with colonial occupation—i.e., indirect British rule and the French and Portuguese *indigénat/indigenato* legal codes—restricted the legal rights and political agency of indigenous colonial subjects relative to colonial settlers. In this regard, the bifurcated legal-administrative institutions associated with colonial occupation were far more extractive and repressive than the legal-administrative institutions that governed emancipated Afro-descendants following the abolition of slavery in forced settlement colonies.

Relation to Existing Typologies of Colonialism

Many readers will be familiar with existing typologies of colonialism that emphasize distinctions between settler and extractive colonization, direct and indirect rule, and formal and informal empire. Consequently, the final section of this chapter situates this historical overview of forced settlement and colonial occupation in relation to existing typologies of colonialism.

Settler versus Extractive Colonialism

Most readers will be familiar with the conceptual distinction between settler and extractive colonization from Daron Acemoglu, Simon Johnson, and James Robinson's seminal research papers on colonial institutions and economic growth. The term "settler colony" refers to colonial states where "Europeans settled in large numbers, and life was modeled after the home country" (Acemoglu, Johnson, and Robinson 2001, 1374). Most settler colonies were established in temperate regions of the New World that had relatively small indigenous populations and geographic conditions that were suitable for European agriculture and settlement on small family farms. European settler colonies tended to develop representative institutions, strong protections for property rights, and institutional checks against government power, as colonial settlers tried to replicate the economic, political, and legal institutions of their home country (Acemoglu, Johnson, and Robinson 2001, 1370). This is particularly true of British settler colonies like the United States, Canada, Australia, and New Zealand. All of these countries extended voting rights and political participation to white male adult settlers during the nineteenth century, and they were among the first wave of countries to democratize worldwide (Huntington 1991; Rueschemeyer, Stephens, and Stephens 1992). British settler societies have also sustained high levels of economic growth that boosted human well-being and development over the *longue durée* (Sokoloff and Engerman 2000; Acemoglu, Johnson, and Robinson 2001, 2002; Krieckhaus 2006; Fails and Krieckhaus 2010).

In contrast to the settler colonies in temperate regions of the New World, extractive colonies were established in tropical regions where Europeans faced high mortality rates between 1500 and 1900. According to Acemoglu, Johnson, and Robinson (2001), "There were few constraints on state power in the non-settler colonies, [where colonial authorities] set up authoritarian and absolutist states with the purpose of solidifying their control and facilitating the extraction of resources" (1375). Consequently, these colonial states developed extractive economies that exploited the labor of enslaved Africans and/or indigenous nonwhite populations. Their economic and political institutions offered limited protection for indigenous property rights, and there were few institutional checks against the abuse of state power. The main purpose of these extractive institutions was to transfer as much as possible of the colony's resources to the imperial power. Perhaps not surprisingly, Acemoglu, Johnson, and Robinson's research demonstrates poor development outcomes in "extractive" colonies relative to colonial states with extensive European settlement (2002), and historically low mortality rates for European colonial settlers (2001).

Although Acemoglu, Johnson, and Robinson's work is widely cited, their typology of "settler colonialism" versus "extractive colonization" is not useful for understanding this study's conceptual distinction between forced settlement and colonial occupation. Both forced settlement and colonial occupation would be considered "extractive" forms of colonization in Acemoglu, Johnson, and Robinson's terminology. After all, forced settlement colonies developed large-scale agricultural plantations with imported African slaves and Asian indentured laborers, while colonial occupation exploited the labor and natural resources of indigenous African, Asian, and Arab populations and territories. Acemoglu, Johnson, and Robinson's research is correct in demonstrating a historical relationship between high settler mortality rates and extractive institutions in the Global South. Nevertheless, my research demonstrates that many forced settlement colonies implemented liberal reforms that expanded the legal rights and political agency of emancipated Afro-descendants following the abolition of slavery. These reforms ultimately contributed to favorable development outcomes in forced settlement colonies relative to Global South countries that experienced colonial occupation.

In contrast to other Global South countries, the developmental trajectory of forced settlement colonies was shaped by extractive institutions during the seventeenth and eighteenth centuries, and inclusive legal-administrative institutions during the late nineteenth and early twentieth centuries. Because forced settlement colonies developed relatively inclusive legal-administrative institutions following the abolition of slavery, they experienced favorable development outcomes relative to colonies of occupation that maintained extractive institutions for indigenous colonial subjects. This is why most forced settlement colonies have intermediate development outcomes that lag behind European settler societies in the New World (see Sokoloff and Engerman 2000), but they exceed the developmental outcomes of Global South countries that emerged from colonial occupation after World War II (Owolabi 2015).

Direct versus Indirect Rule

Another well-known typology from existing literature is the conceptual distinction between direct and indirect forms of colonial rule. This conceptual distinction originates from the writings of colonial administrators and historians from the early and middle decades of the twentieth century (see Lugard 1922; Perham 1937; Hailey 1957; Crowder 1964). Indirect rule is generally understood as "a form of political control in which agents of the state delegate day-to-day governance to local power-holders in areas considered beyond the reach of the state's direct authority" (Naseemullah and Staniland 2016, 14). Indirect rule empowered local chiefs, princes, sultans, and other indigenous elites that collaborated with colonial state officials to govern rural indigenous populations in peripheral districts, where the administrative control of colonial state officials was limited (Lange 2009, 4). By contrast, direct rule is a much more hegemonic form of political control in which "the state maintains and administers a monopoly of law, policy, and administration to the population without intermediaries, through bureaucrats without independent means of coercion" (Naseemullah and Staniland 2016, 14). Although these basic definitions of direct and indirect rule are largely uncontested, there are vigorous and ongoing debates about the political determinants of direct and indirect rule, and which colonial territories employed these contrasting methods of governance.

Some scholars argue that indirect rule was favored by conservative colonial officials that prioritized social stability and the preservation of traditional authority structure, whereas liberal universalists favored the transformative power and assimilationist institutions of direct colonial rule. These views are often espoused in older Africanist studies that emphasize distinctions between British and French administrative in colonial Africa (see Perham 1937; Crowder 1964, 1968; Ajayi and Crowder 1973; Mazrui 1983). It is certainly true that British colonial officials were more accommodating of traditional authority structures than their French counterparts in colonial Africa (see Crowder 1964, 1968; Ajayi and Crowder 1973; Wucherpfennig, Hunziker, and Cederman 2016). This partly reflects the fact British officials tended to prioritize social order and political stability in colonial territories with large and widely dispersed indigenous populations, whereas legal and political assimilation became an important objective for republican French officials following the revolutionary upheavals of the nineteenth century (Betts 1961; Lewis 1962; Conklin 1997). Nevertheless, it is clear—even in these older studies—that the high cost of state-building and the constant threat of indigenous rebellion forced all colonial rulers to employ indigenous intermediaries in outlying rural districts of continental African states (see Deschamps 1963; Crowder 1964; Ajayi and Crowder 1973; Geschière 1993; Young 1994, 107–13; Herbst 2000, 81–84) and in outlying districts of British India, where the administrative reach of colonial state officials remained limited (see Naseemullah and Staniland 2016; Mukherjee 2018). The historical overview in this chapter also highlights the extent to which all colonial rulers developed distinctive legal frameworks for colonial settlers and indigenous subjects in colonial territories with large and widely dispersed indigenous populations. The arbitrary and exclusionary nature of these colonial "native legal codes" is also highlighted in existing studies by Mahmood Mamdani (1996), Isabelle Merle (2002), and Gregory Mann (2009) and in my earlier research (see Owolabi 2015, 2017).

My conceptual distinction between forced settlement and colonial occupation is consistent with more recent studies that acknowledge variations of direct and indirect rule within the British and French colonial empires (see Young 1994, 107–13; Mamdani 1996; Conklin 1997; Lange 2004, 2009; Gerring et al. 2011, 400–404; Naseemullah and Staniland 2016; Lawrence 2020). My analysis of British forced settlement and colonial occupation also builds on Matthew Lange's seminal research on the distinctive developmental legacies of direct and indirect British rule. Lange (2004, 2009) argues that direct British rule established effective states that were able to promote inclusive human development and effective governance over the *longue durée,* whereas indirect British rule established extractive and ineffective states that impeded human development and undermined postcolonial democratization. Lange's measurement of indirect rule is based on the percentage of legal cases that were handled by traditional chiefs in "customary courts" during the mid-1950s, and it demonstrates varying degrees of direct and indirect rule in all British colonies with large and widely dispersed indigenous populations. Using this indicator, all British-occupied colonies apart from Sri Lanka employed varying degrees of indirect rule, and British indirect rule was most widespread in continental African states like Nigeria, Sierra Leone, Sudan, and Uganda. By contrast, all British forced settlement colonies that were included in Lange's data analysis are classified as directly ruled colonies (see Lange 2009, 48).[12]

Lange's conceptual distinction between direct and indirect British rule, and his theoretical model of distinctive patterns of state-building within the British colonial empire, are useful for understanding the favorable development legacies of British forced settlement colonies relative to British colonial occupation. Nevertheless, it is important to remember that direct British rule also generated inclusive human development and early democratization in British settler colonies like Australia, Canada, and New Zealand. In city-state colonies like Hong Kong and Singapore, direct British rule promoted spectacular economic growth without significant democratization. These directly ruled British colonies lacked the type of extractive institutions and coercive labor policies that characterized British forced settlement prior to the abolition of slavery. This shows significant variation in the extent to which directly ruled British colonies enforced coercive labor policies and "centralized despotism" (see Mamdani 1996) or inclusive economic and political institutions that facilitated long-term development (see Acemoglu and Robinson 2012). The fact that forced settlement colonies were able to promote inclusive long-term development despite the legacies of slavery is an important empirical puzzle that is not adequately addressed in existing studies of direct and indirect rule (see Mamdani 1996; Lange 2004, 2005, 2009; Gerring et al. 2011; Acemoglu, Reed, and Robinson 2014; Naseemullah and Staniland 2016). Consequently, my conceptual distinction between forced settlement and colonial occupation moves beyond existing frameworks of direct and indirect rule to explain the diverse developmental trajectories of Global South countries with predominantly nonwhite populations that emerged from colonial domination after 1945.

Formal versus Informal Empire

Another important and well-known typology highlights the conceptual distinction between formal and informal methods of imperial control. Atul Kohli (2020) distinguishes between formal methods of imperial control that establish colonial states whose sovereignty is controlled by an external power and informal methods of imperial control in which an external imperial power maintains de facto control over the key economic and security interests of "client states" in the Global South. In situations of informal empire, the imperial metropole does not legally control the dependent peripheral country, but "it maintains effective control—veto power—over policies in the periphery that infringe on the real or perceived interests of the metropole" (Kohli 2020, 7). Informal imperialism sustains clientelistic relations between national political elites in the dependent client states and imperialist elites that expand their economic, political, and military power in dependent client states. By contrast, formal imperialism establishes colonial states that lack sovereign control over their external relations and domestic political affairs. According to Atul Kohli (2020), the concept of formal empire—or colonialism—is useful for understanding Britain's legally recognized political control over India or Nigeria during the first half of the twentieth century, whereas the concept of informal empire is useful for understanding the expansion of British economic and military power in Egypt, China, and Latin American countries like Argentina during the nineteenth century. The concept of informal empire is also useful for understanding the expansion of US economic and military power in Latin America throughout the twentieth century, and the expansion of US economic and military power in Pacific Asia and the Middle East after World War II.

It should be clear from these definitions that forced settlement and colonial occupation are both examples of formal colonization, rather than informal imperialism in the Global South. Colonial powers like Britain, France, and Portugal maintained formal control over their forced settlement colonies and colonies of occupation into the twentieth century. Most of these colonial territories gained independence after World War II, although France, to a greater extent than Britain or Portugal, has maintained many vestiges of imperial control over its forced settlement colonies, which became French overseas departments in 1946. Nevertheless, the relationship between Britain or France and their colonial territories in the Global South was very different from the British or US relationship to Latin American countries following their independence from Spanish or Portuguese rule.

Kohli (2020) argues that the main motivations for imperialism—whether formal or informal—are to expand the economic and military interests of imperial powers in the global periphery. Yet global powers are more likely to pursue informal methods of imperial control when global conditions are not conducive to the establishment of colonies. Kohli also argues that formal methods of imperial control, such as the British colonization of Nigeria or India, tended to generate worse developmental outcomes than informal British or American imperialism in the Middle East, Latin America, or Pacific Asia. This argument is generally persuasive, but Kohli's (2020) research primarily focuses on informal examples of imperialism. His research also overlooks the extent to which forced settlement colonies have outperformed colonies of occupation on key indicators of human well-being and postcolonial democratization.

Summary and Discussion

This chapter presents a historical overview of forced settlement and colonial occupation that advances existing empirical studies of imperialism, state-building, and long-term development in the Global South. This conceptual distinction between forced settlement and colonial occupation differs significantly from existing typologies that emphasize distinctions between formal and informal imperialism (see Kohli 2020) and the distinction between European settler colonialism and extractive colonization in the Global South (see Acemoglu, Johnson, and Robinson 2001, 2002; Krieckhaus 2006). There is some overlap between forced settlement colonization and the type of direct rule that was employed in British plantation colonies, but direct British rule was also implemented in city-state colonies like Hong Kong and Singapore and British settler colonies like Australia, Canada, and the United States (see Lange 2009). British colonial occupation relied on varying degrees of indirect rule to control indigenous populations in the Indian subcontinent and continental Africa (see Lange 2004, 2009; Kohli 2020; Naseemullah and Staniland 2016), but continental European powers also established "native legal codes" to control indigenous populations in their colonies of occupation (see Mamdani 1996; Owolabi 2017).

Consequently, the historical overview in this chapter highlights the distinctive legal-administrative institutions that distinguished forced settlement colonies from colonies of occupation following the abolition of slavery in the New World. This is a novel and important contribution that extends beyond existing typologies of settler versus extractive colonization, and formal versus informal imperial control.

Figure 2.1 situates forced settlement and colonial occupation with other varieties of Western imperial domination that emerged after 1500. Moving from left to right, the horizontal axis of Figure 2.1 shows variations in the degree of political control, from informal imperialism to the formal establishment of colonial states. The vertical axis shows variations in the extent of European settlement from low to high. Forced settlement and colonial occupation are both located in the lower-right quadrant of Figure 2.1, indicating low levels of European settlement and a highly formalized pattern of political control. The left side of Figure 2.1 is populated by examples of informal imperialism with low, intermediate, or high levels of European settlement. These examples of informal British and US imperialism are excluded from this study, which primarily examines the divergent developmental legacies of forced settlement and colonial occupation in the Global South. The more formalized nature of colonial domination in forced settlement colonies is indicative of direct rule, and the establishment of European legal-administrative institutions following the abolition of slavery. The degree of political control established in colonies of occupation was somewhat less formal because these colonial states relied on indigenous intermediaries and patrimonial forms of domination to control their vast and widely dispersed indigenous populations. Nevertheless, colonies of occupation experienced a more formalized pattern of political control than British East India Company rule prior to the 1857 Sepoy rebellion (see Kohli 2020) or the British-protected client states in Egypt (see Kohli 2020) or the Persian Gulf region (see Owolabi 2015).

The location of forced settlement colonies in the lower-right quadrant of Figure 2.1 also highlights their intensive and highly formalized pattern of colonial state-building, despite low levels of European settlement. The extent of European settlement in forced settlement colonies—often less than 5% of the population—was significantly lower than in South Africa (~25%) and in Latin American countries like Brazil or Cuba, where European descendants comprised approximately 50% and 66% of their respective populations at the beginning of the twentieth century. This is why the pattern of state-building that occurred in forced settlement colonies is conceptually distinct from that of partial settler colonies that gained independence under the political domination of local white and light-skinned elites during the nineteenth century.

Despite the fact that forced settlement and colonial occupation established extractive colonial states with limited European settlement, most forced

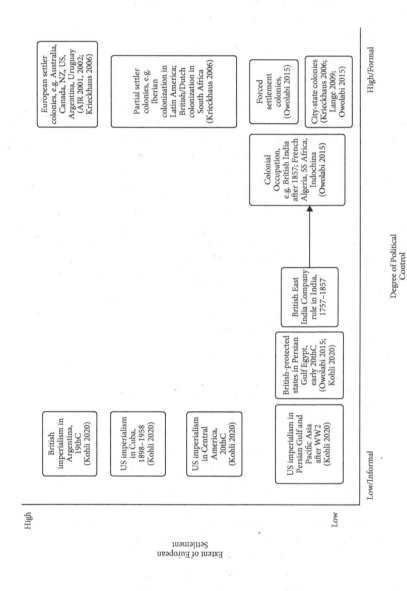

Figure 2.1 Varieties of imperial control in the Global South

European settler colonies, e.g. Australia, Canada, NZ, US, Argentina, Uruguay (AJR 2001, 2002; Krieckhaus 2006)

Partial settler colonies, e.g. Iberian colonization in Latin America; British/Dutch colonization in South Africa (Krieckhaus 2006)

Forced settlement colonies, (Owolabi 2015)

City-state colonies (Krieckhaus 2006; Lange 2009; Owolabi 2015)

Colonial Occupation, e.g. British India after 1857; French Algeria, SS Africa, Indochina (Owolabi 2015)

British East India Company rule in India, 1757–1857

British imperialism in Argentina, 19thC (Kohli 2020)

US imperialism in Cuba, 1898–1958 (Kohli 2020)

US imperialism in Central America, 20thC (Kohli 2020)

British-protected states in Persian Gulf Egypt, early 20thC (Owolabi 2015; Kohli 2020)

US imperialism in Persian Gulf and Pacific Asia after WW2 (Kohli 2020)

Extent of European Settlement

High

Low

Low/Informal

High/Formal

Degree of Political Control

settlement colonies ultimately promoted favorable development outcomes relative to Global South countries that emerged from colonial occupation after 1945.
To explain this surprising divergence, the historical overview in this chapter
emphasizes the importance of liberal reforms that expanded the legal rights and
political agency of emancipated Afro-descendants in forced settlement colonies
following the abolition of slavery. The next chapter advances the book's argument that liberal reforms enabled most forced settlement colonies to promote
favorable development outcomes relative to Global South countries that experienced colonial occupation. This is because the postabolition reforms that expanded the legal rights of emancipated Afro-descendants were seldom extended
to indigenous nonwhite populations that were colonized after the abolition of
slavery in the New World. Instead, most colonies of occupation established
bifurcated legal-administrative frameworks that privileged colonial settlers at
the expense of indigenous colonial subjects. The maintenance of coercive labor
practices and extractive legal-administrative institutions in colonies of occupation undermined the legal rights and political agency of indigenous colonial
subjects until after World War II. Building on existing research by Mahmood
Mamdani (1996), Matthew Lange (2004, 2005, 2009), and others (e.g., Owolabi
2017), I argue that the establishment and maintenance of bifurcated legal-
administrative institutions hindered the long-term development of colonial
states with significant indigenous populations.

3

Historical Institutionalism, Critical Junctures, and the Divergent Legacies of Forced Settlement and Colonial Occupation

This chapter develops a historical-institutional framework that explains the favorable developmental legacies of forced settlement relative to colonial occupation in the Global South. The chapter is organized into four sections. The first section introduces and defines historical institutionalism as a theoretical framework that emphasizes the importance of historical sequence and path dependence that shape the evolution of governing institutions that structure social, economic, and political behavior and outcomes over long periods of time. This chapter builds on the historical overview of forced settlement and colonial occupation in the previous chapter and advances theoretical arguments that highlight the relationship between colonial legal-administrative institutions and postcolonial development in the Global South.

I advance the argument that liberal reforms enabled many forced settlement colonies to promote more inclusive development outcomes that improved the living conditions of emancipated Afro-descendants following the abolition of slavery. Drawing insights from James Mahoney's research on colonial state-building, liberal reforms, and postcolonial development in Latin America, I argue that the liberal reforms implemented by the British and French governments undermined the economic and political dominance of local white planters in British forced settlement colonies and the French Antilles colonies following the abolition of slavery. As British and French officials established more direct political control over their forced settlement colonies, they implemented liberal reforms that expanded the legal rights and political agency of emancipated Afro-descendants. I argue that liberal reforms strengthened the rule of law and expanded economic and social inclusiveness in forced settlement colonies following the abolition of slavery. Liberal reforms also strengthened the administrative capacity of colonial state officials to expand the provision of developmental public goods like state-funded education, sanitation, and poor relief. Consequently, I argue that liberal reforms transformed the legal-administrative

Ruling Emancipated Slaves and Indigenous Subjects. Olukunle P. Owolabi, Oxford University Press.
© Oxford University Press 2023. DOI: 10.1093/oso/9780197673027.003.0003

institutions of forced settlement colonies from "extractive" to "inclusive." The reformed institutional framework of forced settlement colonies ultimately improved the living conditions of emancipated Afro-descendants following the abolition of slavery.

The third section outlines the contrasting experience of Global South countries that experienced colonial occupation and gained independence after 1945. I argue that colonies of occupation lagged behind forced settlement colonies on key indicators of human development because they did not experience the liberal reforms that expanded the legal rights and political agency of emancipated Afro-descendants. Instead, the territorial expansion of colonial occupation generated bifurcated colonial states with distinctive legal-administrative institutions for colonial settlers and indigenous colonial subjects. Drawing theoretical insights from existing literature on colonial state-building and underdevelopment in sub-Saharan Africa (e.g., Young 1994; Mamdani 1996; Herbst 2000; Englebert 2000; Acemoglu and Robinson 2010), I argue that extractive legal-administrative institutions undermined the rule of law, citizenship rights, and administrative effectiveness in Global South countries that experienced colonial occupation. As a result, colonial occupation generated an ineffective and predatory pattern of state-building that hindered inclusive long-term development and postcolonial democratization.

The final section discusses the limitations of existing studies that emphasize the conceptual distinction between "settler" and "extractive" colonization, the distinctiveness of British rule relative to French or Iberian colonization, and the developmental impact of Protestant missionary evangelization. None of these theories sufficiently explain the favorable developmental legacies of forced settlement relative to colonial occupation across multiple colonial empires. I also address the limitations of existing arguments that highlight the importance of ethnic diversity and geographic factors that undermine (or facilitate) long-term development and postcolonial democratization.

Colonial Institutions, Critical Junctures, and the Divergent Developmental Legacies of Forced Settlement and Colonial Occupation

In what ways did colonial institutions favor the long-term development of forced settlement colonies relative to Global South countries that experienced colonial occupation? To answer this question, it is important to recognize two important attributes of institutions that explain their persistence over time and their impact on the long-term developmental trajectories of different countries. Peter Hall defines institutions as "regularized practices" that structure the behavior of economic and political actors (Hall 2010, 204). James Mahoney (2010) recognizes the importance of institutions as distributional instruments that regulate human behavior in ways that generate and reproduce the uneven allocation of economic, social, and political resources. In Mahoney's words, "Individuals and groups . . . enter into social interactions with different endowments of resources, and these differences ensure that any given set of rules . . . will have unequal implications for subsequent resource allocations, no matter how justly these institutions are designed" (Mahoney 2010, 15). Colonial institutions were specifically designed to concentrate economic and political resources among small groups of colonial settlers, administrators, and/or indigenous collaborators that benefited from European rule. Often, the descendants of colonial settlers, indigenous collaborators, and ethnic and religious groups favored by colonial state officials have remained powerful for several generations after independence.[1]

It is important to recognize that economic, social, and political institutions can persist for long periods of time because they tend to benefit powerful elite groups that resist institutional change (Mahoney 2010, 16). Despite the tendency of institutions to persist for a long time, countries also experience "critical historical junctures," that challenge the economic and/or political dominance of elite groups that benefited from long-standing institutional arrangements. These critical junctures are triggered by economic, social, or political crises that transform the relationship between the state, economy, and society. Accordingly, the way that political actors respond to critical historical junctures can produce distinct historical legacies that "establish certain directions of change and foreclose others in a way that shapes [political outcomes] for years to come" (Collier and Collier 1991, 27).

Existing studies also emphasize the importance of historical periodization (i.e., timing) as a critical variable that shapes the response of political actors to critical historical junctures in different countries (Collier and Collier 1991, 31). This is why historical-institutionalists emphasize the importance of "critical historical junctures" as transformative events that shape the development of political institutions and the long-term development trajectory of different countries (see, for example, Lipset and Rokkan 1967; Collier and Collier 1991; Sokoloff and Engerman 2000; Acemoglu, Johnson, and Robinson 2002; Mahoney 2010).

Many existing studies emphasize the importance of World War II and its immediate aftermath as a critical historical juncture for developing countries that gained independence after 1945. World War II undermined European control over their overseas colonies and precipitated a wave of demands for political reforms that stimulated independence movements across the Global South. Colonial authorities responded to nationalist demands for political representation and self-determination in different ways that shaped the political trajectories of Global South countries that emerged from colonial domination after World War II (see Collier 1982; Lawrence 2013; Cooper 2014; Paine 2019a; Garcia-Ponce and Wantchekon n.d.). While acknowledging the importance of postwar reforms for postcolonial development and democratization, this chapter emphasizes two critical historical junctures from the nineteenth century that contributed to the divergent developmental legacies of forced settlement and colonial occupation in the Global South. I first examine the abolition of slavery as a critical juncture that generated liberal reforms that expanded the legal rights and political agency of emancipated Afro-descendants in forced settlement colonies. I also examine the territorial expansion of colonial occupation in the late nineteenth century as a critical juncture that hindered the long-term development of Global South countries that emerged from colonial occupation after World War II. It is important to examine these critical junctures because the favorable developmental legacies of forced settlement relative to colonial occupation were in many cases apparent prior to the outbreak of World War II.

The timing of these events had profound consequences for the subsequent pattern of institutional development associated with forced settlement and colonial occupation. As outlined in previous chapters, the abolition of slavery in forced settlement colonies was strongly impacted by the timing of the British Industrial Revolution and France's revolutionary upheavals during the nineteenth century. The indigenous hinterlands of the Indian subcontinent, Southeast Asia, and the African continent were still independent of European control at this time, and they did not benefit from liberal reforms that expanded the legal rights and political agency of emancipated Afro-descendants following the abolition of slavery. In fact, the impact of abolition was largely limited to forced settlement colonies and the coastal regions of Africa that were under European control during the transatlantic slave trade. This is why liberal reforms were largely limited to these regions. By contrast, the vast indigenous hinterlands of sub-Saharan Africa were only brought under European control during the second global wave of imperialist expansion at the end of the nineteenth century.

The next sections outline the critical junctures that transformed the legal-administrative frameworks that colonial rulers used to control emancipated Afro-descendants vis-à-vis indigenous nonwhite populations in the Global South. As outlined in the previous chapter, the abolition of slavery triggered a series of liberal reforms that expanded the legal rights and political agency of emancipated Afro-descendants in forced settlement colonies. By contrast, the territorial expansion of colonial occupation generated bifurcated legal-administrative institutions that hindered the developmental capacity of indigenous populations that experienced colonial occupation. I argue that these institutional differences ultimately favored the long-term development of forced settlement colonies relative to Global South countries that emerged from colonial occupation after World War II.

The Abolition of Slavery as a Critical Historical Juncture in Forced Settlement Colonies: From Extractive to Inclusive Institutions

Forced settlement colonies present an empirical puzzle that is not adequately addressed in existing studies of colonialism and postcolonial development. On the one hand, forced settlement colonies established agricultural plantations with imported slave labor, and existing studies have correctly emphasized the negative developmental consequences of plantation slavery for Afro-descendant populations in countries like Brazil (Fujiwara, Laudares, and Valencia 2019) and the United States (Bertocchi and Dimico 2012; Achyara, Blackwell, and Sen 2018). At the same time, however, forced settlement colonies show favorable development outcomes relative to Global South countries that emerged from colonial occupation after World War II (Owolabi 2015). Consequently, it is important to identify the historical and institutional factors that facilitated the long-term development and postcolonial democratization of many forced settlement colonies where enslaved Africans were the majority of the population in the eighteenth century. The theoretical framework in this section outlines the specific historical and institutional mechanisms that enabled forced settlement colonies to improve the living conditions of emancipated Afro-descendants following the abolition of slavery in the nineteenth century. Because most of the influential studies from the early 2000s exclude small countries with less than a million inhabitants, there is very little scholarship that systematically compares the developmental legacies of forced settlement to other patterns of European imperial domination in the Global South. Consequently, the theoretical framework in this section draws theoretical and empirical insights from James Mahoney's research on liberal reforms and postcolonial development in Latin America.

In some ways, Iberian colonization in Latin America resembles the initial phase of forced settlement, when European colonists established agricultural plantations in newly settled territories using imported African slaves. Both patterns of imperial control generated extractive and labor-repressive colonial economies with racialized class inequalities. By highlighting the similarities between liberal reforms that promoted greater economic inclusion in certain Latin American countries, and liberal reforms that expanded the legal rights and political agency of emancipated Afro-descendants in forced settlement colonies, the historical-institutional framework in this chapter advances my previous empirical work on the favorable developmental legacies of forced settlement relative to colonial occupation in the Global South (Owolabi 2015).

All Latin American countries experienced at least three centuries of Iberian colonial domination that privileged European settler elites at the expense of indigenous nonwhites and Afro-descendants. Yet despite this shared experience of labor-repressive and extractive colonization, Latin American countries have experienced diverse developmental and political trajectories after independence (Mahoney 2001, 2010; Kurtz 2013).[2] James Mahoney (2010) explains this developmental variation by identifying which Latin American countries were primarily colonized with "mercantilist" or "liberal" institutions.

Mahoney's research identifies two distinct phases of Spanish colonization in the Americas. The mercantilist phase of Spanish colonization (1500–1750) established extractive institutions that restricted trade, landownership, and political participation in a labor-repressive political economy that depended on the extraction of precious metals using indigenous forced labor and/or African slave labor. The economic and political institutions of mercantilism were designed to privilege short-term accumulation and concentrate wealth in the hands of colonial state agents, monopolistic merchants, and wealthy landed elites. Although Spanish mercantilist institutions generated significant wealth for the Spanish Crown and for the privileged descendants of Spanish conquistadors in the Americas, they failed to promote sustained or inclusive development. Over time, this contributed to Spain's long-term secular decline relative to rising liberal capitalist imperial powers like Britain and the Netherlands. To address this decline, Spanish Bourbon elites implemented liberal reforms that loosened trade restrictions and promoted economic diversification during the second half of the eighteenth century. Spanish liberal reforms also weakened the political control of Catholic Church officials and expanded the administrative capacity of state officials to collect taxes and enforce a more uniform and inclusive legal system (Mahoney 2010, 44–46).

Mahoney argues that the extent to which Latin American countries were colonized with mercantilist or liberal institutions has profound consequences for their long-term development. His research highlights the long-term secular decline of Latin American countries that were intensively colonized during the mercantilist phase of Spanish colonization and comparatively neglected during the liberal phase of Spanish colonization. These countries, like Bolivia and Guatemala, have worse development outcomes than Southern Cone countries that were intensively colonized during the "liberal" phase of Spanish colonization but were comparatively neglected during the earlier mercantilist phase. Mahoney's research also demonstrates intermediate development outcomes in Latin American countries that successfully implemented liberal reforms following the mercantilist phase of Spanish colonization (e.g., Mexico, Peru, and Colombia). These countries were partially able to overcome the negative legacies of mercantilist colonialism, but their development outcomes are less inclusive than Latin American countries that were primarily colonized with liberal economic and political institutions. Consequently, Mahoney's (2010) research emphasizes the extent to which eighteenth-century liberal reforms have shaped developmental variations across Latin American countries over the *longue durée*.

Liberal Reforms, Inclusive Institutions, and Postcolonial Development in Forced Settlement Colonies: Argument and Theoretical Framework

Building on Mahoney's insights, my theoretical framework highlights the extent to which liberal reforms transformed the legal-administrative institutions of forced settlement colonies that remained under British or French control following the abolition of slavery in the nineteenth century. The liberal reforms in British forced settlement colonies and the French Antilles colonies were far more transformative than the eighteenth-century Bourbon reforms in Spanish America. Whereas the Spanish Bourbon liberal reforms primarily emphasized economic diversification and the administrative capacity of colonial state officials to collect taxes more efficiently (Mahoney 2010), the abolition of slavery also generated liberal reforms that expanded the legal rights and political agency of emancipated Afro-descendants in many forced settlement colonies. These reforms were supported by British liberals and French republican leaders that advanced core elements of liberal ideology, including notions of popular sovereignty, parliamentary representation, individual liberty and freedom, private property, and religious liberty. British liberal reforms generally emphasized the expansion of property rights, religious liberty, and other civil liberties like freedom of speech and association, as well as a modest expansion of political representation and voting rights. French liberal reforms were driven by revolutionary upheavals that significantly expanded political representation and citizenship rights, state-funded education, and secular state authority under a republican system of government that espoused liberty, fraternity, and equality. These reforms transformed the legal-administrative institutions of forced settlement colonies from extractive to inclusive during the transformative years between the 1789 French Revolution and the onset of World War I.

The theoretical argument linking liberal reforms and the abolition of slavery to the successful postcolonial development of forced settlement colonies is outlined in Figure 3.1. The flow chart links the abolition of slavery to the British Industrial Revolution and the French revolutionary upheavals that empowered liberal reformers and undermined the economic and political dominance of conservative landed aristocrats and slaveholders in both countries. The British Industrial Revolution (1780s–1840s) also contributed to the political ascendancy of liberal parliamentary reformers and abolitionists during the 1830s. France experienced a devastating cycle of revolutionary violence that pitted conservative

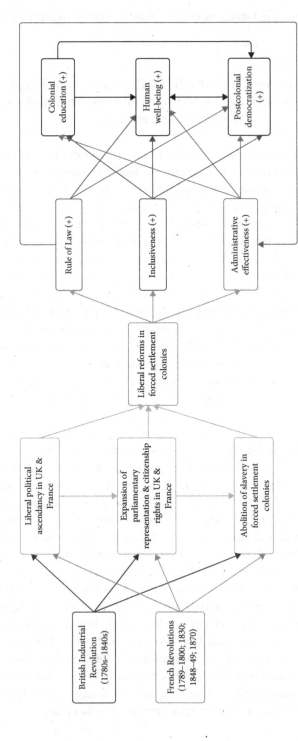

Figure 3.1 How liberal reforms promoted human well-being and postcolonial democratization in forced settlement colonies

monarchists against republican abolitionists that rose to power following the 1848 French revolution. These events contributed to the expansion of parliamentary democracy in the UK and France, where liberal reformers overrode the political preferences of aristocratic landowners and slaveholders and abolished plantation slavery in their forced settlement colonies. The historical evidence in Chapter 5 reveals that British-emancipated slaves were legally recognized as free British subjects, whose personal freedoms—including property rights, religious liberty, and to a somewhat lesser extent, freedom of speech and association—were protected by British common law. Chapter 7 examines how the cyclical pattern of revolutionary violence in France and its Antilles colonies contributed to the abolition of slavery in the French Antilles, and the extension of parliamentary representation and citizenship rights to emancipated Afro-descendants in the French Antilles colonies. These economic and political upheavals generated a reform process that strengthened the rule of law, expanded citizenship inclusiveness, and promotedgreater administrative effectiveness in forced settlement colonies following the abolition of slavery.

My research outlines three specific ways in which liberal reforms enabled many forced settlement colonies to promote more inclusive patterns of long-term development following the abolition of slavery in the nineteenth century. First, I argue that liberal reforms promoted inclusive development and postcolonial democratization in forced settlement colonies by strengthening the rule of law and extending metropolitan (i.e., European) legal rights to emancipated Afro-descendants following the abolition of slavery in the nineteenth century. The rule of law is necessary for protecting individual civil liberties, regulating market transactions, and protecting citizens from arbitrary or despotic abuses of state power (see Law Porta et al. 1998, 1999; Mendez, O'Donnell, and Pinheiro 1999; Bratton and Chang 2006). A uniform and inclusive legal system also protects the individual freedoms that are necessary to build and sustain effective democratic governance (O'Donnell 2004; Bratton and Chang 2006). The historical evidence in this book demonstrates that liberal reforms expanded the legal rights of emancipated Afro-descendants in forced settlement colonies following the abolition of slavery in the nineteenth century. This is particularly true in British forced settlement colonies, where British common law protected key personal freedoms, including religious liberty, property rights, and to a lesser extent, freedom of speech and association (Ledgister 1998, 13–15). The extension of legal rights enabled emancipated Afro-descendants to acquire small plots of land, educate their children in state-funded denominational schools, and establish cooperatives, labor unions, and other civil society organizations that expanded their political agency prior to the introduction of universal suffrage elections after World War II. Outside of the British Empire, all forced settlement colonies apart from Portuguese-ruled São Tomé and Príncipe developed a uniform and inclusive legal system based on French (or Iberian) civil law following the abolition of slavery. Building on the insights from previous research studies by James Mahoney (2001, 2010), Matthew Lange (2009), Guillermo O'Donnell (2004), and others, I expect to find favorable development outcomes in colonial states that extended metropolitan (i.e., European) legal rights to emancipated Afro-descendants and other nonwhite populations following the abolition of slavery. I also expect the early extension of metropolitan legal rights to favor the long-term development of forced settlement colonies relative to Global South countries that experienced colonial occupation.

The historical evidence in this book also highlights the extension of metropolitan citizenship rights to emancipated Afro-descendants in the French Antilles and in Portuguese forced settlement colonies following the abolition of slavery. Citizenship laws define membership and political inclusion within the state, and citizenship laws were inextricably linked to the expansion of state-funded education, political representation, and electoral participation in Western European countries (Weber 1976; Brubaker 1992; Howard 2009, 3–8), throughout the Americas (Engerman, Mariscal, and Sokoloff 2009), and across the globe (Meyer et al. 1992). Therefore, my theoretical framework also builds on existing literature on citizenship rights and political inclusiveness (or exclusion) in Western European states and their overseas colonial territories (see Brubraker 1992; Mamdani 1996; Marx 1996, 1998; Howard 2009; Janoski 2010). Democratization theorists also highlight the importance of inclusive citizenship rights for facilitating democratic consolidation following transitions from authoritarian rule.[3] This is because inclusive citizenship rights generate the political consensus that is necessary to *sustain democratic governance over the longue durée* (Linz and Stepan 1996, 27–28). Linz and Stepan argue that although many countries have established democratic institutions under challenging economic and political circumstances, the ability to maintain democratic governance over long periods of time is invariably linked to effective state-building and inclusive citizenship. They note that "without a state, there can be no citizenship; without citizenship, there can be no democracy" (Linz and Stepan 1996, 28). Colonial states generally lagged their imperial masters in extending citizenship, education, and voting rights to nonwhite populations, but forced settlement colonies were among the first colonial states to expand citizenship rights, voting, and state-funded education following the abolition of slavery. Consequently, I expect to find favorable development outcomes in forced settlement colonies relative to Global South countries that emerged from colonial occupation.

My theoretical framework also builds on existing studies that explore the ways in which inclusive state-building enhances administrative effectiveness in ways that support human well-being (see Kohli 2004; Krieckhaus 2006; Lange 2009; Mahoney 2010; Acemoglu and Robinson 2012) and facilitate stable and effective democratic governance (Lange 2004, 2009; Angell 2010; Andersen et al. 2014). Andersen et al. (2014) define administrative effectiveness as the ability of state officials to provide public goods other than political order. In other words, administrative effectiveness enhances the capacity of state officials to provide public goods like state-funded education, sanitation, and public infrastructure. These public goods enable individuals and communities to engage in economic, social, and political activities that support/enhance their well-being. This suggests that human well-being and political development are directly linked to the administrative capacity of the colonial state.

But how do states develop the administrative capacity to efficiently distribute public goods across their population and territory? The administrative capacity of state officials depends on a centralized bureaucracy that is autonomous from religious institutions and/or economic elites in the society. The state bureaucracy must be sufficiently centralized and uniformly integrated to ensure that its subnational divisions are formally coordinated with one another (Weber 1978; Tilly 1975, 70; Lange 2009, 35–38). The development of an efficient administrative state also enhances the provision and distribution of public goods and services that promote human well-being and development, such as education, sanitation, public infrastructure, and poverty reduction (Lange 2009; Krieckhaus 2006; Kohli 2004; Angell 2010). The efficient provision of public goods also enhances the legitimacy of the state, which sustains democratic institutions once they have been established (Andersen et al. 2014). In other words, effective state institutions also facilitate democratic consolidation following the establishment of mass electoral competition. Because liberal reforms expanded the administrative effectiveness of forced settlement colonies to provide public goods like state-funded education, sanitation, and public infrastructure, I expect to find favorable development outcomes in forced settlement colonies relative to Global South countries that emerged from colonial occupation.

Colonial Occupation, Extractive Institutions, and Underdevelopment: Theoretical Insights from Sub-Saharan Africa

The theoretical framework in this section builds on existing empirical literature on extractive institutions that hindered effective state-building in ways that limited human development and postcolonial democratization in continental Africa (see Rodney 1981; Young 1994; Mamdani 1996; Herbst 2000; Acemoglu and Robinson 2010). This literature is relevant because sub-Saharan Africa accounts for more than half of the countries under colonial occupation during the first half of the twentieth century. Because my case studies of colonial occupation are primarily drawn from sub-Saharan Africa, it is important to examine the vast literature on the pathologies of colonial state-building that generated persistent underdevelopment in this region. The insights from sub-Saharan Africa are useful for understanding the poor development outcomes of Global South countries that emerged from colonial occupation after 1945.

The Territorial Expansion of Colonial Occupation and the Persistence of Extractive Institutions in Continental Africa

The territorial expansion of colonial occupation occurred after the Industrial Revolution and the emergence of modern nation-states in Western Europe. Consequently, many scholars have argued that indigenous Africans were subject to a pattern of colonial domination very different from the "plantation" colonies in the Caribbean Basin or the Iberian colonial states in Latin America (see Young 1994; Krieckhaus 2006). For example, Crawford Young's (1994) research highlights the extent to which advances in Western medicine, military technology, transportation, and communication infrastructure empowered industrialized European nations relative to their African colonial subjects. Consequently, Young argues that the industrialized European states that controlled Sub-Saharan Africa after 1880 had far greater capacity for economic extraction and hegemonic political control than the pre-industrial European states that had colonized Latin America and the Caribbean during sixteenth and seventeenth centuries (73–74). The twin processes of industrialization and national integration also enabled European colonizers to construct more rigid status and legal distinctions between themselves and their colonial subjects during the late nineteenth and early twentieth centuries (Young 1994; Mamdani 1996; Krieckhaus 2006, 40–44, 53–59).[4]

Crawford Young (1994) uses the metaphor of *Bula Matari*—a Congolese term that denotes intrusive alien domination—to describe how indigenous Africans encountered the extractive and repressive institutions of colonial states with an unprecedented capacity for institutionalized violence, and insatiable demands for taxation and forced labor recruitment. Forced labor was used to construct roads, railways, and other public infrastructure projects that enabled Europeans to control vast indigenous populations and territories, to transport indigenous laborers from their home villages to European-owned commercial mines and plantations, and to transport agricultural produce and mineral resources from Africa to export markets in Europe. In contrast to other parts of the world, Africa's transportation and communications infrastructure was developed to support resource extraction that benefited Europeans. It was never intended to promote national integration or inclusive development. Colonial powers also established extractive economic institutions like punitive head taxes and co-ercive labor recruitment that supported the development of European-owned agricultural plantations and commercial mines throughout continental Africa (Young 1994, 134–48). These coercive labor practices were maintained long after the abolition of slavery in forced settlement colonies. Consequently, the colonial states in continental Africa never developed the administrative capacity to effi-ciently provide public goods and services like education, sanitation, and poor relief (Young 1994, 168–76). Not surprisingly, this has hindered the long-term development of postcolonial African states relative to other developing regions in the Global South.

I also draw insights from Jeffrey Herbst's research on the geographic and envi-ronmental factors that hindered state-building efforts on the African continent. Herbst (2000) argues that continental African states face unique geographic and environmental challenges that have hindered their long-term development. These challenges include a hostile disease environment, large and expanding deserts, poor soil conditions, erratic rainfall patterns, few navigable rivers, and an exposed coastline that provides few natural harbors for ships and seaborne trade. These conditions hindered Africa's long-term economic growth and po-litical development from precolonial times until the present day (also see Sachs and Warner 1997; Collier and Gunning 1999, 8–9; Sachs 2005). Herbst (2000) also argues that Africa's challenging natural environment is responsible for the continent's unusually low population density (relative to Europe, China, India, or Japan) at the beginning of the twentieth century. Low population density increased the relative value of African people (and labor) compared to the land that they occupied. This seems to have incentivized European colonial rulers and the indigenous African rulers that preceded them to prioritize the control and regulation of human labor over the physical control of sparsely inhabited territo-ries (Herbst 2000).[5]

In contrast to Crawford Young, Jeffery Herbst's theoretical framework downplays the extent to which colonial African states relied on systematic vi-olence and coercive labor practices to control their indigenous populations. Herbst (2000) also downplays the historical impact of the Atlantic slave trade in undermining state-building efforts and economic development in precolo-nial Africa. As Europeans became increasingly involved in the transatlantic slave trade, the purchase and sale of African slaves became so lucrative that it sucked away investment from technology and human capital in Africa (Acemoglu and Robinson 2010, 28–33). The globalization of slave trading also generated a dev-astating cycle of warfare that undermined the continent's population growth and economic development (Nunn 2008; Acemoglu and Robinson 2010, 28–31; Krieckhaus 2006, 55–56; Rodney 1974; Ibikwe 1975) and reduced contempo-rary levels of social trust (Nunn and Wantchekon 2011). For these reasons, my theoretical framework downplays Herbst's claim that environmental and geographic constraints hindered effective state-building and postcolonial development in Africa.[6] Despite my skepticism toward Herbst's claims, it is useful to consider the environmental and geographic challenges obstacles to controlling vast and widely dispersed indigenous populations under foreign domination.

Instead of emphasizing geographic determinism, my theoretical framework builds on Mahmood Mamdani's (1996) research on the "bifurcated" legal-administrative institutions that undermined Africa's long-term development and postcolonial democratization. Mamdani's concept of the "bifurcated African colonial state" is useful for understanding the colonial practice of maintaining two separate legal-administrative frameworks to govern "indigenous colonial subjects" and "colonial settler minorities." This type of legal-administrative bifurcation was first developed in French-ruled Algeria (see Lawrence 2020) and in British India following the 1857 Sepoy Mutiny (Lange 2009, 23–24, 176–78; Naseemullah and Staniland 2016; Mukherjee 2018). It was later extended to South Africa, where European colonial officials encountered significant anticolonial resistance from large and well-organized indigenous populations (Mamdani 1996, 62–72; Lange 2009, 180). The institutionalization of a bifurcated legal-administrative framework enabled the British and French to subdue anticolonial indigenous resistance in these territories during the nineteenth century. As a result of their success in India, Algeria, and South Africa, this practice of legal-administrative bifurcation was later extended throughout sub-Saharan Africa at the turn of the twentieth century (Mamdani 1996, 72–93).

Mamdani (1996) describes how the bifurcated colonial state was based on a series of dichotomies that reinforced legal differences between colonial settlers (i.e., citizens) and indigenous colonial subjects (i.e., "natives") using distinct administrative practices known that British administrators referred to as direct versus indirect rule (Lange 2004, 2009; Naseemullah and Staniland 2016), and French administrators referred to as *assimilation versus association* (Betts 1961; Conklin 1997). Regardless of the imperial power, the bifurcated colonial state had a thin bureaucratic apparatus that was largely concentrated in the administrative capital. In rural districts, by contrast, colonial officials (known as district commissioners in British colonies, *commandants de cercle* in French colonies, or *chêfes de posto* in Portuguese colonies) oversaw a vast network of local intermediaries that enforced distinctive "native legal codes" or "customary laws" that applied only to indigenous subjects. In French-occupied Algeria, Indochina, and sub-Saharan Africa, most indigenous colonial subjects lived in rural areas where the state was organized along patrimonial lines. Local chiefs combined legislative, executive, judicial, and administrative authority and were responsible only to the local district administrator (Mamdani 1996, 56–61). Whereas colonial settlers and nonnatives were subject to European laws, which typically recognized their individual civil liberties, native populations were subject to customary laws "dispensed . . . by chiefs and commissioners" (Mamdani 1996, 109). As European commissioners lacked the administrative capacity to control the population and territory in their district, they devolved significant judicial and legislative autonomy to indigenous "chiefs" that were responsible for tax collection, labor recruitment, and maintaining law and order in rural indigenous communities. Mamdani's (1996) detailed ethnographic research provides important evidence that bifurcated legal-administrative institutions strengthened the arbitrary and despotic power of indigenous "chiefs" far beyond the traditional power and legitimacy that they enjoyed in precolonial times. This is because the personal authority of the local "chief" or "commissioner" was backed up the repressive power of the modern colonial state.[7]

I consider Mamdani's concept of the "bifurcated colonial state" more useful and relevant than Crawford Young's *Bula Matari* or Jeffrey Herbst's emphasis on environmental and geographic challenges that hinder effective state-building and postcolonial development in sub-Saharan Africa. This is because Mamdani's (1996) institutionalist framework is the only one that explains the "Janus-faced nature" of colonial state-building in Africa. Mamdani's emphasis on the bifurcated nature of colonial state authority accounts for the institutionalized violence of *Bula Matari* as well as the limited administrative capacity of colonial African states in outlying rural districts. Mamdani's theoretical framework concurs with Jeffrey Herbst's (2000) argument that the administrative capacity of colonial African states was primarily limited to their capital cities and outlying areas with significant European settlement. Most indigenous colonial subjects lived in outlying rural areas, where the administrative capacity of colonial state officials was extremely limited. Consequently, Mamdani's concept of the bifurcated African colonial state is useful for understanding the ineffective and uneven nature of colonial state-building as well as the limited extent of postcolonial democratization in mainland African countries.

The expansion of political representation and voting rights after World War II generated expectations that postcolonial African states would expand public services, promote broad-based development, and provide employment opportunities for political supporters, especially in the rapidly growing urban sectors (see Ekeh 1975, 103). Instead, most African bureaucracies became heavily politicized after independence, and most scholars recognize that African states remained bureaucratically weak, despite their significant repressive capacity (Young 1994; Mamdani 1996; Goldsmith 1999; Herbst 2000). This suggests that the pathologies of the bifurcated colonial state persisted long after independence, contributing to ineffective governance, widespread corruption, and poor provision of public goods and services (see Mamdani 1996; Englebert 2000; Collier and Gunning 1999; Easterly and Levine 1997; Bates 1981, 2008). Moreover, the hybrid fusion of traditional African authority structures with the rational-legal authority of the modern postcolonial state allowed neopatrimonialism to flourish in the decades after independence. In many postcolonial African states, "Big Man" rulers used the existing networks of traditional intermediaries or newly established party cadres to dispense patronage benefits to their political supporters; civil service appointments and promotions were often based on political loyalties, rather than merit; and political leaders abused public resources for their own private or political gains (see Ekeh 1975; Bratton and Van de Walle 1997, 61–96; Meredith 2005). These practices persist in many African countries despite the restoration of mass electoral competition in the 1990s (see Lindberg 2003; Driscoll 2018). This is why recent empirical studies have demonstrated poor developmental outcomes and limited postcolonial democratization in countries that maintained bifurcated legal-administrative institutions during the colonial era (see Lange 2004, 2005, 2009; Owolabi 2017; Mukherjee 2018).

The Bifurcated Colonial State, Extractive Institutions, and Underdevelopment in Colonies of Occupation: Argument and Theoretical Framework

Building on insights from these works, I present a theoretical argument that links the extractive legal-administrative institutions of the bifurcated colonial state to persistent underdevelopment and limited democratization in Global South countries that experienced colonial occupation. The argument is summarized in Figure 3.2, which presents a flow chart that outlines the expected development outcomes associated with colonial occupation. The theoretical model presumes that the territorial expansion of colonial occupation occurred after the Industrial Revolution and the emergence of modern nation-states in Western Europe. These forces generated brutal "wars of pacification" to control indigenous populations and territories in the Global South. Perhaps not surprisingly, many indigenous populations resisted the territorial expansion of European colonial occupation during the final decades of the nineteenth century. As a result of this resistance, European colonizers established bifurcated colonial states with extractive institutions that controlled and repressed indigenous colonial subjects: indirect rule became the preferred means of administration in British-occupied colonies following the 1857 Sepoy rebellion in India. Continental powers like France and Portugal established their own "native legal codes" that restricted the citizenship rights and legal rights of indigenous colonial subjects. I argue that the establishment of bifurcated legal systems undermined the rule of law and limited the administrative effectiveness and inclusiveness of Global South countries that experienced colonial occupation. This pattern of state-building ultimately

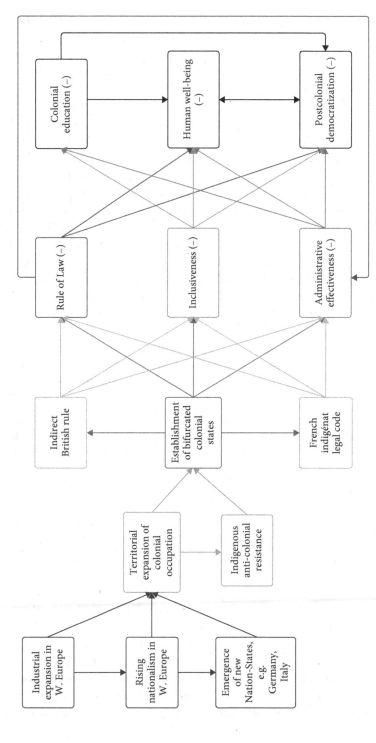

Figure 3.2 How colonial occupation and bifurcated legal-administrative institutions undermined human well-being and postcolonial democratization

hindered the expansion of developmental goods such as colonial occupation, human well-being, and postcolonial democratization.

The three parts of my argument are elaborated as follows: first, I argue that bifurcated colonial states established extractive legal-administrative institutions that undermined the rule of law and limited the political agency of indigenous colonial subjects. The limited institutionalization of British common law expanded the arbitrary and despotic power of traditional chiefs and "customary laws" in British-occupied colonies (see Mamdani 1996; Lange 2009; Acemoglu, Reed, and Robinson 2014). French and Portuguese "native legal codes" also restricted the legal rights and political agency of indigenous colonial subjects (Mamdani 1996; Merle 2002; Mann 2009). Because the rule of law is necessary for protecting individual civil liberties, regulating market transactions, and protecting citizens from the arbitrary or despotic abuse of state power (see La Porta et al. 1998, 1999; O'Donnell 2004; Bratton and Chang 2006), I expect to find poor development outcomes and limited postcolonial democratization in countries that maintained bifurcated legal-administrative frameworks into the twentieth century.

Second, bifurcated legal-administrative institutions also limited political inclusion and citizenship rights in colonial states with significant indigenous populations (Mamdani 1996; Lange 2009). The bifurcated colonial state excluded indigenous colonial subjects from citizenship, so there was no real incentive to educate indigenous colonial populations. This is why primary schooling remained limited in most colonies of occupation until after independence. The exclusion of indigenous colonial populations from citizenship also politicized ethnic differences in ways that hindered national integration and democratization efforts in many Global South countries that emerged from colonial occupation after World War II. Empirical evidence from countries like Sri Lanka (see Horowitz 2000; Lange 2012), India (Stepan, Linz, and Yadav 2011; Horowitz 2000), Malaysia (Horowitz 2000), and Rwanda (Mamdani 2001; King 2014) suggests that it is very difficult to promote national integration and democratic consolidation in countries with ongoing disagreements about citizenship or exclusionary citizenship laws that marginalize or exclude minority groups within the national polity. African countries that maintained rigid legal distinctions between "Creole" and indigenous African populations—like Liberia, Sierra Leone, and Guinea-Bissau—have also struggled to promote national integration or postcolonial democratization. Consequently, I expect to find limited postcolonial democratization in colonies of occupation that restricted the citizenship rights of indigenous colonial subjects prior to independence.

The third part of my argument is that bifurcated legal-administrative institutions generated poorly integrated states with limited administrative capacity/effectiveness. The limited administrative capacity of bifurcated colonial states hindered the development of inclusive linkages between the colonial state and societal actors in outlying rural areas. This is why so many postcolonial states with bifurcated institutions continue to struggle with public service provision and policy implementation in outlying rural areas (see Lange 2009; Mamdani 1996). The limited administrative capacity of postcolonial states also makes it difficult for state officials to implement governmental policies that advance long-term economic growth and human well-being. In postcolonial states with limited administrative capacity, political leaders are more likely to emphasize the consolidation of political power over the promotion of broad-based development (see Bates 1981, 2008; Englebert 2000; Kohli 2004; Kriekchaus 2006; Lange 2009, ch. 5). For these reasons, I expect to find poor development outcomes and limited postcolonial democratization in European-occupied colonies that maintained bifurcated legal-administrative institutions into the twentieth century.

Implications for Existing Literature on Colonialism and Postcolonial Development

The theoretical framework in this chapter challenges some widely held assumptions from existing studies that overlook the important conceptual distinction between forced settlement and colonial occupation in the Global South. Consequently, the remainder of this chapter outlines the contributions, and shortcomings, of previous theoretical frameworks that do not convincingly explain the favorable developmental legacies of forced settlement relative to colonial occupation.

Settler versus Extractive Colonization

Perhaps the most widely cited argument in the existing literature is that European settler colonization facilitated inclusive long-term development and postcolonial democratization because European settlers established inclusive economic and political institutions that protected property rights and individual civil liberties. Where European settlement was limited, by contrast, colonial officials imposed "extractive" institutions that enabled them to expropriate resources and exploit nonwhite populations for their labor. Based on these assumptions, many influential studies have demonstrated favorable development outcomes and greater postcolonial democratization in European settler colonies relative to "extractive" colonies with limited European settlement (Easterly and Levine 2016; Acemoglu, Johnson, and Robinson 2001, 2002; Sokoloff and Engerman 2000; Krieckhaus 2006, 6–10, 36–44, 53–57).

The robust empirical association between European settlement and postcolonial development is not particularly useful for understanding the favorable developmental legacies of forced settlement relative to colonial occupation. After all, both forced settlement and occupation were labor-repressive modes of colonialization with limited European settlement. To provide a specific example, colonial Barbados and Rhodesia (present-day Zimbabwe) had similar levels of European settlement—about 5% of the population—during the 1950s. Yet Barbados has been far more successful at promoting postcolonial development and democratization. In contrast to Barbados, Zimbabwe's white settlers established a white supremacist state (the Republic of Rhodesia) that repressed the country's indigenous African majority during the 1960s and 1970s. Zimbabwe's black Africans had to resort to insurgency and political violence to obtain independence from white settler rule after 1980, and the country degenerated into single-party authoritarian rule after independence. Today, Zimbabwe is one of the most impoverished countries on the African continent. Clearly, Barbados and Zimbabwe have had very different development trajectories despite similar levels of European settlement during the colonial era. This suggests that the extent of European settlement does not convincingly explain the favorable developmental legacies of forced settlement relative to colonial occupation in the Global South.

British versus Continental European Colonization

Another popular argument is that British colonization generated favorable development outcomes relative to French or Iberian colonization (see Bollen and Jackman 1985, 1995; Hadenius 1992; Grier 1997, 1999; La Porta et al. 1998, 1999), and that the British were more likely than other continental European powers to establish democratic institutions in their colonies prior to independence (Huntington 1984; Weiner 1987; Lee and Paine 2019a). Existing studies have explored various causal mechanisms that might have promoted favorable developmental outcomes in former British colonies relative to other postcolonial states. Some studies emphasize the comparatively liberal economic and political institutions of British imperialism relative to French or Iberian colonization (see Landes 1998; La Porta et al. 1998, 1999; Lange, Mahoney, and Vom Hau 2006; Lee and Paine 2019a; Paine 2019, 549–551). Others emphasize the liberal nature of British common law—with its strong protection of individual civil liberties and property rights—relative to French or Iberian civil laws (La Porta et al. 1998, 1999). More recent studies have examined the role of Protestant missionaries in expanding civil society, mass education, and capitalist development, which facilitated postcolonial democratization in many former British colonies (Woodberry 2004, 2012; Gallego and Woodberry 2010). Scholars have also argued that British colonization facilitated postcolonial democratization by encouraging mass electoral competition (i.e., "tutelary democracy") prior to independence (Huntington 1984; Weiner 1987; Lee and Paine 2019a). Perhaps not surprisingly then, many empirical studies demonstrate that British colonization generated favorable developmental outcomes in terms of education (Brown 2000), economic development (La Porta et al. 1998, 1999; Grier 1997, 1999), and postcolonial democratization (Bernhard, Reenock, and Nordstrom 2004; Lee and Paine 2019a).

My research casts some doubt on these assumptions. British colonization did not always generate inclusive development and postcolonial democratization, and there is a wide range of developmental and political outcomes across the former British Empire. In general, indirectly ruled British colonies—like Nigeria, Sierra Leone, Sudan, and Uganda—have significantly worse development outcomes than directly ruled British colonies like Australia, Barbados, Canada, Hong Kong, Singapore, New Zealand, and the United States. British colonies that combined direct and indirect rule—like Fiji, Ghana, Kenya, and India—tend to have intermediate development outcomes (see Lange 2004, 2005, 2009). This variation is consistent with my theoretical framework because indirect British rule generated bifurcated colonial states with ineffective and predatory legal-administrative institutions. Moreover, indirect rule was primarily implemented in British-occupied colonies with significant indigenous populations. By contrast, direct British rule was established in European settler societies like Australia and Canada, forced settlement colonies like Barbados, Jamaica, and Mauritius, and city-state colonies like Singapore and Hong Kong. Because direct rule and indirect rule were based on very different legal-administrative principles, it is incorrect to assume a common pattern of state-building and institutional development in all countries that experienced British colonization.

Protestant Missionary Evangelization

Recent empirical studies have also examined the developmental and political legacies of Protestant missionary evangelization in the Global South (see Woodberry 2004, 2012; Gallego and Woodberry 2010; Lankina and Getachew 2012, 2013). This is because Christian missionaries were often responsible for educating and "civilizing" colonial subjects, given the limited administrative capacity of the colonial state officials. Protestant missionary evangelization was particularly transformative because Protestant missionaries sought to promote Bible literacy in indigenous languages. They also established denominational schools that advanced the development of civil society in many colonial territories.

These denominational schools educated many activist leaders who lobbied colonial state officials for social, political, and labor reforms in the years leading
up to independence (see Woodberry 2012). Perhaps not surprisingly then, existing studies demonstrate higher levels of educational attainment (Gallego and
Woodberry 2010; Lankina and Getachew 2012, 2013), household wealth (Okoye
and Pongou 2014; Wantchekon, Klasnja, and Notva 2015), and postcolonial democratization in colonial states and subnational districts that were most heavily
exposed to Protestant missionary evangelization (see Woodberry 2012).

These arguments are persuasive, but they do not explain why forced settlement also generated favorable development outcomes relative to colonial occupation in the French and Portuguese colonial empires, where the impact of
Protestantism was limited.[8] While recognizing the contributions of Protestant
missionaries in expanding literacy, educational access, and household wealth in
many British colonies, my research advances an alternative theoretical framework that emphasizes the liberal reforms that expanded the legal rights and political agency of emancipated Afro-descendants in forced settlement colonies.
We will see in subsequent chapters that these reforms were implemented by secular liberal officials in French and Portuguese colonies where Protestant missionary evangelization was historically limited.

Ethnic Fractionalization

Many scholars have also argued that high levels of ethnic diversity can hinder
economic and political development in postcolonial states (Easterly and Levine
1997; Habiyarimana et al. 2007; Laitin and Ramachandran 2016). Many postcolonial states with ethnically diverse populations have suffered from political
instability and civil conflict, as political leaders mobilize ethnic identities to attract votes from coethnic supporters (Horowitz 2000). These behavioral patterns
often resulted from colonial state policies that politicized ethnic, racial, or religious differences and exacerbated social inequalities prior to independence
(see Bates 1974; Mamdani 1996, 2001; Posner 2003; King 2014). The politicization of ethnic differences was especially common in sub-Saharan Africa,
where European colonizers established arbitrary borders with little regard for
preexisting social and political units. Many colonial states in the Global South
recruited foreign migrant laborers that significantly altered their ethnic or racial
composition (Lange and Dawson 2009), and administrative practices like British
indirect rule tended to privilege certain ethnic groups (or ethnic elites) at the expense of others (see Lange and Dawson 2009; King 2014; Palagashvili 2018; Ray
2018, 370–71).[9] Despite the widespread practice of "divide and rule" policies (see
Lange and Dawson 2009), there is considerable variation in the extent to which

postcolonial states have been able to manage their ethnic and religious diversity without resorting to conflict (see Lieberman and Singh 2012; Lange 2012; Stepan, Linz, and Yadav 2011).

In general, forced settlement colonies have done a better job of managing their ethnic differences than colonies of occupation. This partly reflects the fact that forced settlement colonies have avoided the devastating "sons of soil" conflicts that pit indigenous communities against migrant groups and/or minority ethnic groups that are perceived as foreign. "Sons of soil" conflicts are especially common in African countries that recruited foreign labor migrants during the colonial era (see Coté and Mitchell 2016; Bah 2010), and in postcolonial states that sought to reverse the economic and political advantages of nonindigenous groups and/or ethnic minorities that had been privileged during the colonial era (see Mamdani 2002, 2009; Palagashvili 2018). Over the years, many postcolonial states—from Indonesia and Malaysia to Côte d'Ivoire, Ghana, and the Democratic Republic of Congo / Zaire—have manipulated their citizenship laws to empower indigenous ethnic groups and disenfranchise the descendants of colonial-era migrants who have lived in these countries for generations (Herbst 2000, 232–42; Bah 2010). By contrast, there are no "sons of soil" to claim preferential treatment or citizenship rights based on ethnicity or ancestry in Creole societies like Barbados, Cape Verde, Jamaica, or Trinidad and Tobago. This is because forced settlement colonies were either uninhabited prior to colonization (like Cape Verde and Mauritius) or their indigenous populations were decimated by European conquest, forced labor, and diseases during the sixteenth century. As a result, virtually all those living in forced settlement colonies are the descendants of African slaves, South Asian or Chinese indentured labor migrants, and/or European colonists.

The absence of "sons of soil" in forced settlement colonies likely helped to facilitate inclusive legal-administrative institutions during the late colonial era, and to promote civic (rather than ethnic) forms of nationalism after independence. Thus, even though forced settlement colonies often have racialized class inequalities and deep political divisions between their Afro-Creole and South Asian communities, they have generally avoided the devastating ethnic conflicts and poor development outcomes that have plagued countries like Rwanda, Sudan, Sri Lanka, and Uganda. For example, Trinidad and Tobago and Mauritius experienced significant ethnic political mobilization during the late colonial era and after independence, yet both countries have promoted significant improvements in human well-being and successful postcolonial democratization (see Lange 2009, ch. 4; Edwards 2018; Premdas 2007). Guyana experienced more ethnic political violence than other forced settlement colonies after World War II, although its colonial institutions and socioeconomic development were not significantly different from other British forced settlement colonies prior to independence (see Lange 2009, ch. 6). And for all its shortcomings, Guyana continues to outperform ethnically divided colonies of occupation (e.g., Nigeria, Rwanda, Sudan, or Uganda) on key indicators of human development and postcolonial democratization. Overall, forced settlement colonies with ethnically divided populations (like Guyana, Mauritius, Trinidad and Tobago, and Suriname) have avoided the worst development problems that have plagued colonies of occupation with ethnically divided populations (like Côte d'Ivoire, Nigeria, Rwanda, Sri Lanka, Sudan, and Uganda).

Geography, Population, and Colonial Duration

It is also important to reconsider the extent to which geography, population, or colonial duration might explain the divergent developmental legacies of forced settlement and colonial occupation. As we saw in the previous chapter, forced settlement was primarily concentrated in small Atlantic islands that were relatively easy for Europeans to control. This is why most forced settlement colonies experienced more than three centuries of colonial domination, and many have retained political ties as overseas dependencies of their former colonizer. The lengthy duration of colonial rule and the unique political geography of small island states might contribute to the favorable developmental legacies of forced settlement relative to colonial occupation colonies. After all, small island states tend to have more highly educated populations and higher postcolonial democracy scores than other developing countries (Anckar 2002, 2006).

Countries that experienced a lengthy duration of colonization also have favorable developmental outcomes and greater postcolonial democratization than countries that were colonized during the second global wave of imperialist expansion after 1885 (Feyrer and Sacerdote 2009; Olsson 2009). This partly reflects the significant challenges that European colonists faced in controlling vast territories with large and widely dispersed indigenous populations. Indeed, "The rapid increase in the geographic scope of colonialism [after 1885] led Europeans to run [their] territories cheaply, while simultaneously extracting whatever they could" (Krieckhaus 2006, 9). Moreover, many scholars have argued that the second wave of imperialist expansion was more exploitative, overtly racist, and hegemonic than the earlier wave of colonial expansion in the Atlantic World (see Young 1994, ch. 3; Krieckhaus 2006, 8–9). In reality, however, the political economy of forced settlement was far more extractive and labor-repressive during the first global wave of imperialist expansion (1500–1750) than during the second global wave of imperial expansion in the second half of the nineteenth century. Indeed, most forced settlement colonies abolished slavery during the first half of the nineteenth century, and they continued to implement liberal reforms during the second half of the nineteenth century. Consequently, my research advances the alternative argument that the favorable developmental legacies of forced settlement likely emanate from the liberal institutional reforms that expanded the legal rights and political agency of emancipated Afro-descendants in forced settlement colonies. I contend that liberal reforms, rather than the lengthy duration of colonial rule, account for the favorable developmental legacies of forced settlement relative to colonial occupation. Both of these arguments will be tested with statistical evidence in Chapter 4.

Existing studies have also examined the impact of environmental factors in contributing to the late colonization and limited postcolonial development of sub-Saharan African countries. Jeffrey Herbst (2000) argues that Africa's vast indigenous hinterlands were especially difficult for Europeans to control because Europeans faced high mortality rates in malaria-endemic regions until the early twentieth century.[10] Africa's low population density and widely dispersed population settlements also increased the cost of state-building and infrastructural development during the colonial era. Jeffrey Herbst (2000) argues that Africa's low population densities, harsh disease environment, and difficult terrain posed unique challenges for broadcasting state power over sparsely inhabited territories. Herbst's research suggests that Africa's difficult "political geography" hindered the developmental and administrative capacity of African colonial states and their postcolonial successors. Tragically, many postcolonial African governments maintained destructive policies that extracted economic surplus from the productive sectors of the economy and maintained authoritarian control over widely dispersed populations and territories. These destructive policies contributed to the poor developmental outcomes and devastating civil conflicts that have plagued many African countries after independence (Bates 1981, 2008; Herbst 2000, esp. chs. 6 and 7; Englebert 2000; Acemoglu and Robinson 2010, 39–44).

Geography, population, and colonial duration undoubtedly impacted the favorable divergent developmental legacies of forced settlement relative to colonial occupation. It was easier and less costly for Europeans to control the limited territory and population of forced settlement colonies than the much larger territories and widely dispersed indigenous African populations that experienced colonial occupation after 1880. This is precisely why European colonists never established large-scale agricultural plantations in sub-Saharan Africa during the seventeenth and eighteenth centuries. Instead, they established these plantations in forced settlement colonies using imported African slaves. By the time Europeans were able to control the vast indigenous hinterlands of the African continent, they had already abolished slavery in their forced settlement colonies, and emancipated Afro-descendants were already starting to reap the benefits of liberal reforms that accompanied the abolition of slavery. Nevertheless, these liberal reforms were seldom extended to the vast indigenous populations and territories that experienced colonial occupation. This partly reflects the limited extent of European control over the African continent when slavery was abolished in forced settlement colonies. Consequently, postabolition reforms were typically limited to culturally assimilated Creole African populations in directly ruled areas coastal areas like Freetown, Sierra Leone (see Chapter 5), the French-controlled coastal towns in Senegal (Chapter 7), and the Portuguese African Creole minority in Guinea-Bissau (Chapter 6). It was easier and cheaper to implement liberal institutional reforms in small colonial states with culturally assimilated Creole populations that in many ways were more similar to rural and working-class Europeans than to indigenous Africans or Asians.

Adria Lawrence (2013) explores how population size affected the French government's response to demands for political reforms in different French colonies, but her argument overlooks the different approaches that were used to control Creole versus indigenous colonial populations in small islands. At the turn of the twentieth century, there were more than six times as many people living in the French Antilles than in French Polynesia and New Caledonia in the Pacific region. If a small population was the primary criterion that favored liberal reforms and inclusive citizenship rights, one would expect to find a more inclusive legal-administrative framework in the Pacific islands relative to the Antilles colonies. In reality, however, it was the Antilles colonies that benefited from liberal institutional reforms following the abolition of slavery. On the eve of World War II, more than 98% of the population in the French Antilles colonies enjoyed French citizenship rights, compared with 15% of the population in Polynesia and 29% in New Caledonia (France 1944). The repressive *indigénat* legal code was also used to control the small population of indigenous Pacific Islanders in Polynesia and New Caledonia (Merle 2002), whereas emancipated Afro-descendants in the Antilles were legally recognized as French citizens (France 1944). This suggests that a small colonial population did not guarantee liberal reforms and inclusive citizenship laws prior to World War II.

This suggests that the impact of small island geography on long-term development is not so simple or straightforward. The small size and island geography of forced settlement colonies undoubtedly made it easier for Europeans to implement liberal institutional reforms following the abolition of slavery. But these geographic factors also made it easier for Europeans to control enslaved Africans in forced settlement colonies prior to the abolition of slavery. Consequently, it is important to examine the reforms that enabled forced settlement colonies to promote more inclusive development outcomes following the abolition of slavery in the nineteenth century. By providing a long-term historical perspective that traces the institutional development of forced settlement colonies back to the sixteenth century, my research highlights the importance of liberal reforms that expanded the legal rights and political agency of emancipated Afro-descendants following the abolition of slavery. Consequently, the remaining chapters of this book provide statistical evidence and comparative-historical evidence that liberal reforms, rather than geographic and environmental factors, favored the long-term development and postcolonial democratization of forced settlement colonies relative to colonial occupation in the Global South.

Summary

This chapter developed a historical-institutional theoretical framework that explains the comparatively successful long-term development of forced settlement colonies relative to Global South countries that emerged from colonial occupation after World War II. Although forced settlement colonies established agricultural plantations with imported African slaves and Asian indentured laborers, they were able to promote favorable development outcomes relative to Global South countries that experienced colonial occupation. I argue that the favorable developmental legacies of forced settlement relative to colonial occupation reflect the different legal-administrative frameworks that governed emancipated Afro-descendants vis-à-vis indigenous colonial subjects. Building on theoretical insights from James Mahoney's research on liberal reforms and postcolonial development in Latin America, the theoretical framework in this chapter advances the argument that liberal reforms enabled forced settlement colonies to expand the legal rights and political agency of emancipated Afro-descendants following the abolition of slavery in the nineteenth century. I also argue that liberal reforms helped strengthen the rule of law, promote inclusive citizenship norms, and expand the administrative capacity of colonial state officials to provide public goods like state-funded education, basic healthcare, and poor relief to emancipated Afro-descendants. In doing so, liberal reforms fundamentally altered the relationship between state and society in ways that facilitated inclusive human development and postcolonial democratization in many forced settlement colonies.

The theoretical framework in this chapter also examined the negative developmental legacies of colonial occupation in the Global South. Building on previous research by Mahmood Mamdani, Matthew Lange and others, I argued that European colonial occupation generated bifurcated legal-administrative institutions that undermined the rule of law, restricted citizenship rights, and limited the administrative capacity of colonial officials to provide public goods like education, sanitation, and poor relief. The development of distinctive legal-administrative frameworks for colonial settlers and indigenous subjects had lasting negative consequences for inclusive human development and postcolonial democratization in Global South countries that emerged from colonial occupation after World War II. By tracing the distinctive patterns of institutional development associated with forced settlement and colonial occupation over the *longue durée*, these arguments are useful for understanding important developmental variations within and across multiple colonial empires. The next chapter provides an empirical test of these arguments using statistical data from more than 90 Global South countries that emerged from colonial domination after 1945.

4

A Global Statistical Analysis of Forced Settlement and Colonial Occupation

Colonial Institutions and Postcolonial Development

This chapter presents a global statistical analysis of the long-term development trajectories of 92 developing countries and nine dependent territories with predominantly nonwhite populations that emerged from colonial rule after World War II. In contrast to earlier studies that explore the impact of national colonial legacies on educational attainment (Brown 2000; Frankema 2012), economic growth (Grier 1997), or postcolonial democratization (Bernhard, Reenock, and Nordstrom 2004; Lee and Paine 2019a), the OLS regression models in this chapter highlight the distinctive developmental and political legacies of forced settlement and colonial occupation in Global South.

The statistical evidence in this chapter demonstrates that forced settlement is associated with higher levels of educational attainment, life expectancy, and economic development relative to colonial occupation. These developmental advantages were already apparent at the end of the colonial era, and forced settlement continues to predict higher HDI scores in 2015 relative to colonial occupation. Consequently, the data models in this chapter confirm that forced settlement generated more inclusive human development outcomes relative to colonial occupation. The OLS models in this chapter also demonstrate the relationship between greater exposure to mass electoral competition during the colonial era and higher mean postcolonial democracy scores in forced settlement colonies relative to colonies of occupation. These empirical results are robust to statistical controls for British colonization, European settlement, ethnic fractionalization, religious composition, geography, and other factors that might have produced developmental advantages in forced settlement colonies. Moreover, both British and continental European forced settlement generated favorable developmental legacies relative to colonial occupation.

The data analysis in this chapter further examines whether the favorable developmental legacies of forced settlement were driven by Protestant missionary evangelization or liberal reforms that expanded the legal rights and political agency of emancipated Afro-descendants following the abolition of slavery. The statistical results are conclusive: forced settlement continues to predict favorable

Ruling Emancipated Slaves and Indigenous Subjects. Olukunle P. Owolabi, Oxford University Press.
© Oxford University Press 2023. DOI: 10.1093/oso/9780197673027.003.0004

development outcomes relative to colonial occupation in OLS models that control for Protestant missionary evangelization. By contrast, the impact of forced
settlement is statistically insignificant after controlling for the extension of metropolitan (i.e., European legal rights) prior to World War II. The historical evidence
in subsequent chapters reveals that these reforms were not unique to the British
colonial empire; continental European powers like France and Portugal also
recognized the citizenship rights of emancipated Afro-descendants following
the abolition of slavery. By contrast, most colonies of occupation maintained
bifurcated legal-administrative institutions that restricted the legal rights of indigenous colonial subjects until after World War II. Perhaps not surprisingly,
the statistical evidence in this chapter demonstrates favorable developmental
outcomes in colonial states that developed an inclusive legal-administrative
framework that resembled their Western European colonizers. Consequently,
the OLS results in this chapter support the book's central claim that liberal institutional reforms following the abolition of slavery promoted favorable development outcomes in forced settlement colonies relative to Global South countries
that emerged from colonial occupation after 1945.

Empirical Strategy and Data Analysis

OLS regression analysis is useful for testing whether the divergent developmental legacies of forced settlement and colonial occupation are robust to statistical controls for European settlement, ethnicity, religion, geography, and other
confounding factors that might have shaped the long-term development and political trajectories of postcolonial states in the Global South. Most data models
in this chapter are based on the subset of 92 developing countries and nine dependent territories with predominantly nonwhite populations that emerged from
colonial rule after 1945. This is because most countries that experienced forced
settlement or colonial occupation gained independence after World War II. At
the same time, the inclusion of dependent territories like the French and Dutch
Antilles enables us to examine the development trajectories of forced settlement
colonies that never gained independence. By contrast, my primary data analysis
excludes developing countries that gained independence prior to World War II.
Most of the excluded states are Latin American countries with intermediate to
high levels of European settlement, and diverse populations of mixed European,
African, and/or indigenous ancestry. Because these countries gained independence during the nineteenth century, their decolonization and state-formation
occurred under historical circumstances very different from the developing
countries that emerged from colonial domination after 1945. In Latin American
countries and South Africa, local whites maintained their economic and political

dominance long after independence. Furthermore, the developing countries that gained independence in the nineteenth century were not significantly exposed to mass electoral competition prior to independence. Consequently, it is not ideal to directly compare their long-term development to Global South countries that emerged from colonial domination after World War II.

There are additional reasons for limiting my primary data analysis to developing countries with predominantly nonwhite populations that emerged from colonial rule after 1945. Most development indicators were not widely available for colonial populations in the Global South until the United Nations compelled European states to report on the economic and social well-being of their colonial territories after World War II. The wartime mobilization of colonized populations also generated demands for political representation and self-determination, and political reform in colonial territories after World War II. Consequently, it is relatively straightforward to connect colonial institutions from the early and mid-twentieth century to the developmental and political trajectories of Global South countries that gained independence after 1945. For these reasons, the primary data analysis in this chapter is limited to the subset of developing countries that emerged from colonial rule after 1945.[1] This strategy enables us to draw reliable conclusions about why specific patterns of colonization are associated with positive or negative developmental outcomes during the second half of the twentieth century. The 92 developing countries and nine overseas dependencies in my primary data analysis are listed in Appendix 1. Table 4.1 provides summary statistics for the key dependent variables, focal independent variables, and control variables included in my data analysis.

Dependent Variables

The statistical models in this chapter examine the distinctive developmental legacies of forced settlement and colonial occupation for various measures of human well-being and postcolonial democratization.

Colonial-Era Development and Human Well-Being

The first set of data models examines three indicators of human well-being at the end of the colonial era: educational attainment in 1960, life expectancy at birth in 1955–60, and per capita GDP in 1973. The adult literacy rate in 1960 measures educational attainment at the end of the colonial era. Because most people learn to read in primary school, the adult literacy in 1960 proxies the extent to which colonial states provided access to primary schooling during the first half of the twentieth century. The 1960 literacy rates were obtained from the United Nations *Compendium for Social Statistics*, and they vary from less than 5% in French- and

Table 4.1 Summary Statistics

Dependent Variable	N	Mean	Std. Dev.	Min.	Max.
Adult literacy rate (%), 1960	101	41.73	30.17	1	97
Life expectancy at birth (years), 1955–60	101	47.60	9.91	28	66
Per capita GDP (logged), 1973	92	7.54	0.94	6.07	10.68
HDI Score, 2015	101	62.65	15.21	28.50	91.20
Years of "tutelary democracy" under colonial rule	101	6.69	9.98	0	34
Mean postcolonial democracy score, 1972–2012	92	4.67	2.72	0.69	9.97
Focal Independent Variables					
Forced settlement	101	0.20	0.40	0	1
British forced settlement	101	0.13	0.34	0	1
Non-British forced settlement	101	0.07	0.26	0	1
Mixed colonization	101	0.06	0.24	0	1
City-state	101	0.03	0.17	0	1
British-protected state	101	0.09	0.29	0	1
Metropolitan legal rights, 1936	101	0.28	0.45	0	1
Key Control Variables					
British colonization	101	0.50	0.50	0	1
% European settlers	101	2.12	3.56	0	25
% Asian settlers	101	5.12	14.60	0	81.20
Ethnic fractionalization	101	0.48	0.28	0	0.93
% Protestant, 1900	101	8.97	20.33	0	100
% Muslim, 1900	101	25.16	37.21	0	100
Protestant missionaries per 10,000 pop. 1923	92	1.24	1.92	0	9.91
Years exposure to Protestant missionaries, 1960	92	99.81	62.40	0	335
Years of colonization prior to 1960	101	146.5	123.00	17	500
Years since independence, 2012	92	47.83	9.89	28	67
% Urban, 1955	101	25.24	23.37	1.40	100

Table 4.1 Continued

Key Control Variables					
Real GDP/capita (logged), 1972–2004	92	7.93	1.07	6.23	10.65
Oil exporter	101	0.14	0.35	0	1
Small island	101	0.30	0.46	0	1
Landlocked	101	0.14	0.35	0	1
Latitude	101	0.16	0.10	0	0.39
Sub-Saharan Africa	101	0.44	0.50	0	1

Portuguese-occupied African states like Angola, Burkina Faso, Central African Republic, Mali, and Niger to more than 90% in forced settlement colonies like Barbados, the Netherlands Antilles, and Trinidad and Tobago (United Nations 1967).[2]

I obtained life expectancy data for 1955–60 from the United Nations (2017) electronic database. All human beings aspire to a long and healthy life, but most colonial states did not provide sufficient access to healthcare, clean water, sanitation, or economic opportunities to support human well-being or longevity. Consequently, the life expectancy at birth in 1955–60 was less than 40 years in one-quarter of the political units in my dataset, including India and more than 20 colonial states in sub-Saharan Africa (United Nations 2017). By contrast, life expectancy at birth already exceeded 60 years in forced settlement colonies like Jamaica, Trinidad and Tobago, and the Netherlands Antilles, and in city-state colonies like Hong Kong and Singapore (United Nations 2017).

I used Angus Maddison's per capita GDP indicator from 1973 to measure economic development at the end of the colonial era. These data are measured in 1990 international Geary-Khamis dollars, and they are available for most of the countries and territories in my dataset.[3] The per capita GDP for countries and territories in my dataset varied widely from less than $600 in Bangladesh, Burundi, Cape Verde, and Guinea to more than $40,000 in oil-rich Qatar (in 1990 international Geary-Khamis dollars). Because of this wide variation, the economic development models were estimated using the natural log of per capita GDP in 1973.

Finally, the United Nations Human Development Index (HDI) provides a broad-based measure of human well-being that encompasses educational attainment, life expectancy, and per capita GDP in 2015.[4] I obtained HDI scores from 2015 to examine whether the developmental legacies associated with each pattern of colonization have persisted until the present day.

Indicators of Tutelary Democracy and Postcolonial Democratization

I also explore the postcolonial regime trajectories associated with each mode of colonization. I developed a "tutelary democracy" indicator that measures the number of years that each colonial state maintained a multiparty electoral system with universal adult suffrage prior to independence. This indicator was primarily constructed using electoral data from Przeworski et al.'s (2011) Political Institutions and Political Events database.[5] Nearly two-thirds of the colonial states in my dataset held at least one competitive election with universal suffrage prior to independence. The main exceptions to this pattern are the British-protected states that maintained traditional Islamic monarchies after independence, and French or Portuguese colonies that gained independence following revolutionary violence, like Algeria, Angola, Guinea-Bissau, Mozambique, and Vietnam. By contrast, most forced settlement colonies— including Barbados, Jamaica, Trinidad and Tobago, and Suriname—experienced at least 15 years of tutelary democracy prior to independence.

Finally, Freedom House Imputed Polity (FHIP) scores measure the extent to which postcolonial states have been able to support highly democratic political regimes between 1972 and 2012. FHIP scores combine the imputed average of two widely used democracy indicators—i.e., Freedom House scores (measuring civil liberties and political rights) and Polity scores (measuring political participation and electoral competition, executive recruitment, and constraints on executive authority). These indicators are merged into a single 0–10 scale, with higher scores indicating higher levels of democracy. This provides a nuanced and intuitive measure of postcolonial democratization that is more reliable than either of its component parts.[6] Freedom House Imputed Polity scores are available for all independent countries in my dataset, so this indicator provides better geographic coverage than alternative democracy indicators from the V-DEM project (Coppedge et al. 2016). The mean postcolonial democracy score for countries in my dataset ranges from 0.69/10.0 in Syria to 9.97/10.0 in Barbados.

Focal Independent Variables

The focal independent variables denote different patterns of colonial domination in the Global South. The "forced settlement" dummy variable denotes colonial states that established agricultural plantations with imported African slaves and/or Asian indentured laborers whose descendants comprise at least three-quarters of the postcolonial population.[7] Some data models also distinguish British forced settlement colonies (such as Barbados, Jamaica, and Trinidad and Tobago) from other forced settlement colonies (such as Cape Verde, Guadeloupe, Martinique, and Suriname) to determine whether non-British forced settlement also generated positive developmental outcomes relative to colonial occupation.

The dummy variable for "mixed colonization" denotes colonial states that experienced diverse patterns of colonization within the same territory. Mixed plantation colonies often attracted significant European settlement (e.g., French Polynesia) or indentured labor migration (e.g., Malaysia and Fiji), despite having sizable indigenous populations. Other mixed colonies established agricultural plantations using African slave labor, but they attracted significant white settlement (e.g., French Guiana and the US Virgin Islands) and/or foreign migration (e.g., Belize) following the abolition of slavery. In accounting for their distinctiveness, the developmental outcomes of mixed colonies are estimated separately from that of forced settlement colonies.

The dummy variable for colonial "city-states" denotes directly ruled city-state colonies that were established to promote and expand European commercial trade with China. Hong Kong, Macau, and Singapore exemplify this pattern of colonization. Last, the dummy variable for "British-protected states" denotes traditional Islamic states that entered into a subordinate relationship with British resident advisers in exchange for protection against third powers. This includes the small Arab kingdoms in the Persian Gulf region as well as Yemen and the Malay Kingdom of Brunei.[8]

Last, colonial occupation refers to European domination over indigenous populations and territories that were exploited for their labor and natural resources. This was the most common pattern of colonial domination in the Global South, so it is the omitted reference category in my data analysis. Consequently, the statistical data models compare the developmental legacies of forced settlement, mixed colonization, city-state colonies, and British-protected states relative to colonial occupation in the Global South.

Table 4.2 summarizes the developmental outcomes associated with each pattern of imperial domination. For each of the indicators outlined above, forced settlement is associated with favorable development outcomes relative to colonial occupation. The developmental advantage of forced settlement relative to colonial occupation has largely persisted over time. In 1960, for example, the mean adult literacy rate was 83% for forced settlement colonies versus 22% for colonies of occupation; life expectancy at birth averaged nearly 58 years in forced settlement colonies compared to 43 years in colonies of occupation; the mean per capita GDP of forced settlement colonies in 1973 was 3.5 times higher than in colonies of occupation. The HDI scores in Table 2.2 also suggest that forced settlement colonies continue to enjoy significant developmental advantages relative to Global South countries that experienced colonial occupation. The summary data in Table 2.2 also reveal important differences in the political legacies of forced settlement relative to colonial occupation. Forced settlement colonies experienced

Table 4.2 Mean Developmental Outcome by Mode of Colonization

Type of Colonial State	Human Development Outcomes				Colonial Elections and Postcolonial Democracy	
	Adult Literacy Rate, 1960 (%)	Life expectancy at birth, 1955–60 (years)	Per capita GDP (logged), 1973 ($)	HDI Score, 2015	Tutelary Democracy under Colonial Rule (years)	Freedom House Imputed Polity Score, 1972–2012
Forced settlement	83.0	57.7	3,727	74.8	22.0	8.95
(n = 20)	(19.6)	(4.0)	(3,634)	(7.3)	(10.4)	(1.6)
Colonial occupation	22.0	42.8	1,057	54.7	1.0	3.71
(n = 63)	(25.4)	(7.4)	(1,282)	(10.9)	(5.2)	(2.3)
City-state colony	70.0	64.6	5,977	90.5	0.0	3.98
(n = 3)	(12.9)	(1.3)	(2,211)	(1.1)	(0.0)	(NA)
Mixed colonization	71.0	57.5	3,423	78.2	20.5	6.57
(n = 6)	(16.7)	(3.0)	(1,025)	(5.6)	(12.2)	(2.0)
British-protected states	28.0	46.4	4,376	71.8	0.0	1.82
(n = 9)	(15.3)	(11.6)	(15,361)	(19.8)	(2.9)	(2.1)

Note: Standard deviations in parentheses.

Sources: 1960 adult literacy rates are from the United Nations 1980. Life expectancy data are United Nations 2017). Per capita GDP data are measured in 1990 international Geary-Khamis dollars to control for purchasing power parity (see Maddison 2006). HDI scores for 2015 are from the United Nations Development Program 2016. Tutelary democracy prior to independence is based on author's calculations using data from Przeworski et al. 2011. I used secondary sources to obtain electoral data on small Pacific islands and dependent territories whose colonial elections are missing from Przeworski's dataset (see Appendix 2). Postcolonial democracy is estimated using Freedom House Imputed Polity scores obtained from the Quality of Government Database, http://www.qog.pol.gu.se.

a much longer period of "tutelary democracy" prior to independence, and they have experienced greater postcolonial democratization than any other type of colonial state in the Global South. From 1972 until 2012, the mean postcolonial democracy score for forced settlement colonies was 8.95 on the 10-point Freedom House Imputed Polity scale. By contrast, the mean postcolonial democracy score for colonies of occupation was only 3.71. These data confirm that forced settlement colonies experienced favorable development outcomes relative to Global South countries that emerged from colonial occupation after World War II.

Control Variables

The statistical models control for confounding factors that may have impacted the favorable developmental legacies of forced settlement relative to colonial occupation.

British Colonization

Thirteen of the 20 forced settlement colonies in my primary dataset experienced at least 150 years of British colonial rule, so it is important to examine whether the favorable developmental outcomes associated with forced settlement were unique to British forced settlement. Existing studies demonstrate favorable developmental outcomes in former British colonies and Anglo-Saxon countries common relative to former French or Iberian colonies (see Bollen and Jackman 1985; Weiner 1987; Huntington 1984; Hadenius 1992; Lipset, Seong, and Torres 1993; La Porta et al. 1998, 1999; Grier 1999; Brown 2000). These developmental advantages stem from a variety of historical legacies including the strong protection of private property rights and individual civil liberties under British common law (La Porta et al. 1998, 1999), Protestant missionary evangelization (Woodberry 2004, 2012; Gallego and Woodberry 2010; Lankina and Getachew 2012, 2013), and the British preference for organizing mass competitive elections in their colonial territories prior to independence (see Huntington 1984; Weiner 1987; Lee and Paine 2019a). Consequently, most OLS models include a dummy variable for former colonies of Britain or one of its settler offshoots (i.e., the United States, Australia, or New Zealand). Some OLS models also provide separate regression estimates for British forced settlement and continental European forced settlement relative to colonial occupation.

Colonial Settlers

Existing studies also suggest that colonial states with extensive European settlement established economic and political institutions that facilitated inclusive human development and postcolonial democratization (see Sokoloff and Engerman 2000; Acemoglu, Johnson, and Robinson 2001; Engerman, Mariscal, and Sokoloff 2009; Acemoglu, Gallego, and Robinson 2014; Easterly and Levine 2016). Consequently, most OLS models control for the percentage of European descendants in each colonial state during the late colonial era. This information was obtained from diverse data sources listed in Appendix 2. There was limited European settlement in most developing countries that emerged from colonial rule after 1945, but several colonial states were partially developed by indentured labor migrants from China and the Indian subcontinent.

Asian settlement had mixed consequences for colonial development and post-colonial democratization. On the one hand, Indian labor migration contributed to the politicization of ethnic differences in postcolonial states like Fiji, Guyana, Malaysia, Sri Lanka, Suriname, Trinidad and Tobago, and Uganda. The politicization of ethnic differences can institutionalize ethnic inequalities in ways that undermine democratic governance (Horowitz 2000) and the effective provision of developmental goods and services (Collier 2000; Easterly and Levine 1997). On the other hand, Chinese and Indian settlers contributed to the long-term development of colonial states like Malaysia and Singapore. Indian and Chinese indentured labor migration may have also facilitated broad-based human development in forced settlement colonies where sugar estates were sustained with indentured plantation labor following the abolition of slavery. This is because indentured labor migration enabled forced settlement colonies like Trinidad, Mauritius, and Guyana to expand their agricultural production after emancipated Afro-descendants moved into towns and villages where they had greater access to primary schooling and small-scale landownership. Consequently, my data models control for the proportion of Asian settlers in each country or territory at the end of the colonial era (c. 1975), using data from the *World Christian Encyclopedia* (Barrett, Kurian, and Johnson 2001).

Ethnicity and Religion

The politicization of ethnic differences can also generate communal violence that impedes development (Lange 2009, 125–29; 2012) and undermines democracy (Horowitz 2000; Lieberman and Singh 2012; King 2014). Consequently, the OLS models include a statistical control for the extent of ethnic fractionalization in each colonial state (Alesina et al. 2003).[9] Religious beliefs, institutions, and actors also shape the developmental and political trajectories of different societies. Previous empirical research suggests that Protestant missionaries expanded educational access and empowered civil society in ways that supported postcolonial democratization (Woodberry 2012; Lankina and Getachew 2012, 2013; Tusalem 2009; Grier 1997; Bollen 1979). By contrast, other scholars have argued that the fusion of clerical and civil authority that underpins many Islamic societies is antithetical to capitalist development (Kuran 2012) and liberal democracy (Huntington 1993). Scholars have also argued Islamic law and cultural practices can reinforce traditional social norms that exacerbate gender inequalities (Fish 2011, 173–215). If girls and women do not have equal access to education, property rights, and other individual liberties, this will perpetuate gender-based inequalities that undermine broad-based development. These conclusions are disputed in recent studies that suggest that religious traditions like Protestantism and Islam are not inherently favorable or antithetical to democracy or inclusive development (see Stepan 2000, 2012; Noland 2005; Fish 2011). Nevertheless, it is important to determine whether Protestant Christianity or Islam has shaped the developmental trajectories of postcolonial states. Consequently, many OLS models include statistical controls for the percentage of Protestants and Muslims in each political unit in 1900 or 1970.[10]

Socioeconomic Development

Socioeconomic modernization is also an important predictor of democratization and human well-being. For example, urbanization often expanded access to public goods and services like education, sanitation, and poor relief because the administrative capacity of colonial state officials was primarily concentrated in modern urban settlements, rather than peripheral rural districts with significant indigenous populations (Herbst 2000; Mamdani 1996). Consequently, it is important to examine whether urbanization contributed to the developmental advantage of forced settlement colonies and of city-state colonies like Hong Kong and Singapore. For this reason, the regression models that examine adult literacy and life expectancy during the colonial era include a statistical control for the percentage of the population living in urban areas in 1955.

The dummy variable for oil-exporting countries tests Michael Ross' (2001) hypothesis that oil exports hinder democratization in developing countries. Finally, the postcolonial democratization models also control for the mean per capita GDP between 1972 and 2004. This provides an empirical test of the "modernization" hypothesis linking socioeconomic development to political democracy (see Lipset 1959; Dahl 1971; Hadenius 1992; Przeworski et al. 2000).[11]

Geography

Geographic factors may have also shaped the divergent developmental and political trajectories associated with forced settlement and colonial occupation. Consequently, most OLS models control for distance from the equator (i.e., latitude) because previous studies suggest that tropical disease environments are less conducive for long-term development (see Sachs and Warner 1997; Collier and Gunning 1999; Sachs 2005). The "small island" dummy variable identifies island microstates with less than 500,000 inhabitants in 1960. Small island populations were easier for colonial rulers to control, which explains why many island microstates experienced more than three centuries of colonial rule. The early integration of many island microstates into the Atlantic world economy likely facilitated their economic development, high levels of educational attainment, and successful postcolonial democratization (Ankar 2006; Feyrer and Sacerdote 2009). By contrast, landlocked states were harder for Europeans to control and less deeply integrated into the European-dominated Atlantic economy. Consequently, landlocked populations remain impoverished and underdeveloped in many parts of the Global South (Sachs and Warner 1997). Consequently, most OLS models include a dummy variable for landlocked states.

I also include a regional dummy for sub-Saharan African countries to capture the late colonization of this region and other unmeasured factors that might have hindered the long-term development of sub-Saharan African countries relative to other Global South regions. Because half of the colonies of occupation in my primary dataset are sub-Saharan African countries, it is important to ensure that the poor developmental outcomes associated with colonial occupation are not driven by unmeasured factors that are unique to this region.

Diagnostic Tests

I conducted several diagnostic tests to ensure that the regression models do not suffer high levels of collinearity, which occurs when two or more independent variables are highly correlated. OLS regression results are highly sensitive to small changes if there is significant collinearity in the data model. Moreover, it is difficult to estimate the unique developmental consequences of independent variables that are highly correlated. I obtained the variance inflation factors for each statistical model to ensure that they do not suffer from excessive collinearity.[12] I also examined the standardized residuals for each model to identify outlying observations, and I obtained the DF-beta statistics for each independent variable to identify influential observations in each model. There are very few outlying or influential observations in these models. Finally, I inspected each model for heteroscedasticity, using Breusch-Pagan's test for linear homoscedasticity and White's test for homoscedastic variance. There is significant heteroscedasticity in the economic development models in Table 4.4, but the remaining data models do not violate the OLS assumption of homoscedastic error terms. Consequently, I reported all statistical results with robust standard errors, which are appropriate for homoscedastic or heteroscedastic conditions.

Hypotheses for Empirical Testing

The statistical models test the following hypotheses that emerged from the theoretical arguments in Chapter 3.

H1: Forced settlement generated favorable development outcomes during the colonial era relative to colonial occupation.

H2: The favorable developmental legacies of forced settlement relative to colonial occupation have persisted to the present day.

H3: Forced settlement is associated with greater exposure to tutelary democracy during the colonial era relative to colonial occupation.

H4: Forced settlement predicts favorable democratization outcomes relative to colonial occupation in the Global South.

H5: Both British and continental European forced settlement are associated with favorable development outcomes relative to colonial occupation.

Empirical Results

Human Well-Being at the End of the Colonial Era

Models 1–3 in Table 4.3 demonstrate that forced settlement is associated with favorable developmental outcomes relative to colonial occupation in terms of adult literacy in 1960. Model 1 estimates separate regression coefficients for forced settlement, mixed colonization, colonial city-states, and British-protected states relative to colonial occupation. Here forced settlement predicts a 45-percentage point advantage in the 1960 adult literacy rate relative to colonial occupation (p < 0.01). Mixed colonization and city-state colonies also demonstrate statistically significant literacy advantages relative to colonial occupation, although the magnitude of this advantage is smaller than in forced settlement colonies. Model 2 includes statistical controls for confounding factors. Here the predicted 1960 literacy rate for forced settlement colonies is 18 percentage points higher than for colonies of occupation, ceteris paribus, and this result is statistically significant at p < 0.01. None of the other modes of colonization predict statistically significant advantages for adult literacy 1960 after controlling for confounding factors. Remarkably, the only control variables that impacted educational attainment during the colonial era at statistically significant levels are the extent of Protestantism in 1900 (+), the extent of Islam in 1900 (−), and the dummy variable for sub-Saharan African countries (−). In Model 3, both British forced settlement and non-British forced settlement are associated with favorable developmental legacies relative to colonial occupation, ceteris paribus, and both results are statistically significant at p < 0.01. This model also tests whether the higher adult literacy rates in forced settlement colonies were driven by their higher rates of urbanization relative to colonies of occupation. This outcome is likely because the administrative capacity of colonial states to provide public goods like education and sanitation

Table 4.3 Education and Life Expectancy at the End of the Colonial Era

Variables	Adult Literacy Rate, 1960			Life Expectancy, 1955–60		
	(1)	(2)	(3)	(4)	(5)	(6)
Forced settlement	45.29** (5.46)	23.73** (5.44)		14.94** (1.31)	10.39** (2.20)	
British forced settlement			18.95** (5.16)			8.56** (2.61)
Non-British forced settlement			15.99** (6.27)			6.89* (2.75)
Mixed colonization	43.51** (7.17)	7.21 (10.15)	9.18 (7.35)	14.68** (1.49)	6.69* (3.04)	7.57* (3.06)
City-state	33.51** (7.02)	16.64 (9.19)	−18.98 (11.71)	21.76** (1.13)	17.53** (2.80)	2.68 (5.07)
British-protected state	−0.38 (5.91)	1.81 (8.29)	−1.80 (7.40)	3.57 (3.85)	4.63 (3.96)	3.29 (3.78)
British colonization		5.49 (2.92)			2.58* (1.21)	
Years since independence		0.72 (0.63)	0.64 (0.54)		0.50 (0.26)	0.47 (0.20)
% European settlers		0.66 (0.54)	−0.43 (0.56)		0.40* (0.17)	−0.06 (0.20)
% Asian settlers		0.04 (0.14)	0.04 (0.13)		0.07 (0.05)	0.07 (0.05)
Ethnic fractionalization		−9.00 (9.05)	−25.16** (9.21)		−0.31 (3.46)	−7.10* (3.34)
% Protestant (1900)		0.39** (0.07)	0.44** (0.07)		0.03 (0.04)	0.05 (0.04)
% Muslim (1900)		−0.17* (0.09)	−0.19* (0.08)		−0.05 (0.03)	−0.05* (0.02)
% Urban (1955)			0.44** (0.09)			0.18** (0.05)
Small island		4.83 (5.95)	−0.11 (5.37)		2.51 (2.49)	0.49 (2.77)
Landlocked		−3.63 (3.79)	−2.71 (4.10)		−0.84 (1.91)	−0.47 (1.91)
Latitude		−17.34 (21.18)	−28.98 (19.70)		12.80 (9.20)	8.04 (8.15)
Sub-Saharan Africa		−21.16** (5.85)	−15.54** (5.17)		−2.87 (1.70)	−0.55 (1.65)

Table 4.3 Continued

Variables	Adult Literacy Rate, 1960			Life Expectancy, 1955–60		
	(1)	(2)	(3)	(4)	(5)	(6)
Constant	29.16**	46.25**	51.43**	42.80**	40.37**	42.72**
	(3.26)	(7.29)	(6.44)	(0.95)	(3.28)	(2.99)
Observations	101	101	101	101	101	101
R-squared	0.44	0.82	0.85	0.51	0.70	0.75

Note: Robust standard errors in parentheses, **$p < 0.01$, *$p < 0.05$.

was often concentrated in urban areas. Model 3 reveals a positive and significant relationship between urbanization and educational attainment (significant at $p < 0.01$), but this does not change the fact that the forced settlement variables maintain statistically significant advantages for educational attainment relative to colonial occupation.

Models 4–6 examine the relationship between the initial mode of colonization and expected human longevity at the end of the colonial era. The statistical relationships in the life expectancy models are similar to the literacy models. In Model 4, forced settlement is associated with 15 additional years of life expectancy relative to colonial occupation, and this result is statistically significant at $p < 0.01$. Mixed colonization and colonial city-states also predict statistically significant advantages in expected human longevity relative to colonial occupation. The regression coefficients for forced settlement, mixed colonization, and city-state colonies remain positive and statistically significant at $p < 0.01$ with the addition of statistical controls for confounding factors. Forced settlement continues to predict 10 additional years of life expectancy relative to colonial occupation after controlling for confounding factors in Model 5. Furthermore, both British and continental European forced settlement are associated with substantial developmental advantages in life expectancy relative to colonial occupation in Model 6. The relative advantage of British forced settlement is somewhat larger than that of European forced settlement, but both variables are statistically significant at $p < 0.05$. Most of the control variables are statistically insignificant in Models 5 and 6. Urbanization is the only control variable with positive and significant consequences for life expectancy at the end of the colonial era. This result is consistent with previous empirical studies that suggest higher levels of administrative state capacity in core urban areas relative to peripheral rural districts. This likely explains why the developmental advantage of city-state colonies is statistically insignificant after controlling for urbanization in 1955. By contrast, forced settlement continues to predict favorable developmental legacies relative to colonial occupation even after controlling for urbanization and other confounding factors in Model 6.

The data models in Table 4.4 examine how different modes of colonization affected economic development at the end of the colonial era. These results are based on a smaller sample of 92 former colonies because Angus Maddison's economic database lacks GDP data for the US Virgin Islands and eight Pacific island microstates.[13] Once again, the initial model examines the developmental legacies of each mode of colonization with no statistical controls for confounding factors. In Model 1, forced settlement, mixed colonization, city-states, and British-protected states all predict significantly higher levels of economic development than colonial occupation in 1973 ($p < 0.01$). Models 2–4 include statistical controls for confounding factors that might have influenced long-term patterns of economic development. I also included a dummy variable for major oil exporters because the oil price shocks of the 1970s would have affected the per capita GDP of many developing countries in 1973. The statistical results for these models are as follows: the most substantial developmental advantages are in city-state colonies and British-protected states, but forced settlement is also associated with a statistically significant developmental advantage relative to colonial occupation.

In Model 2, the predicted developmental advantage of forced settlement relative to colonial occupation remains large and statistically significant at $p < 0.01$ after controlling for confounding factors.[14] The predicted developmental advantage of forced settlement relative to colonial occupation in Model 2 is similar to the actual difference in per capita GDP between a middle-income Caribbean nation like Jamaica ($4,130) and an impoverished African state like Sudan ($780) in 1973. In Model 3, British forced settlement is associated with favorable long-term development relative to colonial occupation ($p < 0.01$), but the regression coefficient for non-British forced settlement is statistically insignificant. Diagnostic tests identify Cape Verde as a major outlier that explains the insignificant result for non-British forced settlement in Model 3. The historical and institutional origins of Cape Verde's economic exploitation and underdevelopment will be explored in detail in Chapter 6, but a short version of this history is that the Portuguese exploitative labor policies and the repressive nature of Portugal's *Estado Novo* dictatorship (1930–74) limited the economic and political development of Portuguese forced settlement colonies relative to their British, French, or Dutch counterparts. Consequently, Model 4 provides an alternative regression estimate that excludes the Portuguese forced settlement colonies: i.e., Cape Verde and São Tomé and Príncipe. Here both British and continental European forced settlements are associated with favorable patterns of economic development relative to colonial occupation (significant at $p < 0.01$). Furthermore, the larger coefficient for non-British forced settlement demonstrates a larger developmental

Table 4.4 Economic Development during the Colonial Era

Variable	Per Capita GDP (logged), 1973			
	(1)	(2)	(3)	(4)
Forced settlement	1.03** (0.19)	0.72** (0.28)		
British forced settlement			0.74** (0.28)	0.84** (0.28)
Non-British forced settlement			0.69 (0.38)	1.08** (0.31)
Mixed colonization	1.04** (0.16)	0.26 (0.43)	0.27 (0.42)	0.44 (0.41)
Colonial city-state	1.43** (0.25)	1.25** (0.39)	1.24** (0.40)	1.38** (0.44)
British-protected state	1.55** (0.48)	0.98* (0.40)	0.98* (0.39)	1.09** (0.40)
British colonization		0.00 (0.14)		
Years since independence (1973)		−0.01 (0.01)	−0.01 (0.01)	−0.01 (0.01)
% European settlers		0.05* (0.02)	0.05* (0.02)	0.05* (0.02)
% Asian settlers		0.00 (0.00)	0.00 (0.00)	0.00 (0.00)
Ethnic fractionalization		0.54 (0.34)	0.54 (0.34)	0.54 (0.35)
% Protestant (1900)		0.01 (0.00)	0.01 (0.00)	0.00 (0.00)
% Muslim (1900)		−0.00 (0.00)	−0.00 (0.00)	−0.00 (0.00)
Oil exporter		0.79** (0.29)	0.79** (0.28)	0.81** (0.29)
Small island		−0.16 (0.24)	−0.15 (0.24)	−0.09 (0.24)
Landlocked		−0.38* (0.15)	−0.38* (0.15)	−0.42** (0.14)
Latitude		2.26* (0.94)	2.27* (0.91)	2.55** (0.88)

(continued)

Table 4.4 Continued

Variable	Per Capita GDP (logged), 1973			
	(1)	(2)	(3)	(4)
Sub-Saharan Africa		−0.35	−0.35	−0.19
		(0.22)	(0.22)	(0.22)
Constant	7.08**	6.82**	6.82**	6.61**
	(0.08)	(0.39)	(0.38)	(0.39)
Observation	92	92	92	90
R-squared	0.41	0.67	0.67	0.70

Robust standard errors in parentheses, ** $p < 0.01$, *$p < 0.05$

advantage for French and Dutch forced settlement colonies relative to British forced settlement colonies. It is perhaps not surprising, then, that the French and Dutch Antilles colonies became overseas dependencies of their respective imperial metropoles after World War II.

Overall, the OLS results in Tables 4.3 and 4.4 support the hypothesis that forced settlement generated favorable developmental outcomes relative to colonial occupation (H1). Moreover, both British and continental European forced settlement generated statistically significant advantages for educational attainment and life expectancy in 1960 relative to colonial occupation (H5). Nevertheless, the OLS results in Table 4.4 provide limited support for H5 because of the limited economic development in Portuguese forced settlement colonies.

Human Well-Being in 2015

To what extent do developmental outcomes from the colonial era affect contemporary variations in human well-being across the Global South? The OLS models in Table 4.5 examine whether the developmental trajectories established during the colonial era have persisted until today. The HDI scores in Table 4.5 provide an aggregate measure of educational attainment, life expectancy at birth, and per capita GDP for postcolonial states in 2015. To facilitate the interpretation of the OLS results, I rescaled the HDI scores from 0 to 100. The OLS results in Table 4.5 confirm that the developmental trends from the late colonial era have persisted until the present day (H2): forced settlement, mixed colonization, city-state colonies, and British-protected states all predict substantially higher HDI scores in 2015 relative to colonial occupation in Model 1. These results are significant at p < 0.01. In Model 2, forced settlement (+6.74, p < 0.05) and city-state colonization

Table 4.5 Human Well-Being in 2015

Variable	HDI Scores in 2015					
	(1)	(2)	(3)	(4)	(5)	(6)
Forced settlement	20.16** (2.15)	6.74* (3.25)		4.74 (3.24)	4.20 (3.11)	1.20 (3.05)
British forced settlement			7.06* (3.18)			
Non-British forced settlement			10.47* (5.11)			
Mixed colonization	23.53** (2.54)	7.38 (4.80)	9.47 (5.06)	7.65 (4.89)	6.11 (4.98)	3.03 (4.22)
City-state	35.80** (1.49)	17.90** (5.62)	20.80** (6.18)	6.12 (6.61)	17.44** (5.64)	8.84 (5.46)
British-protected state	17.14** (6.52)	4.33 (5.58)	6.57 (5.30)	2.54 (5.38)	4.87 (5.68)	3.43 (5.49)
British colonization		2.44 (2.05)		2.27 (1.95)	1.80 (2.02)	1.09 (1.75)
Years since independence (2015)		−0.07 (0.08)	−0.01 (0.08)	−0.08 (0.07)	−0.05 (0.07)	−0.08 (0.07)
% European settlers		0.43** (0.16)	0.44** (0.16)	0.12 (0.19)	0.43* (0.16)	0.30 (0.16)
% Asian settlers		0.12 (0.06)	0.12 (0.07)	0.12 (0.06)	0.11 (0.06)	0.08 (0.06)
Ethnic fractionalization		−1.50 (3.51)	−2.22 (3.58)	−6.16 (3.68)	−0.65 (3.37)	−1.13 (2.81)
% Protestant (1970)		−0.14* (0.06)	−0.10* (0.05)	−0.14* (0.06)	−0.19** (0.06)	−0.15** (0.05)
% Muslim (1970)		−0.10** (0.03)	−0.10** (0.03)	−0.09** (0.02)	−0.07* (0.03)	−0.05* (0.02)
% Urban (1955)				0.14** (0.05)		
Adult literacy rate (1960)					0.13** (0.05)	
Life expectancy at birth (1955–60)						0.63** (0.11)
Oil exporter		11.68** (2.60)	11.97** (3.18)	10.71** (3.28)	11.98** (3.47)	10.54** (3.35)

(continued)

Table 4.5 Continued

Variable	HDI Scores in 2015					
	(1)	(2)	(3)	(4)	(5)	(6)
Small Island		4.91	4.70	3.43	4.60	3.88
		(2.60)	(2.62)	(2.55)	(2.36)	(2.00)
Landlocked		−4.70*	−4.66	−4.38	−3.99	−3.63
		(2.34)	(2.48)	(2.29)	(2.25)	(2.08)
Latitude		29.80**	30.83**	25.61**	29.46**	17.56
		(10.79)	(10.91)	(10.22)	(10.33)	(9.10)
Sub-Saharan Africa		−10.54**	−10.48**	−8.52**	−7.27**	−7.22**
		(2.59)	(2.76)	(2.62)	(2.72)	(2.52)
Constant	54.67**	63.24**	60.86**	64.08**	56.04**	35.69**
	(1.39)	(5.49)	(6.42)	(5.09)	(5.88)	(6.72)
Observations	101	101	101	101	101	101
R-squared	0.50	0.80	0.80	0.82	0.81	0.85

Note: Robust standard errors in parentheses, **$p < 0.01$, *$p < 0.05$.

(+17.90, $p < 0.01$) continue to predict significant advantages in human well-being relative to colonial occupation after controlling for confounding factors. Both British and non-British forced settlement predict higher HDI scores in 2015 relative to colonial occupation in Model 3, and these results are statistically significant at $p < 0.05$.

Models 4–6 examine whether current cross-national variations in human well-being reflect the developmental outcomes established during the colonial era. These models include additional statistical controls for socioeconomic modernization and human development during the colonial era. The focal independent variables are statistically insignificant in these models. This means that the extent of urbanization (Model 4), educational attainment (Model 5), and life expectancy at the end of the colonial era (Model 6) continue to explain disparities in human well-being among postcolonial states in 2015.

Tutelary Democracy Prior to Independence

The OLS models in Table 4.6 explore the relationship between the initial mode of colonization and mass electoral competition during the colonial era. The dependent variable, "tutelary democracy," is the number of years that a colonial state maintained mass representative institutions and a competitive electoral system with universal adult suffrage. I estimated the duration of tutelary democracy for dependent territories using the median independence year associated with its type of colonization. Consequently, the data results in Models 1–3 assume 29 years of tutelary democracy in the French Antilles colonies (1946–75), 26 years of tutelary democracy for the Netherlands Antilles (1949–75), and no years of tutelary democracy for Hong Kong and Macau.

The OLS results in Table 4.6 support the hypothesis that forced settlement colonies experienced a longer period of tutelary democracy during the colonial era relative to Global South countries that emerged from colonial occupation after 1945 (H3). In Model 1, forced settlement predicts 16 additional years of tutelary democracy relative to colonial occupation (p < 0.01). Mixed colonization also predicts 16 additional years of tutelary democracy relative to colonial occupation (p < 0.01). By contrast, the regression coefficient for city-state colonies is statistically insignificant, given the absence of mass electoral competition in Hong Kong and Macau. The statistical result for British-protected states is negative and significant (p < 0.01). Overall, the OLS results in Model 1 demonstrate that forced settlement colonies experienced a longer period of mass electoral competition before independence than other colonial states in the Global South.

Forced settlement continues to predict 11 additional years of tutelary democracy relative to colonial occupation (p < 0.01) after controlling for confounding factors in Model 2. Both British forced settlement and continental European forced settlement predict at least 10 additional years of tutelary democracy relative to colonial occupation in Model 3 (p < 0.01), and most of the control variables are statistically insignificant.[15] The significant result for British forced settlement colonies is hardly surprising because Britain was more committed than other colonial powers to promoting mass electoral competition prior to independence (Huntington 1984; Weiner 1987; Lee and Paine 2019a, 2019b). Nevertheless, British forced settlement colonies had far greater exposure to tutelary democracy than other British colonies with nonwhite majorities. Before independence, most British forced settlement colonies experienced at least 15 years of tutelary democracy. In contrast, most British-occupied colonies only held one competitive election with universal suffrage prior to independence. The lengthy period of tutelary democracy in British forced settlement colonies like Barbados, Jamaica, Mauritius, and Trinidad and Tobago might be familiar to readers, but French and Dutch forced settlement colonies also experienced several decades of tutelary democracy under colonial rule. For example, Suriname experienced 26 years of tutelary democracy prior to its independence from the Netherlands in 1975. But the longest period of tutelary democracy actually occurred in French Guiana and the Antilles colonies, where French republican officials established mass electoral competition and universal male

Table 4.6 "Tutelary Democracy" under Colonial Rule

Variable	Duration of "Tutelary Democracy" Prior to Independence (years)					
	Full Sample of Postcolonial States and Dependent Territories			Postcolonial States Only		
	(1)	(2)	(3)	(4)	(5)	(6)
Forced settlement	16.47** (2.44)	11.17** (2.76)		14.16** (2.70)	9.04** (2.80)	
British forced settlement			10.85** (2.59)			10.90** (2.55)
Non-British forced settlement			11.89* (5.04)			1.74 (4.74)
Mixed colonization	15.72** (4.73)	11.29* (4.79)	11.16* (4.70)	9.22 (6.45)	2.43 (4.43)	2.92 (4.59)
City-state	−1.11 (1.55)	−6.98 (4.30)	−6.85 (4.37)	2.22** (0.67)	−5.51 (6.55)	−5.69 (6.70)
British-protected state	−2.78** (0.67)	−12.08** (3.30)	−12.11** (3.36)	−2.78** (0.67)	−15.03** (3.75)	−14.7** (3.47)
British colonization		−0.14 (1.28)			0.82 (1.21)	
Year of independence		0.40** (0.10)	0.40** (0.01)		0.51** (0.10)	0.52** (0.10)
% European settlers		−0.13 (0.28)	−0.12 (0.27)		−0.85** (0.26)	−0.92** (0.24)
% Asian settlers		−0.12** (0.04)	−0.12** (0.04)		−0.10* (0.05)	−0.10* (0.05)
Ethnic fractionalization		−2.88 (3.77)	−2.81 (3.73)		−1.40 (3.48)	−1.59 (3.19)
% Protestant (1900)		0.02 (0.03)	0.02 (0.04)		0.04 (0.04)	0.04 (0.03)
% Muslim (1900)		0.05 (0.03)	0.05 (0.03)		0.06* (0.03)	0.06* (0.03)
% Urban (1955)		0.10** (0.03)	0.10* (0.04)		0.12** (0.04)	0.12** (0.04)
Small island		−2.43 (2.08)	−2.52 (1.99)		−4.62* (2.16)	−4.30 (2.17)
Landlocked		0.88 (1.23)	0.90 (1.20)		1.28 (1.09)	1.12 (1.12)

Table 4.6 Continued

Variable	Duration of "Tutelary Democracy" Prior to Independence (years)					
	Full Sample of Postcolonial States and Dependent Territories			Postcolonial States Only		
	(1)	(2)	(3)	(4)	(5)	(6)
Latitude		−16.78	−16.80		−17.59*	−18.14*
		(8.94)	(8.91)		(7.82)	(7.33)
Sub-Saharan Africa		−4.67	−4.72		−6.14**	−5.76**
		(2.60)	(2.53)		(2.14)	(2.18)
Constant	2.78**	−773.8**	−771.9**	2.78**	−997.3**	−1008.6**
	(0.67)	(196.3)	(193.9)	(0.67)	(196.3)	(198.4)
Observations	101	101	101	92	92	92
R-squared	0.55	0.71	0.71	0.45	0.71	0.74

Note: Robust standard errors in parentheses, **p < 0.01, *p < 0.05.

suffrage during the 1870s. This history is presented in greater detail in Chapter 7. The data models in this chapter only capture the post–World War II years, when women also participated in competitive elections. Nevertheless, the OLS results confirm the hypothesis that British and continental European forced settlement are associated with a longer period of tutelary democracy relative to colonial occupation (H5).

Models 4–6 exclude seven colonial states that are still classified as European overseas dependencies (like the French and Dutch Antilles colonies), and two colonial states that became Special Administrative Regions of China during the 1990s (i.e., Hong Kong and Macau). Here, forced settlement predicts 14 additional years of tutelary democracy relative to colonial occupation in Model 4 (p < 0.01). Forced settlement continues to predict nine additional years of tutelary democracy relative to colonial occupation after controlling for confounding factors in Model 5 (p < 0.01). British forced settlement predicts 11 additional years of tutelary democracy relative to colonial occupation (p < 0.01), but the regression coefficient for non-British forced settlement is insignificant in Model 6. Here the insignificant result for continental European forced settlement is unsurprising because two of the three remaining examples of continental European forced settlement did not establish mass electoral competition prior to independence. As we will see in Chapter 6, Portugal's *Estado Novo* dictatorship (1930–74) prevented the establishment of mass electoral competition

in Cape Verde and São Tomé and Príncipe. After removing the French and
Dutch overseas dependencies from Model 6, only British forced settlement is
associated with a lengthier period of tutelary democracy relative to colonial
occupation.

Postcolonial Democratization

To what extent does the initial mode of colonization affect the democratization trajectory of former colonies after independence? The statistical models in
Table 4.7 support the hypothesis that forced settlement is associated with greater
postcolonial democratization than colonial occupation (H4). The coefficient for
forced settlement is positive and significant at $p < 0.01$ in every model. In Model
1, forced settlement predicts a democratic advantage of +4.10 points on the 0–10
Freedom House Imputed Polity scale between 1972 and 2012. Forced settlement
is the only mode of colonization that consistently predicts higher mean postcolonial democracy scores relative to colonial occupation in Table 4.7, and this result
remains robust to statistical controls for confounding factors.[16] Furthermore,
both British and non-British forced settlement colonization are associated with
higher mean postcolonial democracy scores than colonial occupation in Model
3 ($p < 0.05$). This result is striking because Portugal's forced settlement colonies
did not democratize until the 1990s. Nevertheless, the data results in Model 3
provide strong empirical support for H5. The data results in Model 4 also show
that forced settlement continues to predict higher postcolonial democracy
scores relative to colonial occupation remains after controlling "tutelary democracy" during the colonial era ($p < 0.05$).[17]

My research also demonstrates that many of the control variables that are
typically associated with democratization are statistically insignificant after accounting for the initial mode of colonization. For example, the data results in
Table 4.7 confirm that the postcolonial democratization of forced settlement colonies was not primarily driven by European settlement or economic development during the colonial era.[18] British colonization and Protestantism predict
higher postcolonial democracy scores at statistically significant levels, but forced
settlement continues to predict statistically significant democratic advantages
relative to colonial occupation ($p < 0.01$) after controlling for these confounding
factors. Moreover, the empirical patterns in Table 4.7 are robust to different democracy indicators, including V-DEM's liberal democracy index and Cheibub,
Vreeland, and Gandhi's (2010) dichotomous indicators of democracy (see
Appendix 3). These robustness tests provide additional statistical evidence that
forced settlement generated favorable developmental legacies relative to colonial
occupation.

Table 4.7 Postcolonial Democratization

Variable	Mean Freedom House Imputed Polity Score, 1972–2012			
	(1)	(2)	(3)	(4)
Forced settlement	4.10** (0.49)	2.20** (0.65)		1.61** (0.60)
British forced settlement			2.75** (0.74)	
Non-British forced settlement			1.56* (0.62)	
Mixed colonization	2.48* (1.08)	0.82 (1.35)	1.36 (1.42)	0.71 (1.20)
British-protected state	−1.95** (0.39)	−2.66** (0.64)	−2.01** (0.56)	−1.78** (0.68)
British colonization		1.37** (0.38)		1.31** (0.39)
Years of tutelary democracy prior to independence				0.07* (0.03)
Years since independence (2012)		−0.05 (0.02)	−0.05 (0.03)	−0.01 (0.03)
% European settlers		−0.05 (0.06)	−0.10 (0.07)	0.00 (0.06)
% Asian settlers		−0.01 (0.02)	−0.01 (0.02)	−0.00 (0.02)
Ethnic fractionalization		−0.12 (0.80)	−0.26 (0.84)	−0.38 (0.74)
% Protestant (1970)		0.04** (0.01)	0.04** (0.01)	0.03** (0.01)
% Muslim (1970)		0.00 (0.01)	0.00 (0.01)	−0.00 (0.01)
Mean per capita GDP, 1972–2004 (logged)		0.13 (0.31)	0.18 (0.33)	0.01 (0.32)
Oil exporter		−1.37* (0.63)	−1.31 (0.70)	−1.03 (0.64)
Small island		0.35 (0.56)	0.38 (0.59)	0.56 (0.51)
Landlocked		−0.38 (0.51)	−0.34 (0.56)	−0.33 (0.50)

(*continued*)

Table 4.7 Continued

Variable	Mean Freedom House Imputed Polity Score, 1972–2012			
	(1)	(2)	(3)	(4)
Sub-Saharan Africa		−0.72	−0.88	−0.25
		(0.65)	(0.67)	(0.60)
Constant	4.04**	5.14	5.50	3.74
	(0.29)	(2.62)	(2.80)	(2.45)
Observations	92	92	92	92
R-squared	0.43	0.73	0.69	0.75

Note: Robust standard errors in parentheses, **p < 0.01, *p < 0.05.

Causal Pathways That Facilitated the Long-Term Development of Forced Settlement Colonies

Why did forced settlement promote favorable developmental outcomes relative to colonial occupation? The remainder of this chapter explores this question by examining the impact of Protestant missionary evangelization and liberal institutional reforms as potential causal mechanisms that may have facilitated the inclusive development of forced settlement colonies following the abolition of slavery. The subsequent analysis examines the historical and institutional factors that promoted the expansion of colonial education and voting rights that facilitated postcolonial democratization in the Global South. These developmental outcomes are emphasized because forced settlement colonies displayed the greatest developmental advantages in expanding educational access, tutelary democracy, and postcolonial democratization relative to other Global South countries that emerged from colonial domination after 1945.

Recent empirical studies suggest that Protestant missionary evangelization promoted the expansion of education and literacy (Gallego and Woodberry 2010; Woodberry 2012; Lankina and Getachew 2012, 2013; Okoye and Pongou 2014), household wealth (Okoye and Pongou 2014), and postcolonial democratization in many parts of the Global South (Woodberry 2012). This partly reflects the transformative role of missionary activists and reformist Protestant church leaders—i.e., Baptists, Methodists, and Quakers—that actively supported the British antislavery movement (Stamatov 2010; Porter 2004) and the establishment of denominational schools that educated emancipated slaves and their descendants in British forced settlement colonies (Latimer 1965; Wesley 1938), and in coastal regions of West African states like Sierra Leone and Nigeria (see

Spitzer 1974; Wyse 1991; Okoye and Pongou 2014) . Perhaps not surprisingly, then, existing studies demonstrate higher levels of educational attainment and household wealth in Global South countries and subnational regions that were significantly exposed to Protestant missionary evangelization (Woodberry 2012, 249–53; Gallego and Woodberry 2010; Frankema 2012; Lankina and Getachew 2012, 2013; Okoye and Pongou 2014). Robert Woodberry's research also demonstrates higher mean postcolonial democracy scores in non-Western countries and Global South countries with the greatest exposure to Protestant missionaries during the first half of the twentieth century (Woodberry 2012). Consequently, it is essential to examine whether Protestant missionary evangelization contributed to the favorable developmental outcomes associated with forced settlement relative to colonial occupation (H6).

The second potential causal mechanism is the impact of liberal institutional reforms that expanded the legal rights and political agency of emancipated Afro-descendants in forced settlement colonies. Many British colonies were heavily exposed to Protestant missionary evangelization, but the historical evidence in Chapter 2 emphasizes the liberal reforms that expanded the legal rights of emancipated Afro-descendants following the abolition of slavery in the New World. British-emancipated slaves were legally recognized as metropolitan (British) subjects whose civil liberties and property rights were protected by British common law. In the more centralized French and Portuguese colonial empires, emancipated Afro-descendants were recognized as metropolitan citizens with the same legal and political rights as their counterparts in Europe. This is why French republican laws that expanded parliamentary representation, universal male suffrage, and compulsory education were extended to the French Antilles colonies after 1870. By the end of the nineteenth century, nearly all forced settlement colonies had inclusive legal-administrative institutions based on British common law or continental European civil law. By contrast, colonial administrators developed "native legal codes" that restricted the civil and political rights of rural indigenous subjects in colonies of occupation. In the statistical models that follow, I expect to find favorable developmental outcomes in colonial states that developed inclusive legal-administrative institutions prior to World War II and poor developmental outcomes in colonial states that maintained distinct "native legal codes" that restricted the legal rights of rural indigenous subjects (H7). These assumptions test the arguments advanced in previous empirical research on the distinctive developmental legacies of direct versus indirect British rule (see Lange 2004, 2009) and the negative developmental legacies of the bifurcated colonial state (see Mamdani 1996; Owolabi 2017).

The OLS models in Table 4.8 examine whether Protestant missionaries (H6) or colonial legal-administrative institutions (H7) provide a more convincing explanation for the high levels of educational attainment and tutelary democracy in forced settlement colonies. Models 1–4 include statistical controls for the number of Protestant missionaries per 10,000 inhabitants in 1923, and the duration of Protestant missionary activity in each colonial state prior to 1960 (see Woodberry 2004, 2012; Woodberry et al. 2010). Robert Woodberry's missionary data do not cover dependent territories, so the OLS results in Models 1–4 are limited to the 92 postcolonial states that gained independence between 1945 and 1985. Here forced settlement continues to predict significantly higher adult literacy rates in 1960 (Models 1 and 2) and greater exposure to "tutelary democracy" prior to independence (Models 3 and 4) even after controlling for Protestant missionary evangelization during the colonial era. Both results are statistically significant at $p < 0.05$. The Protestant missionary variables, by contrast, are mostly insignificant, although the percentage of Protestants in 1900 continues to predict significantly higher literacy rates in 1960 ($p < 0.05$). This result suggests that Protestant missionary evangelization did not directly contribute to the expansion of literacy and tutelary democracy in forced settlement colonies prior to independence. Consequently, H6 is not supported by statistical evidence.

In Models 5 and 6, I constructed a binary variable that distinguishes colonial states that extended metropolitan (i.e., European) legal rights to nonwhites prior to World War II vis-à-vis colonial states that maintained "native legal codes" that restricted the individual liberties of indigenous colonial subjects during the 1930s. This time period is instructive because colonial rule remained strongly institutionalized into the 1930s, and few would have predicted the tidal wave of decolonization that swept across the Global South after World War II. Furthermore, the extent of legal rights during the 1930s reflects the unique institutional development of each colonial state from the late nineteenth century until World War II.

The striking variation in the legal-administrative institutions of colonial states largely resulted from the liberal institutional reforms that extended metropolitan legal rights to emancipated Afro-descendants in forced settlement colonies. All forced settlement colonies maintained a uniform and inclusive legal-administrative system that recognized the legal rights of emancipated Afro-descendants by the mid-1930s. Only Portuguese-ruled São Tomé and Príncipe maintained a separate "native code" for indentured African labor migrants and their descendants until the mid-1950s (see Portugal 1960; Duffy 1959, 295). City-state colonies like Hong Kong and Singapore also recognized the legal rights of nonwhite residents by the early twentieth century. By contrast, all colonies of occupation, apart from Sri Lanka, Nauru, and the Solomon Islands, maintained bifurcated legal-administrative systems with distinctive "native legal codes" for indigenous colonial subjects. The only other colonial states that protected the legal rights of nonwhites were mixed plantation colonies where emancipated

Table 4.8 Causal Mechanisms Linking Forced Settlement to Education and Voting Rights

Variable	Adult Literacy, 1960		Tutelary Democracy		Adult Literacy, 1960	Tutelary Democracy
	(1)	(2)	(3)	(4)	(5)	(6)
Forced settlement	18.20** (5.93)	14.34* (7.20)	8.12** (2.86)	7.88** (2.92)	7.36 (6.37)	0.04 (3.97)
Mixed colonization	−6.78 (15.66)	−5.47 (15.35)	1.44 (4.30)	1.73 (4.39)	5.17 (6.88)	7.63* (3.53)
City-states	Omitted	Omitted	Omitted	Omitted	−25.80* (12.06)	−16.53** (4.69)
British-protected states	−4.36 (8.02)	−9.95 (9.07)	−13.62** (3.55)	−13.90** (3.61)	−1.41 (7.11)	−9.17** (2.96)
British colonization	8.43** (3.13)	9.87** (3.63)	0.12 (1.31)	0.30 (1.32)	2.92 (2.81)	−1.84 (1.13)
Metropolitan legal rights prior to WWII					14.77* (6.32)	15.39** (3.77)
Years since independence (1960)	0.93 (0.62)	0.37 (0.67)			0.73 (0.52)	
Year of independence			0.55** (0.10)	0.55** (0.00)		0.34** (0.00)
% European settlers	−0.19 (0.76)	−0.36 (0.80)	−0.78** (0.24)	−0.77** (0.25)	−0.52 (0.54)	−0.36 (0.22)
% Asian settlers	0.07 (0.19)	0.10 (0.19)	−0.12* (0.05)	−0.12* (0.05)	0.03 (0.12)	−0.09* (0.04)
Ethnic fractionalization	−18.36 (9.71)	−13.04 (10.01)	−1.18 (3.08)	−0.58 (3.09)	−23.35* (9.14)	−2.78 (3.10)
% Protestant (1900)	0.46** (0.07)		0.04 (0.03)		0.47** (0.08)	0.06 (0.03)
% Muslim (1900)	−0.14 (0.08)	−0.17 (0.08)	0.07* (0.03)	0.06* (0.03)	−0.16* (0.08)	0.06* (0.03)
Protestant missionaries per 10,000 pop. (1923)	0.80 (0.87)	2.20 (1.34)	−0.19 (0.35)	−0.02 (0.39)		

(continued)

Table 4.8 Continued

Variable	Adult Literacy, 1960		Tutelary Democracy		Adult Literacy, 1960	Tutelary Democracy
	(1)	(2)	(3)	(4)	(5)	(6)
Years of missionary presence (1960)	−0.01 (0.03)	−0.01 (0.03)	0.02 (0.02)	0.02 (0.02)		
% urban (1955)	0.32** (0.11)	0.27* (0.12)	0.10** (0.04)	0.10** (0.04)	0.38** (0.09)	0.05 (0.04)
Small island	0.45 (6.51)	7.20 (7.08)	−3.99 (2.26)	−3.27 (2.21)	0.01 (5.06)	−2.24 (2.24)
Landlocked	−2.47 (3.62)	−3.90 (3.76)	1.95 (1.29)	1.90 (1.30)	−2.47 (3.72)	0.90 (1.10)
Latitude	−32.16 (20.45)	−19.64 (21.37)	−16.42* (7.91)	−15.77* (8.06)	25.52 (17.82)	−12.03 (7.37)
Sub-Saharan Africa	−13.98 (5.78)	−20.05** (6.66)	−5.70** (2.04)	−6.05** (2.02)	−13.14* (5.24)	−2.72 (2.30)
Constant	43.08** (7.47)	44.97** (9.27)	−1075.5** (210.8)	−1081.5** (209.9)	46.28** (6.40)	−660.8** (182.0)
Observations	92	92	92	92	101	101
R-squared	0.84	0.79	0.72	0.72	0.86	0.79

Note: Robust standard errors in parentheses, **$p < 0.01$, *$p < 0.05$.

Afro-descendants comprised more than 50% of the total population (i.e., Belize, French Guiana, and the US Virgin Islands). By contrast, the remaining colonies of occupation maintained bifurcated legal-administrative systems with distinctive "native legal codes" for indigenous colonial subjects. And traditional Muslim rulers continued to control the domestic political affairs of indigenous colonial subjects in British-protected states.[19] Consequently, the bivariate correlation between forced settlement and metropolitan legal rights exceeds r = 0.75.[20]

The high bivariate correlation between forced settlement and metropolitan legal rights reduces the likelihood of a statistically significant result for either variable. Consequently, the regression coefficient for forced settlement is statistically insignificant in Models 5 and 6. By contrast, the extension of metropolitan legal rights prior to World War II predicts a literacy advantage of nearly 15 percentage points in 1960 (p < 0.05) and 15 additional years of tutelary democracy (i.e., mass electoral competition) prior to independence (p < 0.01). These results provide strong empirical support for H7. This suggests that the expansion of adult literacy and mass electoral competition in forced settlement colonies was primarily driven by liberal institutional reforms that extended metropolitan legal rights to emancipated Afro-descendants during the nineteenth century.

Table 4.9 presents similar models with alternative statistical controls as an additional robustness test. These OLS models do not control for the initial mode of colonization to avoid the collinearity problems between forced settlement colonization and liberal institutional reforms prior to World War II. Instead, they test whether metropolitan legal rights remain associated with educational attainment and postcolonial democratization after controlling for the duration of colonial rule and the logged population of each colony in 1900. Existing studies have suggested that the second global wave of imperialist expansion colonization was more extractive and disruptive than the first wave of European imperialist expansion during the "Age of Discovery" (Krieckhaus 2006, 9). If this assumption is true, one would expect to find favorable long-term development and greater postcolonial democratization in countries that experienced a long duration of colonial rule. Nevertheless, it is important to remember that forced settlement colonies were brutally exploited during the seventeenth and eighteenth centuries, when they established agricultural plantations using African slave labor. These colonial states only benefited from liberal institutional reforms after slavery was abolished in the mid-nineteenth century. Consequently, the duration of colonial rule should be considered separately from the liberal reforms that expanded the legal rights of emancipated Afro-descendants following the abolition of slavery.

The OLS models in Table 4.9 also control for the logged population of each colonial state in 1900, and this replaces the "small island" dummy variable in the earlier models. The population control is relevant because previous research suggests that smaller populations and territories were easier and cheaper for Europeans to control (Herbst 2000) and that colonial administrators were more likely to promote inclusive legal systems in colonies with small populations (Lawrence 2013, 101). Consequently, it is important to examine whether metropolitan legal institutions promoted favorable long-term development even after controlling for the duration of colonial rule and the logged population of each colony in 1900.

The data results in Table 4.9 are as follows: the extension of metropolitan legal rights prior to 1936 is associated with higher adult literacy rates in 1960 (Models 1 and 2), greater exposure to mass electoral competition prior to independence (Models 3 and 4), and higher mean democracy scores after independence (Model 5). In Model 6, 10 additional years of tutelary democracy are associated with a one-point increase on the 10-point Freedom House Imputed Polity scale of postcolonial democratization (Model 6). These results are all statistically significant at $p < 0.05$. This suggests that the legal-administrative reforms that extended

Table 4.9 Colonial Institutions, Colonial Education, and Postcolonial Democracy

Variable	Adult Literacy, 1960		Tutelary Democracy		Mean Democracy Score, 1972–2012	
	(1)	(2)	(3)	(4)	(5)	(6)
Metropolitan legal rights before WWII	13.07* (5.42)	14.66** (4.86)	16.74** (2.47)	15.62** (2.52)	2.14** (0.71)	
Years of tutelary democracy before independence						0.10** (0.03)
Colonial duration (1960)	0.02 (0.02)	0.03 (0.02)	0.00 (0.01)	−0.00 (0.01)	0.00 (0.00)	0.00* (0.00)
British colonization	4.05 (3.24)	7.04* (3.52)	−0.93 (1.19)	−1.84 (1.22)	1.03** (0.37)	1.27** (0.36)
Dependency	5.64 (5.60)	Omitted	6.19 (3.40)	Omitted	Omitted	Omitted
Year of independence		−0.60* (0.24)		0.31** (0.10)	0.03 (0.03)	−0.00 (0.03)
% European settlers	−0.47 (0.43)	0.16 (0.74)	0.16 (0.21)	−0.49 (0.32)	0.01 (0.07)	0.07 (0.07)
% Asian settlers	0.07 (0.13)	0.05 (0.12)	−0.05 (0.04)	−0.09** (0.03)	−0.01 (0.02)	0.00 (0.02)
Ethnic fractionalization	−11.78 (9.60)	−15.16 (12.22)	4.09 (3.97)	0.27 (4.06)	0.84 (0.77)	−0.88 (0.68)
% Protestant (1900)	0.41** (0.08)	0.40** (0.08)	0.09* (0.04)	0.10* (0.03)	0.04** (0.01)	0.03* (0.01)
% Muslim (1900)	−0.18* (0.07)	−0.17* (0.07)	0.04 (0.03)	0.03 (0.03)	−0.01 (0.01)	−0.01* (0.01)
% Urban (1955)	0.12 (0.10)	0.08 (0.14)	−0.14** (0.05)	0.01 (0.04)		
Per capita GDP (logged), 1972–2004					−0.04 (0.37)	−0.08 (0.34)
Oil exporter					−1.42* (0.71)	−1.20 (0.66)
Population (logged), 1900	−1.26 (0.86)	−2.91* (1.40)	−0.84* (0.02)	0.52 (0.49)	−0.02 (0.16)	−0.11 (0.16)
Landlocked	−4.70 (3.75)	−6.02 (3.55)	−0.15 (1.04)	0.59 (1.08)	−0.51 (0.53)	−0.59 (0.54)

Table 4.9 Continued

Variable	Adult Literacy, 1960		Tutelary Democracy		Mean Democracy Score, 1972–2012	
	(1)	(2)	(3)	(4)	(5)	(6)
Latitude	−4.39	−7.31	−7.51	−4.98	0.73	1.40
	(19.10)	(17.39)	(7.14)	(6.76)	(2.17)	(2.06)
Sub-Saharan Africa	−20.12	−16.48**	−2.91	−2.12	−0.11	0.05
	(4.96)	(5.87)	(2.45)	(2.39)	(0.70)	(0.67)
Constant	53.57**	1233.2*	8.86**	−604.6**	−51.62	13.10
	(7.86)	(470.6)	(3.17)	(207.2)	(58.17)	(59.54)
Observations	101	92	101	92	92	92
R-squared	0.84	0.85	0.71	0.70	0.72	0.73

Note: Robust standard errors in parentheses, **p < 0.01, *p < 0.05.

metropolitan legal rights to emancipated slaves contributed significantly to forced settlement colonies' favorable postcolonial development outcomes. Most control variables fail to reach conventional levels of statistical significance in Table 4.9. Only the percentage of Protestants in 1900 predicts favorable development in terms of colonial literacy, tutelary democracy, and postcolonial democracy. After controlling for metropolitan legal rights, the duration of colonial rule does not significantly impact any of the developmental outcomes. Moreover, colonial states with fewer inhabitants in 1900 do not have favorable patterns of long-term development or postcolonial democratization. This suggests that a lengthy duration of colonial rule, and small populations do not generate favorable development outcomes once you control for the legal-administrative institutions of different colonial states. By contrast, the extension of metropolitan legal rights is associated with favorable long-term development and greater postcolonial democratization. This suggests that the postabolition reforms played a significant role in promoting inclusive development and postcolonial democratization in forced settlement colonies, despite the legacy of plantation slavery.

Final Robustness Tests

It is also important to consider the experience of Brazil and Cuba as the Iberian colonies that imported the largest numbers of enslaved Africans in the New World. Brazil and Cuba were the last countries to abolish slavery in the Western Hemisphere, and local whites continued to dominate their economic and political institutions long after independence. These countries are excluded from the core data results because of their early independence from colonial rule, and because of their extensive levels of white colonial settlement. Haiti is also excluded from the core statistical results because of its early independence from French colonial domination. Haiti is an important country to consider given its historical significance as the first forced settlement country to establish an independent black state following a successful slave revolt against white planter control. Nevertheless, Haiti remains the most impoverished country in the Americas, despite its early independence from French rule in 1804. Consequently, it is important to determine whether the core statistical results from this chapter are consistent in data models that classify Brazil, Cuba, and Haiti as forced settlement colonies. These questions are explored in data models in Appendix 4, which examines a larger sample of developing countries that gained independence after 1800.

Forced settlement is still associated with favorable developmental outcomes relative to colonial occupation in the expanded data sample in Appendix 4. Haiti is classified as a forced settlement colony in the expanded sample of countries in Appendix 4, and it is an extreme negative outlier in these models. The dummy variable "forced settlement2" expands the definition of forced settlement to include Brazil and Cuba, as well as Belize, French Guiana, and the US Virgin Islands. These countries had large slave populations during the colonial era, but emancipated Afro-descendants no longer comprise an overwhelming majority of the population. Other Spanish Caribbean territories, like the Dominican Republic and Puerto Rico, are classified as mixed colonies because African slaves never comprised more than 15% of their colonial populations (Engerman and Higman 1997, 52; Yelvington et al. 1997, 286–87). The expanded definition of forced settlement2, which includes Brazil, Cuba, and Haiti, also predicts favorable developmental outcomes relative to colonial occupation in the data models of Appendix 4. These tests confirm that the favorable developmental outcomes of forced settlement (relative to colonial occupation) are robust to different data samples and different definitions of forced settlement.

Summary and Discussion

The statistical results in this chapter demonstrate four important conclusions regarding the distinctive developmental legacies of forced settlement and colonial occupation in the Global South. First, the multivariate OLS models in this chapter demonstrate that forced settlement is consistently associated with favorable development outcomes relative to colonial occupation. Forced settlement consistently predicts statistically significant developmental advantages in human well-being at the end of the colonial era (Tables 4.3 and 4.4), and higher HDI scores in 2015 (Table 4.5). Compared with colonial occupation, forced settlement is also associated with greater exposure to mass electoral competition prior to independence (Table 4.6), and higher mean democracy scores after independence (Table 4.7). These statistical results suggest that the favorable developmental legacies of forced settlement relative to colonial occupation have persisted until the present day. All of these statistical results are significant at $p <$ 0.05, and they are robust to statistical controls for British colonization, European and Asian settlement, ethnic fractionalization, religious composition, and geography.

Second, the favorable developmental legacies of forced settlement relative to colonial occupation challenge previous empirical studies that predict poor developmental outcomes in countries that experienced "extractive" and labor-repressive forms of colonization with limited European settlement (see Acemoglu, Johnson, and Robinson 2001, 2002; Sokoloff and Engerman 2000; Easterly and Levine 2014). The prevailing conclusion from previous empirical research is that the labor-repressive plantation economies generated persistent poverty, structural inequality, and underdevelopment (see Sokoloff and Engerman 2000; Beckford 1983; Best 1968; Best and Polanyi 2009; Williams 1941). This conclusion is primarily derived from implicit or explicit comparisons with European settler colonies that significantly expanded educational access, voting rights, and mass electoral competition during the nineteenth century. It is certainly true that forced settlement colonies experienced delayed development and democratization relative to British settler societies like Canada and the United States (see Sokoloff and Engerman 2000; Acemoglu, Robinson, and Johnson 2001; Engerman, Mariscal, and Sokoloff 2009). It is also undeniable that plantation slavery left a lasting legacy of racial and regional inequalities in countries like Brazil and the United States (Marx 1998; Soares, Assunção, and Goulart 2012; Bertocchi and Dimico 2012; Acharya, Blackwell, and Sen 2018). Nevertheless, the statistical data models in this chapter demonstrate favorable development outcomes in forced settlement colonies relative to Global South countries that experienced colonial occupation. Although forced settlement colonies lag behind European settler societies on key indicators of human development, they emerged from the colonial era with favorable developmental outcomes relative to Global South countries that emerged from colonial occupation after 1945.

The third conclusion is that the favorable developmental legacies of forced settlement were not primarily driven by Protestant missionary efforts to expand educational access and civil society following the abolition of slavery. Protestant missionary evangelization was primarily limited to the British colonial era, as French, Portuguese, and even Dutch colonial officials limited Protestant missionary evangelization in ways that hindered the expansion of state-funded education and voting rights (see Woodberry 2004, 2012). Nevertheless, the data results in this chapter demonstrate that continental European forced settlement also generated favorable developmental legacies relative to colonial occupation. This is because all European countries implemented liberal institutional reforms that expanded the legal rights and political agency of emancipated Afro-descendants following the abolition of slavery. French republican leaders extended citizenship rights and political representation to emancipated Afro-descendants in the French Antilles colonies after the 1870 Franco-Prussian War. Portuguese officials initially recognized the citizenship rights of emancipated Creoles in Cape Verde and São Tomé and Príncipe, although the social and political benefits of metropolitan citizenship were undermined by the repressive policies enacted by Portugal's *Estado Novo* dictatorship after 1930. The partial reversal of liberal institutional reform during the *Estado Novo* dictatorship (1930–74) undermined the long-term development and postcolonial democratization of Portuguese forced settlement colonies relative to their British, French, or Dutch counterparts. Notwithstanding the delayed democratization of Portuguese forced settlement colonies, OLS results demonstrate that both British and continental European forced settlement are associated with favorable developmental legacies relative to colonial occupation.

Last, the data results support the book's central claim that liberal institutional reforms enabled most forced settlement colonies to promote inclusive human development following the abolition of slavery. By contrast, most British- or European-occupied colonies maintained distinctive "native legal codes" that undermined the legal rights of indigenous colonial subjects in ways that hindered their long-term development. This claim is supported by statistical evidence that demonstrates favorable patterns of development outcomes and greater postcolonial democratization in forced settlement colonies relative to countries that emerged from colonial occupation after World War II. The OLS results clearly suggest that the favorable developmental legacies of forced settlement (vis-à-vis colonial occupation) were primarily driven by liberal institutional reforms that extended metropolitan legal rights to their emancipated populations following the abolition of slavery. As a result of these reforms, the legal-administrative institutions of forced settlement colonies were far more inclusive than the "native legal codes" that limited indigenous colonial subjects' legal and political rights in colonies of occupation during the first half of the twentieth century. The statistical models in Tables 4.8 and 4.9 demonstrate higher levels of literacy and greater postcolonial democratization in colonial states that recognized metropolitan legal rights prior to 1936. This is consistent with previous empirical studies that explore the ways in which liberal institutional reforms and colonial legal-administrative institutions either facilitated or hindered broad-based human development (Mamdani 1996; Lange 2009; Mahoney 2010; Acemoglu and Robinson 2012; Owolabi 2017) and postcolonial democratization (see Mamdani 1996; Mahoney 2001; Owolabi 2015; Acemoglu and Robinson 2019). My data analysis builds on these previous studies by demonstrating the extent to which institutional reforms enabled many forced settlement colonies to promote inclusive human development and postcolonial democratization despite the legacy of plantation slavery.

Although the OLS results are robust to different model specifications and data samples, it is important to acknowledge some of the limitations of quantitative data analysis. First, data collection over a large number of countries is always imperfect, given the inconsistent measurement of development outcomes like adult literacy across different countries, and the potential sources of bias in cross-national indicators of democracy. Moreover, it is impossible to find perfect statistical indicators to measure "thick" and multidimensional concepts like forced settlement, metropolitan legal rights, human well-being, and postcolonial democracy.[21] Nevertheless, it is important to recognize that the statistical results in this chapter remain remarkably consistent in OLS models that employ different definitions of forced settlement, different indicators of democracy, and different samples of countries. Despite these consistent results, OLS analysis cannot tell us whether the empirical relationships between variables are causal or spurious, and the cross-national data sample is not useful for understanding developmental changes over time. The statistical models only tell us that forced settlement predicts favorable long-term development relative to colonial occupation. They suggest that the favorable developmental outcomes in forced settlement colonies resulted from the institutional reforms that extended metropolitan legal rights to their emancipated populations. But to test the extent to which institutional reforms promoted the expansion of education and voting rights, it is necessary to provide comparative-historical evidence of the divergent developmental legacies of forced settlement and colonial occupation.

Furthermore, OLS analysis is not useful for understanding individual countries whose developmental legacies diverged from the dominant empirical trends. The OLS models indicate that forced settlement colonies implemented liberal institutional reforms that extended metropolitan legal rights to emancipated Afro-descendants following the abolition of slavery. This was largely true in the British and French colonial empires, but Portugal's mid-twentieth century *Estado Novo* dictatorship undermined many liberal reforms that had been implemented in Portuguese forced settlement colonies during the nineteenth century (see Chapter 6). The historical evidence in Chapter 7 also highlights the extent to which Haiti was also victimized by French and US neocolonial exploitation that hindered the implementation of liberal institutional reforms after independence. Haiti's crippling underdevelopment and limited democratization

provide a tragic reminder that liberal institutional reforms are necessary to promote literacy and democracy following the abolition of slavery. The second half
of this book presents comparative-historical evidence that liberal institutional
reforms enabled many forced settlement colonies to significantly expand educational access and voting rights following the abolition of slavery. It is because of
these reforms that forced settlement is generally associated with favorable developmental outcomes relative to colonial occupation in the Global South.

5

Comparing British Forced Settlement and Colonial Occupation

Jamaica and Sierra Leone

Jamaica, the largest and most populous island in the English-speaking Caribbean, conjures up powerful images of an idyllic tropical paradise, blessed with gorgeous palm-fringed beaches, soaring verdant mountains, and warm temperatures year-round. Yet Jamaica's idyllic beaches and all-inclusive resorts obscure the most brutal aspects of the island's colonial history. The vast majority of Jamaicans are descendants of African slaves brought to the island between 1660 and 1807. During these years, British planters imported more than 1 million enslaved Africans to work on Jamaican sugar estates (Eltis and Richardson 2010, 18). To put this into perspective, this was more than twice the total number of enslaved Africans shipped to the United States between 1619 and 1860 (Eltis and Richardson 2010, 18). Moreover, enslaved African slaves comprised more than 80% of Jamaica's population when the British Parliament abolished slavery in the 1830s (Engerman and Higman 1997, 50). The establishment of Jamaica's colonial plantations was partly fueled by the commercial success of the British Royal African Company, which established one of its largest slave-trading operations on Bunce Island in present-day Sierra Leone. During the 1780s, however, British abolitionists established Sierra Leone's capital city, Freetown, as a free settlement for liberated Africans and emancipated slaves returning from the New World. Sierra Leone's early colonial settlements were a powerful symbol of freedom, hope, and liberty for liberated Africans rescued from slave ships. By the middle of the nineteenth century, Freetown had emerged into a thriving bourgeois and predominantly Christian Creole African city that boasted one of the most literate societies in the tropical Atlantic world (Peterson 1969; Spitzer 1974).

It would be entirely reasonable to expect favorable development outcomes in Sierra Leone relative to Jamaica, given Sierra Leone's historical origins as a British settlement for emancipated slaves and liberated Africans. At the same time, one might expect uneven development and limited postcolonial democratization in Jamaica, given the island's long history of forced settlement colonization and plantation slavery. In reality, however, Jamaica emerged from British colonial domination with favorable development outcomes and greater postcolonial

Ruling Emancipated Slaves and Indigenous Subjects. Olukunle P. Owolabi, Oxford University Press.
© Oxford University Press 2023. DOI: 10.1093/oso/9780197673027.003.0005

democratization relative to Sierra Leone. More than 80% of Jamaican adults were literate by the end of the colonial era, and the island state was able to establish an inclusive and competitive parliamentary democracy following its independence from British rule. Despite Jamaica's considerable economic and political challenges, the country has promoted significant improvements in education and life expectancy during the second half of twentieth century. Sierra Leone's long-term development trajectory is significantly worse than Jamaica's. Only 8% of Sierra Leonean adults were literate when Sierra Leone gained independence from British rule, and the country's first elected government was overthrown in a bloody military coup following a disputed election. By the end of the 1960s, Sierra Leone had already experienced three military coups, and the country endured a lengthy and repressive single-party dictatorship under the predatory leadership of Siaka Stevens (1967–85) and his successor Joseph Momoh (1985–92). These leaders decimated the country's economy and infrastructure while enriching themselves on its vast diamond resources. Momoh's dictatorship collapsed in a decade-long civil war when a rebel group known as the Revolutionary United Front (RUF) invaded the country from neighboring Liberia. Throughout the 1990s, Liberia's warlord president, Charles Taylor, supported the RUF's brutalization of Sierra Leone's civilian population as they fought to control the country's rich diamond deposits. Today, Sierra Leone remains one of the most impoverished and underdeveloped countries on the planet, ranking 184th out of 189 countries on the United Nation's Human Development Index in 2012.

This chapter explores the historical-institutional origins of Jamaica's inclusive long-term development and postcolonial democratization in comparison to Sierra Leone's underdevelopment and limited democratization. At first glance, this outcome seems highly paradoxical because Jamaica's agricultural plantations were developed using enslaved African labor, whereas the Sierra Leone colony was initially established as a British settlement for freed slaves and liberated Africans. Nevertheless, the distinctive developmental trajectories of Jamaica and Sierra Leone are consistent with the theoretical framework in Chapter 3 and the statistical results in Chapter 4. The comparative-historical evidence in this chapter supports the argument that Jamaica's more inclusive long-term development and postcolonial democratization are the results of liberal reforms that extended metropolitan legal rights to Jamaica's emancipated population following the abolition of slavery. This chapter traces Jamaica's institutional transformation from a slave society dominated by local white planters (1660s–1830s) to a directly ruled British colony that protected the legal rights of emancipated Afro-descendants and limited the political dominance of local white planters (1838–1944). Even though direct British rule restricted the voting rights of most Jamaican adults until World War II, British liberal reforms enabled nonwhite activists to lobby colonial state officials for social and political advances during the first half of the twentieth century. Consequently, Jamaican politicians were able to organize four competitive elections with universal adult suffrage in the decades leading up to independence.

Sierra Leone followed the opposite trajectory. The early Sierra Leone colony was established as a settlement of freed slaves and liberated Africans living under direct British rule. After 1896, however, Britain established a vast protectorate over 70,000 square kilometers of indigenous African territory. For the remainder of the colonial era, Sierra Leone maintained bifurcated colonial institutions that hindered its long-term development. Sierra Leone's capital city and surrounding areas remained under direct British rule after 1896, whereas indirect British rule reinforced the social and political dominance of "paramount chiefs" in the Sierra Leone protectorate. This chapter examines how the institutional transformation of Jamaica and Sierra Leone affected educational outcomes during the colonial era and democratization after independence. In general, direct British rule promoted effective governance and the expansion of primary schooling in postabolition Jamaica and the Sierra Leone colony. By contrast, indirect rule hindered the development of effective governance and mass education in the Sierra Leone protectorate, where the majority of indigenous Africans resided. Perhaps not surprisingly, I find that liberal reforms in postabolition Jamaica helped to facilitate the colony's democratization after World War II, whereas Sierra Leone's bifurcated institutions generated a fragile, ineffective, and deeply divided state that was unable to sustain democracy after independence.

State and Society in Colonial Jamaica

British Forced Settlement and Plantation Agriculture in Jamaica, 1660–1833

When Britain seized Jamaica from Spanish control in 1655, the island was still a remote and sparsely inhabited backwater colony of Iberian and Jewish settlers with a few hundred African slaves and indigenous Arawaks (Dunn 1972, 151). During the 1660s, however, British planters began to establish large-scale agricultural plantations using imported African slave labor. From 1660 until 1807, white Jamaican planters imported more than a million African slaves as plantation laborers (Eltis and Richardson 2010, 18, 51–52), and Jamaican plantations produced more sugar than in any other British forced settlement colony.[1] A small number of white planters, less than 5% of the total population, dominated Jamaica's economy and society.[2] By contrast, African slaves comprised more than 80% of Jamaica's population by the mid-eighteenth century (Dunn 1972, 312; Engerman and Higman 1997, 48–50).

The legal-administrative institutions of the early Jamaican colony were adapted from Tudor English norms to fit the needs of a white supremacist colony with a large enslaved population. In other words, aristocratic white planters enjoyed significant legal and political privileges, but they enforced racially discriminatory laws and a draconian slave code that gave plantation owners and managers unlimited control over the lives and livelihoods of their slaves.[3] The Jamaican House of Assembly was dominated by local white planters who held annual elections with a narrow electoral franchise of white male property holders. The legislative autonomy of Jamaica's elected assembly enabled local white planters to control public expenditures and limit the executive power of the British-appointed governor (Wrong 1923, 43–45; Hurwitz and Hurwitz 1971, 23–24). In 1664, Jamaica's planter-dominated assembly enacted a brutal slave code that enforced a rigid racial-case hierarchy and legitimized white planter control over African slaves and their descendants (Dunn 1972, 238–41). Jamaica's 1664 slave code denied even the most basic liberties to enslaved African laborers, who remained subject to special legal tribunals that often included their owners (Hurwitz and Hurwitz 1971, 84–86). Gross abuses remained an everyday aspect of plantation life, and the vast majority of Jamaican slaves died from disease, torture, suicide, or overwork. At the time, Britain's commercial and political elites supported this status quo, given the massive profits derived from the Atlantic slave trade and slave-based sugar production. Indeed, for 20 years between 1787 and 1807, the planter-dominated legislatures of the British West Indies worked with the West Indian lobby (a powerful alliance of aristocrats and commercial elites in the British Parliament) to stave off the abolition of the slave trade and protect the economic and political interests of West Indian sugar producers (Green 2016, 75; Hurwitz and Hurwitz 1971, 26; Wrong 1923, 48–49; Dunn 1972; Williams 1994).

Abolition and Reform in Britain and Jamaica, 1807–38

During the first half of the nineteenth century, the economic and political dominance of Jamaican white planters was undermined by the British Industrial Revolution, which empowered industrial capitalists, humanitarian activists, and Protestant reformist activists in the British Liberal (Whig) Party. As Britain emerged into a global industrial power, industrial capitalists and political reformers in the Liberal Party became increasingly opposed to the transatlantic slave trade and plantation slavery in the West Indies (Williams 1994). Protestant missionary activists mobilized an effective transnational movement against the transatlantic slave trade (see Stamatov 2010; Woodberry 2004), and the British Parliament enacted a wave of liberal reforms that extended civil and political equality to free peoples of color (Wesley 1934) and abolished plantation slavery in the forced settlement colonies (Wesley 1938; Campbell 1976, 118–53). The 1832 Reform Act extended voting rights to industrial capitalists, and weakened the political dominance of landed aristocracy (Williams 1994, 133–36; Ertman 2010, 1008). The following year, Parliament passed the Emancipation Act to abolish plantation slavery in the British colonial empire. The abolition of slavery weakened the economic and political dominance of white planters in forced settlement colonies, where reformist British officials enacted legal-administrative reforms that extended metropolitan legal rights to emancipated slaves.

The abolition movement precipitated a severe institutional crisis between Jamaica's planter-dominated assembly and the reformist British Parliament. In 1833, Jamaica's planter-dominated House of Assembly condemned the Emancipation Act as "unjust, unlawful, and unconstitutional" on the grounds that it deprived slave owners of their property rights and individual liberty (Jamaica Royal Gazette, April 12–19, 1834). Nevertheless, the Jamaican House of Assembly ultimately adopted its own emancipation bill in exchange for monetary compensation from British taxpayers to Jamaica's plantation owners (Wesley 1933, 1938; Latimer 1964; Draper 2010, 107). Between 1834 and 1838, Parliament paid more than £6 million in compensation to liberate more than 340,000 slaves in Jamaica (Draper 2010, 139; Beauvois 2017, 217). This compensation was paid to colonial planters as well as British aristocrats and parliamentarians who owned slaves in the Caribbean.[4]

The cruel irony of emancipation is that Jamaica's liberated slaves did not any receive financial compensation or economic support from the British government. Instead, the Emancipation Act required freed slaves to work as wage laborers for their former owners for an additional seven years under a program known as "apprenticeship." Nevertheless, British magistrates were sent to monitor the working conditions of freed slaves and to mediate labor disputes between freed slaves and their employers (Hall 2002, 115; Wrong 1923, 57). Abolitionists and Protestant church leaders uncovered many labor abuses in the West Indies, and apprenticeship became a major campaign issue in the 1837 British parliamentary elections (Latimer 1964; Wesley 1938). After William Lamb's Liberal government was re-elected in 1837, it abolished the apprenticeship program the following year (Wesley 1938), declaring that all plantation laborers were now "free [British] subjects" (Jamaica Royal Gazette, June 23, 1838). British common law protected the individual civil liberties, property rights, and religious liberty of emancipated slaves, who now enjoyed the right to purchase land and homes and to live independently with their families in "free villages" established away from the plantations (Hall 2002, 119–39).

The constitutional standoff between Jamaica's planter-dominated assembly and the British Parliament persisted well into the nineteenth century, as British liberal reforms undermined the legislative autonomy of Jamaican planters. In 1838, for example, Parliament passed the West India Prisons Act, which authorized British-appointed inspectors to close colonial prisons that did not meet metropolitan standards. The Jamaican House of Assembly protested by refusing to adopt any of the metropolitan legislation that was necessary to improve the conditions of emancipated slaves (Wrong 1923, 56–57). Parliament threatened to close down Jamaica's planter-dominated assembly, which the colonial undersecretary of state Henry Taylor condemned as "representative of slavery" and "eminently disqualified for the great task of educating and improving a people born into freedom" (Wrong 1923, 56–57). Although British liberal reforms undermined the economic and political dominance of West Indian planters, they did not significantly expand the *political rights* or electoral representation of emancipated Afro-descendants (see Wrong 1923, 56–70; Hall 1994; Smith 1994). In part, this reflects the fact that Britain itself maintained significant restrictions on parliamentary representation and voting rights until the early twentieth century. Despite the restrictions on electoral participation, British liberal reforms strengthened parliamentary oversight over colonial affairs and empowered the Colonial Office relative to local white planters in Jamaica and other forced settlement colonies.

Why did the British government enact reforms that undermined West Indian planter interests during the first half of the nineteenth century? Historians have articulated a number of moral, economic, and political arguments in previous scholarly research. Moral arguments emphasize the rise of Enlightenment ideology among British liberal elites following the political revolutions that swept across the Atlantic world—from Britain's North American colonies to France and its Caribbean colonies to Spanish America—between 1775 and 1820. These revolutions undermined support for slavery in the Atlantic world, as many liberal elites—including industrial capitalists, reformist church leaders, and secular humanitarians—increasingly regarded slavery as morally repugnant. These groups gained ascendancy in the British Liberal Party at the beginning of the nineteenth century (Smith 1994, 131; Ertman 2010). Protestant missionary activists and reformist church leaders played a significant role in mobilizing British public opinion against the Atlantic slave trade and plantation slavery (Stamatov 2010; Beauvois 2017, 34–35; Woodberry 2012; Hall 2002, esp. ch. 1; Latimer 1965; Williams 1994, ch. 11; Wesley 1938). Reformist church leaders also lobbied the British Parliament to establish denominational schools that educated emancipated populations in the forced settlement colonies following the abolition of slavery (Latimer 1965). They also helped to mobilize British public opinion against the apprenticeship program that required emancipated slaves to continue working for their former owners (Wesley 1938; Latimer 1964). This highlights the important role of reformist church leaders in mobilizing British public and parliamentary opinion against slavery and planter dominance in the West Indies.

Economic considerations are also important. The British Industrial Revolution began during the 1780s, when the Atlantic world was rocked by a series of political revolutions that destabilized the transatlantic slave trade, and increased the price of African slaves relative to global sugar prices in British currency (Eltis and Richardson 2010, 3). Britain's industrial transformation empowered industrial capitalist elites relative to conservative landed aristocrats during the first half of the nineteenth century. As Britain emerged into a global industrial power, British economic and political elites increasingly favored a liberal capitalist economy that promoted free trade and the export of British manufactured goods to foreign markets. Consequently, the sugar plantations in British forced settlement colonies became increasingly marginal to the needs of an industrial capitalist economy (Williams 1994, 150–51; Drescher 1987, 139). The economic marginalization of the British forced settlement colonies was further exacerbated by the abolition of slavery in the 1830s.[5] As Britain emerged into a global industrial powerhouse, its industrial capitalist elites became less interested in protecting West Indian sugar production, and more interested in free trade policies that expanded foreign export markets in the United States, China, India, and Latin America (Williams 1994, 132–33).

Many economic historians, including Eric Williams, the independence leader of Trinidad and Tobago, believe that economic factors far outweigh moral considerations in explaining British efforts to undermine West Indian planter interests during the nineteenth century. By the early 1800s, British West Indian sugar was far more expensive than imported sugar from Brazil or Cuba, given the larger plantations and slave populations of these colonies (Williams 1994, 141, 152). In the words of Eric Williams, British capitalism "continued to thrive on Brazilian, Cuban, and American slavery" even after it had destroyed West Indian slavery (Williams 1994, 176). West Indian cane sugar was also more expensive than European beet sugar by the middle of the nineteenth century (Knight 1997, 333). Thus, Britain's empowered industrial elites lost interest in propping up an inefficient, increasingly repugnant system of sugar production in forced settlement colonies like Jamaica if they could obtain cheaper sugar from elsewhere. As the British economic model shifted toward industrial capitalism and free trade, British elites and consumers came to prioritize cheap imported (foreign) sugar rather than the continued subsidy of inefficient and indebted plantation owners in British forced settlement colonies.[6]

Political factors also undermined support for slavery and colonial planters in the British Parliament during the 1830s and 1840s. Britain's emergence into a global industrial power contributed to its political transformation from a competitive oligarchy into an expanding parliamentary democracy. It is impossible to separate the British abolition of slavery from the 1832 Reform Bill that extended voting rights to Britain's industrial capitalist elites. The Reform Bill strengthened Britain's rising industrial capitalists at the expense of landed aristocrats (Ertman 2010). Because many British aristocrats owned plantations in the West Indies, the political decline of Britain's landed aristocracy undermined the "West India Lobby" that once defended planter interests in Parliament (Williams 1994, 87–92). Britain's emergence as a global industrial power also generated support for liberal reforms and free-market capitalism among political elites in both major political parties by the middle of the nineteenth century. Both Liberal and Conservative Party elites supported Britain's global economic expansion and free trade by the middle of the nineteenth century (Black 2015, 121–24), and both parties enacted electoral reforms that expanded voting rights between 1867 and 1918 (Ertman 2010; Hall 1994). These electoral reforms were not extended to forced settlement colonies like Jamaica, but British colonial officials implemented legal-administrative reforms that strengthened the protection of individual civil liberties in the forced settlement colonies (Ledgister 1998, 13). The extension of civil rights to emancipated Afro-descendants undermined the economic and political dominance of local white elites, and it transformed the nature of state-society relations in forced settlement colonies over the *longue durée*.

Planter Decline and Social Unrest in Postabolition Jamaica, 1838–65

The legal-administrative reforms that accompanied the abolition of slavery contributed to the economic and political decline of Jamaica's planter elites. In the decades following abolition, ruined planters abandoned more than 600 sugar and coffee estates that had once housed more than 50,000 slaves (Sheller 2000, 50; Satchell 1990, 39–46). Jamaican sugar production declined by 62% between 1834 and 1865, and coffee exports declined by 76% between 1834 and 1850 (Sheller 2000, 50). During these years, reformist church leaders and Protestant missionary activists helped former slaves to acquire land (Dick 2003, 7–11; Sheller 2000, 157–59; Holt 1992). As Jamaican plantations were abandoned, the number of small (and mostly black-owned) family farms increased from 883 in 1840 to about 60,000 in 1865 (Sherlock and Bennett 1998, 242). The emergence of an independent class of black landowners dramatically transformed Jamaica's social and political structure, generating racial tensions between small black landholders and the declining planter elites.

By 1863, people of color comprised the majority of Jamaica's electorate (Satchell 1990, 62), so local whites in the House of Assembly imposed voter registration fees, as well as income and taxation requirements that disenfranchised most small landowners. These restrictions reduced the Jamaican electorate to only 1482 voters in 1865, even though at least 50,000 black peasants met the property (but not tax or income) qualifications for voting (Colony of Jamaica 1865; Hurwitz and Hurwitz 1971, 127; Sherlock and Bennett 1998, 242, 251–52). Black church leaders, peasant farmers, and middle-class activists responded by lobbying for democratic political reforms, which gave way to racialized violence during Jamaica's 1865 Morant Bay rebellion. In October 1865, a group of black Jamaicans led by Paul Bogle, a political activist and Jamaican Baptist clergyman, broke into a local courthouse to free a black man who had been accused of illegally entering a plantation to retrieve his horse. The chief magistrate appealed to local militia to protect the courthouse, which was burned to the ground by armed protesters who attacked the local prison and liberated its inmates. Much of the village was destroyed in rioting and looting that claimed 24 lives, including two white militia that had been deployed to protect the courthouse and prison (Wrong 1923, 73–74; Chivallon and Howard 2017).

The response of Jamaica's colonial government was draconian and unlawful. The British governor, Colonel Eyre, suspended Jamaica's constitution and imposed martial law over the island during a monthlong reign of terror in which more than 350 black and mixed-race Jamaicans were court-martialed and executed. The two most prominent victims of this repression were Paul Bogle and George William Gordon, a prominent black Baptist minister, landowner, and elected member of the Jamaica House of Assembly, who was not even present at the site of the rebellion. Both men were court-martialed and executed during the British reign of terror. Hundreds more were summarily executed without trial. Thousands more were arrested, tortured, and forced to bury the bodies of those who had been court-martialed and executed without trial (Chivallon and Howard 2017, 541–42; Sheller 2000, 198–203; Sherlock and Bennett 1998, 254–62; Smith 1994, 134–35; Hurwitz and Hurwitz 1971, 145–51; Wrong 1923, 74–75).

The 1865 Morant Bay rebellion was an important turning point in Jamaica's political development. This was the final straw for Jamaica's elected assembly, which ultimately bent to British pressure to abolish itself in favor of direct rule by British colonial administrators (Smith 1994, 141; Hall 1994, 11; Wrong 1923, 75–77). This was also the last time in which Jamaica's colonial authorities would respond to social unrest with indiscriminate violence. Governor Eyre's unlawful political repression was widely criticized in Britain, where the governor was recalled and forced to stand trial. Governor Eyre was ultimately acquitted, though he was never appointed to another colonial posting (Chivallon and Howard 2017, 548–49). In the aftermath of the 1865 Morant Bay rebellion, the Colonial Office imposed direct "crown colony" rule over Jamaica and other forced settlement colonies (Wrong 1923, 77).[7]

Crown Colony Rule and Liberal Administrative
Reforms in Jamaica, 1866–1944

The Jamaican-born political scientist F. S. J. Ledgister describes three main features of crown colony direct rule as implemented in Jamaica in other British forced settlement colonies.

1. "Respect for civil liberties, in particular the right to own property, including freedom of religion and [freedom of] expression."
2. "Continued local [participation] in government, even though legislatures could be dominated by [colonial governmental officials] and the suffrage . . . was often restricted. Even though this was intended to secure upper-class participation in the operation of the state, it created an opening for the emergent middle class. It nonetheless provided the [metropolitan] subject with a means of lobbying the state authorities for assistance or redress."
3. "Authoritarian government by bureaucrats whose primary concern was social discipline in the interests of the colonizer but who were also concerned with social amelioration" (Ledgister 1998, 13–14).

Direct crown colony rule had profound consequences for Jamaica's institutional development. Its official objective, according to an 1868 colonial dispatch, was "to establish a system of government and legislation by which the financial condition of the [Caribbean] colonies should be improved, and their agricultural and commercial interests be promoted, by which industry might be encouraged, crime repressed, and the welfare of all classes be better provided for" (Wrong 1923, 79). British officials also favored direct crown colony rule as a way of improving the administrative effectiveness of West Indian colonial governments, and protecting them from US imperialist expansion after 1865 (Smith 1994, 132).

Crown colony rule was largely successful at achieving these goals. Direct British rule weakened the political control of Jamaica's local elites, as British officials enacted reforms that improved the administrative effectiveness and developmental capacity of Jamaica's colonial state (see Smith 1994; Hurwitz and Hurwitz 1971, 181–88; Wrong 1923). Historian James Patterson Smith highlights the "wave of administrative and social reforms [that] followed the removal of oligarchic obstruction and the shift of sweeping powers to [Jamaica's] new colonial executives" (Smith 1994, 141). These reforms were largely intended to reverse the economic decline that resulted from the abolition of slavery. British officials favored more centralized methods of administrative control to strengthen the rule of law, diversify the economy, and encourage the small-scale production of secondary crops like bananas. During the late 1860s and early 1870s, Jamaica's colonial governor, Sir John Peter Grant, centralized the island's police administration and established a new rural police force to improve law and order in the countryside (Smith 1994; Bryan 1991, 23). He also introduced a new system of district courts and land reforms that expanded small property ownership among black Jamaicans. His administration also introduced Jamaica's first government medical service, and invested in schools, roads, sanitation, and irrigation projects (Smith 1994, 142). Jamaica also enacted a new constitution that allowed for limited voting rights after 1884, although the elected members of the legislative council were always outnumbered by the British governor's appointed nominees (Wrong 1923; Ledgister 1998, 66). Nevertheless, Jamaica's colonial government began to provide a wider range of public goods and services. Jamaica's municipal councils began to provide poor-relief programs (Bryan 1991, 161), and the island's medical service provided free treatment for yaws and malaria, vaccinations for smallpox, and improved sanitation regulation (Hurwitz and Hurwitz 1971, 183; Bryan 1991, ch. 9). As a result of these improvements, childhood and infant mortality declined sharply, and life expectancy soared from 38 years in 1913 to 55 years by 1950 (Riley 2005, 28, 35).

British colonial officials tended to prioritize law and order and the protection of property rights over social and political reforms. These policies were broadly supported by Jamaican landowners and conservatives (Bryan 1991, ch. 3; Satchell 1990, 66–74), but they also appealed to the large and growing class of small black farmers, mostly banana producers, who experienced a net economic gain relative to the island's large sugar producers. Whereas Jamaica's sugar production continued to decline after the 1865 Morant Bay rebellion, banana production increased more than twenty-fold between 1874 and 1900 (Bryan 1991, 2–7). By 1900, bananas had displaced sugar as Jamaica's primary export, and banana producers (mostly independent black farmers) became increasingly important to the colony's economic well-being (Bryan 1991, 7).

Direct British rule also expanded the legal rights and political agency of emancipated Afro-descendants in the early decades of the twentieth century. By the 1930s, all Jamaicans—regardless of race, ethnicity, income or social status—enjoyed freedom of speech and association, religious liberty, and the right to join trade unions and professional associations (Ledgister 1998, 39). Moreover, the Jamaican press and legislature could freely criticize government policies. Thus, despite its political limitations, and the deeply rooted socioeconomic inequalities that persisted along race and color lines, British crown colony rule institutionalized a "liberal-authoritarian state" that fused "paternalistic authoritarian government with civil and economic liberalism" (Ledgister 1998, 66). Direct British rule protected the property rights and individual civil liberties of emancipated Afro-descendants, but most working and middle-class Jamaicans remained politically disenfranchised until after World War II.[8] From 1866 until

1944, Jamaica's legal-administrative framework was similar to other directly ruled crown colonies, including Ceylon (Sri Lanka), Hong Kong, Mauritius, Trinidad, and Singapore. Jamaica's legal-administrative framework was also similar to the early Sierra Leone colony (1808–96), where emancipated slaves and liberated Africans lived under British laws and institutions.

State and Society in Colonial Sierra Leone

Liberated "Creole" Africans in the Province of Freedom, 1788–1896

During the 1780s, British abolitionists established Sierra Leone as a settlement colony for freed and repatriated African slaves. The early Sierra Leone colony was built around the capital city of Freetown, whose early settlers included black loyalists from the Canadian province of Nova Scotia,[9] African American settlers,[10] emancipated Afro-descendants from the British West Indies,[11] and more than 80,000 liberated Africans that the British Royal Navy rescued from slave ships destined from the New World (Wyse 1991, 2; Fyfe 1973, 43; Fyfe 1967, 51). Most Creole blacks settled in Freetown, whereas liberated Africans established small farms in the surrounding "free villages" with quintessentially British names like Aberdeen, Dublin, Gloucester, Hastings, Wellington, and York. Liberated Africans also served in the Royal Navy's antislavery patrols that operated out of Freetown's harbor. Sierra Leone's diverse community of liberated Africans assimilated into the Anglo-bourgeois norms of Freetown's Creole society, while maintaining aspects of indigenous African culture (Spitzer 1974; Fyfe 1973). Over time, the colony's diverse settlers developed their own Creole English and forged a common ethnic identity as Krio (Creole). Many Krios developed a genuine attachment to the British Crown and regarded themselves as free British subjects at the vanguard of Britain's "civilizing mission" in Africa (Wyse 1991, 7–8; Fyfe 1973, 48–49; Spitzer 1974, 9–36).

Sierra Leone's early colonial economy was primarily based on commerce and cash crop production (primarily groundnuts and palm oil) during the nineteenth century. The expanding colonial settlement also attracted Mende, Temne, and Limba migrants from Sierra Leone's adjacent indigenous hinterlands as British legal institutions provided commercial opportunities, political stability, and protection from slavery (Fyfe 1967, 101). Sierra Leone was one of the first British colonies to establish denominational Christian schools for liberated Africans during the first half of the nineteenth century (Sumner 1963, 12–34; Cole 2013, 70–71), and one of Sierra Leone's most prestigious schools, Fourah Bay College, became the first "European" university in West Africa during the 1870s (Paracka 2002).

As Freetown emerged as a vibrant commercial center with a sizable middle class, Sierra Leone Creoles developed "a strong sense of their own rights" as free British subjects (Fyfe 1973, 52). Nevertheless, British administrators never permitted extensive political representation in the early Sierra Leone colony, and educated Krios were increasingly squeezed out of senior administrative positions after 1890 (Spitzer 1974, 45–50; Kup 1975, 50–68). This exclusion only hardened after Britain established a vast "protectorate" over more than 70,000 square kilometers of indigenous African territory in 1896.

Territorial Expansion and the Historical Origins of Sierra Leone's Bifurcated State, 1896–1951

The territorial expansion of colonial occupation in Sierra Leone was primarily motivated by British efforts to expand trade and commerce in West Africa and to limit the territorial expansion of French rule in the region. The initial British plan was to employ Freetown Creoles to collect taxes from indigenous Africans in Sierra Leone's interior districts, but indigenous Mende patriots massacred nearly a thousand Creole administrators, traders, and missionaries during the anticolonial Hut Tax War of 1898. The monetary and human cost of this war forced Freetown's British officials to rethink their administrative strategy and devolve local authority to protectorate African "chiefs." Thus, Sierra Leone developed a bifurcated state after 1900: the British maintained direct political control over Freetown and its immediate vicinity (i.e., the Sierra Leone colony), whereas indirect rule empowered indigenous African chiefs in the Sierra Leone protectorate (Acemoglu, Reed, and Robinson 2014, 326; Lange 2009, 95; Spitzer 1974, 89–107).

The Sierra Leone protectorate was organized into 10 administrative districts, each overseen by a British district commissioner (DC). Each British DC supervised a hierarchical network of paramount chiefs, subchiefs, and village chiefs that managed the day-to-day affairs of indigenous African communities (Lange 2009; Acemoglu, Reed, and Robinson 2014). Consequently, Sierra Leone's colonial administration was "tiny, infrastructurally weak, and detached from the majority of the population" (Lange 2009, 96), in keeping with Mahmood Mamdani's conceptualization of the bifurcated African colonial state. Only five British administrators, 10 DCs, and a single court judge oversaw more than 1 million indigenous Africans between 1896 and 1921 (Kup 1975, 198). By the end of World War I, there were only 1800 colonial officials—roughly 12 for every 10,000 inhabitants—in all of Sierra Leone, and most were based in the capital city, Freetown (Lange 2009, 95). As late as 1950, there were only 33 state employees for every 10,000 inhabitants in Sierra Leone (Lange 2009, 96).

Consequently, Sierra Leone's colonial officials "could not contemplate basic government functions outside of Freetown," where indirect British rule reinforced the political authority of paramount chiefs—i.e., indigenous African elites who had supported the British during the 1898 Hut Tax War (see Abraham 1978, 181; Lange 2009, 99).[12] Sierra Leone's paramount chiefs were authorized to collect colonial taxes, recruit indigenous labor, and maintain law and order through "customary courts" whose rulings were enforced by "native police" (Lange 2009, 97–100). Their descendants still comprise the majority of "ruling houses" in Sierra Leone today (Acemoglu, Reed and Robinson 2014, 326).

Indirect British rule also expanded the arbitrary and despotic power of Sierra Leone's chiefs (Acemoglu, Reed, and Robinson 2014; Lange 2009; Reno 1995; Migdal 1988). Prior to 1896, Sierra Leone's African kingdoms were not hereditary, and there were traditional checks and balances that limited the despotic power of African rulers. For instance, African subjects could always appeal to a neighboring king in the event of a legal dispute. The relative abundance of land also enabled Africans to "vote with their feet" and relocate to a new area if their rulers became too despotic (Herbst 2000, 39–44). Indirect rule severed the accountability of paramount chiefs by making them responsible to their British overlords. Through their control of "customary courts," protectorate chiefs controlled access to "tribal lands," and they could generate personal revenues through fines and court fees (Acemoglu, Reed, and Robinson 2014; Lange 2009, 99–100). These customary courts were largely unregulated because British colonial officials lacked the administrative capacity to supervise them (Lange 2009, 99; Abraham 1978, 175). As late as the 1950s, customary courts heard 81% of the legal cases in Sierra Leone, and British DCs revised only 7% of these rulings (Lange 2009, 48, 98). Moreover, Sierra Leone's customary courts decided all rural land claims, matrimonial and/or inheritance disputes, and cases involving indigenous Africans where the matter of dispute was less than £50 (Sierra Leone, 1955, 67). Thus, even Sierra Leone's Supreme Court had no jurisdiction over the vast majority of court cases involving rural African claimants.

Indirect rule also generated significant labor abuses in the Sierra Leone protectorate. Despite the fact that the Sierra Leone colony had been established as a safe haven for liberated slaves, Sierra Leone's 1902 Protectorate Ordinance recognized domestic slavery on chiefly estates, and authorized chiefs to recruit unpaid labor and to punish those who challenged their authority (Reno 1995, 37). British officials maintained that compulsory labor was necessary for the economic well-being and social stability of protectorate Africans, although forced labor enabled chiefs to profit from cash crop farming by using unpaid labor on their estates (Sawyer 2008, 390). Given the limited bureaucratic and legal-administrative capacity of the colonial state, Sierra Leone's protectorate chiefs continued to rely heavily on unpaid forced labor long after it was formally abolished in 1928 (Harris 2014, 25). Unpaid agricultural labor became even more important after the colonial government established extractive marketing boards that paid low prices to rural producers (Reno 1995, 44). The maintenance of extractive economic institutions contributed to widespread rural unrest that culminated in the antichief revolts of 1955–56. Despite widespread allegations of forced labor on chiefly estates, Sierra Leone's chieftaincy system was never reformed, and paramount chiefs remain important power brokers in national politics more than 50 years after independence (Acemoglu, Reed, and Robinson 2012; Lange 2009; Sawyer 2008; Richards 2005).

The discovery of alluvial diamond deposits in Sierra Leone's Kono District only increased the scope for labor abuses and governmental corruption after 1930. British efforts to monopolize the diamond trade under the Sierra Leone Selection Trust (SLST) proved unsuccessful, as Kono chiefs argued that they were the rightful owners of Sierra Leone's mineral wealth, given their constitutional rights as "custodians of the land." Thus, Kono chiefs enriched themselves by extracting rents from "strangers," including Freetown Krios, Liberians, and Syrian-Lebanese merchants who participated in illicit diamond mining and retail. To entice the chiefs to work with government-licensed dealers, the colonial government increased their monthly stipends and expanded their administrative responsibilities (including control over local schools, health clinics, and development grants) under the "native administrations" established during the 1930s. Nevertheless, many chiefs pocketed the money while ignoring the government's regulations. Over the next two decades, chiefs' incomes increased 20-fold despite the limited expansion of education, public health, or agricultural development (Reno 1995, 45–53; Lange 2009, 102–3; Acemoglu, Reed, and Robinson 2014, 327–28). In the end, the SLST came to accept the de facto limits on its formal monopoly, in exchange for side payments that reached a quarter of total government expenditure in 1955 (Reno 1995, 61–62). Thus, in contrast to Jamaica, where direct crown colony rule institutionalized administrative reforms that generated significant improvements in primary schooling, sanitation, and medical services at the end of the nineteenth century, the consolidation of indirect rule hindered similar advances in Sierra Leone's indigenous hinterlands after 1900.

Consequences of British Expansion for Sierra Leone's Educated Creoles

The legal-administrative bifurcation of Sierra Leone's had negative consequences for Freetown Krios during the twentieth century. With the expansion of British rule into Sierra Leone's indigenous hinterlands, Freetown officials increasingly regarded the civil liberties and high educational attainment of Sierra Leone Krios as a "threat to the [new] colonial order." Indirect British rule also shifted the balance of power away from Sierra Leone's educated Creoles toward protectorate chiefs (Whyte 2008, 86). Historians have suggested that this was part of a deliberate British strategy to undermine Sierra Leone's nascent political bourgeoisie (Reno 1995, 43; Wyse 1991; Spitzer 1974). Indirect British rule also eliminated employment opportunities for British-educated Creole lawyers in the Sierra Leone protectorate, where protectorate chiefs presided over customary courts. Creole Africans were also pushed out of senior administrative roles as a result of increased European settlement made possible by Western medical advances. Consequently, the proportion of Sierra Leone Creoles employed in senior administrative positions declined from 45% in 1892 to 16% by 1912 (Lange 2009, 95; Reno 1995, 41). The West African Medical Service also closed its doors to African doctors after 1902, as the colonial government attempted to establish a segregated residential district for white government employees (Wyse 1991, 62–63; Spitzer 1974, 52–69). The colonial government also blamed Afro-Creole newspapers and journalists for every episode of social or political unrest following the 1898 Hut Tax War (Spitzer 1974, 103). Seen from this vein, it is perhaps not surprising that Freetown Krios became increasingly vocal in their criticisms of British rule following the establishment of the protectorate.

Comparisons with Jamaica

Jamaica and Sierra Leone experienced very different patterns of institutional development, even though both countries can be described as "extractive" colonies with limited European settlement. For a brief period during the late nineteenth century, both Jamaica and Sierra Leone were directly ruled crown colonies with similar legal-administrative institutions. Over time, however, Jamaica's administrative structure became increasingly bureaucratic, with a uniform legal framework that protected individual civil liberties and economic rights regardless of race, creed, or ethnicity (Ledgister 1998, 18–19). By contrast, Sierra Leone's colonial administration became increasingly bifurcated, as direct British rule in the early Sierra Leone colony gave way to indirect rule over indigenous Africans in the Sierra Leone protectorate. Consequently, for most of the twentieth century, direct British rule was limited to Sierra Leone's capital city, Freetown, with its predominantly Creole population. By contrast, indirect British rule empowered local chiefs in the indigenous rural hinterlands. These distinctive legal-administrative institutions produced very different developmental consequences for Jamaica and Sierra Leone. Direct crown colony rule gave British administrators greater political autonomy from Jamaica's planter elites and strengthened the rule of law and the protection of individual civil liberties

(Ledgister 1998, 18–19; Rueschemeyer et al. 1992, 236–44; Smith 1994). Direct British rule also contributed to the significant expansion of primary schooling in nineteenth-century Jamaica. In Sierra Leone, by contrast, the shift from direct to indirect British rule undermined the political status of Sierra Leone's educated Creoles (Spitzer 1974) and strengthened the authority of Sierra Leone's protectorate chiefs after 1896 (Lange 2009; Reno 1995). As we will see in the next section, these distinct institutional trajectories had profound consequences for the expansion of primary schooling in colonial Jamaica and Sierra Leone.

The Expansion of Primary Schooling in Colonial Jamaica and Sierra Leone

British Colonial Office records contain valuable information on the expansion of primary schooling in colonial Jamaica and Sierra Leone. The Colonial Office *Blue Books* contain valuable information on the historical development of denominational and government-funded schools after 1830, the expansion of primary school enrollment, and the extent of public expenditure on colonial schools in Jamaica and Sierra Leone. *The Blue Books for Sierra Leone* also provide disaggregated records for the directly ruled colony and indirectly ruled protectorate. Consequently, I was able to the distinctive developmental consequences of direct versus indirect British rule for the expansion of primary school enrollment in Jamaica and Sierra Leone.

I estimated gross primary enrollment rates for each colonial state by multiplying the percentage of primary school children in the total population by a factor of five. This assumes that children aged six to thirteen comprised about one-fifth of the total population in both colonies.[13] I used the six to thirteen age range because primary schooling in British colonies was based on a six-year cycle. Colonial Office records demonstrate that primary schooling became increasingly widespread in Jamaica following the abolition of slavery in the 1830s. In Sierra Leone, by contrast, primary schooling was largely confined to the directly ruled colony, and there was little emphasis on educating indigenous Africans in the indirectly ruled protectorate.

Jamaica

Table 5.1 highlights the significant expansion of primary schooling in colonial Jamaica following the abolition of slavery in the 1830s. The data show that the most significant expansions of primary school enrollment occurred during periods of liberal administrative reform. The first major expansion of primary

Table 5.1 The Expansion of Primary Schooling in Colonial Jamaica, 1834–1961

Year	Total Number of Schools	Total Enrollment	Most Recent Population Estimate or Census	Primary Enrollment / Total Population (%)	Estimated Gross Primary Enrollment Rate (%)
1834	7	NA	378,050	NA	NA
1837	183	12,580	378,050	3.3	16.5
1838	296	31,865[a]	378,050	8.4	42.0
1851	212	16,303	377,433	4.3	21.5
1868	286	19,764[b]	441,264	4.5	22.5[c]
1884	701	57,557	580,804	9.9	49.5
1900–1901	720	84,491	745,104	11.3	56.5
1913–14	697	96,757	808,987	12.0	60.0
1928	672	127,785	1,050,667[d]	12.1	60.5
1946	681	177,000	1,314,025	13.5	67.5[e]
1961	728	281,799	1,639,395	17.2	86.0

[a] This total is inflated because it includes Sunday schools, day schools, and evening schools. Disaggregated data are not available for 1838 (Jamaica 1838).

[b] Data obtained from Jamaica 1885.

[c] Hurwitz and Hurwitz (1971) estimate 20% primary enrollment in 1864 (124).

[d] Population data from Jamaica's 1931 census.

[e] The British Colonial Office estimated Jamaica's primary enrollment rate at 70% in 1946 (Jamaica 1948a, 40).

schooling occurred immediately after the abolition of slavery, between 1834 and 1838. This is because reformist Protestant church leaders successfully lobbied the British government for parliamentary funds to establish denominational schools for British-emancipated slaves and their descendants (Wesley 1933, 69; Wesley 1932; Campbell 1996, 262; Klingberg 1939).[14] British parliamentary grants covered two-thirds of Jamaica's education expenditures between 1835 and 1842. This enabled reformist Protestant denominations (such as Quakers, Baptists, and Wesleyan Methodists) to compete on an even playing field with the established Church of England (Wesley 1933). The British parliamentary grant also enabled the Lady Mico Charity to establish Jamaica's first teacher training college during the 1830s (Klingberg 1939, 305; Wesley 1933; Latimer 1964). Jamaica's white planter elite initially opposed using local funds to educate emancipated children. Nevertheless, senior British government officials, including the prime minister, Lord Grey, favored the education of emancipated slaves, even though there was no compulsory education legislation in Britain at that time (Wesley 1933, 81). The British government's position is clearly articulated in this 1836 dispatch from the Colonial Office to the governor of Jamaica:

> Whatever objections may exist in more advanced societies to the principle of compulsory education, they can have no place in reference to a colony in which the great mass of people have just emerged from slavery.... In such a case, it will be a substitution of the name of liberty if we should not hold ourselves bound to acknowledge and respect amongst the Negroes the freedom to choose between knowledge and ignorance. (Hurwitz and Hurwitz 1971, 122)

Historical sources suggest that many Jamaican parents supported the education of their children to prevent local planter efforts to reinstate slavery. Emancipated Afro-descendants also valued education as a means to empower their children and promote upward social mobility (Klingberg 1939, 301). Thus, by the end of apprenticeship, nearly 32,000 Jamaican adults and children—approximately 8% of the island's total population—were enrolled in primary day schools, evening classes, and Sunday schools (see Table 5.1). This was a remarkable achievement for a predominantly rural and agricultural colony that had just liberated more than 300,000 slaves.

The initial expansion of primary schooling in Jamaica was limited by the vocal opposition of local white planters and the significant reduction, and subsequent elimination of the British parliamentary grant for denominational schools after 1845 (Engerman, Mariscal, and Sokoloff 2009, 104). This partly reflected the religious cleavage in British party politics, as British Conservatives strongly favored the official Church of England, whereas Liberals supported religious liberty and the social activism of reformist Protestant churches (Ertman 2010) that were more supportive of nonwhite colonized populations (Latimer 1965; Wesley 1938; Stamatov 2010; Woodberry 2004, 2012). Like their Conservative counterparts in Parliament, the "Country Party" that dominated Jamaica's House of Assembly openly favored Church of England schools that primarily catered to local whites. By 1851, most Jamaican primary schools were no longer receiving government funding (Jamaica 1851). The Jamaican assembly spent less than 2% of its budget on education during the 1850s (Jamaica 1858, 1865), as local planters argued that mass education would limit the supply of plantation labor (Campbell 1996; Sires 1942, 303).

Nevertheless, Jamaica experienced a second expansion in primary school enrollment after reformist British officials established direct control over the colony in 1866. The dissolution of Jamaica's planter-dominated assembly enabled reformist British officials to increase Jamaica's educational expenditures during the final third of the nineteenth century. During the late 1860s, Governor Grant's

administration established a board of education that supported all denominational schools that met government inspection and curricular standards (Smith
1994, 142; Hurwitz and Hurwitz 1971, 180–81). Consequently, Jamaica's educational expenditures increased from 0.8% of the colonial budget in 1865 to 7.5%
by 1901 (Jamaica 1865, 1885, 1901). These expenditures enabled Jamaica's colonial authorities to provide free primary schooling after 1890 (Dick 2003, 35–
36; Bryan 1996, 119), and Jamaica's estimated gross primary enrollment rate
increased from 23% in 1868 to nearly 60% by 1914 (see Table 5.1).

The final expansion resulted from the expansion of political representation and
mass electoral competition after World War II. Jamaica's elected governments significantly increased public spending on education to more than 15% of total government expenditure following the introduction of mass electoral competition.
By the mid-1950s, nearly 70% of Jamaican children were enrolled in primary
schools (Jamaica 1956, 220). This enabled Jamaica's postcolonial governments to
focus on expanding access to secondary schools after independence.

Sierra Leone

Colonial Office records show vast educational disparities between Sierra Leone's
directly ruled colony and indirectly ruled protectorate (see Table 5.2). It is difficult to comprehend the vast disparity in primary school enrollment between
Sierra Leone's colony and protectorate without understanding the very different
rationales and institutions used to control Creole versus indigenous African
populations in these territories. For most of the nineteenth century, British
officials and Christian missionaries prioritized the education, evangelization,
and cultural assimilation of emancipated Creoles and liberated Africans in the
directly ruled Sierra Leone colony. British officials and Protestant church leaders
regarded Sierra Leone's liberated Africans as useful allies for promoting "legitimate" commerce, Christianity, and (Western) civilization in West Africa (Wyse
1991, 1–2; Spitzer 1974, 9–10; Kilson 1969, 97–99).[15] Consequently, the UK-
based Christian Missionary Society (CMS) established its first primary schools
in Sierra Leone in 1804 (Sumner 1963, 4–12), and Sierra Leone's earliest colonial governors actively supported CMS efforts to educate and assimilate the
growing population of liberated Africans during the first half of the nineteenth
century. British officials also established English-style "parishes" as the basis of
local administration in the directly ruled Sierra Leone colony, where CMS clergy
were frequently employed as "village managers." British parliamentary grants
also paid for the construction of schoolhouses, churches, and administrative
buildings (Peterson 1969, 83–85; Cole 2013, 71–73). The colonial government's

Table 5.2 The Expansion of Primary Schooling in Colonial Sierra Leone, 1838–1956

Year	Number of Schools	Number of Pupils Enrolled	Most Recent Population Estimate	Primary School Enrollment as % of Population	Estimated Gross Primary Enrollment Rate (%)
1822 (colony)	NA	~2,000[a]	~12,000	16.7	83.5
1838 (colony)	36	7,518[a]	40,592	18.5	92.5
1851 (colony)	38	6,586	44,501	14.8	74.0
1884 (colony)	85	9,154	81,614	11.2	56.0
1901 (colony)	92	7,543	76,655	9.8	49.0
1901 (protectorate)	22	671	949,000[b]	< 0.1	< 0.5
1913 (colony)	89	8,206	75,572	10.8	54.0
1913 (protectorate)	74	2,320	935,592[c]	0.2	1.0
1928 (colony)	59	8,321	85,153	9.8	49.0
1928 (protectorate)	121	5,352	1,450,903	0.4	2.0
1937 (colony)	68	10,128	96,422	10.5	52.5
1937 (protectorate)	176	10,161	1,672,048	0.6	3.0
1946 (colony)	65	10,294	96,422	10.7	53.5
1946 (protectorate)	185	13,000	1,672,048	0.8	< 4.0
1951 (colony and protectorate)	307	40,235	2,000,000	2.0	10.0
1956 (colony and protectorate)	460	61,796	2,100,000	2.9	14.5

Notes:

[a] Includes both children and adults.

[b] No census records are available for the Sierra Leone protectorate in 1901. I generated this population estimate by subtracting the population of the Sierra Leone colony from the estimated population for all of Sierra Leone in 1900, as listed in the *World Christian Encyclopedia* (Barrett, Kurian, and Johnson 2001).

[c] No census records are available for the Sierra Leone protectorate in 1911. I generated this population estimate by multiplying the 1901 population estimate by 0.986, reflecting the population difference in the Sierra Leone colony between 1901 and 1911. The Colonial Office did not take its first population census for the Sierra Leone protectorate until 1921, highlighting the limited administrative capacity of Sierra Leone's colonial state at the beginning of the twentieth century.

"liberated African department" also established its own schools for emancipated Africans rescued from slave ships destined for the New World. Consequently, the number of primary day schools in Sierra Leone increased from five in 1828 to 47 by 1840, and one-third of Sierra Leone's schools received funding from the colonial government's liberated African department (Sumner 1963, 50).

It is hard to overstate the significant expansion of primary schooling in the early years of the Sierra Leone colony. A British commission inquiry stated that nearly all Freetown children (approximately one-fifth of the colony's entire population) were enrolled in primary schools by 1840—a significantly higher proportion than in most European countries at that time (Spitzer 1974, 79). This suggests that Sierra Leone's early colonial governors were even more supportive of mass education than in early postabolition Jamaica, where local planters resisted the expansion of state-funded education to emancipated Afro-descendants until the establishment of direct British rule in 1866.

Sierra Leone's primary school enrollment rate declined during the second half of the nineteenth century. This seems to reflect Sierra Leone's declining strategic importance to Britain following the successful eradication of the transatlantic slave trade.[16] There were no European-controlled plantations in Sierra Leone at mid-century, and British officials were not aware of any mineral resources that might have attracted European investment in the colony. Furthermore, the high mortality rates for European soldiers, administrators, and clergy in West Africa fueled the dominant view that tropical African colonies were burdensome and expensive. As late as 1865, a British parliamentary committee warned against expanding Britain's territorial possessions in West Africa (Herbst 2000, 62). Thus, British parliamentary grants, which accounted for 16% of Sierra Leone's public revenues in 1851, had been entirely phased out by 1865 (Sierra Leone 1851; Sierra Leone 1865).

By the end of the nineteenth century, resurgent nationalism rekindled Europe's expansionist interests in the African continent, although British priorities had clearly shifted from educating and assimilating liberated Africans toward territorial aggrandizement and resource control. Between 1870 and 1890, British officials in Sierra Leone made several unsuccessful attempts to annex indigenous African territories claimed by the neighboring Republic of Liberia (Mark-Thiesen and Milhatsch 2019, 899–901). With the extension of indirect rule over the Sierra Leone protectorate, British officials came to regard Sierra Leone's westernized and educated Krios as "a threat to the stability of the [new] colonial order" (Whyte 2008, 86). Thus, Sierra Leone did not benefit from the type of education reforms implemented in late nineteenth-century Jamaica. Whereas Jamaica's educational expenditures increased from 2% of the colonial budget in 1865 to nearly 8% by 1914 (Jamaica 1865, 1914), Sierra Leone's consistently hovered around 2% of budgetary expenditure (Sierra Leone 1865, 1884, 1901). Consequently, the Sierra Leone colony's primary school enrollment rate stagnated at around 50% of the school-aged population during the first half of the twentieth century (Sierra Leone 1901, 1914, 1928, 1943).

Primary schooling was severely neglected in Sierra Leone's indirectly ruled protectorate, as many mission schools were destroyed during the 1898 Hut Tax War. In the aftermath of the Hut Tax War, British colonial officials envisioned a very different type of school system that was more in keeping with the norms of indirect rule (Sierra Leone 1939). Consequently, Governor Leslie Probyn (1904–10) sought to establish "technical and agricultural schools" that would expand the economic viability of indigenous communities in the Sierra Leone protectorate. The technical curriculum of these schools was designed to ensure that indigenous African leaders were not "educated enough to encourage or lead opposition against the colonial government" (Corby 1990, 320).

The protectorate government established its first primary school in the provincial town of Bo in 1906. The Bo school's mission was to educate "the sons and nominees of chiefs" in a traditional African setting to reinforce "tribal loyalties," and to instill respect for chiefly authority (Corby 1990, 320–22). The Bo school became the model for future government schools in the Sierra Leone protectorate (Whyte 2008), where British colonial policies reinforced chiefly authority over rural indigenous African communities. During the 1930s, many of Sierra Leone's protectorate schools were placed under the control of "Native Authorities" (NA), and many protectorate chiefs continued to prioritize personal expenses and the education of their own relatives over mass education and other developmental priorities. In 1948, for example, 58% of all NA expenditures went toward chiefs' salaries and allowances, compared with just 4.5% for education and 3.5% for agricultural development (Reno 1995, 57). Primary schooling only became a serious concern during the 1950s, when protectorate African leaders began to fear a Krio political takeover during the transition to independence (Sumner 1963, 321–28). Although these fears never materialized, the legal-administrative bifurcation of Sierra Leone's colony and protectorate meant that the Freetown-based Creole minority was far better educated than the indigenous African majority. As late as 1946, only 4% of protectorate African children were attending primary schools, compared to more than 55% of children in the directly ruled colony (Sierra Leone 1947). By independence, perhaps 15% of Sierra Leone's children were attending primary schools in the amalgamated colony and protectorate.

Comparing the Expansion of Primary Schooling in Jamaica and Sierra Leone

Colonial Office records demonstrate that Jamaica was able to develop a much more comprehensive and inclusive network of primary schools than Sierra Leone

prior to independence. This seems to reflect the unique institutional development of each colony. In directly ruled Jamaica, British colonial officials supported
Protestant missionary efforts to educate Jamaica's emancipated population following the abolition of slavery in the 1830s. Jamaica's denominational schools
were initially established by Protestant missionaries supported by a British parliamentary grant, yet Jamaica's colonial authorities assumed financial respon-
sibility for the island's denominational schools after 1890 (Dick 2003, 35–36;
Bran 1996, 119). A similar dynamic was at play in the directly ruled Sierra Leone
colony, where British colonial officials supported Protestant missionary efforts to
educate and assimilate Sierra Leone's liberated Africans. In the indirectly ruled
Sierra Leone protectorate, by contrast, British colonial officials sought to limit
Protestant missionary evangelization that might threaten the conservative social order enforced by local chiefs and Islamic elites. Instead, British officials es-
tablished their own protectorate schools that primarily catered to ruling elites.
British colonial policies in Sierra Leone failed to promote the type of expan-
sion in primary schooling that occurred in Jamaica after 1866. Consequently,
Sierra Leone's primary school enrollment rate lagged significantly behind that of
Jamaica's during the first half of the twentieth century (see Figure 5.1).

It is also important to consider the impact of cultural and religious preferences
that may have promoted greater demand for primary schooling in Creole
societies such as colonial Jamaica or nineteenth-century Freetown relative to
the indigenous African communities in Sierra Leone's interior. Jamaica's emancipated Afro-descendants and Sierra Leone's liberated Africans were (relatively)
westernized Creole populations that had been deeply and forcibly integrated
into the Atlantic world economy for several generations. The significant role of
Protestant church leaders in the abolition of slavery would have only increased
the demand for primary schooling among emancipated slaves and liberated

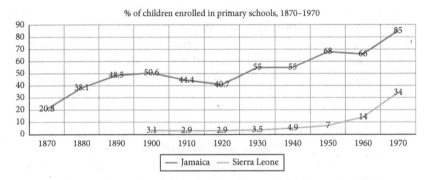

Figure 5.1 Primary school enrollment rates for Jamaica and Sierra Leone,
1870–1970

Africans. By contrast, Sierra Leone's indigenous African communities had their own informal education systems that predate the onset of colonial rule. Koranic schools also offered an alternative type of formal education in many parts of Sierra Leone. Because Islam has significantly older roots in traditional West African society, many indigenous African parents favored these Koranic schools over Christian denominational schools that offered a British academic curriculum. This reasoning is entirely consistent with the statistical evidence from Chapter 4, where Protestantism was generally associated with higher adult literacy rates, and Islam was associated with lower adult literacy rates in 1960.

Nevertheless, religious and cultural differences are unlikely to explain the significant increase in primary schooling in colonial Jamaica relative to Sierra Leone. Muslims only accounted for 10% of Sierra Leone's indigenous African population in 1900 (Barrett, Kurian, and Johnson 2001), and Islam was largely concentrated in northern regions of the Sierra Leone protectorate. Muslim parents may have sent their children to Koranic schools in indirectly ruled areas that lacked British schools, but Freetown's Muslim leaders lobbied the colonial government to establish and finance Muslim schools that offered a British academic curriculum during the nineteenth century (Cole 2013). This suggests that it was the British policy of indirect rule rather than the preference of Muslim elites that hindered the expansion of primary schooling in the Sierra Leone protectorate after 1896. Moreover, the government schools in the Sierra Leone protectorate primarily catered to the sons and nominees of local chiefs, and most of the mission schools were not financially supported by the colonial government (Sierra Leone 1939). This suggests that it was the British policy of indirect rule that hindered the expansion of primary schooling in the Sierra Leone protectorate after 1896.

Postwar Reforms and Postcolonial Regime Trends in Jamaica and Sierra Leone

Both Jamaica and Sierra Leone introduced mass electoral competition prior to independence, but their decolonization processes were built on very different legal-administrative foundations. This generated distinctive forms of nationalist politics after World War II, and distinctive regime trajectories after independence. In both colonies, outgoing British officials favored conservative reformers over radical nationalist leaders who might have threatened British interests after independence. Despite these similarities, Jamaica introduced universal suffrage and mass electoral competition significantly earlier than Sierra Leone. Moreover, Sierra Leone gained independence under an elite ruling party that maintained the political authority of paramount chiefs in the country's rural districts.

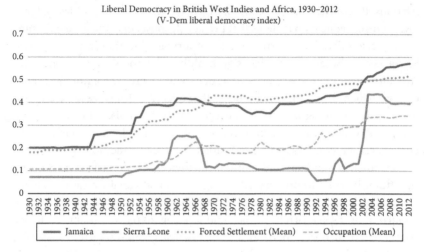

Figure 5.2 Liberal democracy in Jamaica and Sierra Leone

Figure 5.2 graphs the distinctive regime trajectories of Jamaica and Sierra Leone from 1930 until 2012, using the liberal democracy index from the Varieties of Democracy (V-DEM) dataset (Coppedge et al. 2016). V-DEM's liberal democracy index provides an aggregate measure of democracy that encompasses free, fair, and competitive elections with widespread electoral participation, the protection of individual civil liberties (including freedom of expression and freedom of association), and checks and balances on executive authority. The V-DEM liberal democracy index suggests that Jamaica's electoral system, and protection of individual civil liberties was significantly more inclusive than in Sierra Leone from the 1930s until independence in the 1960s. Jamaica has also maintained solid to high democracy scores since gaining independence from British rule in 1962. Consequently, postcolonial Jamaica has maintained significant democratic advantages relative to Sierra Leone, which failed to consolidate democracy after independence.

Postwar Reforms and Jamaica's Democratic Transition to Independence

Jamaica's independence transition was led by elected politicians from rival political parties with deep ties to the country's labor unions and middle-class professional associations. Jamaica's first prime minister, Alexander Bustamante, was a conservative populist and moneylender who mobilized the island's agricultural and industrial workers into a nationwide labor organization that he established following the labor unrest of the 1930s. His cousin Norman Manley established Jamaica's first mass political party, the People's National Party (PNP), in 1938. Initially, Bustamante's Industrial Trade Union was affiliated with Manley's PNP, but the two men broke ranks to contest Jamaica's first universal suffrage election in 1944. Bustamante used his control over unionized agricultural and factory workers to mobilize political support for his conservative Jamaica Labor Party (JLP) in the 1944 elections (Dawson 2016, 190–200; Rueschemeyer, Stephens, and Stephens 1992, 237–38). Bustamante promised his working-class supporters that their demands for better wages and improved living conditions would be better met within the existing capitalist framework, and without the additional burden of self-government. By contrast, Manley's PNP campaigned for political reforms, self-government, and greater public ownership within the domestic economy (Wallace 1977, 58; Sives 2010, 8–10; Edie 1994, 26–27; Munroe and Bertram 2006, 80, 121–23). Bustamante's JLP won Jamaica's first democratic election in 1944, and held power for two consecutive terms until 1955. In response to their electoral losses, Manley established his own affiliated trade unions—representing teachers, nurses, and other government employees—to mobilize middle-class votes for the social democratic PNP (Rueschemeyer, Stephens, and Stephens 1992, 37–38). Consequently, both of Jamaica's political parties mobilized unionized workers from different economic sectors. At the same time, however, both party leaders were firmly committed to mass electoral competition (Ledgister 1998, 73–74, 86–87), although late colonial Jamaica developed an institutionalized pattern of partisan electoral violence that polarized the country after independence (see Dawson 2016; Sives 2010).[17]

Jamaica's elected postwar governments successfully lobbied the British government for greater political autonomy leading up to the island state's independence in 1962. The first JLP governments (1944–55) resisted calls for independence in exchange for promoting economic growth and distributing patronage benefits (i.e., jobs, contracts, and public housing) to their political supporters (Ledgister 1998, 72–73; Dawson 2016; Sives 2010). Manley's PNP openly called for Jamaica's independence from Britain, but the party also adopted the JLP's style of distributing patronage benefits to its supporters after gaining power in 1955 (Dawson 2016; Ledgister 1998, 71–75).

In the years after 1955, both of Jamaica's political parties emerged into "cross-class, vote-getting machines" that mobilized their political supporters in favor of independence from Britain (Ledgister 1998, 74). Both political party leaders used their control over labor unions and professional associations to reward their political supporters with patronage benefits.[18] Consequently, the socioeconomic distinctions between the two parties became increasingly blurred, as the social democratic PNP adopted stronger protections for property rights, and the working-class JLP maintained conservative economic and social policies that attracted support from agricultural and business elites.

By the late 1950s, there was only important political difference between the PNP and the JLP: Norman Manley's PNP wanted to pursue Jamaica's independence within a larger federation of British West Indies colonies that included Barbados and Trinidad and Tobago, whereas Bustamante's JLP campaigned for Jamaica's independence as a sovereign state during a 1961 referendum on the British West Indies federation (Sives 2010, 56–59; Wallace 1977, 207–8; Ledgister 1998, 75–76). Jamaican voters ultimately rejected the island's continued membership in the British West Indies Federation, which paved the way for Bustamante's return to power in April 1962. During the next four months, a bipartisan committee of legislators from both parties agreed to a constitution that established a bicameral legislature, enshrined the rights of political opposition leaders, and established a bill of rights that protected individual civil liberties (Ledgister 1998, 76). Jamaica gained independence under Bustamante's leadership on August 6, 1962, but Norman Manley continued to serve as the leader of the opposition until his retirement in 1969 (Ledgister 1998, 77). Manley's gracious acceptance of Bustamante's electoral victory helped to consolidate and legitimize Jamaica's democratic institutions after independence (Sives 2010; Dawson 2016).

The Maintenance of Chiefly Control in Postwar Sierra Leone

Whereas Jamaica's political leaders shared a common vision for the country's political future after World War II, Sierra Leone's paramount chiefs and Creole nationalist politicians had very different visions for the country's political future. The deep social divide between Creole and indigenous African elites made it difficult for political leaders to build electoral support in both communities. Freetown's middle-class Krios were highly critical of indirect British rule, which excluded them from administrative positions and left them powerless against the political domination of paramount chiefs in the country's rural districts (Spitzer 1974; Cole 2013, 135–36, 138). The low level of education in the Sierra Leone protectorate only reinforced the vast social divide, and growing mistrust between Sierra Leone's Creole and indigenous African communities. The small number of Western-educated Africans mostly came from chiefly families, and they often regarded the colony's Krio minority as "foreigners." For the most part, British colonial officials favored Sierra Leone's protectorate elites throughout the decolonization process.

Whereas labor unrest in Jamaica gave way to democratic political reforms after World War II, British officials steadfastly resisted any constitutional reforms that might have strengthened Sierra Leone's Krio minority at the expense of indigenous African elites (Cole 2013, 140–43; Spitzer 1974, 184–90). Thus, when Krio labor organizer Isaac Wallace-Johnson became the first African politician to successfully organize trade unions in the colony and protectorate during the 1930s, British officials responded by removing Wallace-Johnson from office, and imprisoning him during World War II (Spitzer 1974, 184–85; Cole 2013, 140; Harris 2014, 29). After Wallace-Johnson was released from prison, the extension of voting rights in postwar Sierra Leone took a backseat to the more vexing question of how to distribute political power between protectorate and colony elites.

Sierra Leone's Creole and indigenous African political leaders disagreed vehemently over questions of citizenship rights and political representation in the emerging national polity. Krio politicians argued that their civil liberties and political rights should be respected throughout the country, and many assumed that they would become its "natural leaders" after independence, given their educational advantages. By contrast, protectorate African leaders began to assert their political rights as "natives" while dismissing the Creole minority as privileged "foreigners." As an example of this dynamic, one of Freetown's leading politicians, Dr. Bankole-Bright, favored an English-language literacy requirement (in addition to the existing tax and income qualifications) for voters and political candidates. Bankole-Bright reasoned that his proposed literacy requirement might incentivize educated protectorate politicians to side with Freetown's Creole middle class and elites, rather than with the rural indigenous masses and their chiefs. At the time, more than 80% of Sierra Leone's chiefs were illiterate, so their exclusion from mass politics would have empowered educated Krios in Sierra Leone's legislative council. Bankole-Bright argued that because Sierra Leone's protectorate chiefs were not British subjects, they should not be in a position to legislate over the rights of British subjects (i.e., Creoles) in the colony (Kilson 1969, 167).

In contrast to Bankole-Bright's position, Sierra Leone's protectorate chiefs mobilized their political support behind Sir Milton Margai's conservative SLPP, established in 1951. Margai openly blamed Sierra Leone's Krios (rather than the British) for the country's "backwardness," and he expressed regret that his forefathers had "given shelter to a handful of foreigners (i.e., Creoles) who ha[d] no will to cooperate with us and imagine[d] themselves to be our superiors because they are aping the Western mode of living" (Kilson 1969, 169). As the political rift between Margai and Bankole-Bright grew, many Creoles rallied behind Bankole-Bright's demands for a separate Krio state (Kilson 1969, 226–27).[19] British officials refused to entertain Krio separatist demands.

The mutually exclusive political visions of indigenous African and Creole political leaders turned Sierra Leone's electoral politics into a zero-sum game after Sierra Leone's colony and protectorate merged into a single national polity. Sierra Leone's first limited suffrage elections were dominated by chiefly elites, who coalesced under Sir Milton Margai's conservative SLPP. Most Freetown Krios continued to support Bankole-Bright, despite his confrontational attitude toward protectorate African elites (Kilson 1969, 226–30). Throughout the 1950s, Bankole-Bright and other Creole opposition leaders continued to disagree with Milton Margai's SLPP about voter eligibility, citizenship rights, and the role of chiefs in the country's emerging representative institutions. Their political compromises always left Sierra Leone's chiefs in a strong position, as the 1954 constitution maintained different voting criteria in urban and rural areas and reserved 12 out of 57 seats for paramount chiefs in the (partially elected) legislative council. These regionally distinctive voting criteria were maintained after universal suffrage was adopted in 1957. In the only universal suffrage election prior to Sierra Leone's independence, direct voting was limited to the capital city and surrounding towns. In the rest of the country, legislative representatives were indirectly elected by local district councils that were dominated by protectorate chiefs (Collier 1982, 39). Not surprisingly, the 1957 election generated a massive electoral victory for the conservative SLPP, which used chiefs to mobilize the country's rural masses against a divided and powerless Creole opposition (Reynolds 1999, 789). The SLPP captured 23 of Sierra Leone's 39 electoral districts (Reynolds 1999, 799), but the party also gained 12 additional seats that were automatically reserved for paramount chiefs (Cartwright 1970, 95–96).

Because of the SLPP's electoral dominance before and after independence, Sierra Leone developed a very different style of political mobilization and electoral competition from postwar Jamaica. The SLPP relied almost entirely on paramount chiefs to mobilize rural voters, thus eliminating the need for local grassroots chapters or political affiliations with organized labor unions. Chiefs were only too happy to support the SLPP, as the ruling party protected their interests and privileges (Lange 2009, 107; Cartwright 1970; Kilson 1969, 227–33). Indeed, most of the SLPP's electoral candidates, including Sir Milton Margai, came from chiefly families that had enjoyed privileged access to the protectorate's colonial schools. In the last election before Sierra Leone's independence, 59% of all electoral candidates and 72% of SLPP candidates came from chiefly families. After independence, 84% of the elected representatives in Sierra Leone's National Assembly came from chiefly families (Harris 2014, 38). Seen from this lens, it is hardly surprising that the SLPP never reformed Sierra Leone's rural authority structure.[20]

In the years leading up to independence, Sierra Leone's independence leader, Sir Milton Margai, began to face challenges from younger and more militant party members like Siaka Stevens, who defected from the party to establish the All People's Congress (APC) in 1960. Stevens also unveiled plans for a general strike after gaining political control over Freetown's municipal government. The

SLPP government responded by declaring a state of emergency and arresting and imprisoning Stevens and other APC representatives (Harris 2014, 43). Thus, in contrast to Jamaica, which established the principle of democratic electoral alternation prior to independence, Sierra Leone gained independence with its chief opposition leader behind bars.

The Jamaica Paradox: Democratic Consolidation Despite Ideological Polarization and Electoral Violence

Jamaica has maintained an unbroken tradition of parliamentary democracy with regular electoral alternation between the center-left PNP and center-right JLP, despite significant economic and political challenges after independence. Jamaica's postwar economic expansion ended shortly after independence, when rising oil prices generated ideological polarization between the social democratic PNP and the conservative JLP (Edie 1994, 31–37; Edie 1991, 87–141; Stone 1986, 151–77; Stephens and Stephens 1986).[21] Kingston's working-class neighborhoods became the site of a violent turf war between rival gangs affiliated with the PNP or JLP (Sives 2010; Fearon and Laitin 2006; Stone 1986, 56–58; Stephens and Stephens 1986, 45–46). These turf wars gained worldwide notoriety during the 1980 elections, in which more than 800 people were killed in partisan violence (Edie 1991, 107). Jamaica's ideological polarization and electoral violence subsided after 1980 (Sives 2010, esp. 118–42), but the island state continues to suffer from extreme levels of lethal criminal violence fueled by the international narcotics trade (Watson 2013).

Despite these challenges, Jamaica has maintained an unbroken parliamentary democracy since its independence from British rule. How was Jamaica able to consolidate democracy despite significant economic and political challenges after independence? In many ways, Jamaica's democratic consolidation was made possible by the historical legacy of liberal reforms that established a relatively effective and inclusive administrative state during the second half of the nineteenth century. British crown colony rule established a liberal-authoritarian state that protected the individual civil liberties and property rights of nonelites. This prevented white planter elites from dominating Jamaica's legal, political, and economic institutions following the establishment of direct British rule after 1866 (Rueschemeyer, Stephens, and Stephens 1992, 236–44; Ledgister 1998). Direct British rule also expanded the administrative capacity of colonial state officials to provide public goods like education, sanitation, and poor relief. Direct British rule also strengthened the rule of law in ways that enabled emancipated Afro-descendants to lobby state officials for social and political reform (Ledgister 1998, 13–19). This is why Jamaica's colonial authorities responded to the labor and political unrest of the 1930s by introducing mass electoral competition after World War II.

As a result of this institutional legacy, Jamaica experienced nearly two decades of "tutelary democracy" after World War II, when the country's political leaders supported the principles of mass electoral competition and inclusive political representation. Moreover, Jamaica's emerging political parties built effective patronage networks that distributed material benefits to their working- and middle-class supporters (see Edie 1991, 1994; Stone 1986; Sives 2010). The fact that the political supporters of both parties have benefited from this patronage system also generates political support for electoral competition and democratic alternation. The Jamaican political scientist Carlene Edie highlights the importance of Jamaica's elected representatives (both MPs and municipal councilors) as the primary link between ordinary citizens and patronage benefits:

> The MP's clout has become almost supreme in getting assistance for the poor. For the poor, the necessities of day-to-day life—documents required for admission to school or a hospital, for a passport, for application for a job, and so on—are not so easily achieved. It is often only by personal intervention of an influential intermediary that a poor person can obtain an immediate result. The poor person then becomes dependent on bureaucratic intermediation performed by the party politicians and their clients working in the state bureaucracy. The MP's intervention secures the political support of the constituent (Edie 1994, 29).

Consequently, the elected representatives from both of Jamaica's major political parties have played an important role in maintaining popular support for the legitimacy of Jamaica's electoral institutions by rewarding their political supporters with patronage benefits (see Dawson 2016; Edie 1991; Edie 1994, 25–43).

As with many mature democracies, popular support for Jamaican political parties has diminished over time, yet popular and elite support for Jamaica's constitutional order remains high. Writing in 1994, Carlene Edie described this as "a reflection of the strength of Jamaica's democracy. Instead of rejecting the system as a whole, [Jamaican] voters have consistently ousted the administration in power and replaced it with the opposition. The professional classes are now engaged in public debates about reform and the state of the economy, with the intended objective of extending democracy and not replacing it" (39). More recently, Freedom House's 2017 report gave Jamaica strong marks (34 out of 40) for protecting key political rights, including political pluralism and citizen participation in the electoral process. Jamaica does less well in protecting individual civil liberties (41 out of 60), given the widespread prevalence of gang violence, extrajudicial police killings (especially against poor, black, young men), and the state's failure to protect LGBT citizens from randomized violence.[22] Despite these imperfections, Freedom House has classified Jamaica's political system as "Free" since its rankings began in 1972 (Quality of Government 2015). Cheibub, Gandhi, and Vreeland (2010) also code Jamaica's political system as continuously democratic since its independence from Britain in 1962.

The continued popular support for Jamaica's democratic institutions also reflects the success of its postcolonial governments in boosting important aspects of human well-being, despite the country's significant economic limitations. Jamaica's economy went into a tailspin following the oil price shocks of the early 1970s, and the country experienced limited economic growth between 1973 and 2000 (Maddison 2006). During the late 1970s, for example, Michael Manley's PNP government invested heavily in primary health facilities in Jamaica's rural communities, and Jamaican governments built 365 new rural health clinics between 1978 and 2000. Most of these facilities focused on expanding maternal and childcare in Jamaica's rural communities. With support from the World Bank, UNICEF, and Dutch foreign aid, Jamaican governments continued to invest heavily in education and health, even as the country became heavily indebted during the 1980s (Riley 2005, 178–81). As a result of these investments, Jamaica's infant mortality rate declined from 78.3 deaths for every 1000 live births in 1955–60 to just 9.6 deaths for every 1,000 live births in 2015. Jamaica's life expectancy soared from 62.6 years in 1960 to 76.1 years in 2017, and secondary school enrollment increased from 15% of Jamaican youths in 1960 to nearly 80% by 2008 (United Nations 1967; United Nations 2017). This improvement in human well-being likely helped to bolster popular support for Jamaica's democratic institutions. After all, many existing studies demonstrate that the state's ability to provide developmental goods like schooling, healthcare, and sanitation is important for maintaining popular support for democracy over the *longue durée* (Przeworski et al. 2000; Glaeser, Ponzetto, and Shleifer 2007; Andersen et al. 2014).[23]

Political Violence and Regime Instability in Postcolonial Sierra Leone

Sierra Leone initially seemed to be a model of democratic multiparty competition compared to other African countries that established single-party authoritarian regimes shortly after independence. The small Western African country boasted a highly educated Krio elite, a relatively autonomous (albeit Krio-dominated) civil society, a free press, and regular electoral competition between the ruling SLPP and the opposition APC (Harris 2014, 48). Moreover, Sierra Leone's first postindependence government was decidedly pro-British and conservative: Sir Milton Margai maintained the capitalist and export-oriented economic policies from the colonial era, and supported the political dominance of local chiefs who mobilized rural voters in support of the SLPP. Underneath the surface, however, the ability to sustain democracy in Sierra Leone was limited by the outsized political influence of elite chiefs (who did not necessarily value or support democracy), and the increasingly "tribal" nature of Sierra Leone's political leadership after Milton Margai's death in 1964.

Sir Milton Margai's half brother, Albert Margai, took over the reins of power as prime minister and SLPP leader after 1964. Unfortunately, Albert lacked his brother's broad-based legitimacy as an independence hero and trusted elder statesman, so the SLPP adopted a more "tribalist" approach to government. Many of the northern and Temne members of Sierra Leone's Cabinet were fired and replaced by coethnic Mendes from the country's southern region. The remaining British officers in Sierra Leone's armed forces and civil service were also retired and replaced by ethnic Mendes (Wyse 1991, 117; Kup 1975, 215; Harris 2014, 54). Albert Margai also expanded the assembly powers of chiefs and ordered them to "make life more difficult for the (opposition) APC in the countryside" (Harris 2014, 54). The new government also clamped down on press freedoms and jailed at least four opposition MPs for "unlawful assembly." More disturbingly, Albert Margai's government also initiated legislation to transform Sierra Leone into a single-party state (Harris 2014, 55).[24]

Sierra Leone's initial experiment with multiparty democracy ended in a series of military coups that followed a disputed parliamentary election in 1967. This election was disputed because the governor general invited opposition leader Siaka Stevens to form a new government before the results had been finalized for the election of paramount chiefs (Harris 2014, 55; Kup 1975, 216). Just minutes after Stevens' government had been sworn in, one of Margai's political appointees, Brigadier Lansana, staged a military coup and arrested Stevens and several members of his newly appointed Cabinet. Many Sierra Leoneans regarded the coup as a show of support for Albert Margai, and 10 of the 12 paramount chiefs declared their support for Margai's SLPP just hours after the coup (Harris 2014, 57). Forty-eight hours later, Lt. Sam Hinga Norman staged a countercoup to prevent Albert Margai's return to power. The leader of the military junta denounced the corruption and nepotism of the deposed SLPP government, while extolling "the virtues of Paramount Chiefs" as "the natural rulers of the country" (Harris 2014, 60). Sierra Leone's independence constitution granted considerable political authority and influence to paramount chiefs who were constitutionally obliged to remain apolitical and support the victorious party in any election. Nevertheless, the close political ties between paramount chiefs and the SLPP hindered the peaceful transition of power following

Sierra Leone's disputed election in 1967 (Cartwright 1970, 251–55; Harris 2014, 57–50).

Siaka Stevens came to dominate Sierra Leone following the disputed election of 1967. Stevens established a brutal dictatorship under the political control of the APC and installed himself as Sierra Leone's life president in 1977. Despite his earlier support and popularity among Sierra Leone's urban youth, Stevens' APC government also came to rely heavily on paramount chiefs to maintain political influence in the countryside. After deposing a handful of powerful chiefs, Stevens persuaded the country's remaining chiefs to support him in exchange for patronage benefits (Lange 2009, 109). Consequently, even under APC rule, Sierra Leone's paramount chiefs continued to control land allocation in the countryside, extract resource rents, and underprovide public goods and services in rural areas. In fact, Stevens' APC government enacted local government reforms that eliminated the elected members of Sierra Leone's district councils and allowed chiefs to rule them as they wished. Chiefs were also given discretionary powers to distinguish between "natives" and "strangers" in their communities, and only those regarded as "natives" had access to land rights (Lange 2009, 108; Fanthorpe 2001, 381).

Various scholars have argued that increasing chiefly authority over customary courts, land rights, and inheritance contributed to the impoverishment of Sierra Leone's rural communities and generated many of the political grievances that contributed to support for the RUF insurgents during Sierra Leone's 1991–2002 civil war (see Richards 2005; Fanthorpe 2001). Paul Richards' (2005) research also demonstrates that chiefly controlled customary courts imposed heavy fines and levies that kept rural "young men" in poverty and economically dependent on their chiefs and elders. Chiefly control over customary land rights, and in some cases, even marriage and inheritance laws, forced many rural young men from modest backgrounds to leave their communities, contributing to a growing population of shiftless, hungry, and underemployed young men in Freetown. Driven away from their ancestral homelands that protected their customary rights, yet trapped in a repressive authoritarian dictatorship that denied their individual civil liberties and political rights, Freetown's growing population of poor and underemployed migrants from the countryside were completely disenfranchised by both the modern and traditional authority structures. In other words, they were "neither citizens nor subjects" with few legal protections under civil or customary law (Fanthorpe 2001).

Despite the collapse of Sierra Leone's once-profitable agricultural sector, Stevens was able to maintain power by positioning himself atop a complex patron-client system that was financed by the diamond trade. To begin with, Stevens emasculated the country's armed forces and established an elite presidential guard that was personally loyal to him (Lange 2009, 109). This protected his government from the threat of a military coup. It also enabled him to amass incredible wealth from his neopatrimonial control over Sierra Leone's alluvial diamonds trade. At the same time, many of Sierra Leone's rural producers were increasingly impoverished by the state's extractive marketing boards, which depressed agricultural prices and impoverished rural producers. Stevens' government even tore up colonial-era railway lines that benefited Mende coffee and cocoa farmers in rural districts that supported the opposition SLPP (Acemoglu and Robinson 2012, 336–37). As highlighted in previous research (see Bates 1981, 2008; Collier and Gunning 1999; Englebert 2000), these extractive policies had devastating economic consequences that impoverished the entire country. Between 1977 and 1986, Sierra Leone's public revenues declined by more than 80%. The drastic reduction in public revenues, coupled with rising levels of foreign debt, forced the government to reduce real social spending by 85% during the 1980s, resulting in a generation of Sierra Leonean children and youth losing access to free primary education and primary healthcare. Indeed, by the end of the 1980s, only 40% of Sierra Leone's children were enrolled in primary schools (Harris 2014, 74–75).

The APC regime was finally toppled in 1992, when the RUF, a rebel army of Sierra Leonean exiles and political dissidents, invaded the country from neighboring Liberia. The RUF pledged to overthrow the bankrupt APC and restore multiparty democracy. Yet they brutalized and terrorized Sierra Leone's civilian population in their efforts to control Sierra Leone's valuable diamond resources. The RUF relied heavily on child soldiers, who were often abducted from their villages, drugged, and forced to kill their parents at gunpoint (Fanthorpe 2001, 364). Sierra Leone's security forces responded with predictable violence, but the armed forces had been so thoroughly emasculated by the APC regime that they were unable to defeat the RUF. Consequently, the bloody civil war dragged on for more than a decade. The RUF was only defeated in 2002, following military intervention by Nigerian and Economic Community of West African States Monitoring Group forces, reinforced by British troops and United Nations peacekeepers (Abebajo 2002, 79–104). More than 75,000 Sierra Leoneans lost their lives during this conflict, and over 2 million people were displaced. In the aftermath of this conflict, Sierra Leone remains one of the most impoverished and underdeveloped countries on the planet, ranking 184th out of 188 countries in the United Nation's Human Development Index for 2012.[25]

Summary and Discussion

This chapter began with a puzzling empirical question. Why did British forced settlement generate favorable long-term development and greater postcolonial democratization in Jamaica relative to British colonial occupation in Sierra Leone? The early colonization of each country would lead us to expect significantly better development outcomes in Sierra Leone because the West African country was initially colonized as a British settlement for emancipated slaves and liberated Africans. Nevertheless, Jamaica experienced a significant increase in education and literacy following the abolition of slavery in 1834, and the island state has successfully maintained a competitive electoral democracy since its independence from British rule in 1962. By contrast, Sierra Leone had one of the lowest literacy rates in British Africa at the time of its independence in 1961, and the country has suffered from significant regime instability that has limited its postcolonial democratization.

The comparative-historical evidence in this chapter suggests that the divergent developmental trajectories of Jamaica and Sierra Leone result from the distinctive legal-administrative institutions and state-society relations that emerged in each colony during the nineteenth and early twentieth centuries. Although Jamaica was initially colonized using imported slave labor, British colonial officials implemented liberal reforms that expanded the legal rights and political agency of Jamaica's emancipated Afro-descendants following the abolition of slavery in 1834. British legal reforms strengthened individual civil liberties like property rights, religious liberty, and freedom of expression, which enabled many emancipated slaves to become small property holders and to lobby colonial state officials for labor and political reforms. Direct British rule also expanded the administrative capacity of colonial state officials to provide public goods like primary schools, sanitation, and poor relief during the late nineteenth century. Although voting rights and political representation remained limited until World War II, three-quarters of Jamaican youths and adults (aged 10 and up) were already literate when Jamaica held its first universal suffrage election in 1944 (see Engerman, Mariscal, and Sokoloff 2009, 103). Jamaica also experienced nearly two decades of "tutelary democracy" between 1944 and 1962, holding five competitive universal suffrage elections prior to independence. The lengthy period of tutelary democracy helped to institutionalize democratic practices and electoral alternation prior to independence. It also enabled the country's two major political parties to establish deep roots in the country's labor unions and professional associations, and both parties have used their affiliated unions to distribute patronage benefits to their supporters. This distribution of patronage benefits, coupled with the significant expansion of state-funded public goods like education, healthcare, and subsidized housing, has helped to maintain grassroots popular support for Jamaica's democratic institutions over the *longue durée* (see Dawson 2016; Sives 2010; Edie 1991, 1994; Stone 1986).

In Sierra Leone, by contrast, direct British control was only established in the capital city of Freetown, where emancipated slaves and liberated Africans lived under British laws and institutions. Direct British rule facilitated the significant expansion of primary schooling in the Sierra Leone colony during the first half of the nineteenth century, but direct British rule was never extended to the indigenous African territories that were annexed in 1896. By contrast, indirect British rule limited the administrative capacity of the colonial state and strengthened the arbitrary and despotic power of indigenous elites (i.e., paramount chiefs) in Sierra Leone's rural communities. The legal-administrative distinction between Sierra Leone's directly ruled colony and indirectly ruled protectorate generated a deep social divide between Sierra Leone's highly educated (and predominantly urban) Creole minority and its indigenous (and rural) African majority. There was limited access to primary schooling in Sierra Leone's rural indigenous districts, where paramount chiefs remained influential, and illiteracy remained widespread into the 1950s. Perhaps not surprisingly then, Sierra Leone's urban-based Creole-dominated political parties were unable to mobilize rural African votes prior to independence. Instead, Sierra Leone's paramount chiefs mobilized the country's rural voters in support of the conservative SLPP before and after independence.

Whereas Jamaica's elected representatives used trade unions and professional associations to distribute patronage benefits to their supporters, Sierra Leone's political parties used paramount chiefs to fulfill this role. At the same time, the political leadership of Sierra Leone's political parties—both the SLPP and the APC—became less and less committed to democracy as their political leadership became increasingly "tribalized" after 1964. Consequently, Sierra Leone's political parties were never able to mobilize popular support for democracy among the country's rural masses. Under SLPP rule (1957–66) and throughout the long period of single-party APC rule (1968–92), Sierra Leone's paramount chiefs have remained the primary patronage brokers and agents of local government, as the administrative capacity of the national government has remained extremely limited. This has continued to hinder the state's ability to provide developmental goods like education, healthcare, and sanitation in Sierra Leone's rural communities, contributing to poor developmental outcomes over the *longue durée* (see Lange 2009, ch. 5; Acemoglu, Reed, and Robinson 2014).

Table 5.3 summarizes the colonial legal-administrative institutions, Protestant missionary history, and postcolonial developmental trajectories of Jamaica and Sierra Leone, as well as the median developmental outcomes associated with British forced settlement and colonial occupation in the West Indies and sub-Saharan Africa. This sample includes all former British African and Caribbean colonies apart from South Africa and Belize, which are classified as mixed colonies. The distinction between forced settlement and colonial occupation largely corresponds with the regional divide between the West Indies and sub-Saharan Africa, although Creole African islands (i.e., Mauritius and the Seychelles) are classified as forced settlement colonies, as outlined in Chapter 2. In Table 5.3, the long-term developmental trajectories of Jamaica and Sierra Leone are broadly similar to other British colonies that experienced similar modes of colonization. Like Jamaica, most British forced settlement colonies developed a comprehensive network of primary schools that generated extremely high rates of adult literacy prior to independence. Most British forced settlement colonies also experienced at least 15 years of tutelary democracy prior to independence, generating a median postcolonial democracy score of 9.32/10.0 between 1972 and 2012. By contrast, the median adult literacy rate for British occupation colonies in sub-Saharan Africa was only 21% in 1960, and the median postcolonial democracy score for these countries was only 3.85/10.0 between 1972 and 2012.

The data trends in Table 5.3 are consistent with the statistical results demonstrating superior developmental outcomes and greater postcolonial democratization in forced settlement colonies relative to colonial occupation in Chapter 4. They are also consistent with the theoretical argument that the superior developmental outcomes in forced settlement colonies are the result of liberal reforms that extended metropolitan legal rights to emancipated populations following the abolition of slavery. Direct British rule extended metropolitan legal rights that protected the civil liberties of emancipated populations following the abolition of slavery. Direct British rule also strengthened the administrative capacity of colonial state officials to provide developmental goods like primary schooling, which generated high adult literacy rates in forced settlement colonies prior to independence. British forced settlement colonies also experienced a lengthy period of "tutelary democracy," which helped to strengthen democratic political norms and institutions prior to independence. Consequently, the extension of metropolitan legal rights to emancipated slaves and the introduction of direct British rule generated a legal-administrative structure that promoted inclusive development and facilitated postcolonial democratization in British forced settlement colonies. By contrast, British colonial occupation often relied heavily on an indirect rule, which previous studies have associated with poor developmental outcomes, ineffective governance, and limited postcolonial democratization (see Lange 2009; Mamdani 1996).

The data trends in Table 5.3 also suggest that Protestant missionary evangelization may have contributed to Jamaica's more inclusive long-term development and greater postcolonial democratization relative to Sierra Leone. Protestant missionaries played a significant role in educating emancipated populations in both colonies, but Protestant missionary activity was more widespread in Jamaica than in Sierra Leone, at least during the 1920s. Nevertheless, the data models in Chapter 4 showed that Protestant missionary evangelization did not significantly affect colonial education and postcolonial democracy independently from the impact of extending metropolitan legal rights to emancipated populations.

Table 5.3 Colonial Institutions and postcolonial development in Jamaica and Sierra Leone, with median outcomes for British Caribbean and African colonies

British African and Caribbean colonies	Colonial Population and Legal-Admin. Institutions		Protestant Missionary History		Education Attainment and Democratic Experience prior to Independence		Postcolonial Democracy and Development	
	Pop. 1900	% Indirect Rule, 1955	Protestant missionaries per 10,000 inhabitants, 1923	Years of exposure to Protestant missions, 1960	Adult Literacy Rate, 1960	Years of Tutelary Democracy before independence	Mean Democracy Score, 1972-2012 (FHIP)	HDI, 2012
Jamaica (forced settlement)	720	0%	1.81	206	82%	18	8.80	0.721 (High)
Sierra Leone (occupation)	1026	81%	0.70	165	7%	4	3.92	0.407 (Low)
British forced settlement colonies (median)	53	0%	1.81	173	86%	17	9.32	0.756 (High)
British-occupied colonies (median)	888	62.5%	0.57	99	21%	1	3.85	0.505 (Low)

Sources: 1900 population estimates from Barrett, Johnson and Kurian (2001); % Indirect rule from Lange (2009), p. 48; Protestant missionary data are from Woodberry (2012); 1960 Adult literacy rates from United Nations (1967); Tutelary Democracy is calculated based on electoral data from Przeworski et al's *Political Institutions and Political and Political Events (PIPE)* dataset; FHIP scores are obtained from the *Quality of Government* dataset, *http://qog.pol.gu.se/data/datadownloads/qogstandarddata*); 2012 HDI scores from https://en.wikipedia.org/wiki/List_of_countries_by_Human_Development_Index

Consequently, the distinctive developmental legacies of British forced settlement and British occupation seem to stem from the legal-administrative differences between direct British rule in the former and indirect British rule in the latter. These legal-administrative differences resulted in superior long-term development and greater postcolonial democratization in forced settlement colonies relative to colonies of occupation. Although Protestant missionary evangelization helped to expand primary schooling in postabolition Jamaica, this does not explain why forced settlement also generated better developmental outcomes than the colonial occupation in countries with limited Protestant missionary evangelization. The next chapter turns to this question by exploring the divergent developmental legacies of Portuguese forced settlement in Cape Verde and Portuguese colonial occupation in Guinea-Bissau.

6

Comparing Portuguese Forced Settlement and Colonial Occupation

Cape Verde and Guinea-Bissau

This chapter explores the divergent developmental legacies of Portuguese forced settlement in Cape Verde and Portuguese colonial occupation in Guinea-Bissau. The geographic proximity between the two countries, and their shared historical and cultural and ties provide a strong empirical incentive for comparing the developmental legacies of Portuguese forced settlement and Portuguese colonial occupation. The Cape Verdean islands are a Creole African archipelago nation in the Atlantic ocean, about 600 kilometers west of Dakar, Senegal (see Map 6.1). These islands were uninhabited at the time of their "discovery" by Portuguese explorers in the 1460s, and Portuguese colonists developed the islands with imported slave labor from the nearby "Guinea Coast" of West Africa. For more than three centuries, the Cape Verdean islands were a strategic entrepôt and supply station for transatlantic slave ships en route to the New World (Mentel 1984, 84). Five centuries of Portuguese colonization generated a hybrid Creole society of mixed Portuguese and African ancestry in the archipelago.[1] Cape Verde emerged from Portuguese rule as the second poorest country in sub-Saharan Africa, but the Creole African nation now boasts the highest living standard in West Africa. It is also the only consolidated democracy in Lusophone (i.e., Portuguese-speaking) Africa.

One thousand kilometers southeast of Cape Verde, the small West African nation of Guinea-Bissau occupies 28,120 square kilometers of swampy coast and interior savanna, sandwiched between the Republic of Guinea and Senegal's Casamance region. The entire "Guinea Coast" of West Africa has a long history of interaction with Portuguese slave-traders, Creole merchants, and Catholic missionaries dating back to the fifteenth century. After Britain gained control of the Gambia River basin and present-day Sierra Leone, and France occupied Senegal and the territories that make up the Republic of Guinea, Portugal's territory was reduced to the coastal territories and interior savanna that make up present-day Guinea-Bissau. This territory was primarily inhabited by indigenous African ethnicities (e.g., Pepels, Fulas, Balantas, Mandingas), and a small Luso-African Creole minority of Cape Verdean ancestry.[2] Guinean Creoles share

Ruling Emancipated Slaves and Indigenous Subjects. Olukunle P. Owolabi, Oxford University Press.
© Oxford University Press 2023. DOI: 10.1093/oso/9780197673027.003.0006

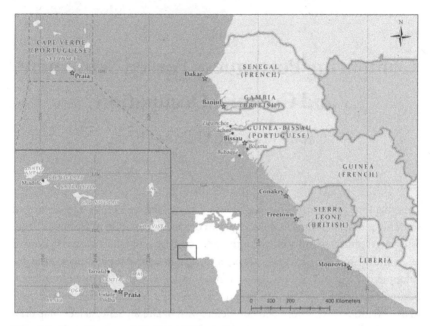

Map 6.1 Cape Verde and the West African Coast

a common language and culture with their Cape Verdeans relatives, and most Guinean Creoles developed a binational identity that resulted from their close family ties and shared political aspirations with Cape Verde. Guinea-Bissau and Cape Verde also share a common history of anticolonial resistance against Portugal's *Estado Novo* dictatorship (1930–74). The two countries fought a joint liberation struggle against Portuguese colonial rule, and the African Party for the Independence of Guinea-Bissau and Cape Verde—more commonly known by its Portuguese acronym, PAIGC—established single-party authoritarian control over both countries during the mid-1970s.

Despite these shared experiences, Cape Verde and Guinea-Bissau have experienced very different developmental and political trajectories since their independence from Portuguese rule. Cape Verde's ruling party was able to promote robust economic growth and social improvements that significantly boosted human well-being after independence. Cape Verde's ruling elites were also far more tolerant of political contestation; Cape Verde was one of the first African countries to experience democratic electoral turnover during the 1990s. Since then, Cape Verde has matured into one of Africa's most competitive and strongly consolidated democracies (Evora 2004; Baker 2006; Meyns 2002). By contrast, Guinea-Bissau struggled to promote inclusive broad-based development, and the country has been plagued by chronic regime instability, frequent military coups, and predatory strongman rule (Forrest 2002, 2003, 2010). Like Sierra Leone in the previous chapter, Guinea-Bissau remains one of the most impoverished and underdeveloped countries on the planet after more than 45 years of independence from Portuguese rule.

This chapter explores the historical and institutional factors that contributed to Cape Verde's favorable postcolonial development relative to Guinea-Bissau, formerly known as Portuguese Guinea. The statistical evidence in Chapter 4 demonstrates that Portuguese forced settlement colonies—i.e., Cape Verde and São Tomé and Príncipe—lagged behind their British counterparts in expanding literacy, developing the economy, and democratizing the postcolonial society. This is because Portugal was significantly weaker and poorer than other major colonial powers like Britain and France. Moreover, Portugal, like its Iberian neighbor, Spain, did not experience significant liberalization and industrialization during the nineteenth century. Consequently, the Portuguese state remained heavily dependent on the extraction of resources and coercive labor practices in its vast overseas empire. To a greater extent than their British counterparts, Portugal's African colonies continued to rely on forced labor migration and coercive labor practices throughout the nineteenth and twentieth centuries. For most of the twentieth century, the Portuguese state and colonial empire were governed by a conservative, corporatist, and highly repressive political regime—the *Estado Novo* dictatorship (1930–74)—which limited electoral competition in Portugal and its overseas colonies. The comparative-historical evidence in this chapter explores these factors in greater detail and acknowledges the extent to which they hindered the long-term development and postcolonial democratization of Portuguese African colonies.

At the same time, however, the comparative-historical evidence in this chapter demonstrates distinctive patterns of institutional development and state-society relations in Cape Verde and Portuguese Guinea. Cape Verde is primarily inhabited by the mixed-race Creole descendants of Portuguese colonists and African slaves who were brought to the islands as plantation laborers, and it is the only Luso-African state that developed and a uniform legal-administrative framework with inclusive citizenship rights following the Portuguese abolition of slavery. By contrast, colonial occupation generated restrictive citizenship laws and bifurcated legal-administrative institutions that privileged emancipated Creoles over indigenous African subjects in Portuguese Guinea-Bissau.

The comparative-historical evidence in this chapter demonstrates that Cape Verde's uniform administrative structure and inclusive citizenship laws facilitated greater access to state-funded education and more inclusive voting rights in colonial Cape Verde than in Portuguese Guinea. Portugal's more effective administrative control over Cape Verde also prevented the type of anticolonial violence that broke out in Guinea-Bissau (and other Portuguese-occupied African

colonies) after 1961. I argue that Cape Verde's longer history of effective administrative control and inclusive citizenship rights facilitated inclusive development
and democratization after independence. By contrast, Guinea-Bissau inherited a
weak and ineffective postcolonial state that continues to suffer from chronic regime instability and persistent underdevelopment. These case studies highlight
the extent to which inclusive legal-administrative institutions can facilitate postcolonial development and democratization in countries that experienced labor-
repressive economic underdevelopment and limited democratization prior to
independence.

Extractive Colonization and Underdevelopment in Portuguese African Colonies

Existing studies highlight four factors that contributed to the underdevelopment of Portuguese African colonies relative to their British counterparts.
First, Portugal was the poorest and weakest of Europe's colonial powers during
the twentieth century (Newitt 1981). Whereas Britain's Industrial Revolution
propelled its emergence into the world's dominant imperial power after 1815,
Portugal did not industrialize until the 1960s.[3] Consequently, Portugal remained
a comparatively impoverished country with very little capital to invest in
Portuguese African colonies. Instead, the political economy of Portuguese colonialism remained heavily dependent on forced labor and resource extraction
(Duignan and Gann 1975, 8–10).

Second, Portugal's democratization was significantly delayed relative to other
Western European colonizers.[4] As the poorest and least developed country in
Western Europe, Portugal did not experience the significant expansion of political representation and voting rights that followed Britain's Industrial Revolution.
Portugal's constitutional monarchy maintained significant restrictions on parliamentary representation and voting rights throughout the nineteenth century, and
the country's first democratic experiment was short-lived (Tavares de Almeida
2011). The First Portuguese Republic (1910–26) was overthrown in a military
coup that established a repressive and reactionary single-party dictatorship that
lasted until 1974. Moreover, the long-standing leader of Portugal's *Estado Novo*
dictatorship (1930–74), Antonio de Salazar, strongly resisted African demands
for political reforms and independence.[5] The rejection of African demands for
political reform and democratic representation generated anticolonial wars
against Portuguese colonial rule during the 1960s. The repressive nature of the
Portuguese dictatorship, coupled with the country's long-standing underdevelopment, ultimately hindered the long-term development and democratization
of Portuguese African colonies.

Third, Portuguese African colonies relied on coercive labor recruitment, forced migration, and forced cultivation long after these practices were phased out in British colonies (see Newitt 1981; Carreira 1982; Ferreira 1974; Duffy 1959, 1961, 1967). Whereas British forced settlement colonies implemented legal-administrative reforms following the abolition of slavery, the Portuguese abolition of slavery was linked to ambitious plans to expand their colonial plantations with indigenous African labor.[6] The dominant view among Portuguese colonial officials was that compulsory labor, rather than state-funded education, was the most effective way to develop African colonies (Silva Cunha 1949, 153). Consequently, Portuguese officials established a special labor bureau to recruit indigenous Africans for indentured plantation labor in São Tomé and Príncipe (Seibert 2006, 46; Silva Cunha 1949, 141–44). Portuguese officials also established a Native Labor Code that enforced compulsory labor recruitment in Angola, Mozambique, and Portuguese Guinea after 1899. These labor practices persisted into the 1960s.

Whereas existing studies emphasize the coercive and repressive labor practices in Portuguese African colonies (Newitt 1981; Carreira 1982; Ferreira 1974; Duffy 1959, 1961, 1967), my research presents important legal distinctions between "civilized" and "indigenous" populations in the Portuguese colonial empire (see Duffy 1961). Creole African populations (i.e., emancipated Afro-descendants in Cape Verde and São Tomé and Príncipe, and mixed-race Creoles in other Portuguese African colonies) were exempted from the Native Labor Code that subjected indigenous colonial populations to forced labor recruitment. Chinese and Indian populations were also exempted from the Native Labor Code, given the importance of Portugal's commercial relations with China (via Macau) and India (via the former Portuguese colony in present-day Goa). Consequently, Chinese, Indian, and Creole African populations were legally classified as *civilisados*, i.e., civilized populations with the same legal rights as white Portuguese citizens. By contrast, indigenous Africans and Timorese were subject to the harsh provisions of Portugal's repressive *indigenato* legal code. This legal distinction between *civilisados* (i.e., metropolitan citizens) and *indigenas* (i.e., indigenous subjects) was maintained until 1961 (O'Laughlin 2000, 12), and it favored the long-term development of Portuguese forced settlement colonies (i.e., Cape Verde and São Tomé and Príncipe) and city-state colonies (i.e., Goa and Macau) relative to Portuguese-occupied colonies like Angola, Mozambique, Guinea-Bissau, and Timor-Leste (see Owolabi 2017).

The comparative-historical evidence in this chapter demonstrates that Cape Verde's inclusive citizenship laws contributed to more inclusive development outcomes relative to Portuguese-occupied colonies like Guinea-Bissau. Whereas plantation slavery was phased out in Cape Verde during the eighteenth and nineteenth centuries, forced labor recruitment became even more pervasive and widespread in Portuguese African colonies with large indigenous populations, rich natural resource endowments, and sizable European settler minorities (i.e., Angola and Mozambique).[7] In Portuguese Guinea, forced labor recruitment was also used to supply Guinean Creole plantation owners and managers with indigenous African laborers. Labor conscripts were often paid with food, rather than cash, and state officials could conscript laborers for two months' work on public projects (Bigman 1993, 53–59). Indigenous Africans remained subject to forced labor recruitment in Guinea-Bissau and other Portuguese-occupied colonies until 1961.

By contrast, Creole Africans were largely protected from forced labor recruitment after 1869. Because Cape Verdeans were legally recognized as Portuguese citizens, they could seek employment in the colonial administration, and they could not be forced to work as indentured laborers. Nevertheless, the Cape Verdean islands became increasingly impoverished by Portuguese administrative neglect, political repression, and poor resource management following the abolition of slavery. More than 30,000 Cape Verdeans died from famine and starvation during the 1860s, and there were 80,000 more famine deaths during the first half of the twentieth century (Davidson 1989, 38–39, 63; Carreira 1982, 167). Instead of providing poor relief, Portuguese officials responded to these crippling famines by encouraging starving Cape Verdeans to "volunteer" for indentured plantation labor in other Portuguese African colonies. Historians estimate that more than 120,000 Cape Verdeans left the islands for indentured plantation labor in Angola or São Tomé and Príncipe between 1940 and 1973 (Davidson 1989, 63).[8] Educated and middle-class Cape Verdeans fared somewhat better, as their education and Portuguese citizenship facilitated government employment or emigration to the United States or Western Europe. In fact, most of Cape Verde's middle class—more than 130,000 people—emigrated to the United States or Western Europe between 1940 and 1973 (Carreira 1982, 178). As a result of Portugal's repressive labor policies and the mass emigration of its colonial middle class, Cape Verde gained independence with the second lowest per capita income in sub-Saharan Africa (Maddison 2006).

The long-term development of Portuguese African colonies was also hindered by the limited extent of Protestant missionary evangelization during the colonial era. Neither Cape Verde nor Guinea-Bissau had any Protestant missionaries at the beginning of the twentieth century (Woodberry 2012), and this likely undermined the expansion of education and the postcolonial democratization of Portuguese African colonies. Despite the limited extent of Protestant missionary evangelization in Portuguese Africa, my research reveals that Cape Verde's inclusive citizenship laws generated significantly greater access to state-funded primary schools than in Portuguese-occupied colonies like Angola, Mozambique, or Guinea-Bissau. By 1960, Cape Verde's adult literacy rate was 27%, compared with 3% in Angola, 8% in Mozambique, and 5% in Guinea-Bissau (United Nations 1967). My research also reveals that Cape Verde's inclusive citizenship laws expanded primary school access during the colonial year, despite the lack of Protestant missionary evangelization in the archipelago nation. This suggests that effective legal-administrative institutions and inclusive citizenship laws can expand access to state-funded education, even in impoverished societies with limited exposure to Protestant missionaries.

Colonial State and Society in Cape Verde and Guinea-Bissau

The remainder of this chapter traces the distinctive development of colonial state and society in Cape Verde and Portuguese Guinea (i.e., present-day Guinea-Bissau). I also explore the impact of these distinctive trajectories for colonial education, voting rights, anticolonial resistance, and postcolonial development.

Cape Verde

Like most forced settlement colonies, Cape Verde developed very different legal-administrative institutions and state-society relations than those of nearby Guinea-Bissau. Because the Cape Verdean islands were uninhabited prior to colonization, Portuguese civil and clerical institutions were introduced *tabula rasa* during the sixteenth century. The first municipal government was established in Ribiera Grande, the first Portuguese municipality in the tropics, in 1533, and local mulattos have served in municipal administration from 1546 (Seibert 2014, 48-49). Portuguese official records demonstrate that Cape Verde was organized into municipalities (i.e., *concelhos*) and parishes (*freguesias*), which formed the basis of colonial administration during the nineteenth century (see Cabo Verde, Secretaría do Governo Geral 1881, 1890).[9] From the very beginning, Cape Verde's colonial economy and society were sustained by the transatlantic slave trade. Enslaved Africans comprised more than 80% of Cape Verde's population by the late 1580s, when Cape Verde became an important strategic entrepôt in the Portuguese Atlantic slave trade. Over time, however, Cape Verde's dry climate and rugged terrain proved unsuitable for intensive plantation agriculture, so the proportion of slaves declined to less than 10% of the archipelago's population by the early 1800s (Mentel 1984, 84-89; Seibert 2014, 51-54).

With the decline of slavery in the 1800s, Cape Verde developed the most inclusive citizenship laws of any Portuguese African colony. This was partly an unintended consequence of Napoleon's invasion of the Iberian Peninsula, which forced the Portuguese royal family into exile in Rio de Janeiro, Brazil, in 1808.

This empowered Brazilian political elites to increase their demands for political representation. With the royal family in exile in Brazil, Portuguese liberal reformers seized power in Lisbon and introduced a new constitution that extended political representation and citizenship rights to free Creoles in the Portuguese colonial empire. The liberal constitution of 1822 was intended to secure the political loyalty of Brazil's colonial elites, who opted instead for independence from Portugal rule (Nogueira da Silva 2011, 94). At the time of Brazil's independence, Cape Verde was primarily inhabited by emancipated Creoles of mixed Portuguese and African descent, so the small archipelago nation became the primary beneficiary of Portuguese liberal reforms during the nineteenth and early twentieth century. The Portuguese civil code became the sole legal system in Cape Verde following the abolition of slavery in 1869 (Nogueira da Silva 2011). And Portuguese republicans formally extended citizenship rights to all Cape Verdeans in 1914, after establishing a republican government in Lisbon. The extension of citizenship rights gave Cape Verdeans greater access to state-funded education and allowed them to compete for administrative positions throughout the Portuguese colonial empire (Davidson 1989, 40–44). As one might expect, metropolitan citizenship rights provided Cape Verdeans with educational and employment advantages that were denied to indigenous African subjects. In the words of the British historian Basil Davidson,

> Literate Cape Verdeans were employed in junior and sometimes even in senior administrative grades in every part of the empire, as far as Timor and Macau. Regarded as Portuguese citizens, although of low degree, a small but important segment of more or less urbanized Cape Verdeans could have access to primary education, and after the First World War, even to secondary education in the archipelago's single *lycée* at Mindelo on São Vicente Island. These and a few others, educated in Portugal, were to provide a catalytic element in crystallizing an immanent sense of Cape Verdean nationalism, and to lead, however, indirectly, to the slow building of anti-colonial revolution (Davidson 1989, 41).

Guinea-Bissau

Portuguese Guinea experienced a very different pattern of colonial state-building. Despite the fact that Portuguese officials claimed sovereignty over Cape Verde and the adjacent Guinea Coast of West Africa during the 1460s, the mainland territories were actually "governed" by colonial officials in Cape Verde until the first municipal government was established in Bissau in 1858 (Cabo Verde, Boletim Oficial 1858). This is because Portuguese military officials faced significant indigenous resistance to the territorial expansion of colonial rule on the

African mainland. According to Portuguese official records from the National Archives of Cape Verde, Portuguese military officials organized dozens of military campaigns to suppress indigenous African resistance during the second half of the nineteenth century (Cabo Verde, Boletim Oficial 1862, 1864, 1871). This resistance prevented the establishment of a separate colonial administration for Guinea-Bissau until 1879 (Cabo Verde, Boletim Oficial 1879).

The Portuguese "pacification" of Guinea-Bissau involved at least 81 separate military campaigns between 1879 and 1920. During this time, de facto Portuguese control remained limited to the coastal towns of Bissau, Cachéu, and Bolama (Bigman 1993, 50; Davidson 1969, 22–23). As late as 1915, a Brazilian visitor described the colonial capital, Bissau, as a "Portuguese camp" where colonial officials "lived behind the defense of their town walls" and could not travel into the interior without first paying tribute to the local Pepel chief (Davidson 1969, 22–23).

Portuguese military officials relied on African mercenary warlords to establish their territorial hegemony over Guinea-Bissau. The French historian Réné Pellisier estimates that the Portuguese military employed more than 8,000 European soldiers and 42,000 African auxiliaries in its "pacification" of Guinea-Bissau between 1879 and 1920 (Bigman 1993, 50). The most notorious of these African mercenaries was the Senegalese warlord Abdoul N'Diaye,[10] who terrorized Guinea-Bissau's ethnic Pepel and Balanta populations. In return for his services to the Portuguese military, N'Diaye was appointed "warrant chief" over the interior province of Oio in 1915. In a cruel twist of fate, Portuguese colonial officials never reimbursed N'Diaye's mercenary army for subjugating the coastal regions of Portuguese Guinea, so they enriched themselves by stealing cattle from local indigenous Pepel and Balanta communities. They also raped large numbers of women and subjected the men to forced labor. As news of these atrocities spread and N'Diaye accumulated vast wealth and power from terrorizing the local communities under his control, Portuguese military officials ultimately deposed N'Diaye from his position as "warrant chief" and exiled him to Cape Verde, where he was imprisoned without trial (Lyall 1938, 190; Forrest 1992, 17–18; Bowman 1986, 475–77).[11] The saga of Abdoul N'Diaye illustrates the arbitrary and extralegal nature of Portuguese colonial authority in Guinea-Bissau. It also shows the extreme fragility of administrative control in Guinea-Bissau, where Portuguese officials remained dependent on indigenous African intermediaries.

Portuguese colonial officials in Guinea-Bissau never established a uniform legal-administrative structure based on civil law. Instead, they created a bifurcated colonial state with distinctive legal-administrative frameworks for Creole versus indigenous African populations. Guinean Creoles, like their Cape Verdean ancestors, were legally regarded as metropolitan Portuguese citizens.

By contrast, indigenous Africans were subject to a repressive legal code (i.e., the *regime do indigenato*) that denied their citizenship rights and subjected them to forced labor. The Portuguese *indigenato* legal code formally distinguished between *indígena* and *civilisado* populations and introduced compulsory labor for able-bodied "native" males between the ages of 14 and 60 (O'Laughlin 2000, 12; Silva Cunha 1949, 147–49).[12] This legal distinction was first imposed in 1899 and remained in place until 1961. In 1929, the Portuguese state legally defined *indígenas* as unassimilated "populations of negro race . . . born or usually living in the provinces of Guinea, Angola, and Mozambique, [who] do not yet possess the education and the social and individual habits demanded for the complete application of the private and public law of Portuguese citizens" (Coissoro 1984, 73).[13] It was extremely difficult for indigenous Africans to become naturalized Portuguese citizens, given the lack of schooling options for indigenous Africans. Consequently, more than 98% of Guinea-Bissau's population was classified as *indígenas* without citizenship rights in 1950 (Portugal, Instituto Nacional de Estatística 1959).

Guinea-Bissau's colonial state was also organized according to Mahmood Mamdani's (1996) concept of legal-administrative bifurcation in colonial Africa. Portuguese municipal institutions (i.e., *concelhos*) were limited to the coastal towns of Bissau, Bolama (the old capital), and Cachéu. The rest of the colony was organized into eight administrative districts (i.e., *circunscrições*) overseen by district commissioners (*chefes de posto*), who were typically Cape Verdeans or local Creoles. Like their British counterparts in Sierra Leone, Guinea-Bissau's district commissioners wielded extensive powers and oversaw a vast network of indigenous "administrative chiefs" (i.e., *régulos*). Whereas British officials tended to favor traditional African authorities, the Portuguese officials tended to appoint former police officers, soldiers, or interpreters to serve as "administrative chiefs" in Portuguese Africa. Like their counterparts in Francophone Africa, these intermediaries were appointed based on their perceived loyalty to Portuguese colonial objectives. African *régulos* were responsible for tax collection, labor recruitment, and maintaining public order, and Guinea-Bissau's colonial officials were significantly less tolerant of traditional authority than their British counterparts in Sierra Leone (see Ajayi and Crowder 1971, 527–28; Lyall 1938, 170–71). Only traditional village chiefs (i.e., *chefes de povoação*) were recognized in Portuguese African territories, and their administrative powers were extremely limited (Teixeira da Mota 1954, 54). Yet despite this difference, it is important to recognize that both Britain and Portugal created bifurcated colonial states with extractive taxation and labor policies, and distinctive legal-administrative frameworks for rural/indigenous and urban/Creole populations. Consequently, Mamdani's (1996) concept of the legal-administrative bifurcation, and Acemoglu and Robinson's (2012) concept of extractive institutions, are useful for understanding Portuguese colonial occupation as well as British colonial occupation in Sierra Leone.

State Institutions, Citizenship Rights, and Colonial Education

Colonial citizenship policies also had profound consequences for state-funded education in Cape Verde and Guinea-Bissau. Perhaps not surprisingly, the early development of an integrated colonial state with inclusive citizenship rights contributed to greater educational opportunities in Cape Verde relative to Guinea-Bissau, which maintained bifurcated legal-administrative institutions throughout the colonial era.

Cape Verde

The early establishment of an effective colonial state with inclusive citizenship rights supported the expansion of state-funded education in Cape Verde. At the turn of the twentieth century, Cape Verde had more students enrolled in primary schools than the rest of Portuguese Africa combined (Portugal, Ministerio dos Negocios da Marinha e Ultramar 1905). According to official Portuguese records, 11% of Cape Verdeans could read and write in 1900, and 4,527 students were enrolled in public primary schools, out of a total population of 147,000 (Portugal, Ministerio dos Negocios da Marinha e Ultramar 1905). In fact, Cape Verde's literacy rate was remarkably similar to that of Portugal, which had the most illiterate population in Western Europe. Less than 20% of Portuguese adults could read and write in 1910 (Cuzán 1999, 120).

In 1910, the Portuguese monarchy was replaced by a secular republican government that contributed to a period of intellectual flourishing in Cape Verde. The spread of secular liberalism and republican ideals in Cape Verde gave rise to an intellectual movement known as *nativismo*, which a republican colonial governor described as "a love of country, a love of freedom . . . , a desire for moral emancipation and for a higher civilization," and "a hatred of racist prejudice . . . and oppression" (Davidson 1989, 46). Both historical and contemporary sources suggest that Portuguese republican officials favored the expansion of state-funded secular education following the separation of church and state in 1911. Consequently, Cape Verde's public expenditure on education increased from 5.6% to 9.3% of colonial budget during the first decade of republican government in Portugal, 1910–20 (Carvalho 2004, 185). At the same time, Cape Verde's republican governor, Fontura da Costa, established new primary schools in rural parts of the archipelago. Many Cape Verdeans enrolled in these schools, often with the view of migrating to the United States after graduation (Mentel 1984, 135).

Governor Fontura da Costa also established Cape Verde's first *liceu* in 1917. This was the only public secondary school in Portuguese West Africa until the 1950s (Mentel 1984, 135). The *liceu* also offered a training course for primary school teachers, which facilitated a significant increase in primary school enroll-ment. By 1920, 30% of Cape Verdean children were enrolled in primary schools (Carvalho 2004, 109, 126), and Cape Verde's primary enrollment rate exceeded that of Portugal (Benavot and Riddle 1988, 205).[14] Portuguese officials who served in Cape Verde during the republican years often described the Creole African archipelago as "an intellectual oasis in the tropics" (Mentel 1984, 136–37), and they were duly impressed by Cape Verde's vibrant press and rich intel-lectual life (Davidson 1989, 43–46; Carvalho 2004, 86–98).

Nevertheless, the First Portuguese Republic (1910–26) was short-lived, and it was replaced by a repressive dictatorship that hindered Cape Verde's social prog-ress after 1930. Portugal's reactionary *Estado Novo* dictatorship (1930–74) had a decidedly anti-intellectual bent, even though it was dominated by conservative law professors and academics. During the *Estado Novo* dictatorship, Portugal's long-serving prime minister, Antonio de Salazar (1930–68), prioritized tradi-tional Iberian Catholic social norms, anticommunism, national security, and balanced budgets over social progress and development. Salazarist colonial officials were openly hostile to social and political progress in Cape Verde: they imposed rigid press censorship and closed down 88 Cape Verdean schools be-tween 1926 and 1946 (Mentel 1984, 135). They even transformed Cape Verde's oldest and most prestigious secondary school, the Liceu-Seminario São Nicolau, into a concentration camp for political prisoners (Carvalho 2004, 355–62). As Salazarist colonial officials closed down primary schools across the archipelago, primary school enrollment declined by one-third, from 6,693 to 4,977, during the first two decades of the dictatorship (Mentel 1984, 135). By 1940, only 14% of Cape Verdean children were enrolled in primary schools.

Educational opportunities in Cape Verde remained extremely limited until the 1960s when the outbreak of anticolonial violence prompted Portuguese colonial officials to promote education in order to win over African "hearts and minds" for the Portuguese nation and empire. As a result of these initiatives, Cape Verde's primary school enrollment increased fourfold during the 1960s, and more than 40,000 Cape Verdeans—about 70% of the school-age population—were enrolled in primary schools by the mid-1970s (Mentel 1984, 140). In some ways, the sig-nificant increase in primary school enrollment was "too little, too late," because more than 130,000 Cape Verdeans, mostly from the educated middle classes, emigrated to the United States and Western Europe between 1950 and 1973

(Carreira 1982, 178). Consequently, Cape Verde's adult literacy rate was only 37% at the time of its independence in 1975 (United Nations 1977). The repressive and reactionary policies of the *Estado Novo* dictatorship clearly impeded the rise of mass education and literacy in Cape Verde prior to independence. Nevertheless, the comparison with Guinea-Bissau will demonstrate the extent to which Cape Verde's inclusive citizenship laws facilitated the expansion of education and literacy relative to Portuguese occupation colonies, where restrictive citizenship laws denied educational access to indigenous African subjects.

Guinea-Bissau

Guinea-Bissau's bifurcated colonial state and exclusionary citizenship policies severely restricted educational access to indigenous African subjects under Portuguese control. Only *civilisado* (i.e., Creole) children were permitted to attend public schools in Portuguese Guinea, which had the lowest levels of primary school enrollment in Portuguese Africa. Only 303 children were enrolled in official public schools in Portuguese Guinea at the beginning of the twentieth century (Portugal, Ministerio dos Negocios da Marinha e Ultramar 1905). There are no census records from this time period, but the *World Christian Encyclopedia* estimates a population of 120,000 inhabitants in Guinea-Bissau in 1900 (Barrett, Kurian, and Johnson 2001). This suggests that primary school students accounted for about 0.25% of the colony's population, or 1% of the school-aged population. Because the administrative capacity of the colonial state was so limited, official census records only provide information on the *civilisado* population of Portuguese Guinea. Between 1910 and 1938, primary school enrollment hovered around 700 students each year (Guiné 1910; Portugal, Instituto Nacional de Estatística 1950), and the first secondary school only established in 1958 (Pombo-Malta 2006, 2). Thus, for most of the colonial era, Guinean Creoles, including the independence hero Amilcar Cabral, had to pursue their secondary education in Cape Verde (Davidson 1989, 65).

Restrictive citizenship laws further limited educational opportunities for indigenous African subjects in Portuguese Guinea. The colony's secular public schools only catered to Creole children, and indigenous African children were relegated to Catholic mission schools that emphasized catechism and manual labor. Catholic mission schools did not prepare students for the entrance examination that was required for secondary school (Patinha 1999, 38–40; Duffy 1961, 298).[15] Consequently, there was no possibility for indigenous Africans to gain access to secondary schools. Secondary schooling for indigenous Africans was clearly not a priority for Portugal's ecclesiastical hierarchy. As late as 1960, the archbishop of Lisbon maintained that Catholic mission schools should "teach the natives to write, to read and to count, but not . . . make them doctors!" (Ferreira 1974, 113). For most of the colonial era, Catholic missionary evangelization remained limited in Portuguese Guinea, and the Catholic Church maintained a state monopoly over the education of indigenous Africans. Nevertheless, there were only nine Catholic mission schools with a limited teaching staff of 16 priests and 14 nuns in the entire country in 1940 (Teixiera da Mota 1954, 116). By 1950, about 1,000 indigenous African children were enrolled in 45 Catholic mission schools (Pombo-Malta 2006, 165), whereas 10 state schools provided primary education for 700 Creole students (Portugal, Instituto Nacional de Estatística 1959). Consequently, there were only 1,700 primary school students in a colonial state with more than 500,000 inhabitants.

Restrictive citizenship laws also hindered the expansion of education and literacy in Guinea-Bissau relative to Cape Verde. In 1950, Guinea-Bissau had the lowest adult literacy rate in the world, at 1%. Amazingly, UN data suggests that 55% of Guinean Creole (i.e., *civilisado*) adults were literate in 1950, compared with 0% for indigenous Africans (United Nations 1963, 303–4). At the same time, Portuguese census records claimed that 0.5% of Guinea-Bissau's total population could read and write, compared with 13% of Cape Verdean adults in 1950 (Portugal, Instituto Nacional de Estatística 1959, 34–35). By 1975, only 9% of Guinea-Bissau's adults were literate, compared with 37% in Cape Verde (United Nations 1977). The limited extent of education and literacy in these territories partly reflects the absence of Protestant missionaries in territories.[16] Yet despite the limited extent of Protestant missionary evangelization, Cape Verde's inclusive citizenship laws facilitated greater access to state-funded education relative to Portuguese Guinea, where indigenous Africans were denied access to state-funded schools. Consequently, the comparative-historical evidence in this chapter is consistent with my statistical results demonstrating favorable development outcomes in forced settlement colonies that expanded the legal rights of emancipated Afro-descendants following the abolition of slavery.

Metropolitan Citizenship and Voting Rights

Cape Verde's inclusive citizenship laws also contributed to greater electoral participation than in Portuguese Guinea. This is an important and original contribution because previous studies have overlooked the significant variation in electoral participation in Portuguese African colonies. Despite the absence of meaningful electoral competition during Portugal's *Estado Novo* dictatorship (1930–74), Portuguese African colonies elected at least one deputy to the national parliament in Lisbon between 1911 and 1975. Moreover, these elections were genuinely competitive during the First Portuguese Republic, 1910–26.[17]

The *Estado Novo* dictatorship banned multiparty electoral competition after 1930 but maintained plebiscitarian elections in which voters could only accept or reject an official of the ruling party's candidates. The ruling National Union party won every electoral seat in Portuguese parliamentary elections between 1934 and 1973, and the official results of these elections were never published or released to the public (Tavares de Almeida 2010, 1540). Nevertheless, my comparative-historical analysis of Cape Verdean and Portuguese archival sources reveals a surprising amount of variation in the extent of electoral participation in Portuguese African colonies.

The National Archives of Cape Verde contain voter records from selected municipal elections dating back to 1844 and Portuguese parliamentary elections after 1873 (Cabo Verde 1994, 2004). Unfortunately, the electoral results from the First Portuguese Republic are not available in the National Archives of Cape Verde, but the voter registration records from this period suggest that the percentage of registered voters in Cape Verde was not significantly different from in Portugal. Portugal's 1878 electoral law extended voting rights to literate male citizens and male household heads over the age of 21. At the time, registered voters comprised 20% of Portugal's total population, or 70% of the adult male population (Tavares de Almeida 2010, 1532). In 1892, registered voters comprised 15% of Cape Verde's total population, or 60% of adult males (Cabo Verde 1894). In 1911, the Portuguese republic restricted voting rights to literate adult male citizens, reducing Cape Verde's electorate to 7.6% of the archipelago's population, or 30% of adult males. Interestingly, and rather progressively for the time, the racial composition of Cape Verde's electorate was not significantly different from its general population, as blacks and mulattos represented 92% of Cape Verde's registered voters in 1911 (Cabo Verde 1915).

Because Portugal's electoral franchise was largely determined by citizenship and education, Cape Verde had higher levels of electoral participation than Guinea-Bissau and other Portuguese-occupied colonies like Angola or Mozambique. Portuguese citizenship laws excluded the indigenous majority in colonial Guinea-Bissau, where registered voters accounted for less than 0.5% of the total population during the 1950s (Portugal, Assemleia de Apuramento Geral 1953, 1957), compared with 11% in Cape Verde (Cabo Verde 1953, 1957). Cape Verde and Portugal had the same citizenship laws and comparable levels of educational attainment during the first half of the twentieth century. Consequently, the percentage of registered voters in Cape Verde (11%) was almost as high as that in Portugal (15%) during the 1950s (Tavares de Almeida 2010, 1546). Furthermore, Cape Verde's electoral participation in Cape Verde was not concentrated in its colonial capital, as was the case in Guinea-Bissau. During the 1960s, more than 60% of Portuguese Guinea's registered voters lived in the capital city, Bissau, where the colony's educated Creole minority was concentrated (Portugal,

Assemleia de Apuramento Geral 1961, 1965, 1969). By contrast, only one in six Cape Verdean voters lived in the capital city during the 1950s and 1960s (Cabo Verde 1949, 1953, 1957, 1961). This suggests that electoral participation was far more inclusive in colonial Cape Verde relative to Portuguese Guinea. Although the repressive nature of Portugal's *Estado Novo* dictatorship prevented mass electoral competition in both Cape Verde and Guinea-Bissau prior to independence, Cape Verde's inclusive citizenship laws permitted greater electoral participation during the colonial era. This might explain why Cape Verde was in a better position to democratize following the introduction of multiparty elections in the 1990s.

Democratization scholarship highlights the extent to which mass electoral participation tends to strengthen citizenship rights and governmental accountability to voter preferences. Obviously, free, fair, and competitive elections are more conducive for building democratic norms and ensuring governmental responsiveness to voter preferences. Nevertheless, even authoritarian elections require mass representative institutions like political parties that generate notions of accountability between ordinary citizens and elected officials. Over time, this can develop civic norms that generate popular support for democratization, as demonstrated in recent empirical research by Staffan Lindberg (2006, 2009) and Michael Bratton and Nicholas Van de Walle (1997). These authors argue that electoral participation is important for building mass representative institutions such as political parties and legislatures that can challenge authoritarian incumbents and channel popular aspirations for democracy (see Lindberg 2006, 2009; Hadenius and Teorrell 2005). Drawing from these arguments, we would expect Cape Verde's much longer electoral history to facilitate its postcolonial democratization, whereas Guinea-Bissau's limited electoral history would undermine postcolonial democratization efforts.

Colonial State Effectiveness and Anticolonial Resistance

Another factor that facilitated Cape Verde's favorable long-term development relative to Guinea-Bissau is that the archipelago nation did not experience the type of anticolonial resistance that destroyed Guinea-Bissau's state institutions after 1963. During the 1960s, the Marxist-oriented African Party for the Independence of Guinea-Bissau and Cape Verde (PAIGC) recruited nationalist leaders from both territories in their liberation struggle against Portuguese rule. Nevertheless, PAIGC activists pursued very different liberation strategies in each territory. In Cape Verde, PAIGC activists pursued a strategy of urban protest, whereas the party's founding leader, Amilcar Cabral, mobilized a devastating rural insurgency against the Portuguese colonial state control in

Guinea-Bissau. Cabral believed that if the PAIGC defeated the Portuguese military in Guinea-Bissau, it would be possible to negotiate Cape Verde's independence from Portuguese rule. Cabral's two-pronged strategy was ultimately successful, although he never got to see the realization of his dream. Cabral was assassinated by Portuguese agents in Conakry, two years before Guinea-Bissau's independence in 1974 (Davidson 2017). Nevertheless, the PAIGC's distinctive strategies—armed insurgency in Guinea-Bissau versus urban protest and negotiation in Cape Verde—had lasting consequences for the political development of the two countries after independence.

Recent empirical research demonstrates that countries that experienced rural anticolonial insurgencies during their independence transitions have been likely to democratize over the *longue durée* (Garcia-Ponce and Wantchekon, forthcoming). This is because colonial authorities often responded with indiscriminate violence against rural anticolonial insurgents, and this generated a repressive and authoritarian political culture that persisted after independence. By contrast, Garcia-Ponce and Wantchekon argue that countries that experienced urban protest instead of rural insurgencies developed a more activist and inclusive political culture in which citizens used trade unions, labor associations, and urban-based ethnic associations to articulate their political demands and negotiate with state officials. They argue that this type of political culture ultimately facilitated the democratization of African countries whose nationalist movements emerged out of urban protest rather than rural-based insurgencies. Indeed, Garcia-Ponce and Wantchekon's research demonstrates more successful democratization outcomes in African countries that used urban protest to secure their independence. My research builds on their work by placing the PAIGC's bifurcated mobilization strategy in the broader historical context of Cape Verde's comparatively effective and inclusive colonial state institutions relative to the fragile and exclusionary institutions of Guinea-Bissau's colonial state.

Cape Verde

The PAIGC pursued very different anticolonial strategies in Cape Verde than in Guinea-Bissau, even though its founding leader, Amilcar Cabral, favored the political unification of the two countries following their liberation from Portuguese rule. Amilcar Cabral was a Guinean Creole agronomist with strong family ties to Cape Verde on his father's side. Given the lack of schooling opportunities in Portuguese Guinea, Cabral was educated in Cape Verde and Portugal, where he established strong political ties with other anticolonial African leaders. Given Cabral's Creole and Cape Verdean ancestry, it was not difficult for him to mobilize Cape Verdean support for the PAIGC's anticolonial war in Guinea-Bissau.

Cabral's strategy was to mobilize a rural insurgency to liberate Guinea-Bissau from Portuguese rule, and then negotiate Cape Verde's independence from Portugal (Davidson 2017). Cabral recognized that the Portuguese colonial state was too strong for armed struggle to succeed in Cape Verde. Consequently, the PAIGC's liberation war was entirely fought in Portuguese Guinea, even though many Cape Verdeans activists—mostly poor agricultural workers, but also middle-class graduates from the archipelago's prestigious lycées—fought in the anticolonial insurgency that liberated Guinea-Bissau from Portuguese rule. Cape Verdeans also held leadership positions in the party's headquarters in the Republic of Guinea (Conakry), and in underground cells in Dakar, Senegal (Davidson 1989, 76–88). Nevertheless, PAIGC activity in Cape Verde was vigorously repressed by Portuguese officials during the liberation struggle in Guinea-Bissau (Davidson 1989, 55–59, 77–78, 93–98, 102–3).

Portuguese colonial officials used a combination of press censorship, torture, imprisonment, and "disappearances" to silence all political opposition in Cape Verde during the 1960s (Barrows 1990, 179–80; Mentel 1984, 146–47). By contrast, Portuguese forces were unable to control Guinea-Bissau's larger population and territory, which fell under PAIGC control by the late 1960s. Nevertheless, the Portuguese state maintained an active military presence in all of its African territories until the *Estado Novo* dictatorship was overthrown by reformist military officers returning from Guinea-Bissau's anticolonial war in April 1974. The soldiers that toppled the Portuguese dictatorship had become convinced of Portugal's inability to win the anticolonial wars, so they supported a reformist political agenda of decolonization, democratization, and development (Davidson 2017; Linz and Stepan 1996, 118–19; Cuzán 1999, 123; Bermeo 2007). From September 1974 until April 1975, reformist Portuguese soldiers established an interim military government that was supported by the Communist Party (Cuzán 1999, 124–25). The interim Portuguese government recognized Guinea-Bissau's independence in September 1974. It also released Cape Verde's political prisoners and invited the PAIGC to establish a transitional government in Cape Verde (Barrows 1990, 199–216; Davidson 111–12, 116–23).

Nevertheless, the Portuguese military government had no intention of recognizing Cape Verde's independence. Instead, the interim government sought to maintain Cape Verde as a dependent territory, with a similar political status to the Azores islands or Madeira. Yet PAIGC activists organized massive public demonstrations in favor of Cape Verde's independence. Portuguese colonial authorities responded to these protests by sponsoring moderate opposition parties that catered to Portuguese loyalists and Cape Verdean émigrés in Western Europe. The transitional PAIGC government arrested these opposition leaders and forced them into exile (Hodges 1977, 43). The PAIGC's transitional government continued to restrict electoral competition, but extended universal suffrage to all Cape Verdean adults prior to independence. Cape Verde only held one election with universal adult suffrage prior to independence, and the PAIGC's candidate list was approved by 96% of Cape Verdean voters (Clemente-Kersten 1999a, 195–97). Consequently, Cape Verde, like other Portuguese African colonies, gained independence under single-party authoritarian rule. In many ways, Cape Verde's independence was an accidental political outcome that would not have occurred without the armed struggle in Guinea-Bissau. Indeed, José Luis Fernando Lopes, a former PAIGC militant, who later served as Cape Verde's ambassador to the United States, emphasized the importance of Guinea-Bissau's national liberation war for Cape Verde's independence in a 1990 interview in Washington, DC. "It was unrealistic . . . to establish an armed struggle in Cape Verde," where Portuguese authority was strong and well institutionalized. In Guinea-Bissau, by contrast, "The circumstances were more realistic, and this allowed [us] to fight for [our] independence" (Barrows 1990, 152).

Guinea-Bissau

In contrast to Cape Verde's negotiated independence, Guinea-Bissau gained independence following a protracted armed struggle. By the late 1960s, PAIGC militants controlled most of Guinea-Bissau's territory, and Portugal's armed forces were trapped in the imbroglio of a three-front anticolonial war in Angola, Mozambique, and Guinea-Bissau (Newitt 1981; Forrest 1992, 35; Davidson 1969, 99–103; Bermeo 2007, 319). Guinea-Bissau's anticolonial war was particularly destructive, as the Portuguese military adopted a scorched-earth policy that obliterated thousands of African villages and devastated the colony's limited infrastructure and economy. Portuguese repression failed to win over African hearts and minds. By 1968, Portuguese authority had receded to the major towns, whose populations swelled with rural migrants fleeing the physical devastation of their communities (Whitaker 1970, 26). In many ways, this was a throwback to the turn of the twentieth century, when Portuguese authority in Guinea-Bissau was limited to a handful of coastal towns.

The anticolonial wars in Angola, Guinea-Bissau, and Mozambique forced Portuguese colonial officials to liberalize the most repressive aspects of their colonial occupation during the 1960s. The *indigenato* legal code was finally abolished in 1961, bringing and end to the forced labor recruitment of indigenous Africans (Barrows 1990, 181–85; Ferreira 1974, 19; Newitt 1981, 240). Guinea-Bissau's school system was also integrated after 1964 (Pombo-Malta 2006, 180–84, 197), and the colony gained two additional seats in the Portuguese National Assembly. These reforms turned out to be meaningless, because the PAIGC already controlled most of the country's rural districts, and less than 1% of the colony's population was eligible to vote in Portuguese elections (Guiné 1972). Moreover, the PAIGC established its own schools, courts, and health clinics in the country's "liberated zones" during the late 1960s (Diggs 1973; Rudebeck 1972, 9, 12–15; Pombo-Malta 2006; Davidson 1969, 81–90, 125–28). After holding single-party plebiscitarian "elections" in Guinea-Bissau's liberated zones in 1972, PAIGC leaders declared the country's independence from Portuguese rule in September 1973 (Diggs 1973; Forrest 1992, 49; Clemente-Kersten 1999b, 467). At the time, Portuguese military forces still controlled the capital city of Bissau, and they did not recognize Guinea-Bissau's independence until after the military coup and subsequent social revolution that toppled the Portuguese dictatorship in Lisbon. Consequently, Guinea-Bissau gained independence as a crippled state in the aftermath of a brutal and violent colonial occupation. Guinea-Bissau's bifurcated colonial state also institutionalized a deep social divide and lingering mistrust between Creole and indigenous Africans that hindered the country's postcolonial regime stability and democratization efforts.

The Divergent Developmental Trajectories of Postcolonial Cape Verde and Guinea-Bissau

Cape Verde and Guinea-Bissau have had very different developmental and political trajectories since their independence from Portugal. Figure 6.1 shows the

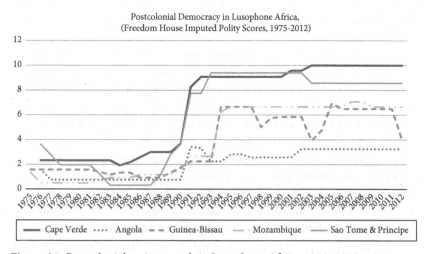

Figure 6.1 Postcolonial regime trends in Lusophone Africa, 1975–2012

Source: Quality of Government 2015. Freedom House Imputed Polity (FHIP) scores are missing for all countries in 1982, so I estimated the scores for that year by averaging the mean score for 1981 and 1983. FHIP scores measure democracy on a 0–10 scale, and higher numbers are more democratic.

significant variation in postcolonial regime trends across Portuguese Africa. The divergent regime trajectories of Cape Verde and Guinea-Bissau are striking because both countries established single-party authoritarian regimes following their independence from Portugal. Nevertheless, Cape Verde significantly liberalized its economic and society during the 1980s, and the country experienced significant democratization following the introduction of multiparty elections in 1991. Today, Cape Verde is one of the few consolidated democracies in sub-Saharan Africa, and it is the only Portuguese African country to consolidate democracy during the 1990s (Baker 2006; Meyns 2002; Owolabi 2017). Guinea-Bissau also introduced economic and political liberalization after independence, but the country has been plagued by frequent military coups and chronic regime instability that persisted following the introduction of multiparty electoral competition in 1994 (Forrest 2002, 2003, 2010). Like many African countries, Guinea-Bissau introduced multiparty electoral competition during the 1990s, yet no elected president has completed a full term in office. Instead, most of the country's elected leaders have been removed from office by military coup, civil war, or assassination.[18] Today, Guinea-Bissau's political violence and regime instability exceed that of neighboring countries like Sierra Leone and Liberia.

Cape Verde has also been far more successful than Guinea-Bissau at promoting broad-based human development after independence. These divergent outcomes are somewhat surprising because both countries were among the poorest in sub-Saharan Africa at the time of their independence, when both countries were heavily dependent on foreign aid. Despite these challenges, Cape Verde was able to maintain one of the highest sustained rates of economic growth in the developing world between 1976 and 2008, when its real per capita GDP increased more than fivefold (see Figure 6.2). The country's population also experienced significant gains in educational attainment, public health, gender equality, and poverty reduction that boosted human well-being and development. By contrast, Guinea-Bissau's economy stagnated after independence, and the country remains one of the most impoverished and underdeveloped nations on the planet.

How do we explain Cape Verde's favorable postcolonial development and democratization relative to that of Guinea-Bissau? The divergent postcolonial trajectories of Cape Verde and Guinea-Bissau clearly reveal the limitations of existing theories on colonialism and long-term development. After all, both Cape Verde and Guinea-Bissau experienced extractive forms of colonization that depended on coerced labor migration (Cape Verde) or indigenous forced labor (Guinea-Bissau). Neither country attracted significant European settlement during the colonial era. Neither colony was significantly exposed to Protestant missionary evangelization during the colonial era. And neither country experienced "tutelary democracy" prior to independence. Cape Verde's electoral system

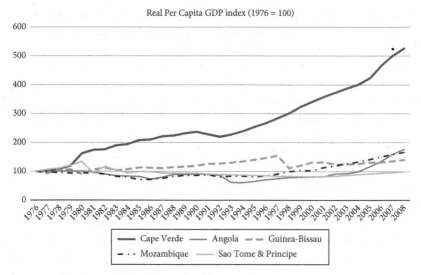

Figure 6.2 Real per capita GDP growth in Lusophone Africa, 1976–2008
Source: Quality of Government 2015.

was more inclusive than Guinea-Bissau's during the colonial era, but Portugal's repressive dictatorship prevented the development of mass electoral competition in either colony prior to independence. As a result of these similarities, existing theories would predict poor development outcomes and limited postcolonial democratization in both countries. Nevertheless, Cape Verde has been much more successful than Guinea-Bissau at promoting broad-based postcolonial development and democratic consolidation after 1991. Consistent with the theoretical framework in Chapter 3, and the statistical evidence in Chapter 4, the empirical evidence in this chapter suggests that Cape Verde's (comparatively) effective and inclusive legal-administrative facilitated broad-based human development and postcolonial democratization after independence. By contrast, the lasting effects of Guinea-Bissau's ineffective legal-administrative institutions and exclusionary citizenship laws undermined postcolonial efforts to promote inclusive human development outcomes after independence.

Explaining Cape Verde's Postcolonial Development and Democratization

Despite gaining independence under single-party authoritarian rule, Cape Verde's effective state institutions and inclusive citizenship laws generated a legal-administrative framework that enabled government leaders to interact with ordinary citizens through corporatist representative channels that represented different groups and interests in civil society. These institutions enabled Cape Verdeans to actively shape the policies and practices that generated political inclusiveness and sustained economic growth after independence. Cape Verde's single-party regime was more inclusive than that of Guinea-Bissau, even though the political leaders of both countries favored their political unification after independence. Amilcar Cabral's dream of uniting the two countries was ultimately shattered after Guinea-Bissau experienced its first military coup in November 1980. The military coup was partly fueled by anti-Cape Verdean propaganda in Guinea-Bissau, where indigenous African soldiers often resented the ruling party's Creole leadership, and the close political ties between Guinea-Bissau's president, Luis Cabral, and the Cape Verdean president, Aristides Pereira. The 1980 military coup severed the institutional link between the two governments, and the two countries went their separate ways (Munslow 1981). Guinea-Bissau's army chief of staff, Nuno Vieira, replaced President Luis Cabral as that country's head of state, and Vieira established a highly repressive, predatory, and personalist dictatorship that remained in place for nearly two decades. By contrast, Cape Verde's ruling party rebranded itself as the African Party for the Independence of Cape Verde (PAICV) and introduced political reforms to expand political participation and representation from independent social and political actors in civil society.

Following the military coup in Guinea-Bissau, Cape Verde's prime minister, Pedro Pires, publicly stated his opposition to military force as a means to resolve political issues (Munslow 1981, 112). Cape Verde's president, Aristides Pereira, also expressed his support for democratic political channels, stating that each citizen must be able to "express . . . his opinion and enrich . . . the collective thought with his suggestions" (Munslow 1981, 112). Building on these ideals, the newly rebranded PAICV began to promote greater political openness that expanded citizens' input in the implementation of governmental policy. Cape Verde's ruling party established cooperatives that empowered local farmers and fishermen to regulate the food supply and prevent excessive price fluctuations (Silva Andrade, 280–81). It also established popular organizations for 60,000 Cape Verdean women, youth, and organized workers that had a direct link to the party's grassroots organizations and elected leaders. Moreover, the Cape Verdean government established independent local tribunals and elected local councils that enabled citizens to express their preferences independently of the ruling party (Davidson 1989, 149, 159–66; Evora 2004, 82). These institutions were sufficiently pluralist to allow for public input on contentious issues such as land reform and governmental efforts to promote gender equality (Davidson 1989, 153–63, 166–77; Barrows 1990, 310–18; Koudawo 2001, 156–58). The Roman Catholic Church and lay Catholic associations also empowered Cape Verde's civil society, which also benefited from the remittance incomes of Cape Verdean emigrants in the United States and Western Europe. Consequently, Cape Verde's civil society was more autonomous than in most single-party regimes, and political independents comprised more than 30% of Cape Verde's elected representatives by the mid-1980s (Baker 2006, 494).

Cape Verde's sociopolitical landscape was also transformed by robust economic growth that boosted living standards after independence. The Cape Verdean economy expanded by 10% per annum during the first decade of independence and 7% annually from 1985 until the early 2000s (Baker 2006, 295). As the Cape Verdean economy improved, primary school enrollment increased from 57% to 95% of the school-aged population between 1975 and 1995 (Livramento 2007, 397). Cape Verde's rapid economic growth and rising living standards also fueled demands for political reforms from middle-class professionals and university students during the 1980s (Koudawo 2001, 93). At the same time, the ruling party's old guard was increasingly displaced by younger technocratic elites who favored economic and political liberalization. As a result, Cape Verde's ruling elites agreed to hold multiparty elections in 1991. They also stepped down without incident after the opposition Movement for Democracy (MpD) defeated the ruling PAICV in the country's first competitive election (Evora 2004, 91–92; Baker 2006, 495).

Since 1991, Cape Verde has quietly emerged into one of the only consolidated democracies in sub-Saharan Africa (Baker 2006). The MpD won consecutive elections in 1991 and 1996 and remained in power until 2001, when the PAICV was restored to power. In recent decades, Cape Verde has experienced regular electoral alternation between the market-oriented MpD and the social democratic PAICV (Baker 2006, 495; African Elections Database 2016). The two parties even experienced a period of partisan "cohabitation," with the MpD controlling the presidency while the PAICV maintained a narrow majority in the National Assembly between 2011 and 2016. As a result, Freedom House has consistently rated Cape Verde as one of the most democratic countries in sub-Saharan Africa. Human rights organizations report widespread respect for civil and political liberties, as the Cape Verdean government respects freedom of speech and freedom of the press (Baker 2006, 502–5; Evora 2004, 109–10). Political analysts also regard the country's judiciary as independent of executive control and largely free of political bias (Baker 2006; Veiga 2007, 44). Furthermore, both political parties have established deep linkages with civil society, and both parties are committed to the democratic constitutional order and a social market economy that promotes economic growth with improvements in public health, education, poverty reduction, and gender equality (Baker 2006).

Cape Verde has continued to enjoy robust economic growth and significant improvements in human well-being since its democratic consolidation in the

1990s. The percentage of Cape Verdean youths attending secondary schools increased from less than 3% in 1980 to 20% in 1990—the last year of single-party authoritarian rule—to 55% by 2004 (Livramento 2007, 397). Public spending on education also increased from 9% of the national budget in 1980 to 14% in 1990 to more than 20% after 2000 (Livramento 2007, 403). Cape Verdean governments have been particularly successful at improving girls' access to education, which had been neglected under colonial rule. Cape Verde also experienced significant gains in life expectancy, and a corresponding decline in infant and maternal mortality. These gains are important because rising education levels tend to boost popular support for democratization (Sanborn and Thyne 2013). Existing studies also demonstrate a positive association between democratization and human development, which tend to be mutually reinforcing (see Przeworski et al. 2000; Angell 2010; Gerring, Thacker, and Alfaro 2012). These dynamics are clearly at work in Cape Verde, which experienced significant improvements in democratization and human development following its independence from Portuguese rule.

State Fragility and Regime Instability in Postcolonial Guinea-Bissau

In contrast to Cape Verde, Guinea-Bissau has been plagued by chronic regime instability that severely impeded its postcolonial development. In many ways, Guinea-Bissau's chronic regime instability results from the limited administrative capacity of its colonial state and extreme militarization during the independence war. Moreover, the limited administrative effectiveness of Guinea-Bissau's colonial state was further eroded by the PAIGC's anticolonial insurgency. This made it very difficult for Guinea-Bissau's postcolonial governments to implement administrative policies in outlying rural districts. Following Guinea-Bissau's independence from Portuguese rule, the ruling party elites became increasingly concerned with securing the political loyalty of urban voters and cultivating urban clients in the capital city (Dávila 1987, 260, 265–66). Ruling party elites came to regard the patronage benefits of government as their reward for the deprivations of the independence war (Forrest 1992, 45–46; Forrest 2003, 228). This caused significant problems for the country's long-term development.

The colonial practice of limiting citizenship rights to Guinea-Bissau's Creole minority also institutionalized a deep social divide and profound mistrust between educated Creole elites and indigenous Africans. Because colonial state policies had favored local Guinea-Bissau's Creole elites over indigenous Africans, the educated Creole minority continued to dominate Guinea-Bissau's state bureaucracy, ruling party, and governing institutions after independence. The army, by contrast, was primarily made up of indigenous African soldiers who resented the political dominance of Guinean Creoles in the ruling party and state bureaucracy. To make matters worse, Guinea-Bissau's Creole elites openly favored political integration with Cape Verde. They also pursued economic policies that clearly benefited government elites and urban consumers at the expense of rural and indigenous Africans. Guinea-Bissau's Creole-dominated government made little effort to develop and maintain a grassroots organizational structure in the countryside (Munslow 1981). Consequently, Guinea-Bissau maintained its deep social and political divide between Creole and indigenous Africans. This ethnic division further reinforced the social and political divide between the national capital and the country's outlying rural districts (see Forrest 2003, esp. chs. 10 and 11).

Guinea-Bissau's postcolonial state-building was also hindered by the legacy of highly restrictive colonial citizenship laws that created a deep social and economic divide between the country's Creole elites and the indigenous African majority. Because colonial state policies had historically favored local Creoles over indigenous Africans, Guinea-Bissau's Creole minority continued to dominate the state bureaucracy after independence. Guinea-Bissau's independence leader, President Luis Cabral (1975–80), pursued economic policies that clearly benefited the country's Creole elites at the expense of rural and indigenous Africans. The Creole minority was heavily concentrated in the capital city, which received 40% of total state investment, despite having only 14% of the national population. Only 11% of government investment was directed toward the agricultural sector, where 80% of the workforce was employed (Dávila 1987). These policies resulted in severe food shortages in the countryside, despite the ostentatious lifestyles of urban government elites (Munslow 1981, 111).

To further complicate matters, Guinea-Bissau's Creole-dominated independence government openly favored political integration with Cape Verde. This generated significant resentment among indigenous Africans (mostly ethnic Pepels and Balantas) who had fought in the country's independence war. Many indigenous Africans resented the Creole domination of the ruling party and state bureaucracy, and they questioned the political loyalty of Creole elites who favored political integration with Cape Verde. As independence provided few material benefits to Guinea-Bissau's indigenous African majority, many began to perceive the ruling party as selling out to Creole and Cape Verdean interests. This perception was only confirmed by an ill-advised constitutional amendment that would have allowed Cape Verdeans to hold the presidency of Guinea-Bissau (Forrest 1992, 56–57). Disgruntled African veterans turned toward the army's chief of staff, João Bernardo "Nino" Vieira, who toppled Luis Cabral's government in a military coup on November 14, 1980 (Forrest 2003, 229; Munslow 1981). The ethnoracial motivation for this coup was emphasized in Vieira's first radio broadcast: he claimed that the military regime sought to "chase off the colonialists" (i.e., Creole elites) still present in Guinea-Bissau (Munslow 1981, 110).

The 1980 military coup brought neither political stability nor effective governance to Guinea-Bissau, despite the transfer of power from Creole to indigenous Africans.[19] Guinea-Bissau's new leader, Nuno Vieira, went on to establish a corrupt, repressive, and highly personalistic dictatorship that persisted for nearly two decades. As Vieira continued to face political opposition from dissident military factions, his leadership became increasingly paranoid, repressive, and violent. He even ordered the execution of several army officers and government ministers following three failed coup attempts against his leadership in 1982, 1983, and 1985 (Forrest 1992, 59–61; Forrest 2003, 229). During the 1980s, Guinea-Bissau's rural sector became increasingly detached from the state bureaucracy, as peasant farmers refused to sell their agricultural produce to state marketing boards that were established to control food prices for urban consumers (Forrest 2003, 223–25). Guinea-Bissau's foreign exchange reserves were significantly depleted by the collapse of the country's export agricultural sector. Consequently, the government's coffers were depleted as Guinea-Bissau's external debt soared to more than 300% of its gross national product in 1988 (Forrest 1992, 102). As Guinea-Bissau's postcolonial state became financially insolvent, the percentage of children attending primary schools declined from more than 60% of the school-aged population in the late 1970s to 37% by 1988 (Forrest 2003, 219).

Guinea-Bissau's economic bankruptcy forced Vieira's government to pursue tepid economic reforms after 1984 and political liberalization after 1991 (Chabal 2002, 96). These reforms were halfhearted, as they were largely implemented to satisfy Western donors. The political incumbent and military strongman Nuno Vieira repeatedly delayed, and ultimately rigged, the country's first multiparty elections to remain in power after 1994 (Chabal 2002, 126; Koudawo 2001, 136–40). Vieira held power until a civil war broke out in 1998, and his government was deposed by an international military intervention in 1999. Vieira returned to power following a brief period of exile, as Guinea-Bissau continued to experience military coups and regime instability after the civil war. Consequently, Vieira was able to dominate Guinea-Bissau's political landscape for nearly three decades, until his violent assassination in 2009 (Forrest 2010).

The contrast between Cape Verde's postcolonial development and democratization and Guinea-Bissau's chronic regime instability and underdevelopment could not be starker. The two countries were among the poorest in sub-Saharan Africa at the time of their independence, and both countries were initially governed by the same authoritarian party. Nevertheless, Cape Verde's single-party regime promoted political liberalization and inclusive human development that paved the way for the country's democratization during the 1990s. By contrast, Guinea-Bissau's ruling party was weakened by frequent military coups and the rise of a political strongman during the 1980s and 1990s. These distinctive postcolonial regime trajectories have had profound implications for human well-being in the two countries. Cape Verde's effective postcolonial governance generated robust economic growth with significant improvements in human well-being. By contrast, Guinea-Bissau remains one of the most impoverished and underdeveloped nations on the planet, ranking in the lowest decile of countries in the United Nations' Human Development Index (United Nations, 2016).

Summary and Discussion

This chapter highlights the extent to which colonial-era legal-administrative institutions shaped the distinctive developmental trajectories of Cape Verde and Guinea-Bissau during the colonial era and after independence. In Cape Verde, Portuguese forced settlement generated an integrated colonial state that established a uniform legal-administrative framework and inclusive citizenship rights following the abolition of slavery. Because Cape Verde was uninhabited prior to its colonization, Portuguese civil and clerical institutions were introduced *tabula rasa* during the fifteenth century. In Guinea-Bissau, by contrast, indigenous African resistance limited the territorial hegemony and administrative control of the Portuguese colonial state. Consequently, Portuguese colonial authority was based on bifurcated legal-administrative institutions that strengthened the arbitrary and despotic power of colonial state officials and their indigenous African intermediaries. Guinea-Bissau's bifurcated colonial state also denied citizenship rights to indigenous Africans, who were subject to the harsh and arbitrary provisions of the Portuguese *indigenato* legal code.

To be sure, both Cape Verde and Guinea-Bissau suffered from extractive economic institutions and repressive political institutions that hindered their social and political development under Portuguese rule. This repressive nature of Portugal's *Estado Novo* dictatorship (1930–74) limited educational opportunities and prevented the expansion of mass electoral competition in both countries prior to independence. Nevertheless, the historical evidence in this chapter emphasizes important legal-administrative differences between the two countries. In contrast to Guinea-Bissau's bifurcated colonial state and restrictive citizenship rights, Cape Verde established an integrated colonial state with inclusive citizenship rights that expanded state-funded education and voting rights following the abolition of slavery. Moreover, Cape Verde did not experience the type of revolutionary violence and colonial state repression that terrorized Guinea-Bissau's indigenous population during the anticolonial war against

Portuguese rule. Consequently, Cape Verde gained independence with effective state institutions and a uniform legal-administrative framework that promoted inclusive development and significant improvements in human well-being after independence. Cape Verde's economic and social progress ultimately generated demands for greater political freedom and mass electoral competition.

In some ways, the historical and institutional factors that facilitated Cape Verde's successful postcolonial development and democratization are not fundamentally different from those of British forced settlement colonies like Jamaica, as outlined in the previous chapter. Nevertheless, the Cape Verdean case is particularly insightful for several reasons: First, Cape Verde was able to promote inclusive human development after independence and to consolidate democracy after the Cold War despite the extractive and repressive nature of Portuguese rule in Africa. This suggests that countries that experienced highly repressive colonial regimes can promote inclusive development and even democratic consolidation after independence. Second, Cape Verde did not benefit from Protestant missionary evangelization that contributed to the establishment of denominational schools in British forced settlement colonies following the abolition of slavery. This suggests that effective administrative institutions and inclusive citizenship laws can promote greater access to state-funded schooling, which is important for promoting mass literacy, education, and the development of civil society. Third, Cape Verde's effective state institutions ultimately promoted inclusive development and facilitated democratic consolidation, despite the authoritarian legacy of Portugal's *Estado Novo* dictatorship. Cape Verde's postcolonial state successfully promoted inclusive development and democratization despite the historical absence of European settlers, Protestant missionaries, or British legal and political institutions—three factors that previous scholarship has often highlighted as important determinants of inclusive long-term development and postcolonial democratization. Despite lacking these historical advantages, Cape Verde's effective legal-administrative apparatus and inclusive citizenship laws facilitated more inclusive socioeconomic and political development after independence than in other Portuguese African colonies.

In many ways, Cape Verde's inclusive postcolonial development and successful democratization support existing arguments that emphasize the importance of effective state institutions and inclusive citizenship laws that facilitate effective governance, inclusive development, and democratic consolidation (Linz and Stepan 1996; Przeworski et al. 2000; Lange 2009; Angell 2010). Cape Verde's inclusive postcolonial development and subsequent democratic consolidation are similar to Portugal's democratic consolidation and inclusive development after 1974. Today, Portugal's democracy is widely celebrated for its high levels of social inclusion and civic engagement. Portugal's successful transition from a despotic colonial power to a democratic European state also highlights the extent to which inclusive citizenship laws and a uniform legal-administrative framework can facilitate social and political inclusion following decades of repressive single-party control (Fernandes 2015; Fishman 2018).

The divergent postcolonial trajectories of Cape Verde and Guinea-Bissau are also indicative of broader trends within Lusophone Africa. Table 6.1 provides comparative data on colonial institutions and postcolonial development across Lusophone Africa. The comparative data in this table clearly demonstrate favorable postcolonial development outcomes in Portuguese forced settlement colonies—i.e., Cape Verde and São Tomé and Príncipe—relative to Portuguese-occupied colonies like Guinea-Bissau, Angola, or Mozambique. Cape Verde and São Tomé and Príncipe had more inclusive citizenship laws than the Portuguese-occupied colonies, where indigenous Africans were excluded from metropolitan citizenship. Cape Verde and São Tomé and Príncipe also gained independence without having to fight a devastating anticolonial war on their home soil; they are the only Luso-African states to avoid a civil war after independence. By contrast, Angola and Mozambique experienced lengthy and devastating civil wars following their anticolonial wars against Portuguese rule. Guinea-Bissau's independence war also generated a heavily militarized state that has been plagued by frequent coup activity and chronic regime instability. Given this history, it is not surprising that Cape Verde and São Tomé and Príncipe experienced greater democratization than Angola, Guinea-Bissau, or Mozambique after multiparty elections were introduced in Lusophone Africa. Cape Verde has the highest democracy score in Lusophone Africa after 1991, and São Tomé and Príncipe is in second place. Mozambique, Guinea-Bissau, and Angola trail Cape Verde and São Tomé and Príncipe on key indicators of postcolonial democratization. Cape Verde also outperforms the HDI scores for São Tomé and Príncipe, Angola, Guinea-Bissau, and Mozambique in 2012 (United Nations 2016). These data suggest that Cape Verde has been more successful than other Portuguese African colonies at promoting human well-being and postcolonial democratization.

One might be tempted to argue that the small size and population of Portugal's forced settlement colonies made them easier and less costly to control, and that this resulted in more effective and inclusive state institutions during the colonial era and after independence. After all, both Cape Verde and São Tomé and Príncipe were effectively colonized by Portugal during the fifteenth and sixteenth centuries, respectively. The Creole populations of these island states were also easier to control using metropolitan European institutions. This is why Portugal never lost control over its Creole African colonies during the independence wars of the 1960s.

Nevertheless, there are important institutional differences between Cape Verde and São Tomé and Príncipe, despite their similar size, island geography, and population composition. Cape Verde lacked was the only Portuguese African colony

Table 6.1 Colonial Institutions and Postcolonial Development in Portuguese Africa

Colonial population and institutions, 1950	Portuguese Forced Settlement		Portuguese Colonial Occupation		
	Cape Verde	São Tomé and Príncipe	Angola	Guinea-Bissau	Mozambique
Population (thousands)	148	60	4,145	511	5,739
Bifurcated legal-administrative framework	No	Yes	Yes	Yes	Yes
% metropolitan citizens/ *civilisado*	100.0	72.1	3.3	1.6	1.6
% indigenous subjects/ *indigena*	0.0	27.9	96.7	98.4	98.4
Anticolonial war after 1961	No	No	Yes	Yes	Yes
Postcolonial Development Outcomes					
Civil war after independence	No	No	Yes, 1975–2002	Yes, 1998–99	Yes, 1977–92
Mean democracy scores, 1972–2012	6.80	6.07	2.12	3.78	3.98
1991–2012	9.57	8.88	2.96	5.41	6.10
HDI score, 2012	0.636	0.551	0.543	0.437	0.412
Life expectancy at birth, 2010–15	72.2	66.2	60.2	56.0	56.0
Youth literacy rate, 2012	98.1	80.2	73.0	74.3	67.1
Alternative Explanations					
% European settlers, 1973	2.0	1.9	7.0	0.4	2.7
Protestant missionaries per 10,000 inhabitants, 1923	0	0	0.47	0	0.52
Real per capita GDP, 1960	$508	$867	$1,253	$501	$1,329
Inhabitants per square kilometer, 1960	48.6	64.0	4.0	16.4	25.3

Sources: Legal-administrative institutions are coded based on % *civilisado* and % *indigena* data based on Portuguese colonial census data for 1950 (Portugal, Instituto Nacional de Estatística 1959); post-colonial democracy is based on Freedom House Imputed Polity Scores for 1972–2012 and 1991–2012 (Quality of Government 2015); HDI scores are from Wikipedia 2016; life expectancy at birth from United Nations 2017; youth literacy rates from United Nations, 2017); % European settlers is from Barrett 1982; Protestant missionary data are from Woodberry 2012; per capita GDP data from Maddison 2006.

to develop an integrated legal-administrative system with fully inclusive citizenship laws prior to World War II. This likely reflects the fact that Cape Verde's agricultural plantations were no longer profitable when slavery was abolished in the Portuguese colonial empire. Because São Tomé and Príncipe's cocoa plantations remained fertile and profitable long after the abolition of slavery, Portuguese colonial officials and local Creole landowners simply recruited indentured labor migrants from other Portuguese colonies. Indigenous African migrant laborers, and their descendants in São Tomé and Príncipe, were denied citizenship rights until the mid-1950s (Duffy 1961, 295). This has had profound consequences for postcolonial governance in the twin-island nation.

Although São Tomé and Príncipe has a smaller geographic area and population than Cape Verde, the twin-island nation gained independence with a deep socioeconomic and political divide between Creole landowners and the descendants of indentured plantation laborers from the African mainland. São Tomé and Príncipe's ruling party sought to address this social divide by nationalizing many Creole-owned plantations after independence. This hindered the country's agricultural production and initiated a lengthy period of economic decline after independence (Seibert 2006, esp. 123–82). São Tomé and Príncipe's economic decline also contributed to significant regime instability, including recurrent coup activity that destabilized the country's ruling party, and undermined democratization efforts after 1991 (Meyns 2002; Seibert 2006). The deep social and political divide between São Tomé and Príncipe's Creole elites and the descendants of indentured plantation laborers is not unlike the deep social and political divide between Creole and indigenous Africans in Guinea-Bissau. Both countries maintain deep social and political divides that result from their colonial history of discriminatory citizenship laws and bifurcated legal-administrative institutions. Thus, even in a small, densely populated, and predominantly Creole island nation, the deep socioeconomic and cultural cleavages exacerbated by the bifurcated colonial state continue to undermine socioeconomic development and effective governance after independence.

The tragic postcolonial trajectories of Angola and Mozambique suggest that European settler minorities can, in fact, hinder inclusive development and postcolonial democratization, as demonstrated in recent research by Jack Paine (2019b). European settler minorities often supported extractive economic institutions and discriminatory citizenship laws that privileged their economic and social well-being at the expense of indigenous Africans. Consequently, indigenous African grievances against settler control and domination contributed to devastating anticolonial wars against Portuguese rule in Angola and Mozambique. Despite the mass exodus of white settlers from Angola and Mozambique, following the collapse of Portuguese rule in 1975, both countries suffered lengthy and devastating civil wars after independence. In part, these civil wars were fueled by US and South African attempts to destabilize the Marxist-oriented single-party dictatorships that emerged after independence (see Krieckhaus 2006, ch. 6; Frynas and Wood 2001). Angola's civil war quickly morphed into a power struggle over that country's vast oil reserves and diamond deposits, with international actors remaining engaged in that conflict until 2004 (Frynas and Wood, 2001). The rich agricultural plantations and vast mineral resources that once attracted hundreds of thousands of Portuguese settlers to Angola continue to enrich that country's ruling elites. Indeed, Angola maintains one of the most corrupt and longest-lived single-party dictatorships in sub-Saharan Africa. Guinea-Bissau and Mozambique have been more democratic than Angola since the mid-1990s, although Freedom House still ranks both countries as "partly free." Both Mozambique and Guinea-Bissau remain at the bottom of the United Nations' Human Development Index. The disappointing postcolonial trajectories of Guinea-Bissau, Angola, Mozambique, and even São Tomé and Príncipe relative to Cape Verde demonstrate the lasting negative developmental consequences of bifurcated colonial states that denied citizenship rights to indigenous Africans.

In conclusion, this chapter's historical evidence demonstrates that Cape Verde established more effective and inclusive legal-administrative institutions than Guinea-Bissau during the colonial era and after independence. Despite the extractive and repressive nature of Portuguese rule throughout Africa, Cape Verde developed more effective bureaucratic administrative institutions and more inclusive citizenship laws that contributed to more inclusive development after independence, which has facilitated the archipelago nation's democratic consolidation after the Cold War. By contrast, Guinea-Bissau's bifurcated colonial state and highly restrictive colonial citizenship laws impeded effective state-building and the types of inclusive state-societal linkages that might have facilitated democratization and/or successful broad-based development after independence. This suggests that colonial legal-administrative institutions can exert a profound impact on postcolonial regime outcomes and developmental trajectories, even in situations where colonial authorities intentionally limited educational access and mass electoral competition prior to independence. The distinctive developmental trajectories of Cape Verde and Guinea-Bissau are consistent with the theoretical arguments and statistical evidence that demonstrate favorable development outcomes in forced settlement colonies relative to Global South countries that emerged from colonial occupation after World War II.

7

Forced Settlement and Colonial Occupation under French Rule

From Saint-Domingue (Haiti) and the French Antilles to Algeria and Sub-Saharan Africa

This chapter examines the long-term developmental consequences of the legal-administrative institutions that governed emancipated Afro-descendants and indigenous colonial subjects in former French colonies. The first section of the chapter examines an important puzzle that is not adequately addressed in earlier chapters: why did Haiti remain underdeveloped and impoverished relative to other forced settlement colonies that remained under European colonial domination throughout the nineteenth century? This question is relevant because of Haiti's historical importance as France's wealthiest and most populous colony prior to the 1789 French Revolution. Haiti was also the only forced settlement colony to gain independence following a successful slave revolt against white planter control. The 1791–1804 Haitian Revolution was one of the most transformative revolutions of the Enlightenment, and it threatened the entire system of colonial slavery and white planter domination in the black Atlantic world. Perhaps not surprisingly, slaveholding Atlantic powers like France, Spain, Britain, and the newly independent United States were overtly hostile to Haiti's political independence, and they actively undermined Haiti's political stability and economic development after its independence from French rule in 1804. Consequently, the first section of this chapter examines the external factors and domestic political constraints that hindered Haiti's long-term development following its independence.

The second section examines why the French Antilles colonies of Guadeloupe, Martinique, and Réunion were more successful than Haiti at promoting inclusive long-term development. The French Antilles colonies were also colonized by forced settlement, and they maintained a similar history of plantation slavery and colonial exploitation prior to the Haitian Revolution. Nevertheless, the historical evidence in this chapter highlights the experience of enslaved Africans and free people of color became intertwined with the revolutionary violence that pitted French republicans against the royalist elites of France's *ancien régime*. During the revolutionary upheavals of 1789–1800 and 1848–49, enslaved Africans and

Ruling Emancipated Slaves and Indigenous Subjects. Olukunle P. Owolabi, Oxford University Press.
© Oxford University Press 2023. DOI: 10.1093/oso/9780197673027.003.0007

free people of color in the French Antilles colonies actively supported the French republican struggle to advance liberty, fraternity, and equality for French citizens, regardless of their racial or ethnic background. Because enslaved Africans supported the republican insurgency against royalist white planters in the French Antilles colonies, French republican leaders extended parliamentary representation and citizenship rights to emancipated slaves in the French Antilles colonies. The core argument in this section is that the formal extension of citizenship rights to emancipated Afro-descendants facilitated the expansion of state-funded education, political representation, and economic development in Guadeloupe, Martinique, and Réunion following the democratic consolidation of the Third French Republic.

The political leaders of the Third French Republic also supported the significant territorial expansion of the French colonial empire to avenge France's humiliating territorial losses in the 1870 Franco-Prussian War. As a result of this expansion, the French colonial empire incorporated more than 10 million square kilometers of additional territory in Algeria, West Africa, Equatorial Africa, Madagascar, Indochina, and Oceania between 1870 and 1914. Consequently, the third section of this chapter explores five abbreviated case studies of French imperialist expansion and colonial occupation in Algeria, Senegal, Gabon, Madagascar, and the Comoros Islands. These African territories experienced French colonial occupation into twentieth century, but their indigenous populations were largely excluded from the legal and political benefits of French citizenship in the Third Republic. The historical evidence from Algeria, Senegal, Gabon, Madagascar, and the Comoros Islands demonstrates the negative developmental and political consequences of the repressive and extractive legal-administrative institutions that were used to control indigenous nonwhite subjects in the French colonial empire. Map 7.1 demonstrates the maximum territorial extent of the French colonial empire during the 1920s, and the geographic location of the colonial territories that are highlighted in this chapter. By 1920, Haiti was already independent from French rule, but suffering under the brutality of US military occupation. Haiti is also included in Map 7.1, given its historical importance as the most populous and wealthiest French colony prior to the 1789 French Revolution.

The case studies in this chapter make four important contributions to existing literature on colonial institutions, state-building, and postcolonial development. To the best of my knowledge, this is the first empirical study that systematically compares the institutional development of French territories that were colonized during the first and second waves of European colonial expansion. Most existing studies heavily prioritize French-occupied colonies that were established after 1830, because France lost most of its early colonial possessions to British colonial expansion between 1760 and 1815.[1] In a refreshing change from existing

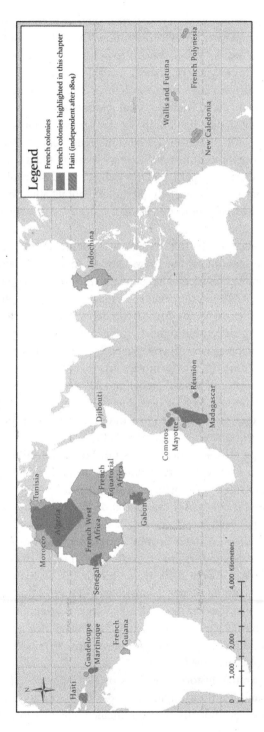

Map 7.1 French Colonial Territories and Haiti, c. 1920

literature, this chapter begins with a historical analysis of forced settlement in French colonies that predate the 1789 revolution. The inclusion of forced settlement colonies from the first global wave of colonial expansion forces us to consider the historical importance of France's unstable political development, and its revolutionary transformation from absolute monarchy to republican democracy between 1789 and 1870. France was unique among Western Europe's colonial powers in establishing a republican democracy with competitive elections and universal (male) suffrage during the late nineteenth century. Because French republicans openly embraced the revolutionary ideals of liberty, fraternity, and equality within an expanding parliamentary democracy, the consolidation of republican democracy raised important questions about whether to extend these rights to emancipated Afro-descendants and indigenous nonwhite subjects in French colonial territories.

The historical evidence in this chapter also highlights the very different legal and political institutions that were used to control emancipated Afro-descendants and indigenous nonwhite subjects in the French colonial empire. In the aftermath of the 1848 French revolution, French republican leaders extended citizenship rights to emancipated Afro-descendants in the French Antilles colonies, while denying citizenship rights to indigenous nonwhite populations in French-occupied colonies like Algeria, Senegal, Gabon, Madagascar, and the Comoros Islands. These colonial territories vary significantly in terms of population, size, resource endowments, religion, and their exposure to Christian missionary evangelization. Nevertheless, French colonial officials used the repressive *indigénat* legal code was to control indigenous nonwhite populations in all of these territories (see Merle 2002; Mann 2009).

Third, the comparative-historical analysis of French forced settlement and colonial occupation in enables us to examine the institutional and political development of colonial territories with limited missionary evangelization. There was limited Protestant missionary evangelization in most French colonies, and France's secular republican elites were often hostile to Catholic missionaries and religious elites. The French state's hostility toward Christian missionary evangelization limited access to Western education in many French colonies (Grier 1997; Gallego and Woodberry 2010; Woodberry 2012). Nevertheless, the limited extent of Protestant and Catholic missionary evangelization in the French colonial empire makes it easier to isolate the unique developmental legacies of colonial institutions that expanded the legal rights and political agency of emancipated Afro-descendants in the French Antilles relative to indigenous nonwhite populations in French-occupied colonies.

Last, the comparative-historical analysis of development outcomes in the French Antilles and Haiti highlights the specific institutional mechanisms that enabled many—but not all—forced settlement colonies to promote more inclusive development outcomes following the abolition of slavery. Most existing studies highlight Haiti's persistent underdevelopment relative to the Dominican Republic, as the two countries are located on the same Caribbean island. The political economy of forced settlement in French-ruled Saint-Domingue was far more extractive and repressive than the mixed pattern of colonization on the Spanish half of the island (i.e., Santo Domingo),[2] and Haiti continues to trail the Dominican Republic on important indicators of human well-being and postcolonial democratization (Harrison 2006; Khan 2010; Valeris 2013). This is why many existing have concluded that Saint-Domingue's brutal and oppressive system of plantation slavery hindered Haiti's long-term development relative to the Dominican Republic.

This chapter offers a different perspective by examining Haiti's long-term underdevelopment in comparative perspective with French Antilles colonies, which experienced similar levels of plantation slavery prior to the 1791–1804 Haitian Revolution. Nevertheless, the developmental trajectories of Haiti and the French Antilles colonies diverged following Haiti's independence from French rule in 1804, and the republican abolition of slavery following the 1848 French revolution. Whereas Haiti's emancipated slaves continued to experience significant exploitation from French and US neocolonial interventions, the Antilles colonies were able to implement liberal institutional reforms that expanded the legal rights and political agency of emancipated Afro-descendants following the French abolition of slavery. The divergent trajectories of Haiti and the French Antilles colonies reinforces the book's central argument that liberal institutional reforms enabled many—but not all—forced settlement colonies to promote inclusive development and postcolonial democratization following the abolition of slavery.

Why Haiti's Development Lags behind Other Forced Settlement Colonies

The forced settlement colony of Saint-Domingue (i.e., present-day Haiti) was France's wealthiest and most populous colony prior to the French Revolution. During the second half of the eighteenth century, Saint-Domingue's coffee, cocoa, and sugar production accounted for nearly 40% of France's overseas trade (Joshi 2005). Like most forced settlement colonies, Saint-Domingue's agricultural production was sustained by a brutal system of plantation slavery, and enslaved Africans accounted for almost 90% of the colony's population. Nevertheless, the Atlantic revolutions of the late eighteenth century disrupted France's political control over its most prized colony, as enslaved Africans rebelled against white planter control and French imperial domination during the Haitian Revolution.

The Saint-Domingue slave insurrection was inspired by the same revolutionary ideals that motivated French republican leaders to overthrow the absolutist Bourbon monarchy and establish a republican government that advanced the political ideals of liberty, fraternity, and equality during the 1790s. France's first republican government was short-lived, as it was toppled by the military strongman Napoleon Bonaparte, who crowned himself emperor in 1802. Napoleon was deeply committed to the restoration of slavery and imperial rule in the Caribbean region, as his wife hailed from a slave-owning family in Martinique. Consequently, one of Napoleon's first decrees was to restore plantation slavery and white planter control in the French colonial empire. Nevertheless, Haiti's revolutionary leaders continued to fight against Napoleon's despotism, and they ultimately prevailed in a brutal independence war against French colonial domination. The victorious Haitian army slaughtered the white colonists that survived the initial slave insurrection, and Haiti became the first forced settlement to permanently abolish slavery following its independence from French rule in 1804.

Despite these early political triumphs, Haiti remains the poorest and most underdeveloped country in the Western Hemisphere more than two centuries after independence from French rule. The data in Table 7.1 demonstrate Haiti's persistent underdevelopment relative to other forced settlement colonies that remained under European control following the abolition of slavery. The contrast between Haiti and Britain's largest forced settlement colony, Jamaica, is particularly striking because the two islands were the largest recipients of enslaved Africans in the Caribbean region. The two colonies also maintained similar levels of plantation slavery during the eighteenth century. Nevertheless, contemporary Jamaica outperforms Haiti on every indicator of human well-being and postcolonial democratization. Haiti also falls well short of the median development indicators for forced settlement colonies that gained independence after World War II.

The contrasting developmental trajectories of Haiti and Jamaica partly reflect the unique nature of British liberal reforms that were implemented following the abolition of slavery. Nevertheless, Haiti is also severely underdeveloped relative to the French Antilles colonies, which maintained similar levels of plantation slavery during the eighteenth century (see Table 7.2). The development gap between the French Antilles and Haiti is striking given their geographic and cultural similarities, and their shared history of forced settlement and plantation slavery. All of these territories developed large agricultural plantations, and enslaved Africans comprised more than 80% of the population during the eighteenth century. Yet, the developmental trajectories of the Antilles colonies and Haiti diverged significantly following the Haitian Revolution. Guadeloupe and Martinique also experienced slave rebellions during the 1790s, but their white

Table 7.1 Slavery, Institutional Reform, and Long-Term Development: Comparing Haiti to Other Forced Settlement Colonies

	% Enslaved Prior to Abolition	Colonial Duration	Legal-Administrative Institutions Following Abolition	Postcolonial Outcomes		
				% Literate, 1960	Mean Democracy Score, 1972–2012	HDI Score, 2015
Haiti (French, 1697–1804)	87 (1791)	French, 1697–1804	Extractive	15	2.90	0.483 (low)
Jamaica (British, 1655–1962)	82 (1830)	British, 1655–1962	Inclusive	82	8.80	0.719 (high)
All forced settlement colonies except Haiti (median)	78 (c. 1830)	1635–1974	Inclusive	83	8.95	0.748 (high)

Sources: Data on the percentage of enslaved persons are primarily drawn from Engerman and Higman 1997, which provides data for all Caribbean societies in 1830 (see 50–52). Data estimates for Mauritius, Seychelles, and Réunion are obtained from Allen 2003, 33. Data for estimates for Cape Verde and Sao Tome and Principe are from Seibert 2014, 53.

Table 7.2 Slavery, Institutional Reform, and Long-Term Development: Haiti versus the French Antilles Colonies

Colonial Conditions	Haiti	French Antilles Colonies		
		Guadeloupe	Martinique	Réunion
% enslaved prior to Haitian Revolution	87 (1791)	81 (1830)	87 (1791) 79 (1830)	~80 (c. 1770) ~60 (1848)
Year(s) of abolition	1793/1804	1794/1848	1848	1848
Duration of colonial rule	1697–1804	1635–1946	1635–1946	1650–1946
Extent of liberal reforms following abolition of slavery	Minimal	Extensive	Extensive	Extensive
Postcolonial development				
Current political status	Independent since 1804	French overseas departments since 1946		
Population (thousands), 2015	10,711	450	386	863
HDI score in 2015	0.483 Low	0.822 Very High	0.813 Very High	0.750 High

Sources: The 1791 data for the percentage of enslaved persons in Haiti and Martinique are from Yelvington et al. 2011, 286–87. Data for Guadeloupe and Martinique in 1830 are from Knight 1997, 51. Estimates for the percentage of enslaved persons in Réunion are from Allen 2003, 33. The HDI scores are obtained from the United Nations Development Program 2016.

planters ultimately survived due to French and British military intervention (see Bénot 2003, 148; Dubois 2004b, 85–89). Consequently, plantation slavery remained legal and widespread in the Antilles colonies until 1848. The Antilles colonies did not implement significant liberal reforms until after the 1848 French revolution and the consolidation of democracy in the Third French Republic (1870–1940). These revolutionary upheavals enabled the Antilles colonies to expand state-funded education, political representation, and voting rights for emancipated Afro-descendants following the abolition of slavery in the nineteenth century. Consequently, Guadeloupe, Martinique, and Réunion now boast very high living standards, whereas Haiti remains severely impoverished, underdeveloped, and mostly undemocratic.

The next section of this chapter highlights the domestic and external factors that hindered the implementation of liberal reforms following Haiti's independence from French rule. The striking contrast between Haiti's persistent underdevelopment and the more inclusive developmental outcomes in the French Antilles colonies demonstrates the extent to which liberal reforms— rather than geographic or cultural conditions—advanced human well-being and postcolonial democratization in forced settlement colonies that emerged from colonial domination after World War II.

Domestic Political Factors That Hindered Haiti's Long-Term Development

The physical destruction of the Haitian Revolution undermined the country's long-term economic viability after independence. Most of Saint-Domingue's agricultural plantations were destroyed during the independence war, and Haiti's export crop production declined by 98% between 1791 and 1798 (Girard 2019). The human cost of the Haitian Revolution was also enormous: most plantation owners were either killed or forced into exile during the Haitian Revolution, and the surviving whites were massacred by the victorious Haitian army after independence. The pent-up anger and violence against colonial white planters is in many ways understandable, but it destroyed Haiti's short-term economic viability and further depleted the newly independent country of its limited human capital.

For black survivors of the Haitian Revolution, the human cost of the revolutionary war was even higher: one-third of Haitian blacks were killed during the independence war, and many survivors refused to continue working as plantation laborers after independence (Phillips 2008, 3–4). Consequently, Haiti's sugar production did not recover to its 1789 levels until the 1960s! (Beauvois 2017, 104). Moreover, the physical destruction of the 1791 slave uprising left Haiti without a functioning state after its independence from France in 1804. The newly established Haitian republic was also forced to pay an insurmountable debt in exchange for diplomatic recognition from France and other slave-holding Atlantic powers. To make matters worse, the constant threat of invasion by hostile foreign powers forced Haiti's early political leaders to maintain a large standing army that consumed more than 50% of government expenditures during the first half of the nineteenth century (Dupuy 1989, 94–95). These geopolitical circumstances forced Haitian leaders to prioritize national security over liberal institutional reforms. Consequently, there was little money available for land reforms, political reforms, or state-funded education after independence.

Haiti's postcolonial development was also hindered by the political dominance of conservative military elites that acquired significant landholdings during the lengthy independence war. The new Haitian military elites had a vested interested in reviving large-scale agricultural production with coercive labor. Consequently, most Haitian governments maintained repressive labor codes that required emancipated slaves to work as agricultural sharecroppers in exchange for one-fourth of the estate profits (Girard 2019).[3] Haiti's 1826 *Code Rurale* exemplifies the type of coercive labor policies that were enacted to ensure the supply of cheap plantation labor after independence. The *Code Rurale* stipulated that all Haitians—apart from plantation owners, government functionaries, military officers, professionals, artisans, and shopkeepers—had a legal obligation to work the land. Haitian peasants were legally bonded to specific plantations, where they were required to work in exchange for a minority share of the estate revenues. Plantation workers could not live in towns without legal authorization, and they were not permitted to sell their own produce. The Haitian government also imposed an internal passport system that restricted freedom of movement. The *Code Rurale* was enforced by military officers who maintained martial law on the country's agricultural estates. The Haitian state also appointed local justices to prevent the breakup of large plantations into smaller estates (Dupuy 1989, 95–96).

Moreover, Haiti's postcolonial rulers never enacted the type of liberal institutional reforms that expanded the legal-administrative capacity of British forced settlement colonies like Jamaica. Instead, Haiti disintegrated into chronic regime instability after independence, as black military elites vied with mulatto economic elites—the descendants of Saint-Domingue's privileged *gens de couleurs*—for control over the Haitian state. In general, black political elites used their military power to control Haiti's largest agricultural estates, whereas mulatto elites used their economic advantage and international connections to dominate the country's largest retail firms. In the face of chronic regime instability and political violence, many Haitian peasants fled to remote villages in the country's mountainous interior to escape forced labor on the agricultural plantations, which remained heavily militarized throughout the nineteenth century. Haitian peasants achieved modest success as small-scale producers of cocoa, coffee, and tobacco, but they remained heavily dependent on mulatto bourgeois elites that controlled the retail and marketing of agricultural exports. Haitian government officials also imposed a heavy tax burden on peasant export crops, and government officials established state monopolies to control the sale and marketing of export cash crops (Dupuy 1989, 92–106). The maintenance of extractive economic institutions prevented Haiti's small peasant farmers from accumulating surplus wealth from their production.

Last, Haitian government officials never established effective administrative control over the country's rural districts. Instead, the early Haitian state used extractive and coercive methods to maintain public order and control agricultural production and retail in the country's rural districts. Haiti's extractive legal-administrative institutions closely resembled the bifurcated state structure that

European colonizers would later use to control indigenous African populations in British-occupied colonies like Sierra Leone (see Chapter 5) and Portuguese-occupied colonies like Guinea-Bissau (Chapter 6). For example, Haitian military administrators appointed "section chiefs" to collect taxes, administer justice, and maintain political order in the country's rural communities. Haiti's rural section chiefs also recruited unpaid corvée labor for road construction and other public works projects. Corvée labor was widely used for road construction and maintenance during the second half of the nineteenth century; peasants could only avoid it by paying daily fees to their "section chiefs." Haiti's section chiefs also established their own "rural police" to enforce law and order in the rural communities. These police forces were not paid or regulated by the Haitian state. Instead, they earned their incomes by extracting fees and payments from the peasant communities that they controlled (Dupuy 1989, 104). These examples highlight Haiti's inability to develop effective state institutions that might have promoted inclusive development after independence. Instead, the early Haitian Republic was plagued by the same chronic indebtedness, endemic corruption, extreme militarization, and regime instability that would afflict many postcolonial African states during the second half of the twentieth century.

External Factors That Hindered Haiti's Long-Term Development

External economic and political constraints also hindered the implementation of liberal reforms in postcolonial Haiti. Because the Haitian Revolution threatened slaveholders throughout the Atlantic world, the early Haitian Republic faced extreme hostility from slaveholding Atlantic powers like France, Britain, and the newly independent United States. France's Bourbon royalist elites were especially hostile to Haiti's independence because of the physical destruction and financial losses suffered by royalist colonial planters during the Haitian Revolution. Many of Saint-Domingue's colonial planters fled to Cuba, to Louisiana, and to nearby British colonies, where they gained a sympathetic ear from colonial officials and local white elites who were determined to prevent similar slave uprisings in their territories. Saint-Domingue's ruined planters also aggressively lobbied the French government for monetary compensation for their "property losses" during the Haitian and French Revolutions. At the time of Haiti's independence, France was still dominated by military strongman Napoleon Bonaparte, whose wife Josephine came from a slave-owning family in Martinique. Consequently, Napoleon was determined to restore plantation slavery and white planter control in the French Antilles, and his government maintained active plans to invade and recolonize Haiti. French government officials also maintained a special bureau to "settle" the financial claims of Saint-Domingue planters after the Bourbon monarchy was restored to power in 1815. Bourbon French officials also leaned on the US government to reject Haitian demands for diplomatic recognition and economic assistance during the first half of the nineteenth century (Sheller 2000, 74).

Successive French governments refused to recognize Haiti's independence until the Haitian government agreed to pay a crippling indemnity of 150 million French francs (FF) to compensate Saint-Domingue's white planters for their "property losses" during the Haitian Revolution. Haitian president Jean-Pierre Boyer was forced to agree to the 1825 indemnity as the French navy maintained 14 warships within striking distance of the Haitian capital (Logan 1930, 418). At the time, the French state was still dominated by conservative royalist elites who supported the restoration of slavery in the Antilles. Indeed, the French prime minister who secured the 150 million FF indemnity from Haiti was one of the largest slaveholders and wealthiest colonial planters from Réunion, which replaced Saint-Domingue as the largest sugar producer in the French colonial empire (Blackburn 1988, 475–76). France's continued support for slaveholding interests was hardly unique. Britain, Denmark, and the Netherlands also refused to recognize Haiti's independence until after Boyer agreed to "settle" the financial claims of Saint-Domingue's defeated planters (see Dupuy 1989, 93–94; Dupuy 2019, 91–94; Gaffield 2015, 13–14). The political leaders of the newly independent United States also maintained an aggressive hostility toward the young Haitian Republic well into the twentieth century.

US political leaders had their own reasons for marginalizing and isolating Haiti after independence. Southern white plantation owners exercised disproportionate power over the United States' foreign policy until 1860, and Haiti's independence was widely perceived as a threat to US slaveholders (Karp 2016). Consequently, the US government did not recognize Haiti's independence until 1862—after the slaveholding Confederate states had seceded from the Union (Saye 2010, 80; Gaffield 2015, 194).[4] To make matters worse, the US relationship with Haiti shifted from diplomatic isolation to economic and political exploitation following the United States' emergence as the preeminent power in the Western Hemisphere following the US Civil War. President Andrew Jackson threatened to annex Haiti after the Civil War, but his expansionist plans were halted by political concerns that this would increase the United States' free black population. The US government stopped short of annexation, but US warships were dispatched to Haiti at least 20 times between 1857 and 1915. Britain, France, and Germany also sent warships to seize money, resources, and debts owed by impoverished Haitian governments in the decades leading up to World War I (Saye 2010, 81).

But how did the Haiti become so indebted and unstable in the first place? Haiti's financial insolvency resulted from its inability to repay the 150 million

FF indemnity that was demanded by French government officials in exchange for recognizing Haiti's independence. The 1825 indemnity was to be paid in five annual installments of 30 million FF, but each payment represented more than twice Haiti's annual tax revenue (Dupuy 1989, 93–94). Consequently, the Haitian government was forced to reschedule its debt payments and take out high-interest loans with French private banks. The compounded interest and fees significantly increased the size of the original loan by more than 50%. By the time the French government loan was paid off in 1883, the Haitian state was heavily indebted to European and American banks. In the decades leading up to World War I, the United States, Britain, France, and Germany regularly dispatched warships to Haitian ports to collect their debts and protect their economic investments in the country. The City Bank of New York (today's Citibank) assumed control over the Central Bank of Haiti following the US military invasion of Haiti in 1915. This forced Haiti's European creditors to settle their claims with Citibank, which continued to charge interest for the debts accumulated by US military administrators in Haiti (Dubois 2012, 204–7, Dupuy 1989, 126–31; Saye 2010, 81). The US military occupation ended in 1934, but the Haitian government did not pay off its outstanding debts to Citibank until 1947—more than 120 years *after* the French government had imposed debt payments to recognize Haiti's independence (Philipps 2008, 6).

Over the long term, Haiti's extreme indebtedness generated severe financial distress and chronic regime instability that undermined the country's postcolonial development. Sixteen of the first 24 Haitian governments were deposed by political uprising, assassination, or military coup (Dupuy 1989, 115–19). By the beginning of the twentieth century, the Haitian state was so insolvent that debt service payments accounted for 80% of government revenues (Dubois 2012, 204–5; Dupuy 1989, 130). Perhaps not surprisingly, the United States used Haiti's chronic indebtedness and regime instability, as well as the geopolitical threat of posed by European warships, to justify its lengthy and brutal military occupation of Haiti between 1915 and 1934. To this day, the US military occupation of Haiti remains the longest neocolonial intervention in any independent republic in the Western Hemisphere.

US Neocolonial Domination and the Revival of Corvée Labor during the Twentieth Century

Haiti's postcolonial development was further undermined by the lengthy US military occupation between 1915 and 1934. During World War I, US military officials dissolved Haiti's national parliament and seized control over Haiti's government ministries. Haitian journalists were subject to the jurisdiction of US military courts, and many prominent Haitian citizens were placed under the surveillance of military intelligence (Bellegarde-Smith 2004, 102). For the duration of the military occupation, the world's oldest black republic became a US colony in all but name. US Marines disbanded the old Haitian army and replaced the Haitian officials that had previously served as regional governors and rural section chiefs. The marines also violently suppressed any type of Haitian resistance. Historians estimate that at least 15,000 Haitian rebels were killed—and entire villages burned—during the early years of the US occupation (Dubois 2012, 211–38; Dupuy 1989, 139).[5]

In 1918, US government officials drafted a new Haitian constitution that paved the way for massive American investment and ownership in the Haitian economy. Haiti's independence constitution had banned foreign ownership of Haitian property, but the US military occupation paved the way for US agro-exporting companies to invest heavily in Haiti's agricultural plantations. Consequently, many Haitian plantations were sold or leased to US companies that produced and sold sugar, coffee, pineapples, bananas, and avocados to American consumers. Countless Haitian farmers lost control over lands that were sold or leased to large US firms, and 300,000 dispossessed Haitian peasant farmers fled the country to work as migrant laborers on US-owned plantations in the Dominican Republic, Cuba, or Central America. In theory, the US-imposed constitution was supposed to make it easier for Haitian farmers to acquire small plots of land, but prospective Haitian buyers had to prove that they could "improve" the land with fertilizers, irrigation, and American technical know-how. This made it very difficult for small Haitian farmers to compete with large US agricultural firms (Dupuy 1989, 135–37; Bellegarde-Smith 2004, 111–12).

To make matters worse, US military officials also revived Haiti's dormant 1865 labor code to conscript Haitian laborers for road construction and other public works projects. The revival of corvée labor generated some important infrastructural improvements, including the expansion of Haiti's road network, and the installation of telephone and telegraph services in Haiti's capital, Port-au-Prince. US military officials also supported public health campaigns to vaccinate schoolchildren, drain Haiti's swamps to reduce the spread of malaria, and chlorinate the water supply (Dupuy 1989, 133; Angulo 2010, 13). Although these were the first significant efforts to increase the administrative capacity of the Haitian state, what many Haitians remember most is the violence and brutality of labor recruitment during the US military occupation. Many Haitians perceived the revival of forced labor conscription as an attempt by a foreign power to restore slavery (Dubois 2012, 241). Indeed, US labor recruitment practices closely resembled the draconian tactics that colonial officials used to recruit indigenous African labor during the first half of the twentieth century.

Last, the US military administration did not expand educational access in Haiti. Instead, US officials slashed Haiti's education budget by more than 50% between 1915 and 1929 (Angulo 2010). This is because many US officials were motivated by the same racist views that generated racially segregated (and chronically underfunded) public schools in southern US states. At the time, many US states did not have a single "Negro" high school that was on par with Haiti's top-ranked *lycées* (Logan 1930, 428). Many US officials felt that it was wasteful to spend money on Haitian public schools (Logan 1930, 428; Angulo 2010; Pamphile 1985),[6] and they preferred to establish vocational schools that trained rural Haitians for agricultural labor and urban working Haitians for industrial labor in US-owned factories. Many educated Haitians criticized the US preference for vocational schools over Haitian public schools. They complained that the vocational schools were unnecessarily expensive, because most of their teachers were white Americans who were paid ten times as much as the black and mulatto teachers in Haiti's public schools. Additionally, the white technical managers of Haiti's vocational schools could be paid a hundred times as much as black Haitian teachers! Overall, the US-run vocational schools received 20 times as much funding per student as Haitian public schools, yet they did little to expand education and literacy among Haitian peasants (Angulo 2010, 6–8).

The US occupation also exacerbated the militarization of the Haitian state and reinforced the social divide between Haiti's black masses and mulatto economic elites.[7] The Haitian army, once the preserve of black military officers, was disbanded and replaced by a militarized police force under US military command. The newly established gendarmes exposed many Haitian peasants to the brutality of American racism: US military officers and Haitian gendarmes frequently abused their powers by executing Haitian prisoners without trial, and destroying entire villages that resisted the US military occupation (Dubois 2012, 233–38). US military officials also expanded the expanded administrative duties of Haitian gendarmes and soldiers to include prison management and corvée labor recruitment. Haitian military officials were also tasked with protecting the property of large landowners, and issuing travel permits that regulated freedom of movement within the country, and protecting the property rights of landowners. US military personnel also enforced Jim Crow laws that excluded Haitians from the exclusive hotels and social clubs favored by white American officials and US investors. They also favored mulatto over black Haitians for promotion in US private companies and the Haitian state bureaucracy. Consequently, economic opportunities for black Haitians were limited to the national police and armed forces (Dupuy 1989, 132–40).

Altogether, the lengthy and brutal US military occupation of Haiti enabled the United States to displace France as Haiti's largest creditor and dominant patron state during the twentieth century. The military occupation also increased Haiti's dependence on US capital, and hindered the development of Haitian public schools. The occupation also expanded the militarization of the Haitian state and reinforced the preexisting social divide between black and mulatto Haitians. Consequently, the lengthy US occupation did little to promote inclusive development or to expand Haiti's legal-administrative capacity in ways that would facilitate democratic political reforms after World War II.

Ruling Emancipated Afro-descendants in the French Antilles

The French Antilles colonies followed a very different pattern of institutional development during the nineteenth century. In contrast to Haiti's diplomatic isolation and neocolonial exploitation, the Antilles colonies were increasingly integrated into the French national polity, which implemented important liberal reforms throughout the nineteenth century. During the 1830s, the Bourbon French monarchy was replaced with a constitutional monarchy that increasingly resembled the British system of parliamentary government, with a modest electoral franchise. At the same time, the British abolition of slavery also generated robust parliamentary debates about whether to implement similar reforms in the French Antilles. French parliamentary records from the 1830 reveal that a growing number of elected officials felt that it was amoral, dangerous, and expensive to support colonial planters and maintain slavery in the French colonies. Moreover, 63% of elected deputies felt that the French parliament had the legal authority to regulate and/or abolish slavery in the colonies (Beauvois 2017, 256–57). These parliamentary records highlight the liberalization of French elite attitudes after 1830.

The Political Consequences of Revolution and Liberal Reforms in France, 1830–52

The onset of electoral competition in France also empowered abolitionists and free people of color to lobby the French state for legal and political reforms, including civil and political equality for free people of color in the Antilles colonies (Blackburn 1988, 475–85). The legal and political reforms of the French constitutional monarchy stopped short of abolishing slavery, but the French constitutional monarchy was ultimately toppled by revolutionary violence in 1848. The 1848 French revolution was supported by republicans, abolitionists, and parliamentary opposition members who established a provisional republican government in 1848–49. Many of the top-ranking officials in government were committed abolitionists, including the colonial secretary of state, François

Arago; the foreign secretary, Alphonse de Lamartine; and the undersecretary of state for the colonies, Victor Schoelcher. Consequently, one of the first acts of the 1848–49 republican government was to abolish slavery in the French colonial empire.

Victor Schoelcher, the lead author of the 1848 abolition decree, was a strong advocate for liberal institutional reforms that advanced the legal rights and political equality of emancipated Afro-descendants (Schoelcher 1998; Blackburn 1988, 499; Welborn 1969; Girolet 2000).[8] Schoelcher was deeply critical of the horrors of plantation slavery, which he had witnessed firsthand in the Antilles colonies and the southern United States. Unlike most abolitionists of his time, Schoelcher supported an antiracist political agenda that advanced the republican ideals of liberty, fraternity, and equality, without racial distinctions or prejudice. He believed the British Emancipation Act, while consequential, was not sufficiently robust to advance the economic and political interests of emancipated Afro-descendants. Schoelcher was deeply critical of the British apprenticeship program that required emancipated slaves to work for their former owners for four to six years (Welborn 1969, 98–99; Schoelcher 1998, 344–49; Girolet 2000, 38–39). Instead, he favored the immediate extension of citizenship rights to emancipated slaves. Schoelcher argued that the only way to incorporate emancipated slaves into French society was to recognize their civil and political rights as French citizens.

In the aftermath of the 1848 French revolution, Schoelcher argued that all aspects of democratic and republican citizenship—including parliamentary representation, universal suffrage, military service, free secular and compulsory education, the free press, and the jury system—should be extended to the French Antilles without delay (Welborn 1969, 101; Schoelcher 1998, 366–81).[9] Consequently, the Antilles colonies were integrated into the French national polity during Schoelcher's tenure as undersecretary of state for the colonies. Consequently, the key democratic and social reforms of the Second French Republic (1848–51) were extended to emancipated Afro-descendants in the Antilles colonies following the 1848 French revolution.

Monetary Compensation and Liberal Reforms in the French Antilles Colonies

The democratization of the Second French Republic ensured that French-emancipated Afro-descendants did not have to pay an insurmountable debt to compensate colonial planters for their "property losses" that resulted from the abolition of slavery. Instead, the French abolition decree provided 26 million FF to establish state-funded schools, nurseries, clinics, and labor arbitration courts for emancipated Afro-descendants in the Antilles colonies (Blackburn 1988, 496). French monetary support for emancipated Afro-descendants was relatively modest relative to the more generous financial compensation of French colonial planters. Nevertheless, French abolitionists reasoned that monetary compensation was necessary to ensure planter compliance with the liberal provisions of the abolition decree. The 1848 abolition decree required the Antilles colonies to provide four years of free schooling for emancipated children and social security benefits (*droits au secours*) for sick or elderly plantation workers. The abolition decree also established jury courts (i.e., *jurys cantonaux*) to adjudicate labor disputes between landowners and employers, and emancipated slaves were empowered to serve on these juries (Cochin 1863, 93–94; Blackburn 1988, 496; Yelvington et al. 2011, 313). These reforms were widely supported by free people of color who had a large presence in the local militias after 1830. These racially integrated militia units were able to register nonwhite voters for the founding elections of the Second French Republic, when emancipated slaves helped to elect a multiracial coalition of (mostly) republican and abolitionist candidates to the 1848 Constituent Assembly and the 1849 French parliament (Blackburn 1988, 496–98; Girolet 2001, 7; Lewis 1962, 135; McCloy 1966, 161–62).[10] This was the first time that nonwhite voters enjoyed political representation in the French government since the revolutionary unrest of the 1790s.

French taxpayers also provided 126 million FF in compensation to colonial planters to ensure their compliance with the abolition reforms and to ease their transition to a wage labor economy. The French republican government clearly sought to balance the planters' demands for monetary compensation with the abolitionists' longer-term interest of promoting land reforms and economic diversification in the Antilles colonies. Consequently, the 1849 indemnity law provided 6 million FF to white planters in immediate cash, plus 20 annuity payments of 6 million FF paid in government bonds earning 5% interest annually (Cochin 1863, 147; McCloy 1966, 150; Blackburn 1988, 501; Girolet 2000, 212–13; Beauvois 2017, 137–42, 215–17). The terms of France's 1849 indemnity law differed significantly from the British emancipation law, which provided £20 million cash compensation to former slave owners over a period of four years. Instead, the French indemnity law required one-eighth of the annuity payments to be held in newly established colonial banks that ensured the financial stability of the Antilles colonies (Blackburn 1988, 504; Beauvois 2017, 135–42).

The fact that the French indemnity law was implemented as a long-term capital grant to colonial planters and financiers prevented the complete collapse of sugar production in the Antilles colonies, which surpassed their preabolition levels of sugar production during the 1860s. The political ascendancy of Louis Napoleon Bonaparte's Second Empire dictatorship temporarily restored the economic and political dominance of white colonial planters during the 1850s and 1860s. Nevertheless, colonial planters were required to hold a portion of their annuity payments in colonial banks. This influx of capital enabled the Antilles colonies to develop and diversify their economic structure during the second half of the nineteenth century. The wealthiest colonial planters allied with local banks to finance the development of sugar refineries and rum distilleries that partially industrialized the economy and labor force of Guadeloupe and Martinique during the 1860s and 1870s. Furthermore, the second Bonapartist dictatorship came to an ignominious end during the France's humiliating national defeat in the 1870 Franco-Prussian War. The political rights of emancipated Afro-descendants were ultimately restored and expanded with the consolidation of democracy in the Third French Republic (1870–1940). Consequently, elected officials in the Antilles colonies enacted modest land reforms that enabled emancipated Afro-descendants to become independent producers of cocoa, coffee, pineapples, and bananas after 1880 (Heath 2011; Church 2017, 27–30).

The Consolidation of Democracy in the Third French Republic, 1870–1940

The implementation of liberal reforms in the Antilles colonies was strongly dependent on the consolidation of republican government in France after 1848, and the Antilles colonies benefited handsomely from the consolidation of democracy in the Third French Republic (1870–1940). During the final decades of the nineteenth century, the French Antilles colonies benefited from liberal institutional reforms that undermined the political dominance of royalist white planters, and expanded the legal rights and political agency of emancipated Afro-descendants. The early political leaders of the Third French Republic actively courted the political support of emancipated nonwhite voters from the Antilles colonies. This is because republican leaders faced significant electoral challenges from conservative rural voters that favored the restoration of the deposed Bonapartist dictatorship or the restoration of the French Bourbon monarchy. Because many rural voters continued to support nondemocratic alternatives, republican leaders were heavily dependent on colonial voters to establish, and later maintain, their electoral majorities in the National Assembly (see Reinsch 1901; Winnacker 1938; Sablé 1955). This dependence on colonial support incentivized republican leaders to support the political rights and parliamentary representation of emancipated Afro-descendants after 1870.

The election of nonwhite Antillean representatives to the National Assembly enabled emancipated Afro-descendants to benefit handsomely from the democratization of the French state after 1870. For the duration of the Third Republic, the French Antilles and French Guiana were the only colonial territories with inclusive and universal citizenship laws that enabled adult male citizens to elect local representatives to their colonial assemblies and to participate in French parliamentary elections. This ensured that that emancipated citizens in the Antilles colonies also benefited from the key economic and social reforms of the Third Republic. These reforms included the establishment of state-funded education in secular public schools during the 1880s (McCloy 1966; Murch 1971). The Third French Republic also established labor reforms that strengthened workers' rights and promoted the partial industrialization of sugar production during the late nineteenth century (Church 2017, esp. 147–90), and legal reforms that expanded individual civil liberties, including freedom of association, jury trials, and freedom of the press (Reinsch 1901, 483; Miles 1985, 198).

The extension of parliamentary representation and universal male suffrage to the French Antilles colonies enabled black and mulatto elected officials and middle-class professionals to emerge as the dominant political class in Guadeloupe and Martinique after 1880. Réunion's white planters maintained their political dominance during the nineteenth century, but were ultimately displaced by educated nonwhite professionals after World War I (Winnacker 1938, 270–72; Murch 1971, 14–15; Horowitz 1960, 805; Church 2017, 47). Local whites mostly held onto their privileged economic status, but the social and political development of the Antilles colonies was increasingly determined by nonwhite elected officials and their political allies in France. Nonwhite elected officials not only represented the Antilles colonies in the French parliament; they also dominated the local colonial assemblies and municipal offices in the Antilles colonies (McCloy 1966, 164; Church 2017, 25–26).

Most elected officials from the French Antilles colonies strongly favored deeper political integration into the French republic as the best way to advance the political rights and socioeconomic interests of nonwhite Antilleans. Without this, local white elites would use their economic dominance to erode the civil and political rights of nonwhites, as they had done in the past. Consequently, the new mulatto and black political elites of the Antilles colonies proudly asserted their political rights as "black Frenchmen" and republican citizens (see Lewis 1962; McCloy 1966, 164; Church 2017, 42–43). Black agricultural and industrial workers lobbied the French government for stronger protection of labor rights. Middle-class mulattos lobbied elected local officials to expand state-funded education (Church 2017, 42). The elected local assemblies also implemented modest land reforms that enabled many independent black producers to acquire small plots of land (Reinsch 1901, 485; Heath 2011).[11] The elected colonial legislatures also repeatedly lobbied the French government to change their legal status to overseas French departments, with the same constitutional status as the political departments on the French mainland. This would prevent local whites from regaining political control and restricting the citizenship rights of emancipated Afro-descendants. These reforms were not implemented until 1946, but they helped to consolidate an inclusive development model that advanced the economic and social well-being and political democratization of the French Antilles after World War II (Sablé 1955; McCloy 1966; Murch 1971).

The Developmental Consequences of Liberal Institutional Reforms: Comparing Haiti and the French Antilles

Enslaved Africans comprised a similar percentage of the population in Saint-Domingue and the French Antilles colonies prior to the Haitian Revolution, and plantation slavery remained legal and widespread in the Antilles colonies long after its abolition in Haiti. Nevertheless, the historical evidence in this chapter demonstrates that the Antilles colonies implemented more inclusive legal-administrative and political reforms following the abolition of slavery, as French republican governments recognized the citizenship rights of emancipated Afro-descendants in the Antilles colonies after 1848. The extension of citizenship rights enabled nonwhite Antilles to benefit from the democratic reforms of the Second and Third French Republics, and to advance human well-being and political democratization following the abolition of slavery. By contrast, the hostile international response to the Haitian Revolution, and the rise of conservative military elites following Haiti's independence war, generated extractive and predatory institutions that undermined that country's long-term development and postcolonial democratization. The summary data in Table 7.3 demonstrate the extent of Haiti's underdevelopment relative to the French Antilles colonies on several important indicators of human well-being and postcolonial democratization.

Table 7.3 shows the limited expansion of primary schooling in Haiti relative to the French Antilles colonies during the first half of the twentieth century. Less than 2% of Haitian children were enrolled in primary schools in 1890, and only 28% of Haitian children were attending primary schools in 1960. The limited expansion of state-funded education partly reflects Haiti's chronic indebtedness and regime instability during the first half of the twentieth century. It also reflects the fact that US officials repeatedly slashed Haiti's public education budget to develop vocational schools during the lengthy US military occupation between 1915 and 1934 (Logan 1930; Angulo 2010). By contrast, French republican officials had a vested interest in expanding state-funded education in the Antilles colonies following the French abolition of slavery in 1848. Because white Antillean planters had consistently supported France's aristocratic and Bonapartist political regimes during the nineteenth century, French republican

Table 7.3 Divergent Development after Abolition: Haiti versus the French Antilles

Colonial Conditions	Haiti	Guadeloupe	Martinique	Réunion
% enslaved prior to Haitian Revolution	87 (1791)	81 (1830)	87 (1791)	~80 (1791)
Year(s) of abolition	1793/1804	1794/1848	1848	1848
Duration of French colonial rule	1697–1804	1635–1946	1635–1946	1650–1946
Institutional Development following Abolition of Slavery				
Political status after abolition	Independent after 1804	French colonial rule, 1848–1946		
Extent of liberal reforms after abolition	Minimal	Extensive		
Inclusive pol. representation before WWII	No	Yes. Universal male suffrage and parliamentary representation during the Second and Third French Republics (i.e., 1848–51 and 1870–1940)		
Current political status	Independent Republic	French overseas department after 1946		
Educational Access during the Early 20th Century				
Primary school enrollment rate, 1900	1.6% (1890)	26.2%	26.8%	32.6%
Primary school enrollment rate, 1940	11.8%	32.1%	59.2%	54.9%
Primary school enrollment rate, 1960	28.0%	87.0%	91.0%	89.0%
Economic Development during the Late 20th Century				
Per capita GDP, 1950	1,051	1,726	1,350	1,989
Per capita GDP, 1973	1,013	4,766	4,723	3,774
Per capita GDP, 2001	785	5,554	5,788	4,610
Postcolonial governance and human well-being				
Voice and Accountability, 1996–2012	−0.90	[+0.83]	+0.62	+1.26
Governance-4 score, 1996–2012	−1.20	[+0.79]	+0.82	+0.84
HDI score (2015)	0.483 Low	0.822 Very high	0.813 Very high	0.755 High

Sources: The sources for the percentage of slaves are listed in the notes to Table 7.2. Primary enrollment rates are from Benavot and Riddle 1988. Per capita GDP data are from Maddison 2006. Voice and Accountability scores and Governance scores are from the World Bank 2016. HDI scores are from the United Nations Development Program 2016.

leaders sought to expand free, secular, and compulsory schooling to counter the political influence of aristocratic and clerical elites and to inculcate civic and republican values among newly emancipated and nonwhite French citizens. The expansion of state-funded education in the Antilles colonies was part of the same republican project of national political integration that was implemented in peripheral French regions like Provence, Brittany, and Corsica between 1870 and 1914 (Weber 1976; Church 2017, 10–13). Consequently, the French national curriculum was adopted in the Antilles colonies during the 1880s (France 1880), and public school teachers were recruited to ensure metropolitan standards in French Antillean schools (France 1898). Secular public schools were the official medium for inculcating French Antillean youths with republican values that emphasized liberty, fraternity, civil and political equality, and a strong belief in the benevolence of the French republic.[12]

The expansion of state-funded education was enthusiastically supported by nonwhite elected officials, who sought to expand the political influence of educated nonwhite professionals relative to white economic elites in the Antilles colonies (Church 2017, 40–47). Republican newspapers in the Antilles colonies also emphasized the importance of educating Afro-descendants to promote their social well-being and political integration (Abou 1988, 78). Consequently, public education was one of largest budget items for the elected colonial legislatures in the Antilles colonies, accounting for 25% of total government expenditure in Martinique during the 1930s (France 1949). At the same time, public education accounted for 15% and 12.5% of total government expenditure in Guadeloupe and Réunion respectively (France 1949). These investments facilitated the expansion of primary school enrollment from less than one-third of the school-aged population in 1900 to more than 90% in 1960.

Haiti's economic decline after 1950 also contrasts with the robust postwar economic growth in Guadeloupe, Martinique, and Réunion (see Table 7.3). Haiti's economic decline partially reflects the predatory nature of the Duvalier father and son dictatorship that plundered the country's economic resources following the US military occupation. The Duvalier family established extractive state monopsonies that controlled the retail and export of Haitian tobacco, cotton, and sugar during the 1950s and 1960s. The state tobacco monopsony provided $10 million in annual income for the Duvalier family during the 1960s. Haiti's first family also benefited enormously from a controversial agreement to "lease" 16,500 Haitians to work on sugar plantations in the Dominican Republic. These sugarcane workers received almost no pay, as the Haitian government withheld a large portion of their salary to ensure that they returned home. By the 1970s, the Duvalier family was receiving about $20–$30 million annually from its control of the state tobacco monopsony, and $3 million annually from the withheld wages of Haitian agricultural laborers in the Dominican Republic (Khan 2010, 121–22;

Dupuy 1989, 171). The Duvalier family also controlled the import of consumer goods like cement, matches, flour, and automobiles, and pilfered much of the foreign aid that flowed into Haiti during the 1980s (Dupuy 1989, 173–74; Khan 2010, 122; Dubois 2012, 350–51). As a result of these predatory policies, Haiti's per capita income declined by almost a third between 1950 and 2001. By contrast, the postwar economic expansion of the French Antilles partly reflects the massive influx of developmental funds from the French government after 1946, and developmental assistance from the European Union after 1973. This financial support has not transformed the French Antilles into manufacturing or financial centers, but it has significantly boosted educational access, economic development, and general living conditions in these territories.

Table 7.3 also shows the superior performance of the French Antilles relative to Haiti on key indicators of democratic accountability, governance, and human well-being. I used the World Bank's Voice and Accountability indicator to measure democratic accountability in Haiti and the French Antilles between 1996 and 2012 because Freedom House Imputed Polity scores are not available for dependent territories. The Voice and Accountability indicator estimates the extent to which citizens are able to participate in selecting their government, and exercise key individual liberties like freedom of speech, association, and access to information. The Governance-4 index combines the World Bank's indicators for the rule of law, control of corruption, government effectiveness, and political instability into a single indicator. Haiti's negative scores on these indicators are well below the global mean of 0. By contrast, Guadeloupe, Martinique, and Réunion perform well above the global mean scores for democratic accountability, rule of law, control of corruption, and government effectiveness.[13]

The data trends in Table 7.3 also suggest that the French Antilles' longer history of democratic accountability and effective governance has significant advantages for human well-being. Guadeloupe, Martinique, and Réunion had high or very high HDI scores by 2015, whereas Haiti's low HDI score (0.483) resembled that of impoverished African states like Benin (0.480), Togo (0.484), and Senegal (0.466). In fact, Haiti's tragic legacy of political instability, predatory rule, and persistent underdevelopment resembles that of several impoverished African states that emerged from French colonial occupation after World War II.

The Negative Developmental Legacies of French Colonial Occupation in Algeria and Sub-Saharan Africa

The final section of the chapter explores the negative developmental legacies of French colonial occupation in Algeria and sub-Saharan Africa. French colonial occupation established extractive and repressive institutions that restricted the legal rights and political agency of indigenous nonwhite populations in colonial territories that were established after the abolition of slavery in the New World. More than 10 million square kilometers of indigenous African territory and more than 20 million indigenous black Africans and North Africans were forcibly incorporated into the French colonial empire between 1870 and 1914. The French colonial empire also acquired 750,000 square kilometers of indigenous territory and 15 million Indochinese colonial subjects during the final decades of the nineteenth century. Yet the vast majority of indigenous colonial subjects were excluded from the legal and political benefits of citizenship rights in the Third Republic (see Lewis 1962; Conklin 1997; Lawrence 2013). In the remainder of this chapter, abbreviated case studies of French colonial occupation in Algeria, Senegal, Gabon, Madagascar, and the Comoros Islands highlight the limits of republican assimilation and citizenship rights in French colonial territories that were established after the abolition of slavery in the New World.

Algeria

Algeria was France's largest and most important colony during the first half of the twentieth century, accounting for more than 40% of French colonial settlers in 1945 (France 1949), and nearly one-third of French imperial trade in the early 1950s (Smith 1975, 185). Algeria's economic and geostrategic importance is also reflected in its geographic proximity to France, and its historical relevance as the first French colony established after the 1789 French Revolution. The French conquest of Algeria began with the seizure of the port of Algiers in 1830, but indigenous Arabs and Berbers continued to resist the territorial expansion of French rule until the 1870s. By 1848, the coastal regions of Algeria were under French military control, and these districts were later organized into three overseas departments in the Third Republic. Algeria's population is mostly composed of Arab and Berber Muslims, but the country was also to a sizable community of North African Jews. Algeria also attracted a large number of colonial settlers (from France, Spain, Italy, Malta, and other Mediterranean islands) during the second half of the nineteenth century. Because Arab and Berber Muslims comprised almost 90% of Algeria's colonial population, the country is classified as a French-occupied colony with a sizable settler minority.

The French military conquest of Algeria was a brutal affair. The country's traditional leaders and social structures were violently dismantled, and indigenous Arab and Berber communities were deprived of their ancestral lands to make room for European settlers and colonists. French military forces used extreme violence to quell indigenous resistance to the territorial expansion of colonial rule after 1830, and the expansion of European settlement between

1848 and 1914. French military officials frequently ordered the destruction of entire villages, and the wholesale confiscation of Arab and Berber agricultural lands and livestock to make room for European colonial settlers. One of France's military commanders, Lieutenant Colonel Lucien-François de Montagnac, described the brutal tactics that were used to quell indigenous Arab resistance to the territorial expansion of French rule in Algeria: "Kill all the men down to the age of fifteen, take all the women and children, put them on boats, and send them to the Marquesas Islands, or somewhere else; in a word, annihilate all who will not grovel at our feet like dogs" (Lawrence 2020, 17, citing Brower 2009, 22). Historians estimate that more than 800,000 Algerians died from the combined effects of French military conquest, the spread of European diseases like typhoid and cholera, and the famines that resulted from the ecological devastation of indigenous lands during the 1850s and 1860s (McDougall 2017, 75–76; Lawrence 2020, 14–20).

Perhaps not surprisingly, more than 150,000 Algerian Muslims rebelled against French colonial rule during the 1870–71 Franco-Prussian War. France mobilized more than 20,000 troops to quell the armed uprising in Algeria, and thousands of Algerians were killed during the 1871–72 uprising against French rule. After quashing the rebellion, French military forces confiscated 450,000 acres of Algeria's best agricultural lands, and the French government imposed an indemnity of 36.5 million FF on indigenous tribal leaders who had organized the rebellion. The leaders of the uprising were either executed, subjected to forced labor, or exiled to the French penal colony in New Caledonia (McDougall 2017, 79–81; Smith 1974, 150). Following the 1871–72 Algerian uprising, French officials also devised a separate set of laws that deprived Algerian Muslims of their civil liberties, and subjected them to summary justice (Smith 1974, 155–56; Merle 2002, 81). This legal code was later codified as the *indigénat* regime, and it was ultimately used to control indigenous populations throughout the French colonial empire (Merle 2002).

Following the establishment of Third Republic, French republican leaders appealed to the expanding minority of colonial settlers to strengthen their political control over Algeria. French citizenship rights were extended to Algerian Jews in 1870, and a second naturalization law extended citizenship rights to the rapidly growing population of Mediterranean immigrants in Algeria (Smith 2006, 104–5). Furthermore, secular public schooling and military service were considered an important aspect of the political socialization of naturalized French citizens in Algeria. Consequently, colonial citizenship laws in Algeria were defined along racial and religious lines: citizenship rights were extended to North African Jews and to white colonial settlers of any nationality. Algerians Muslims were defined as French nationals, but not citizens (McDougall 2017, 122–23). The exclusionary nature of Algeria's citizenship laws generated a white supremacist colonial state that openly favored Algeria's white settlers and North African Jews at the expense of Arab and Berber Muslims. Algeria's Arab and Berber tribes had to renounce their personal status as Muslim in order to qualify for French citizenship, and most would have considered this as apostasy. Algerian Muslims also had to demonstrate knowledge of the French language and French military service, and to adopt an assimilated (i.e., European) lifestyle in order to qualify for French citizenship. Not surprisingly, only 7,000 Algerian Muslims were recognized as French citizens in 1920, and most had served with the French army during World War I (Janoski 2010, 58).

Whereas the French Antilles colonies benefited from the expansion of parliamentary democracy in the Third Republic after 1870, the triumph of republican government in France generated an apartheid-like regime that systematically excluded indigenous Arabs and Muslims from the colonial economy and society. The economic marginalization and political exclusion of Algeria's Muslim population enabled Algeria's white settlers, locally known as *pieds noirs*, to dominate the elected representative institutions that were established during the 1870s. Algeria's white colonial settlers elected six representatives to the French National Assembly after 1870, and 10 elected deputies after 1936. French republican leaders supported the political rights of Algeria's colonial settlers because they tended to elect republican representatives to the French National Assembly (Winnacker 1938, 266–68). White settlers also dominated Algeria's elected colonial assembly, which enacted discriminatory policies that privileged white colonial settlers at the expense of indigenous Algerian Muslims. For example, when France's Popular Front government proposed an extension of citizenship rights to 25,000 Algerian Muslims in 1938, this reform was vetoed by Algeria's colonial settler representatives (Lawrence 2013, 80–81).

Algeria's elected colonial representatives also implemented economic and social policies that benefited white settlers at the expense of indigenous Arabs and Muslims. The colonial legislature provided low-cost loans to white settler farmers, while denying these benefits to indigenous Muslim producers. During the 1930s, for example, 90% of Algeria's agricultural credits were distributed to European farmers, who represented only 3% of the country's agricultural population (Smith 1974, 148). By this time, more than seven million hectares of the most profitable agricultural lands had been confiscated from Algerian Muslims and given to colonial settlers at nominal cost (Young 1994, 173).

The same inequalities existed in Algeria's education system. French colonial officials systematically closed many Arab and Muslim schools in the name of republican assimilation, and colonial settlers were disproportionately favored in the secular public schools that were established in Algeria after 1880. Consequently, indigenous Muslims accounted for less than 10% of secondary school students in Algeria in 1930 (Young 1994, 173). At the start of the Algeria's independence war in 1954, only 8% of Algerian Muslims were literate, compared with 93% of European colonial settlers (United Nations 1963).

Like the apartheid regime in South Africa, France's colonial regime in Algeria was ultimately doomed by its inability to reconcile the generous civil, political, and social rights of its citizen minority with the systematic exclusion of its Arab Muslim majority. Demands for political reform ultimately gave way to anticolonial violence after World War II, when French officials proved unable to reconcile the political demands of these two distinct populations. Although France formally extended voting rights to the Arab Muslim population after World War II, the 1947 Algerian constitution established separate electoral colleges with equal political representation for Algeria's Muslim and settler communities. Of course, this was a flagrant violation of democratic principles, as Algerian Muslims outnumbered European settlers by eight to one (Cooper 2014, 135–36). After a series of rigged elections between 1948 and 1954, Algeria's National Liberation Front (FLN) began its campaign of anticolonial violence, and the French state responded with unprecedented military repression during the bloody Franco-Algerian War, 1954–62. This protracted conflict ultimately brought the Fourth French Republic to its knees, and French troops were ultimately withdrawn from Algeria shortly following Charles de Gaulle's return to power in 1958. Algeria ultimately gained independence in 1962, precipitating a massive exodus of colonial settlers and North African Jews to France. Algerians also paid a heavy human price for their independence from France, as the Franco-Algerian War displaced more than three million Algerians, and resulted in one million Algerian deaths between 1954 and 1962.

Senegal

Senegal is the oldest French colony in West Africa. French political control over Senegal's coastal regions dates back to the 1650s, when the coastal islands of St-Louis-de-Senegal (near the border with Mauritania) and Gorée Island (near present-day Dakar) became important colonial outposts for French slave-trading companies. The territorial expansion of French rule into the country's vast and (mostly arid) interior regions occurred after the French abolition of slavery in 1848. Consequently, Senegal's indigenous Wolof, Jola, Fula, and Mandinga populations only came under French political control during the second half of the nineteenth century. Like Algeria, Senegal's indigenous ethnic groups are overwhelmingly Muslim, but the absence of significant colonial settlement enabled French officials to develop more accommodationist policies toward Senegal's traditional and Islamic authority structures (Robinson 1988, 1999; Stepan 2012). Consequently, the French colonial occupation of Senegal was carried out with significantly less violence and brutality than its counterpart in Algeria.

From 1895 until 1958, the Senegalese capital, Dakar, served as the administrative capital for the French West African Federation, which encompassed nearly 5 million square kilometers of indigenous African territory from the Guinea Coast of West Africa to the shores of Lake Chad. The colonial federation of French West Africa encompassed eight present-day countries: Benin (formerly Dahomey), Burkina Faso (formerly Haut-Volta or Upper Volta), Côte d'Ivoire, Guinea-Conakry, Mali, Mauritania, Niger, and Senegal. Because the French colonial administration for French West Africa was based in Dakar, the Senegalese capital developed into an important political and intellectual hub, with the best schools in French West Africa. Indeed, several of the independence leaders in French West Africa obtained their secondary education in one of Dakar's elite *lycées* (i.e., French-language public schools) before pursuing their university studies in Paris.[14] These *lycées* were initially established as French schools (rather than "native" schools), and their curriculum was designed to educate a Francophile African elite to fill the lower ranks of the colonial civil service.

Senegal also has the longest electoral history of any French colony in sub-Saharan Africa. Like the French Antilles and Algeria, Senegal's electoral representation in the French National Assembly dates back to the Second Republic (1848–51), and the restoration of voting rights to four of Senegal's coastal urban centers in 1879 (Idowu 1968; Winnacker 1938). Given this lengthy electoral history, one might expect to find relatively high levels of human development and postcolonial democratization in Senegal, but the country's record is quite mixed. On the one hand, Senegal is often celebrated as a model of political stability and social tolerance among its diverse ethnic and religious groups (Stepan 2012; Diouf 2013; Gellar 2005). Moreover, Senegal has been broadly democratic since the early 2000s, and it is one of the few African countries that have never experienced a military coup or coup attempt. Nevertheless, like many countries that emerged from colonial occupation after 1945, Senegal experienced several decades of single-party rule after independence, and it remains one of the most impoverished and underdeveloped countries on the planet.

Why has Senegal failed to develop despite the "lighter touch" of French colonial occupation relative to Algeria? Although some studies emphasize the more enlightened aspects of French colonial occupation in Senegal (see Stepan 2012; Robinson 1988), it is important to remember that the "liberal aspects" of French rule were mostly limited to the small number of coastal towns that benefited from the expansion of French citizenship and legal rights during the nineteenth century. The coastal regions of Senegal that were under French control when slavery was abolished in the Antilles colonies also benefited from emancipatory reforms that extended citizenship rights and political representation to (male) freed slaves and their descendants. These reforms were implemented in the coastal island towns of Gorée (the French-controlled slave-trading island adjacent to Dakar) and Saint-Louis (i.e., Senegal's old administrative capital, near the border with Mauritania) during the short-lived Second French Republic (1848–51). Adult males from both towns became naturalized French citizens with parliamentary representation in the National Assembly during the Second Republic and after 1879. French republican elites also extended citizenship rights and political representation to the indigenous inhabitants (i.e., *originaires*) of Senegal's administrative capital, Dakar, and nearby Rufisque, during the 1880s (Idowu 1968; Gellar 2005; Lawrence 2013, 109). Mixed-race Creoles and French colonial merchants initially dominated the representative institutions of these towns, but the *originaires* of these coastal towns (known in Senegal as the *quatre communes*) also benefited from state-funded French-language education in secular public schools. Nevertheless, Blaise Diagne was elected as the first indigenous African representative in the French National Assembly in 1914, and his election gave rise to significant political mobilization and demands for colonial reforms in Senegal after World War I (see Johnson 1971; Lawrence 2013, 110–12; Gellar 2005, 40).

Although the French colonial occupation of Senegal was less violent and repressive than that of Algeria, Senegal also suffers from many of the pathologies of the bifurcated colonial state institutions that were established during the late nineteenth century. The conquest phase of French colonial occupation in Senegal was relatively short, as the French military established control over the entire country between 1880 and 1895. Nevertheless, many indigenous Muslim leaders resisted the territorial expansion of French colonial rule at the end of the nineteenth century. Many prominent Muslim clerics and religious leaders were expelled from Senegal following the late nineteenth-century jihadist revolts against the territorial expansion of French colonial occupation (Robinson 1988, 415; Babou 2013, 128). French military officials also extended the *indigénat* legal code into Senegal's rural districts in 1887 (Merle 2002, 93), and throughout French West Africa after 1904 (Mann 2009; Merle 2002). The *indigénat* legal code empowered French colonial officials to appoint administrative chiefs (locally known as *chefs de cantons*) to collect taxes and recruit labor. These administrative chiefs had little choice but to comply with French demands. Chiefs were generally given a commission on the taxes they collected, and they were severely punished if they failed to collect sufficient taxes or recruit sufficient labor (Mann 2009; Young 1994; Gellar 2005, 39–40).[15] Despite frequent petitions from educated Africans and administrative chiefs to eliminate or reform the French *indigénat* legal code, Crawford Young's research highlights a significant increase in *indigénat* legal convictions in Senegal during the 1930s. French West African governors frequently rejected African petitions to reform or eliminate the *indigénat* legal code during the first half of the twentieth century. Colonial officials clearly benefited from the arbitrary nature of the *indigénat* legal code, and they argued that French law was "much too slow and complex" for indigenous Africans (Young 1994, 155). Consequently, the French *indigénat* legal code, and forced labor recruitment, remained legal and widespread throughout French West Africa until 1946 (Mann 2009; Cooper 2014, 16–18).

Despite the repressive and arbitrary nature of the *indigénat* legal code, the French colonial state in Senegal was far less violent and repressive than its counterpart in Algeria. This is because French officials recognized that they could avoid the type of ongoing violent resistance that they had experienced in Algeria by incorporating the traditional leaders of Senegal's Sufi Muslim brotherhoods (known as *mourides*) into the colonial authority structure of Senegal's rural districts (Babou 2013, 127–28). Consequently, France's *laïcité* laws were relaxed in ways that facilitated a peaceful modus vivendi between French colonial officials and Sufi Muslim groups (Babou 2013, 128; Robinson 1999, 204–11), and mutual accommodation between Catholics and Muslims (Stepan 2012). These policies enabled traditional Islamic leaders, locally known as *marabouts*, to maintain control over customary law, land use, peanut production, and Koranic schools in Senegal's rural areas (Robinson 1999, 210–11). This developmental approach closely resembled that of British indirect rule in Sierra Leone, as outlined in Chapter 5.

The establishment of bifurcated legal-administrative institutions generated vast inequalities between Senegal's indigenous rural hinterlands and the coastal municipalities that established European legal and political institutions during the nineteenth century. As the benefits of British colonization were primarily concentrated in Sierra Leone's capital city, Freetown, the benefits of French rule were similarly concentrated in the Senegalese coastal towns that established European legal and political institutions during the nineteenth century. Only the male indigenous inhabitants of these coastal communities could participate in Senegalese elections prior to 1946. French colonial officials were reluctant to extend voting rights beyond these Senegal's Four Communes because these urbanized coastal communities became hotbeds of political activity during the first half of the twentieth century (Lawrence 2013, 111–15). Consequently, only 46,000 Senegalese adults had voting rights in 1946 (Gellar 2005, 41), and fewer than 26,000 Senegalese children were enrolled in public or Catholic schools that offered a French-language academic education (Kantrowitz 2018, 225). Despite the long history of French rule in Senegal's coastal regions, there were fewer students enrolled in Senegal's French-language schools than in the much smaller Antillean colonies of Martinique (42,510) or Réunion (37,660). Indeed, the number of primary school students in the French Antilles exceeded the entire primary school enrollment for the entire region of French West Africa in 1946! (France, 1949).

Gabon

Gabon is a sparsely populated and resource-rich country in the heavily forested Upper Congo basin of Equatorial Africa. During the first half of the twentieth century, Gabon was one of the four territories in the colonial federation of French Equatorial Africa, which stretched from the Congo River to the northern border between the Republic of Chad and Libya. Like its immediate neighbors, Cameroon, Equatorial Guinea, and the Republic of the Congo, Gabon is a vast and sparsely populated country with immense natural resources. Today, Gabon is one of the wealthiest countries in continental Africa, despite the country's authoritarian political system and deep socioeconomic inequalities: Gabon's relatively diversified economy is largely based on oil production, rubber, logging, and large-scale agricultural plantations. Gabon's physical geography and population are significantly different from that of Senegal or Algeria, which are arid countries with predominantly Muslim populations. By contrast, traditional African religions were widely practiced in Gabon and other parts of Equatorial Africa prior to the onset of European colonization. Christian missionaries evangelized the Congo basin of Equatorial Africa during the late nineteenth and early twentieth centuries, so Gabon emerged from the colonial era with a predominantly Catholic population. This allows us to examine the developmental legacies of French colonial occupation in a black African country with a tiny population and a Catholic Christian majority. When Gabon gained independence from France in 1960, its 470,000 inhabitants occupied a vast and resource-rich territory that is twice the size of England!

Gabon's French colonial occupation began in 1849, when the country's capital city, Libreville, was established as a French colonial settlement for liberated Africans rescued from a slave ship bound for Brazil. For several decades afterward, Libreville served as the administrative capital for French colonial territories in the Congo region of Equatorial Africa (Reed 1987, 289). Like its British namesake, Freetown in Sierra Leone, Libreville's growing population of liberated African slaves was intensely loyal to France. They were heavily evangelized by New England Protestants and French Catholic missionaries, who established the first primary schools in the Congo basin. These mission schools educated, trained, and supported Gabon's small population of Francophile elites during the nineteenth and twentieth centuries (Reed 1987, 285–89).

Despite the cultural assimilation of Libreville's Francophile and educated elites, French colonial officials used ruthless and repressive methods to control Gabon's vast indigenous hinterlands after 1880. Large concessions of land were granted to French companies to develop logging, mining, and agricultural plantations in the French-controlled areas of the vast Congo basin, which encompassed the present-day countries of the Republic of Congo, Gabon, and the Central African Republic.

Moreover, the French *indigénat* legal code was extended across French Equatorial Africa in 1910 (Merle 2002, 93), paving the way for forced labor conscription that enriched French private companies, colonial officials, and indigenous intermediaries. The political scientist Crawford Young describes how French colonial officials used military-style conscription to forcibly recruit African laborers for road construction and other public works projects like the ill-fated Congo-Océan railway line linking the Congolese-Gabonese border town of Mbinda with Brazzaville and the Atlantic coast. The mortality rate for African workers on this project was so high that there is a popular saying: "Every railway tie symbolize[s] the corpse of a worker" (Young 1994, 176). Historian Eric Jennings also highlights the widespread use of forced labor recruitment for rubber production and road construction to support the Allied war effort during World War II. African laborers were also forced to plant rice and collect rubber and palm oil to support the Allied war effort (Jennings 2015, 191).

During the 1920s, a small group of French-educated Gabonese elites joined a human rights organization, the Ligue des droits de l'homme, which was established by elected political leaders from the French Antilles colonies. Their goal was to reform the *indigénat* legal code, and to lobby for the protection of indigenous customary land rights. Nevertheless, French colonial governors repeatedly rejected demands for labor reforms (Reed 1987, 289–91). Ethnic divisions also weakened the bargaining power of Gabon's labor activists relative to the more effective organization of French private companies and colonial state officials. The political demands of Gabon's labor leaders were also subjugated to the interests of French labor unions that advanced the interests of white laborers, so indigenous African workers faced significant labor and political repression from colonial authorities and the militias employed by private French companies. Despite numerous reports of French company officials beating African villagers, raping women, stealing food and livestock from indigenous communities, and diverting indigenous labor for their own personal use, Gabon's colonial authorities did very little to stop these abuses (Edwards 2018, 485–90).

In the end, French colonial occupation had devastating consequences for indigenous Africans in Gabon's rural hinterlands:

> Gabon's small, scattered population was badly deracinated by colonialism, forced labour, [the] regrouping of villages, [the] destruction of religious cults and objects, and by the accompanying diseases and famines. It was never able to generate a sizeable indigenous nationalist movement that had the capacity to overcome extreme French influence (Reed 1987, 228–89).

In contrast to Algeria's violent anticolonial resistance, or the pragmatic accommodation between French colonial officials and in Senegal, Gabon's political leaders have consistently demonstrated their mettle as "elitist, non-radical, ... and almost always pro-French" (Reed 1987, 228–29).

The fact that Gabon failed to develop a bona fide nationalist movement or politicized labor movement enabled French economic and military elites to maintain close ties to Gabon's postcolonial rulers. Gabon's first president, Léon M'Ba, was a Francophile politician and former *chef de canton* (i.e., French-appointed administrative chief) who was personally loyal to French president Charles de Gaulle. He was temporarily deposed in a 1964 coup d'état that was reversed by French military intervention, and his government increased its political repression following the French military intervention. M'Ba's successor, Omar Bongo, was even more repressive, maintaining a repressive single-party dictatorship that was sustained by French troops and foreign mercenaries until Bongo's death in 2009. Gabon's vast oil wealth and natural resources have enriched the country's political leaders and their foreign patrons supported by France's ongoing military presence. Although Gabon is now one of the wealthiest countries in sub-Saharan Africa, the country's population continues to suffer from vast socioeconomic inequalities, corrupt and inefficient government, and a neocolonial authoritarian petro-state that steers the country's vast economic resources toward a small number of political elites and foreign (mostly French) corporations.

Madagascar

Madagascar is the world's fourth-largest island, and its 26 million inhabitants occupy more than 580,000 square kilometers of densely forested and mountainous terrain in the Indian Ocean, about 1000 kilometers east of Mozambique. Madagascar's geographic location is relevant because of its proximity to Arab slave-trading outposts on the Swahili coast of East Africa, and to European forced settlement colonies like Mauritius, Réunion, and the Seychelles islands. Madagascar was first "discovered" by European explorers during the sixteenth century, and its earliest colonial settlements date back to 1643. The first wave of French colonists arrived at the same time as the first colonial plantations were established in Guadeloupe, Martinique, and nearby Réunion. In contrast to the French Antilles colonies, however, Madagascar was already densely populated by indigenous Malagasy, and the island's indigenous inhabitants occupied a vast and rugged territory that is larger than France itself. During the 1670s, indigenous Malagasy massacred many of the early French colonists who were unable to control the island's vast and rugged terrain. The surviving French colonists fled to nearby Réunion island, where they established sugar plantations using imported African slave labor. By contrast, Madagascar's indigenous rulers established a powerful monarchy that successfully repelled European colonization efforts until the end of the nineteenth century (Metz 1995, 9–11).

From the 1600s until the late nineteenth century, Madagascar's indigenous rulers profited from the thriving Indian Ocean slave trade with local Arab merchants and European planters in nearby forced settlement colonies like Mauritius and Réunion. Madagascar's indigenous rulers established a powerful centralized kingdom that successfully repelled the type of French colonial encroachment that occurred in Algeria, Senegal, or Gabon. During the first half of the nineteenth century, Madagascar's King Radama I (1810–28) established a strategic alliance with the British that modernized Madagascar's army and bureaucracy along Western lines. Radama I invited British missionaries to establish schools, churches, and a local printing press during the 1820s. These missionary efforts facilitated the spread of Christianity and Western education under indigenous control prior to the onset of French colonial rule. When France finally gained control over Madagascar in 1896, more than 164,000 indigenous Malagasy children were enrolled in the island's Protestant and Catholic mission schools (Metz 1995, 11). The early expansion of Christian missionary evangelization contributed to significantly higher levels of primary school enrollment in Madagascar relative to French-occupied colonies on the African mainland.[16]

Despite the early spread of Christianity and Western education, Madagascar failed to promote inclusive development during the twentieth century. Like other French-occupied colonies, the island state remains one of the poorest and least developed countries in sub-Saharan Africa. This partly reflects the brutality of French colonial occupation during the twentieth century and the failure of King Radama's successors to build on his early modernization. Madagascar's failure to modernize generated significant political instability that enabled France to expand its control over the island at the end of the nineteenth century. King Radama's immediate successor, Queen Ranavalona I (1828–61) was more reactionary and distrustful of foreign and British influence. Many Protestant converts were killed, and many Europeans fled the island during her reign. Queen Ranavalona allowed Madagascar's ruling elite to monopolize landownership and commerce, including the lucrative Indian Ocean slave trade that was increasingly dominated by Arab slave traders. After Ranavalona I, Madagascar's nineteenth-century rulers alternated between inward-looking reactionary policies and strategic partnerships to promote modernization under British or French tutelage. This generated political instability that enabled France to expand its control over the island at the end of the nineteenth century (Metz 1995, 12–13). French marines ultimately invaded and occupied Madagascar's capital city, Antananarivo, after the Malagasy queen, Ranavalona III, refused to recognize French rights to a protectorate "treaty." The island's queen and prime minister were deposed by French forces following an indigenous insurgency in the southern part of the island. Madagascar officially became a French colony in 1896. Its indigenous political leaders were sent into exile, first to nearby Réunion, and later to faraway Algeria (Metz 1995, 13; Jennings 2001, 33–34).

After 1896, indigenous Malagasy subjects experienced the same heavy-handed political domination and repressive labor practices that were enforced in other French-occupied colonies during the first half of the twentieth century. French colonial officials suppressed the Christian missionary schools that had been established in Madagascar during the nineteenth century. This partly reflects the French republican hostility toward religious orders and instruction following the 1905 law on the separation of church and state. Some French officials even feared that Christian missionaries were agents of the deposed Merina political dynasty, and that missionary schools could be used to advance the political and cultural claims of Madagascar's deposed indigenous elites (Wietzke 2014, 296–97).[17] The *indigénat* legal code was extended to Madagascar in 1901, ensuring that the legal rights of indigenous Malagasy were not recognized under French law (Merle 2002, 93). The denial of legal rights enabled colonial authorities to recruit indigenous Malagasy laborers for colonial infrastructure projects and plantation labor during the first half of the twentieth century. These practices were further intensified during World War II, when the island state fell under the fascist political control of Vichy France (Jennings 2001, 58).

Madagascar also experienced the same type of anticolonial violence that destabilized Algeria after World War II. This partly reflects the fact that French colonial officials systematically rejected demands for labor and political reforms from Madagascar's Western-educated elites during the 1920s and 1930s (Metz 1995, 13). Even Malagasy Marxists initially lobbied the French colonial authorities for civil and political equality, rather than independence from French rule. They argued that Madagascar's indigenous inhabitants should have become ipso facto French citizens after France annexed the island in 1896 (Jennings 2001, 57). Malagasy nationalist leaders only agitated for political independence after Britain seized control of the island during World War II. During the wartime British occupation, Malagasy nationalists established secret societies that mobilized the island's rural population in favor of independence. Malagasy nationalist leaders assumed that the likelihood of independence was high until the British restored the island to French political control in 1946 (Lawrence 2013, 153).

After the British restored Madagascar to French rule, Malagasy nationalists organized a violent armed resistance that encompassed one-third of the island's territory in 1947. France ultimately suppressed the uprising, but more than 60,000 indigenous Malagasy were killed in the ensuing political repression. French officials arrested the political leaders of Madagascar's Democratic Movement for Malagasy Restoration (MDMR) and outlawed the organization. The leaders of the 1947 uprising were tried by French military courts and sentenced to death. Another 5,000 to 6,000 Malagasy were convicted in civilian courts that imposed penalties that ranged from imprisonment to death (Metz 1995, 15). The brutal and violent repression of Madagascar's nationalist leaders had severe long-term consequences that hindered the island state's democratization efforts during the final decades of French rule. Recent research by Omar Garcia-Ponce and Leonard Wantchekon (n.d.) demonstrates that African countries that experienced anticolonial rural insurgencies after World War II have been less likely to democratize after the Cold War. This is because the colonial state's response to anticolonial rural insurgencies generated norms of state repression that hindered the development of democratic institutions and behaviors. This is certainly the case in Madagascar, where French colonial authorities outlawed the MDMR following the 1947 anticolonial insurgency. Although France ultimately recognized Madagascar's independence in 1960, the brutal repression of Madagascar's nationalist movement generated a single-party authoritarian regime that maintained strong economic, cultural, and military ties with France after independence.

Comoros Islands

The Comoros Islands are a little-known archipelago of four tiny islands in the northern end of the narrow channel between Madagascar and the Swahili coast of East Africa (see Map 7.2). Three of the four islands—Grande Comore (Ngazidja), Mohéli (Mwali), and Anjouan (Ndzuani)—are members of the Union of Comoros, which gained independence from France in 1975. The fourth island, Mayotte (Maore), remained a French overseas territory (like French Polynesia or New Caledonia) after 1975, and became a French overseas department in 2011. This chapter analyzes the four Comoros islands as a single political unit, given their shared history of French colonial occupation between 1908 and 1975. The Comoros Islands are the smallest territory that experienced French colonial occupation during the first half of the twentieth century.

One could be forgiven for not having heard of the Comoros Islands. I imagine that many international soccer fans turned to Google or Wikipedia to search for the Comoros Islands after the tiny archipelago nation defeated the mighty Black Stars of Ghana in the qualifying round of the 2021 African Cup of Nations championship. The combined surface area of the four Comoros islands is less than that of nearby Réunion island, where French planters established sugar plantations with imported slave labor during the seventeenth century. Yet the Comoros Islands are home to a diverse population of African, Arab, Persian, Indonesian, and Malagasy origin that predates the onset of European exploration in the

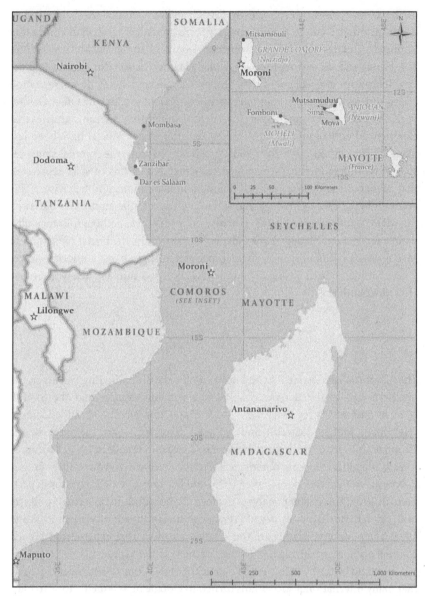

Map 7.2 East African Coast, Comoros Islands, and Madagascar

Indian Ocean region. This is because the Indian Ocean slave trade was already dominated by Sherazi Arabs and Malagasy slave trade traders when European colonists first arrived in the region. Consequently, the Comoros Islands remained under the political control of local Muslim elites that established agricultural plantations for sugar and spice production during the seventeenth and eighteenth centuries. Malagasy slave traders also raided the Comoros Islands to capture slaves that were sold to French planters in Mauritius and Réunion (Walker 2019, 62–77). Sherazi Arab elites also supplied indentured laborers from the Comoros Islands to Creole planters in Mauritius and Réunion island following the British and French abolition of slavery (Walker 2019, 97).

In contrast to the Creole islands of the Indian Ocean, where European colonists established agricultural plantations with imported slave labor, the Comoros Islands remained under the political control of local Muslim elites until the beginning of the twentieth century. Yet the combined population of the four Comoros islands was smaller than that of many forced settlement colonies. Only 70,000 people lived in the Comoros Islands at the beginning of the twentieth century. In fact, the four Comoros Islands had fewer inhabitants than Guadeloupe (182,000), Martinique (208,000) or Réunion island (173,000) in 1900.

Given their similarities of size, population, and slave-based plantation economies, one might reasonably expect to find similar patterns of state-building and institutional development in the Comoros Islands and the French Antilles colonies. Nevertheless, this was not the case. The Antilles colonies implemented liberal reforms that expanded the legal rights and political agency of emancipated Afro-descendants following the French abolition of slavery in 1848. By contrast, the indigenous population of the Comoros Islands remained under the political control of local Muslim elites until the end of the nineteenth century. Although French colonists gained control over Mayotte and abolished slavery there in 1843, the indigenous Muslim rulers of the remaining Comoros islands signed protectorate agreements that enabled them to negotiate labor contracts and commercial relations with French companies that were not subject to French law. These protectorate treaties enabled the sultans of Grande Comore, Mohéli, and Anjouan to maintain control over domestic political affairs, whereas France's official role was largely restricted to foreign affairs and defense. As a result of this arrangement, three of the four Comoros islands were governed as French protectorates until 1912, when the four islands were officially reclassified as a province of French-occupied Madagascar (Walker 2019, 114; Baker 2009, 216). From 1912 until 1946, the four Comoros islands were administered with the same repressive legal-administrative institutions that controlled indigenous populations in other French-occupied colonies.

During the first half of the twentieth century, the colonial economy of the Comoros Islands was dominated by European plantation companies that produced coffee, cocoa, vanilla, cloves, pepper, and other spices. Colonial plantation companies owned most of the productive land on the islands, and the largest plantation company was exempt from all tax payments under the terms of an 1885 agreement between the company's owner and one of the local sultans.

Not surprisingly, the labor and taxation policies of these agreements were abusive toward Comoros natives, who were often forced to sell their labor to local companies to pay their taxes (Walker 2019, 123–25).

The legal-administrative system of the Comoros Islands was also plural and complex: Each island was organized into districts known as *subdivisions*, and subdistricts known as *cantons*. As in other French-occupied colonies, the districts were administered by French officials known as *chefs de subdivisions*; the subdistricts were administered by "native" *chefs de canton*, who were responsible for taxation, labor recruitment, and maintaining public order. Most *chefs de canton* were Islamic magistrates (*cadis*) who enjoyed some traditional legitimacy in their communities. The *chefs de canton* also nominated village chiefs (*chefs de village*) who served as the lowest tier of colonial authority (Walker 2019, 116). Comoros "natives" were governed under a specific legal status, *droit local*, that denied the denied the rights of full French citizens. "Natives" were denied the rights of full French citizens. Like their counterparts in indirectly ruled British colonies, Comoros natives could technically choose whether to present their legal cases in French or "native" courts, but most legal cases were processed outside the legal framework of French courts. Yet even the French courts in the Comoros Islands often imposed collective fines and other arbitrary punishments that would have never been allowed under French civil law (Walker 2019, 116–17).

Perhaps not surprisingly, the Comoros Islands' labor-repressive plantation economy and limited administrative state capacity hindered the archipelago's long-term development during the first half of the twentieth century. Colonial schooling remained extremely limited throughout the colonial era, as most "native schools" (i.e., *écoles indigènes*) only taught the basics of literacy and mathematics, the French language, and manual skills. In 1918, there were only seven "native schools" in the entire archipelago, compared with 652 Koranic schools. In 1931, less than 3% of school-aged children were attending state-funded primary schools, and there were no secondary schools on any of the islands until 1964! (Walker 2019, 134). By the early 1960s, when many African states were gaining independence from European colonial occupation, the Comoros Islands remained woefully underdeveloped, and there was no hint of any demand for independence from French rule:

> Even by the standards of France's much-neglected African colonies, the [Comoros Islands] remained significantly underdeveloped in all domains including education, roads, and health. Although the territory now had a *lycée*, it was unable to meet demand; in 1964, only 12% of school-aged children were attending school—the lowest rate of all French territories—and most of these were from aristocratic families. Teachers were lacking, and several of the few

who were qualified abandoned the profession to enter politics. There were hospitals on all four islands (two of each on the three larger islands, one on Mwali), but they had limited facilities and were often distant from the majority of the population; in 1964 there were only eleven doctors in the territory, several of whom were French military doctors. Roads were still rudimentary—708 km in the entire archipelago of which only 95 km were paved—there was no deep-water port, and although each island had an airstrip, only Moroni-Ikoni was paved, and it was not until 1965 that a local airline was established. (Walker 2019, 138).

On December 22, 1974, the Comoros Islands held a disputed referendum on independence from French rule. Although 95% of voters expressed a preference for independence, the French government decided to retain Mayotte, while recognizing the independence of the three remaining islands on July 6, 1975. Since then, the three independent islands that comprise the Union of Comoros have been plagued by persistent underdevelopment and political instability that have hindered democratization efforts. The Union of Comoros has suffered from significant domestic political challenges, including interisland rivalries and a hostile geopolitical environment that has undermined effective state-building and democratization efforts after independence. The large French military base in Mayotte presents a significant political threat to the sovereignty and independence of the remaining Comoros islands. Perhaps not surprisingly, the Union of the Comoros rejects France sovereignty over Mayotte, which attracts thousands of migrant workers every year from the other islands. Many of these migrant workers die in illegal crossings, and every year, French police deport thousands of migrant laborers back to the Comoros Islands. At the same time, French political and military interventions have destabilized the Comoros Islands, which have experienced more than 20 coups or coup attempts since independence from France (see Baker 2009; Hassan 2009; Walker 2019). Consequently, the Comoros Islands have experienced more coup activity and greater regime instability than continental African states that are much larger and far more ethnically diverse, such as Nigeria, Sudan, and Uganda.

The persistent underdevelopment and chronic regime instability of the Comoros Islands clearly demonstrate that small-island geography does not automatically promote inclusive development and postcolonial democratization. Instead, the experience of the Comoros Islands highlights the extent to which French colonial occupation established extractive and repressive institutions that hindered the long-term development of colonial states with indigenous nonwhite populations. French colonial officials used extractive and repressive institutions to control the small indigenous population of the Comoros Islands during the first half of the twentieth century. These institutions had adversely impacted the islands' long-term development and undermined the regime stability and postcolonial democratization of the small archipelago nation.

Discussion and Conclusion

Table 7.4 summarizes the long-term development trajectories of the various former French colonies that are highlighted in this chapter. This allows readers to compare the duration of French colonial rule, the size of the population in 1900, and the extension of citizenship rights in each colonial territory in 1945. The table also presents five different measures of postcolonial development for the French colonies highlighted in this chapter. These include primary school enrollment as a measure of educational access in 1960, per capita GDP as a measure of economic development in 1973, the aggregate democracy score for 1972–2012 (for sovereign states only), the World Bank's Voice and Accountability indicator as an alternative measure of postcolonial democracy for sovereign states and dependent territories, and the United Nations' HDI score as an aggregate measure of human well-being in 2015.

The summary data in Table 7.4 highlight the extent to which the French Antilles colonies outperform Haiti on all these development indicators, despite their shared history of forced settlement and plantation slavery prior to the French and Haitian Revolutions. Nevertheless, the Antilles colonies were able to benefit from liberal reforms that extended citizenship rights to emancipated Afro-descendants following the French revolutions of 1789, 1848, and 1870–71. As a result of these reforms, Guadeloupe, Martinique, and Réunion were the only French colonies that established inclusive citizenship rights, universal male suffrage, and parliamentary representation after 1870. By contrast, domestic political factors and French and US neocolonial interventions hindered the implementation of liberal reforms in Haiti after 1804. Consequently, the postcolonial Haitian state continues to suffer from poor development outcomes that more closely resemble those of French-occupied colonies in sub-Saharan Africa. In 1960, Haiti's primary school enrollment rate lagged behind that of Gabon or Madagascar; and Haiti's per capita GDP lagged behind Algeria, Senegal, Gabon, and Madagascar in 1973. Haiti's postcolonial democratization is also extremely limited. From 1996 to 2012, Haiti's average Voice and Accountability Score (−1.20) was significantly lower than that of Algeria (−1.04), Senegal (−0.05), Gabon (−0.075), Madagascar (−0.31), and the Comoros Islands (−0.53).[18] Haiti's HDI score in 2015 also lags behind African countries that experienced French colonial occupation during the first half of the twentieth century.

Haiti's persistent underdevelopment is a painful reminder of how other forced settlement colonies might have fared without the liberal reforms that

Table 7.4 Colonial Citizenship and Postcolonial Development in Selected French Colonies

Former French Colonies	Colonial Duration	Population in 1900 (thousands)	% French Citizens, 1945	Postcolonial Development				
				Primary School Enrollment, 1960 (%)	Per Capita GDP, 1973	Mean Democracy Score, 1972–2012	Voice & Accountability, 1996–2012	HDI Score, 2015
Forced Settlement without Liberal Reforms								
Haiti/Saint-Domingue	1697–1804	1,500	<0.1	28	1,013	2.90	−1.20	0.483
Forced Settlement with Liberal Reforms after Abolition								
Guadeloupe	1635–1946	182	100.0	87	4,766	NA	+[0.95]	0.822
Martinique	1635–1946	208	99.8	91	4,723	NA	+0.62	0.813
Réunion	1650–1946	173	100.0	89	3,774	NA	+1.26	0.750
French-Occupied Colonies								
Algeria	1830–1962	4,600	12.3	28	2,357	2.39	−1.04	0.736
Senegal	1895–1960	1,000	1.2–5.0	20	1,315	5.46	−0.05	0.466
Gabon	1880–1960	280	0.5	49	7,286	2.57	−0.75	0.684
Madagascar	1896–1960	2,580	1.4	35	1,144	4.97	−0.31	0.510
Comoros Islands	1886–1975	70	0.5	9	889	4.89	−0.53	0.503

Note: Data evidence on Senegal is inconsistent, but the upper estimates are that 3% to 5% of the Senegalese population were black or mixed-race citizens of France prior to World War II (Lawrence 2013, 109).

Source: Citizenship data for French colonies were obtained from France 1949.

accompanied the abolition of slavery in the British and French colonial empires. Less than 0.5% of Haitians enjoyed political rights comparable to French citizens in 1945.[19] Haiti did not establish direct presidential elections or universal suffrage elections until 1950, and electoral competition was limited by the political repression of the Duvalier family dictatorship after 1957. By contrast, the French Antilles colonies benefited significantly from liberal reforms that extended citizenship rights and political representation to emancipated Afro-descendants during the second half of the nineteenth century. These reforms enabled the French Antilles colonies to promote more inclusive long-term development and to achieve high levels of postcolonial democratization.

By contrast, the limited extension of citizenship rights hindered the long-term development of African states that emerged from French colonial occupation after World War II. In French colonies of occupation, citizenship rights were typically restricted to European settlers and to a small number of urbanized, Westernized, and Francophile indigenous elites like the *originaires* of Senegal's *quatres communes*. These privileged groups enjoyed the benefits of French citizenship—i.e., education, political representation, and voting rights—that were generally denied to indigenous colonial subjects in the French colonial empire. The data in Table 7.4 suggest that the limited extension of citizenship rights hindered the long-term development of French-occupied colonies relative to the French Antilles colonies. This pattern is consistent among Muslim and Christian countries alike. It is also consistent among French-occupied colonies with large or small indigenous populations. For example, the Comoros Islands have not escaped the lasting negative effects of French colonial occupation, despite their tiny population and small-island geography. Gabon and Madagascar also have significant development challenges, despite the greater impact of Christian missionary evangelization relative to predominantly Muslim states like Algeria or Senegal. And Algeria, despite its significant history of European colonial settlement, lags behind the French Antilles on every indicator of postcolonial development.

The historical evidence in this chapter demonstrates that indigenous colonial subjects did not benefit from the liberal reforms that extended citizenship rights to emancipated Afro-descendants in the French Antilles following the abolition of slavery. Neither were these reforms extended to the indigenous African or Arab populations that came under French rule during the final decades of the nineteenth century. Consequently, all French-occupied colonies, regardless of population, size, religion, or ethnicity, have experienced limited postcolonial development relative to the French Antilles colonies that implemented liberal reforms following the abolition of slavery. These trends highlight the lasting legacies of the distinctive legal institutions that were used to control emancipated Afro-descendants and indigenous colonial subjects under French rule.

8

Conclusions, Reflections, and Avenues for Future Research

What conclusions can we draw from this empirical study of the developmental legacies of forced settlement and colonial occupation in the Global South? And how does this study advance empirical research on colonial, state-building, and long-term development in the Global South? The final chapter of this book reflects on these questions and outlines an agenda for future research that builds on this work.

Four Conclusions That Advance Empirical Research on Colonialism, State-Building, and Long-Term Development

This is the first scholarly book to explore the distinctive developmental legacies of forced settlement and colonial occupation in the Global South. This conceptual distinction between forced settlement and colonial occupation is overlooked by previous studies that examine the distinctive developmental legacies of European settler colonialism vis-à-vis extractive colonization with limited European settlement. Existing studies propose that European settler colonies developed liberal economic and political institutions that advanced their long-term development, whereas extractive colonies developed repressive economic and political institutions that hindered their long-term development (see Acemoglu, Johnson, and Robinson 2001, 2002; Sokoloff and Engerman 2000; Krieckhaus 2006; Easterly and Levine 2016). These seminal research papers opened new frontiers that expanded existing knowledge on colonialism, state-building, and long-term development at the beginning of the twenty-first century. Nevertheless, these studies overlooked an important conceptual distinction between forced settlement and colonial occupation as distinctive modes of extractive colonization in the Global South. Neither forced settlement nor colonial occupation generated significant European settlement during the colonial era. Yet this empirical study demonstrates that forced settlement generated favorable developmental legacies relative to Global South countries that emerged from colonial occupation after World War II. The statistical data models and comparative-historical evidence

Ruling Emancipated Slaves and Indigenous Subjects. Olukunle P. Owolabi, Oxford University Press.
© Oxford University Press 2023. DOI: 10.1093/oso/9780197673027.003.0008

in this book generate four important contributions that advance scholarly research on the diverse developmental and political legacies of colonialism in the
Global South.

Forced Settlement and Colonial Occupation Were Distinct Modes of Colonization with Very Different Developmental Legacies

The most important contribution of this book is its conceptual distinction between forced settlement and colonial occupation as distinct modes of colonialism with very different developmental legacies. In forced settlement colonies,
Europeans established agricultural plantations using imported African slave
labor. By contrast, colonial occupation is the more typical pattern of colonial
domination in which Europeans controlled indigenous populations and territories and exploited their labor and natural resources. I find that forced settlement generated favorable development outcomes relative to colonial occupation
in terms of educational attainment, life expectancy, and economic development
at the end of the colonial era. Forced settlement colonies also benefited from
greater exposure to mass electoral competition during the colonial era, which
generated higher mean postcolonial democracy scores relative to Global South
countries that experienced colonial occupation. The favorable developmental
legacies of forced settlement relative to colonial occupation demonstrate the
limits of existing studies that predict persistent underdevelopment in Global
South countries that established labor-repressive agricultural plantations during
the colonial era (Beckford 1983; Sokoloff and Engerman 2000; Bertocchi and
Dimico 2012; Engerman, Mariscal, and Sokoloff 2009). The high levels of human
well-being and postcolonial democracy in many forced settlement colonies
also demonstrate the limits of existing studies that predict poor developmental
outcomes in Global South countries that experienced "extractive" forms of colonization with limited European settlement (Acemoglu, Johnson, and Robinson
2001, 2002).

My research explains this paradox with a historical-institutional approach
that underscores the importance of liberal reforms that expanded the legal
rights and political agency of emancipated Afro-descendants following the abolition of slavery in the New World. As a result of these reforms, most forced
settlement colonies developed legal-administrative institutions that resembled
their respective metropoles. I find that liberal institutional reforms established
effective and inclusive legal institutions that expanded the provision of public
goods like state-funded education, political representation, and mass electoral
competition in forced settlement colonies following the abolition of slavery in

the New World. By contrast, European rulers developed very different legal-administrative institutions to control indigenous populations and territories that were colonized following the abolition of slavery in the New World: British colonial officials favored "indirect" methods of administrative control that strengthened the arbitrary and despotic power of indigenous "chiefs" over indigenous nonelites. French and Portuguese colonial officials were less accommodating toward traditional indigenous elites, but they also established harsh and arbitrary "native legal codes" that restricted the legal rights and political agency of indigenous colonial subjects in their colonies of occupation. Building on existing studies by Mahmood Mamdani (1996), Matthew Lange (2004, 2009), and others, my research demonstrates that the establishment of bifurcated legal-administrative institutions limited the expansion of state-funded education, political representation, and voting rights in colonial states with significant indigenous populations. Bifurcated legal-administrative institutions also undermined the rule of law and the administrative capacity to expand public goods and services in colonial states with large and widely dispersed indigenous populations.

The central claim of this book is that liberal institutional reforms enabled many forced settlement colonies to promote more inclusive human development and postcolonial democratization, despite the legacy of plantation slavery. This claim builds on previous empirical studies that demonstrate the importance of liberal institutional reforms for inclusive human development (see Lange 2009, 2004; Mahoney 2010; Acemoglu and Robinson 2012; Owolabi 2015). It also advances existing studies that demonstrate poor developmental outcomes in colonial states with bifurcated legal-administrative institutions that privileged colonial settlers over indigenous subjects (see Mamdani 1996; Lange 2004, 2009; Owolabi 2017).

Statistical Evidence Demonstrates That Forced Settlement Generated Favorable Developmental Legacies Relative to Colonial Occupation

The second lesson is that forced settlement generated favorable developmental legacies relative to colonial occupation in terms of educational attainment, human well-being, and postcolonial democratization. These empirical claims are supported by statistical evidence from more than 90 developing countries with predominantly nonwhite populations that emerged from colonial rule after 1945. The statistical data models in Chapter 4 confirm that the developmental advantages of forced settlement relative to colonial occupation are robust to statistical controls for confounding factors such as the extent of

European settlement, British colonization, ethnic diversity, religious composition, Protestant missionary evangelization, and geography. The data appendix to Chapter 4 demonstrates similar results in an expanded sample of developing countries that gained independence after 1800, and in data models that provide alternative measurements of forced settlement and different indicators of post-colonial democratization. These robustness tests confirm that forced settlement colonies have large and statistically significant development advantages relative to Global South countries that experienced colonial occupation.

Comparative-Historical Evidence Demonstrates the Favorable Developmental Legacies of Forced Settlement Relative to Colonial Occupation across Multiple Colonial Empires

The comparative-historical evidence in Chapters 5, 6, and 7 demonstrates the favorable developmental legacies of forced settlement relative to colonial occupation across multiple colonial empires. This conclusion is important because many existing studies demonstrate favorable developmental outcomes in former British colonies relative to French or Iberian colonies (Grier 1999, 1997; Brown 2000; La Porta et al. 1998, 1999; Lee and Paine 2019a). The comparative-historical evidence in this book supports a different conclusion, as my research highlights the favorable developmental legacies of forced settlement relative to colonial occupation across multiple colonial empires. This is an important conclusion that builds on earlier research that highlights important development variations within the British and Spanish colonial empires (see Lange, Mahoney, and vom Hau 2006; Lange 2004, 2009; Mahoney 2010).

We already know that Spanish American countries that were intensively colonized with mercantilist economic institutions have worse developmental outcomes than Spanish American countries that were colonized later with liberal economic institutions (Mahoney 2010). Existing studies also demonstrate worse developmental outcomes in indirectly ruled British ruled colonies like Nigeria, Sierra Leone, or Uganda, relative to directly ruled British colonies like Barbados, Jamaica, Mauritius, Hong Kong, Singapore, or the United States (see Lange 2004, 2009). Existing studies also demonstrate worse developmental outcomes in subnational districts of India that experienced indirect British colonization (see Lee 2019; Mukherjee 2018).

The comparative-historical evidence in Chapter 5 is largely consistent with existing studies that highlight the distinctive developmental legacies of direct versus indirect British colonization. After all, direct British rule was established in Jamaica and in Sierra Leone's capital city, Freetown, following the abolition of slavery in the nineteenth century. The establishment of direct British rule in these territories promoted favorable development outcomes following the abolition of slavery, whereas indirect British rule hindered the long-term development of Sierra Leone's indigenous hinterlands. The historical evidence in Chapter 5 also demonstrates the extent to which Sierra Leone's long-term development was undermined by extractive legal-administrative institutions that limited the legal rights and political agency of indigenous colonial subjects in the country's outlying rural districts.

Chapters 6 and 7 also explores important developmental variations within the Portuguese and French colonial empires. The comparative case studies in Chapter 6 highlight the favorable developmental legacies of forced settlement in Cape Verde relative to Portuguese to colonial occupation in nearby Guinea-Bissau. The comparative-historical evidence in Chapter 7 also highlights the favorable developmental legacies of forced settlement in the French Antilles colonies relative to French colonial occupation in Algeria, Senegal, Gabon, Madagascar, and the Comoros Islands. These comparative case studies highlight the experience of French and Portuguese forced settlement colonies that expanded the citizenship rights of emancipated Afro-descendants following the abolition of slavery. By contrast, French and Portuguese colonies of occupation maintained repressive and arbitrary "native legal codes" that restricted the citizenship rights and political agency of indigenous colonial subjects until after World War II. Consequently, my research demonstrates important institutional variations within and across the British, French, and Portuguese colonial empires.

The historical evidence in Chapter 7 highlights the extent to which France's revolutionary upheavals pitted secular republican elites against reactionary Bonapartists, aristocratic landowners, and Catholic Church officials during the long nineteenth century. France's secular republic elites sought to expand the political representation and voting rights of emancipated Afro-descendants in order to weaken the political control of royalist white planters in the French Antilles colonies following the 1848 revolution. Because white colonial planters supported the Bonapartist dictatorship that topped the Second Republic in 1851, the "founding fathers" of the Third Republic supported the extension of key democratic rights—including universal male suffrage, parliamentary representation, and secular public education—to emancipated Afro-descendants in the French Antilles colonies after 1870. These were the only French colonies that maintained democratic institutions during the Third Republic (1870–1940). Consequently, the French Antilles colonies experienced a unique pattern of state-building and institutional development that empowered emancipated Afro-descendants relative to indigenous colonial subjects in French-occupied colonies like Algeria, Senegal, Gabon, or Madagascar after 1870. The successful long-term development of the French Antilles colonies also demonstrates the limits of existing studies that highlight the historical role of Protestant missionary evangelization in expanding educational access and postcolonial democracy in many parts of the Global South (see Woodberry 2012; Gallego and Woodberry 2010; Frankema 2012; Lankina and Getachew 2012, 2013). Instead, the favorable developmental legacies of forced settlement relative to colonial occupation outside of the British colonial empire demonstrates that colonial state institutions have important and lasting consequences for postcolonial development that extend beyond the impact of missionary evangelization during the colonial era.

Liberal Institutional Reforms Enabled Many (but Not All) Forced Settlement Colonies to Promote Inclusive Development following the Abolition of Slavery

The fourth lesson is that liberal institutional reforms enabled many—but not all—forced settlement colonies to generate more inclusive state institutions that expanded the political agency and socioeconomic well-being of emancipated Afro-descendants following the abolition of slavery. This pattern is generally true among forced settlement colonies that remained under European colonial domination following the abolition of slavery in the nineteenth century. Ironically, this pattern of inclusive development does not extend to Haiti, which was the only forced settlement colony to gain independence following a successful slave rebellion against white planter control and French colonial domination. Instead, the 1791–1804 Haitian Revolution empowered black military elites who gained control over the island's agricultural plantations after independence.

The historical evidence in Chapter 7 demonstrates that Haiti's conservative military elites had a vested interested in reviving labor-repressive plantation agriculture following that country's early independence from French rule. Haiti's long-term development was also undermined by neocolonial exploitation, US military interventions, and the crippling debt that France imposed on the impoverished Haitian Republic in exchange for recognizing its independence. Consequently, Haiti's postcolonial rulers were unable to implement the liberal institutional reforms that were enacted in other forced settlement colonies following the abolition of slavery. The French Antilles colonies—i.e., Guadeloupe, Martinique, and Réunion—experienced a very different political and developmental trajectory following the French abolition of slavery in 1848. In contrast to Haiti, the French Antilles colonies benefited from legal and political reforms that extended metropolitan citizenship rights to emancipated slaves following the 1848 French Revolution. Consequently, the emancipated populations of the French Antilles colonies were able to reap the social and political benefits of French citizenship—including parliamentary representation, universal male suffrage, and state-funded education in secular public schools—following the consolidation of the Third Republic in 1870.

The contrasting developmental legacies of the French Antilles and Haiti demonstrate the limits of existing arguments that suggest that formalized colonial rule is more destructive and extractive than neocolonial imperialist interventions in nominally sovereign or semisovereign states (see Kohli 2020). The comparative-historical evidence in Chapter 7 demonstrates that this is not always the case. Domestic political pressures may incentivize colonial rulers to implement institutional reforms that expand the legal rights and political agency of nonwhite colonial populations such as the emancipated Afro-descendants in the French Antilles or the British forced settlement colonies. These reforms ultimately favored the long-term development of the French Antilles colonies relative to Haiti, despite their similar history of white planter domination prior to the Haitian Revolution.

Why Do These Conclusions Matter?

The conclusions of this book matter because they demonstrate the limits of existing studies that predict persistent underdevelopment and limited postcolonial democratization in Global South countries that experienced extractive and labor-repressive forms of colonization with limited European settlement (Sokoloff and Engerman 2000; Acemoglu, Johnson, and Robinson 2001, 2002; Nunn 2008). The conclusions of this book also showcase the limits of large-N statistical data analyses that fail to account for institutional change over time. In contrast to existing studies that assume little change in the legal-administrative framework of colonial states over time (e.g., La Porta et al. 1998, 1999, 2008; Acemoglu, Johnson, and Robinson 2001, 2002; Wucherpfenning, Hunziker, and Cederman 2016), my research demonstrates the extent to which the abolition of slavery transformed the legal and administrative framework of forced settlement colonies across the Global South. Because the abolition of slavery was often connected to a broader project of liberal reform that expanded citizenship rights, political representation, and democratic accountability in Western European countries like Britain and France, this enabled colonial officials to implement liberal reforms that expanded the legal rights and political agency of emancipated Afro-descendants in forced settlement colonies. By contrast, colonial occupation did not produce this type of legal-administrative reform because colonial rulers enforced harsh and repressive "native legal codes" to control indigenous populations that were colonized following the abolition of slavery in the New World. Consequently, my research builds on earlier studies that highlight variations in colonial legal-administrative institutions across time and space (see Lange 2004, 2009; Mahoney 2010).

The mixed methodology in this study highlights important historical variations in the legal-administrative institutions associated with forced settlement and colonial occupation across multiple colonial empires. Consequently, it is important to acknowledge and to further investigate some of these temporal, geographic, and national variations in future empirical studies of colonialism, state-building, and postcolonial development in the Global South.

Avenues for Future Research

The core results of this study were obtained from statistical data analysis and comparative-historical evidence from developing countries that gained independence after World War II. Consequently, my research mostly overlooks the experience of Global South countries that emerged from colonial domination during the nineteenth century. Most of these countries were "mixed" colonies with intermediate to high levels of European settlement, and they were geographically concentrated in Latin America.[1] In contrast to the experience of Global South countries that emerged from colonial domination after 1945, Latin America's independence movements were primarily organized by the descendants of Iberian colonial settlers who maintained their economic and political dominance after independence (see Anderson 1981, 47–76; Centeno and Ferraro 2014). These elites faced significant challenges in integrating racially diverse populations into national states that maintained the economic and political dominance of Iberian colonial settlers and their descendants (see Centeno 2003; Centeno and Ferraro 2014; Safford 2014; Needell 2014; Kurtz 2013). Most Latin American republics abolished slavery during the mid-nineteenth century, following their independence from Spanish rule (Engerman 2012, 600), but indigenous forced labor persisted in many Latin American countries until the early twentieth century (Acemoglu, Johnson, and Robinson 2001, 1376; Dell 2010; Bruhn and Gallego 2012). This partly reflects the legacy of mercantilist institutions that prioritized the extraction of precious metals like gold and silver. Because these mineral deposits were often located in highland regions with significant indigenous populations, indigenous forced labor was far more common than enslaved African labor in the mainland colonies of Spanish America.

The next section of the chapter offers some reflections on the complex developmental legacies of "mixed colonization," and outlines some avenues for future research on the legacies of colonialism in Spanish America, Brazil, and South Africa. All of these countries have extreme levels of socioeconomic inequality and racialized class structures that have persisted since colonial times, and they all struggled, in varying degrees, to promote democratic development since their early independence from colonial rule.

The Complex Developmental Legacies of "Mixed" Colonization in Spanish America

The Spanish colonization of Latin America was based on a hybrid model in which colonial settlers and administrators used indigenous forced labor to extract mineral wealth from resource-rich territories in present-day Mexico, Guatemala, and the Andean countries of South America. Iberian colonists also established sugar, coffee, and cocoa plantations the Caribbean region, and in the tropical lowlands of Latin American countries whose indigenous populations were decimated by the Spanish colonial conquest, colonial forced labor, and exposure to European diseases during the sixteenth century. Cuba was the largest recipient of enslaved African labor in Spanish America,[2] but colonial plantations were also established in Puerto Rico, Spanish Santo Domingo (i.e., the Dominican Republic), and in the low-lying coastal regions of Latin American countries like Venezuela, Colombia, Ecuador, and Peru. The Spanish Caribbean colonies differed from forced settlement colonies in that they also attracted large numbers of white settlers, including poor whites that were engaged in the small-scale production of secondary crops like coffee, cocoa, and tobacco. It was not until much later that US agro-exporting companies established large-scale sugar estates in the Spanish-speaking Caribbean. Because of the late establishment of large-scale sugar production in the Hispanic Caribbean, local white settlers and free people of color always outnumbered enslaved Africans in Spanish Caribbean colonies like Cuba, Puerto Rico, and Spanish Santo Domingo.[3]

Indigenous labor coercion was far more widespread than African slave labor in Spanish American colonies. This is because Spanish colonists were particularly interested in colonizing densely populated indigenous territories that were rich in gold, silver, and other precious metals. Consequently, indigenous labor coercion was particularly widespread in Spanish American colonies with large indigenous populations and significant mineral wealth. During the mercantilist phase of Spanish rule (i.e., 1500–1700), Spanish colonial officials developed the *mita* system of forced labor recruitment that required indigenous community leaders to recruit adult male labor conscripts for compulsory labor in Spanish-owned gold and silver mines. Indigenous leaders that failed to provide the required number of conscripts were forced to pay a hefty fine in gold or silver that would cover the cost of hiring wage laborers (Dell 2010, 1867; also see Mahoney 2010, 68–70, 74–75, and 112–13). The Spanish system of using indigenous community leaders to recruit colonial mining labor closely resembled the pattern of indigenous labor recruitment of labor recruitment that was later used in indirectly ruled British colonies like Sierra Leone, in Portuguese-occupied colonies like Angola and Guinea-Bissau, and in French-occupied colonies like Gabon, Madagascar, and Senegal. This system of forced labor recruitment persisted in many Spanish American colonies until their independence in the 1820s (Dell 2010). Spanish colonists also used forced labor recruitment to generate indigenous labor for small-scale textile production in many parts of Latin America (Bruhn and Gallego 2012, 438).

Existing research has shown that Peruvian districts that employed the *mita* system of forced labor recruitment have worse developmental outcomes today than Peruvian districts that lacked indigenous labor recruitment during the colonial era (Dell 2010). Melissa Dell's research is compelling because she compares Peru's mining districts with rural districts that established hacienda estate agriculture, but their indigenous populations were not subject to forced labor recruitment. Although Peru's hacienda agriculture estates did not depend on forced labor recruitment, they created their own inequalities that enriched wealthy colonial landowners with secure property rights at the expense of the indigenous and mixed-race peasant farmers who lived and worked on these estates. Nevertheless, Dell's (2010) research demonstrates favorable developmental outcomes in Peru's hacienda agricultural districts relative to the rural districts that maintained forced labor recruitment for Spanish colonial mines. Over time, Peru's hacienda agricultural districts developed higher levels of household consumption, better access to public roads, and higher levels of educational attainment relative to rural districts that maintained forced labor conscription for Spanish colonial mines (Dell 2010).[4] In some ways, the subnational developmental variations in Peru are a microcosm of the macro trends that demonstrate favorable developmental outcomes in forced settlement colonies relative to Global South countries that experienced colonial occupation.

In light of this empirical pattern, future empirical research might examine whether Iberian colonization generated developmental disparities between coastal regions of Latin American countries that were colonized with African slave labor versus interior highland regions where Iberian colonists exploited indigenous labor. This question is important because indigenous labor recruitment was far more widespread than enslaved African labor in most Spanish American colonies. Consequently, future studies might examine whether subnational variations in governmental effectiveness and public service provisions in Latin American countries like Peru, Colombia, or Ecuador, might be explained by the historical legacy of indigenous forced labor in interior mining districts versus enslaved African labor in coastal regions that established large-scale agricultural plantations. These countries have the greatest regional disparities in economic development among former Spanish colonies in Latin America (Bruhn and

Gallego 2012, 434). Consequently, Latin American countries can offer important insights for understanding subnational variations in the developmental legacies of Spanish colonial rule.[5]

Future studies might also examine the distinctive developmental trajectories of Spanish American colonies that relied most heavily on African slave imports (i.e., Cuba, Puerto Rico, Dominican Republic) with Spanish American colonies that relied more heavily on indigenous labor coercion (e.g., Peru, Bolivia, Colombia, Guatemala, and Mexico). In contrast to the mainland Spanish American republics that gained independence between the 1820s, Cuba and Puerto Rico continued to rely on enslaved African labor until 1876 and 1886 respectively, and they remained under Spanish colonial domination until the US military intervention in the 1898 Spanish-American War. Cuba and Puerto Rico were arguably more exposed to US neocolonial intervention than any other Latin American countries during the first half of the twentieth century. At the same time, however, both islands showed significant increases in educational attainment, health, and other aspects of human well-being relative to Latin American countries and/or subnational regions with significant indigenous populations. Future studies might investigate the historical origins of human well-being in Cuba and Puerto Rico, which are typically excluded from English-language comparative studies of colonialism, state-building, and postcolonial development in Latin America.[6]

Future empirical research might examine why Cuba and Puerto Rico experienced significant increases in primary school enrollment following their late abolition of slavery in 1886 and 1876 respectively. Cuba's primary school enrollment rate increased from 10% to 41% of the school-aged population between 1880 and 1920, and Puerto Rico's primary school enrollment rate soared from 13% to 59% during the same period (Benavot and Riddle 1988, 205). By contrast, Latin American countries with large indigenous populations had much lower rates of primary school enrollment during the first half of the twentieth century. In Peru, Bolivia, and Guatemala, for example, only 15%–17% of children were enrolled in primary schools by 1920 (Benavot and Riddle 1988, 205).

The limited expansion of state-funded education in Latin American countries with large indigenous populations might reflect the brutal way in Latin America's indigenous communities were dispossessed of their communal land rights at the end of the nineteenth century. Decades after their independence from Spanish rule, most Latin American republics implemented liberal reforms that were designed to weaken the political authority and social control of Catholic Church officials and expand the production of agricultural and mining exports. These reforms were intended to socioeconomic and political modernization, but they were implemented in a brutal manner that devastated Latin America's indigenous communities. Because Latin America's liberal reformers failed to recognize the communal land rights of indigenous communities, these reforms enabled capricious landowners and foreign plantation companies to force the wholesale expropriation and privatization of indigenous communal lands.

The unethical and violent privatization of indigenous communal lands during the second half of the nineteenth century only exacerbated the unequal pattern of landholding that had plagued most Latin American countries since colonial times. Mexico's peasant and indigenous populations responded to the confiscation of their communal lands with political unrest and revolutionary violence that replaced the neocolonial social order of the Porfiriato dictatorship (1876–1910) with a semblance of political inclusion under the single-party hegemony of a corporatist authoritarian dictatorship following the Mexican Revolution of the 1910s (Teichman 2011, 106–14). The Peruvian state, by contrast, remained unable to incorporate its vast and widely dispersed indigenous communities: the persistence of strong regional identities, coupled with extreme land inequality and rural unrest in indigenous and mestizo peasant communities contributed to an unstable competitive oligarchy that was punctuated by frequent military coups during the first half of the twentieth century (Dell 2010, 1890; Kurtz 2009). Central American countries experienced indigenous resistance and revolutionary violence that unleashed the furor of military force backed by conservative landowning elites in Guatemala, and conservative dictatorships that were supported by US capitalist interests in Nicaragua, Honduras, and El Salvador (see Mahoney 2001, 197–235).

The significant increase in landlessness in Latin American countries with significant indigenous populations was likely more intense than in Cuba or Puerto Rico, where local white settlers outnumbered emancipated Afro-descendants during the second half of the nineteenth century. More research is needed to identify the conditions that enabled Cuba, and especially Puerto Rico, to promote favorable development outcomes relative to Latin American countries and subnational regions with significant indigenous populations. Preliminary evidence suggests that US ownership and investment in large-scale agricultural plantations primarily benefited white and light-skinned elites in both islands (Kohli 2020, 229; Bobonis and Toro 2007), so the expansion of primary schooling in these countries probably benefited white and mixed-race citizens more than emancipated Afro-descendants. Puerto Rico's predominantly white population also benefited from the limited expansion of US citizenship rights during World War I. The US decision to extend limited citizenship rights to Puerto Rico was largely motivated by wartime considerations to mobilize the island's population. Nevertheless, this political decision significantly expanded Puerto Rico's educational expenditures and primary school enrollment during the 1920s (Bobonis and Toro 2007, 39–48). It also paved the way for the significant expansion of political representation, electoral competition, and voting rights in Puerto Rico after 1946 (Cámara 2004).

Existing studies suggest that many Latin American countries failed to expand the political agency of emancipated Afro-descendants after independence from colonial rule (Marx 1996, 1998; Paschel 2018). The neglect of Latin America's emancipated Afro-descendant communities partly reflects the fact that plantation slavery was a relatively marginal aspect of economy and society in most Spanish American colonies. Cuba was the obvious exception to this pattern, but even here, enslaved Africans were always outnumbered by local white settlers and free people of color. In mainland countries like Mexico, Colombia, Peru, and Ecuador, enslaved Africans and were also outnumbered by the much larger population of indigenous colonial subjects. Consequently, the abolition of slavery in Latin American countries did not represent the same type of critical historical juncture that generated liberal institutional reforms seen in British forced settlement colonies and the French Antilles colonies. Although Latin America's emancipated Afro-descendants did not make significant political gains following the abolition of slavery, the benign neglect of Latin America's Afro-descendant communities may have been less devastating for their well-being and development than the devastating policies that dispossessed and further impoverished Latin America's indigenous communities during the second half of the nineteenth century.

Brazil and South Africa

Future research on Brazil and South Africa might also build on the conclusions from this work. Existing studies have examined various aspects of state-building and postcolonial development in Brazil and South Africa, but these studies tend to overlook the "reversal of fortune" that enabled Brazil to surpass South Africa's development during the second half of the twentieth century. Brazil was intensively colonized with enslaved African plantation laborers, but the country's southern regions were primarily settled by European immigrants who arrived after Brazil gained independence from Portugal in 1822.

South Africa's colonial history is more complex than Brazil's. South Africa's Cape of Good Hope was initially colonized by Dutch settlers during the seventeenth century, but indigenous African ethnicities long predate the onset of European colonization. The British conquest of South Africa's Cape Colony during the Napoleonic wars generated an intense political rivalry between the descendants of Dutch settlers (locally known as Boers) and the new British colonists. South Africa's Boer white settlers vehemently opposed the British abolition of slavery in South Africa's Cape Colony during the 1830s, so they established their own white supremacist republics—Transvaal and the Orange Free State—in the country's indigenous interior during the 1840s and 1850s. The British also expanded into the eastern half of the country following the Anglo-Zulu wars of the 1870s. The modern state of South Africa only emerged after the 1899–1902 Boer War, when the British army successfully vanquished the independent Boer states and the remaining indigenous territories that had hitherto resisted British colonization.

Consequently, the political construction of modern South Africa was characterized by significant ethnic and racial political violence, whereas Brazil gained independence following a peaceful transfer of power within the Portuguese royal family. Brazil's first emperor, Dom Pedro I, was the eldest son of the Portuguese king, who fled to Rio de Janeiro during the Napoleonic wars and returned to Lisbon following Portugal's Liberal Revolution of 1820. This is why Brazil gained independence with little disruption to its colonial economy and society. The peaceful transition of power from Portuguese to Brazilian royal authority protected the interests of Brazil's landed elites and slave-owners until the Brazilian monarchy was overthrown by a republican uprising in 1889.[7]

In keeping with the core arguments of this book, the modern Brazilian republic never enforced the type of state-sanctioned racial discrimination or institutional segregation that the South African state used to repress and control indigenous black Africans following the Boer War (Marx 1996, 1998). This is not to say to say that Brazilian abolition created the type of racial democracy that is celebrated in Gilberto Freyre's theory of *lusotropicalismo*. The First Brazilian Republic (1889–1930) maintained voting restrictions that disenfranchised many illiterate wage-holders and small property owners, but these rules applied equally to white and black poor. Moreover, all Brazilians—regardless of race or socioeconomic status experienced significant political repression during Getúlio Vargas' populist dictatorship (1930–45) and the military dictatorship that lasted from 1964 until 1985. These policies helped to sustain Brazil's vast socio-economic inequalities and its racialized class structure into the twentieth century.

In contrast to Brazil, South Africa was initially advantaged by British liberal reforms that expanded educational access and political representation following the abolition of slavery in the 1830s. British liberal reforms extended individual civil liberties, political representation, and voting rights to the mixed-race descendants of emancipated slaves, indigenous Xhosa, and European settlers in South Africa's Cape Colony. Indigenous Bantu-speaking property owners also enjoyed voting rights in the Cape Colony during the nineteenth century (Fintel and Fourie 2019, 763). Nevertheless, these reforms were only implemented in directly ruled areas under British authority (i.e., Cape Colony), and they were never extended to indirectly ruled British territories (e.g., Natal province), or the Boer republics of Transvaal and the Orange Free State. The partial implementation

of nineteenth-century liberal reforms privileged South Africa's early development relative to Brazil, but South Africa's long-term development was ultimately
compromised by white supremacist policies that marginalized, repressed, and
impoverished indigenous black Africans after the Boer War. The political rights
and individual liberties of indigenous black South Africans were increasingly
curtailed following the forced merger of the two Boer republics (i.e., Transvaal
and the Orange Free State) and the former British colonies (i.e., Cape Colony and
Natal) into a white supremacist state that gained independence from Britain in
1910 (Marx 1998; Fintel and Fourie 2019, 763).

The racial policies of the modern South African state combined the most repressive aspects of Jim Crow segregation in the southern United States with the
most despicable aspects of "native policies" that expropriated land and resources
from indigenous populations in white settler countries like Canada, Australia,
and the United States. South Africa's 1913 Native Lands Act restricted indigenous African landownership to "native reserves" that accounted for less than
10% of the country's landmass (Fintel and Fourie 2019, 764). This policy was
designed to expand white settlement on the country's best agricultural land
(Acemoglu and Robinson 2010, 36). During the 1920s, the South African government also created a separate system of "tribal councils" that empowered
local chiefs in the native reserves. The government also established segregating
housing units that discouraged African "migrant workers" from permanently
settling in urban areas (Mamdani 1996, 71–72, 95, 257–59). These policies became even more repressive with the formalization of apartheid after 1948. South
Africa's apartheid policies were explicitly designed to remove indigenous black
South Africans from "white" urban space, and to reverse the rural-urban migration that brought black Africans into South Africa's largest cities during the
first half of the twentieth century. Consequently, the South African government
destroyed black neighborhoods and businesses in the country's major cities and
forcibly "deported" many urban black residents back to tribal native reserves
(Mamdani 1996, 29, 102).

There was very little access to employment opportunities, education, or
healthcare in South Africa's impoverished native reserves, where government-
appointed chiefs controlled access to communally held indigenous lands (Fintel
and Fourie 2019, 764; Reed 2020). Black Africans were prohibited from living
in urban areas, although black workers could temporarily settle in peri-urban
shantytowns (known as African townships) if they maintained an internal "pass"
that was linked to a white employer. Indigenous Africans were barred from
owning property or businesses that competed with the "European" sector of the
economy, and indigenous Africans were prohibited from holding skilled jobs
in the mining sector (Acemoglu and Robinson 2010, 37). There was no equivalent to any of these policies in Brazil (see Marx 1996, 1998). South Africa's racial

policies were overtly harmful toward indigenous black Africans; Brazil's policies toward emancipated Afro-descendants are more accurately described as benign neglect.

Future empirical research might examine whether the more inclusive development of the Brazilian state has facilitated certain aspects of human well-being relative to South Africa. Preliminary evidence suggests a reversal of fortune between the two countries. During the first half of the twentieth century, Brazil lagged South Africa on key indicators of human development, including educational access, voting rights, and per capita GDP.[8] Nevertheless, the combined effects of native legal codes (1913–48) and apartheid (1948–94) hindered South Africa's long-term development relative to Brazil. By contrast, the absence of legalized racial distinctions, native legal codes and de jure segregation ultimately seems to have favored Brazil's long-term development relative to South Africa.

Brazil's per capita GDP first surpassed South Africa's during the 1970s, and the country has made impressive economic gains relative to South Africa during the past fifty years (Maddison 2006). Both countries implemented democratic reforms during the 1990s, but Brazil has been far more successful than South Africa at reducing poverty, child mortality, and income inequality in recent years (Avirgan 2006). By contrast, South Africa's ANC governments have been less successful than Brazil's center-left Workers' Party at expanding educational access, employment opportunities, and living standards for the country's poorest households since the end of apartheid in 1994.[9] Consequently, South Africa remains beset by high levels of structural unemployment, entrenched income and wealth inequality, and persistent poverty in indigenous rural communities and working-class black townships nearly three decades after the formal end of apartheid (Fintel and Fourie 2019; Reed 2020; Chatterjee, Czakja, and Gethin 2021).

The Long Afterlife of Slavery and Racial Domination in the United States

Future empirical studies might also explore the unusually long and brutal afterlife of slavery and racial domination in the southern United States in comparative perspective with British forced settlement colonies or the French Antilles colonies. Slavery was far less extensive in the southern United States than in forced settlement colonies like Barbados, Jamaica, or the French Antilles, but the decentralized nature of political authority in the United States enabled southern state governments to block the type of liberal reforms that were implemented in British and French forced settlement colonies following the abolition of slavery. Whereas British and French colonial planters were forced to emancipate their slaves during the 1830s and 1840s respectively, the decentralized nature of the

United States' federal constitution enabled southern state governments to maintain plantation slavery until the 1860s. Slavery was phased out in most northern US states following the American Revolution, but southern planters extended slavery into many parts of the expanding western frontier during the nineteenth century. The western expansion of slavery generated intense political competition between US Republican leaders, who embraced the abolitionists' cause during the 1850s, and the southern and frontier states that maintained plantation slavery into the 1860s. Eleven southern states seceded from the United States following the Republican party's first presidential election victory in 1860. The newly elected Republican president, Abraham Lincoln, called on the Union Army to recapture the secessionist Confederate states in a bloody and lengthy civil war that lasted until 1865.

There was only a brief period of liberal reform in southern US states after the Civil War. This occurred during the early Reconstruction years (1865–70), when the defeated Confederate states lost their political representation in the Republican-dominated US Congress. In the decade following the civil war, the defeated Confederate states were occupied by the abolitionist Union Army and organized into military districts. In many ways, this political arrangement was akin to colonialism, because southern white elites were subject to the political control of military officials appointed by the federal government. This unusual political arrangement facilitated a short-lived period of legal and political reforms in the southern United States in the immediate aftermath of the Civil War.[10] Because the defeated Confederate states were temporarily excluded from the US Congress, the Republican-dominated Congress enacted a series of constitutional amendments that abolished slavery (1865), extended citizenship rights to emancipated slaves (1868) and voting rights to emancipated Afro-descendants throughout the United States (1870). More than 700,000 emancipated black citizens were registered as new voters during the short-lived military reconstruction in the southern United States (Valelly 2004, 32; Gibson 2012, 51). In fact, the proportion of blacks that were eligible to vote in the United States increased from 0.5% at the end of the Civil War to 80.5% in December 1867 (Gibson 2012, 51).

From 1865 until the late 1870s, the southern United States followed a reformist path similar to that of the British and French colonial territories where slavery had been abolished during the 1830s and 1840s. In all of these territories, liberal reforms were implemented by reformist government officials that overrode the preferences of local white planters. This was made possible by institutional arrangements that empowered colonial government officials in British and French territories and federal government officials in the southern United States. Nevertheless, the constitutional amendments and civil rights legislation that protected the legal and political rights of emancipated Afro-descendants in the southern United States were only meaningful if the federal government remained committed to their enforcement. The Republican Party was largely committed to the civil and political rights of emancipated Afro-descendants during Reconstruction, but the party's electoral fortunes declined after 1874 (Frymer 1999, 60–63). And although federal troops were deployed to protect the voting rights of emancipated Afro-descendants in southern state elections, the federal army withdrew from the southern United States following a disputed presidential election in 1876. The Great Compromise of 1877 gave the disputed 1876 presidential election to the Republican candidate Rutherford Hayes in exchange for removing the federal troops that protected Republican (and mixed-race) state governments in Florida, South Carolina, and Louisiana. The removal of federal troops from the United States enabled local whites to intimidate and harass black voters until former Confederate elites regained political control over southern state legislatures (Valelly 2004, 47–52; Frymer 1999, 65–72). At first, the political disenfranchisement of southern black voters was informal and illegal, but US federal courts systematically privileged the institutional autonomy of southern state legislatures over the civil and political rights of emancipated Afro-descendants after 1896 (González and King 2004; Gibson 2012, 55–71). Consequently, the participation of black voters in southern state elections declined from 61% in 1880 to 36% in 1892 to less than 2% from 1912 until 1944 (Gibson 2012, 61).

In contrast to the centralized nature of political authority in British and French forced settlement colonies following the abolition of slavery, the decentralized nature of American federalism and the ineffectiveness of the US federal courts enabled southern state legislatures, beginning with Mississippi, to systematically disenfranchise African American voters after 1890 (González and King 2004; Gibson 2012, 60–63; Woodward 2013, 145–47). The former Confederate states also constructed a brutal and repressive system of racial domination underpinned by Jim Crow segregation, separate and unequal schools, share-crop agriculture, vigilante justice, widespread lynching, and the white supremacist violence of the Ku Klux Klan. The legal rights of southern blacks were further undermined by racialized policing and whites-only juries. And the political rights of emancipated southern blacks were restricted by electoral violence, voter intimidation, unfair literacy tests, poll taxes, single-party control, and white primary elections (see Key 1949; Gibson 2012, 60–67). Many southern US states also constructed oppressive penal codes that revived forced labor on agricultural plantations.[11]

These discriminatory policies were intensified during the early decades of the twentieth century. Racial discrimination and Jim Crow segregation were introduced in the US federal government and bureaucracy after Woodrow Wilson, a southern Democrat and committed segregationist, gained the presidency in 1912 (González and King 2004). Franklin D. Roosevelt was somewhat more sympathetic to northern urban blacks during the Great Depression, when millions of African Americans migrated from southern rural districts into northern and midwestern US cities like Chicago, St. Louis, Cleveland, Pittsburgh, and Philadelphia. The political rights of black voters were not formally restricted in northern states, but Roosevelt's government remained heavily dependent on white supremacist voters from southern US states. This why southern blacks were purposely excluded from New Deal welfare programs that benefited white pensioners and promoted broad-based prosperity among middle-class whites after World War II (González and King 2004, 204). Because the decentralized US Constitution protected the rights of southern state legislatures to enforce racially discriminatory policies, the federal government failed to protect the civil liberties and political rights of emancipated Afro-descendants from the 1880s until the implementation of the 1964 Civil Rights Act and the 1965 Voting Rights Act. Consequently, the southern US states did not fully democratize until the 1960s, when civil liberties and political rights were extended to African American citizens (González and King 2004, 204; Acemoglu and Robinson 2019, 306–23).

Placing the US experience in comparative-historical perspective with other forced settlement colonies, it becomes clear that what differentiates the United States from other countries is not only the extent of plantation slavery during the colonial era. Slaves only accounted for 12% of the US population in 1860, and slavery was heavily concentrated in southern states, where slaves comprised between 25% and 60% of the total population (Bertocchi and Dimino 2012, 593). Demographic data suggests that US slavery was less deadly than in British or French forced settlement colonies, where most enslaved Africans died from disease, abuse, starvation, or suicide within a few short years of their arrival in the New World. The US slave population was able to sustain and reproduce itself without the need for new arrivals from Africa. Although slavery in the United States was less intensive and brutal than in other parts of the New World, the postbellum United States was one of the most brutally repressive countries for emancipated Afro-descendants. There was no equivalent to Jim Crow segregation, white-only juries, the Ku Klux Klan, prison plantations, segregated military units, or racially segregated schools for emancipated Afro-descendants in British forced settlement colonies or the French Antilles colonies. There was also no equivalent to state-sanctioned racial segregation in Latin American societies like Brazil, Cuba, or the Dominican Republic either, except during periods of US military occupation. Consequently, what distinguishes the United States from other forced settlement colonies was not the extent of plantation slavery during the colonial era, but the fact that US state legislatures were able to reverse the liberal reforms that were implemented during the Reconstruction years. As a result of this reversal, slavery had a much longer afterlife in the United States than in forced settlement colonies that successfully implemented liberal reforms following the abolition of slavery.

Final Thoughts

I conclude with a timely reflection on the 1619 project that commemorates the somber memorial of four hundred years since the first enslaved Africans were brought to colonial Virginia. The 1619 project has generated a highly polarized discussion about the complex legacies of plantation slavery in contemporary America. Conservative politicians and media outlets have condemned the 1619 project because it challenges the dominant narrative of the United States as a democratic republic founded on the principles of liberty and equality. This position is highlighted in a recent op-ed by Richard Lowry, the editor-in-chief of the conservative *National Review*. Lowry's op-ed downplays the destructive legacy of slavery in the United States by suggesting that "ninety-five percent of the slaves transported across the Atlantic went to places south of the present-day United States" (Lowry 2019). Because these facts are true, Lowry argues that US public schooling should de-emphasize the corrosive effects of slavery, and celebrate positive things that differentiate the United States from other societies that have been shaped by plantation slavery. In Lowry's words,

> None of the other societies tainted by slavery produced the Declaration of Independence, a Washington, Jefferson, and Hamilton, the U.S. Constitution, or a tradition of liberty that inspired people around the world for centuries. If we don't keep that in mind, as well as the broader context of slavery, we aren't giving this country—or history—its due.

By contrast, the 1619 project makes it impossible to ignore the racialized origins of American democracy, and the racial disparities that have pervaded American life since colonial times. This is why progressive liberals and "woke" activists have used the 1619 project to revive long-held demands for reparations to address the historical injustice of slavery and the continued marginalization of African Americans following the abolition of slavery. In an important critical essay that was published in the *Atlantic* magazine, the celebrated African American activist and writer Ta-Nehisi Coates painted a devastating picture of the long and brutal afterlife of plantation slavery after the US Civil War: Coates (2014) observed that America's deep and persistent racial inequalities have been sustained into the twenty-first century by "ninety years of Jim Crow [segregation]; sixty years of separate but equal; [and] thirty-five years of racist housing policy".

It is the long and brutal afterlife of American slavery that distinguishes the United States from forced settlement colonies where metropolitan officials implemented liberal administrative reforms that expanded the legal (and in some cases, political) rights of emancipated slaves. The decentralized nature of American federalism enabled southern political leaders to construct a racially stratified political order that appealed to poor white voters by disenfranchising black voters. This is what explains the long history of single-party domination based on racial exclusion in southern United States from the 1890s until the mid-1960s (see Key 1949; Gibson 2012; Grantham 1988). Consequently, future research might examine the extent to which the resurgence of racially discriminatory policies after the Civil War may have hindered the social, economic, and political well-being of African Americans relative to emancipated Afro-descendants in British forced settlement colonies or the French Antilles. The consequences of discriminatory policies that followed the abolition of slavery are still evident in the United States today. In 2010, the life expectancy for African Americans (74.9 years) lagged behind that of Barbados (78.1 years), Guadeloupe (79.4 years), Martinique (80.1 years), and Réunion (78.2 years). African American children also suffer from higher mortality rates than children born in Antigua and Barbuda, Barbados, or the French Antilles.[12] The United States continues to suffer from de facto racial segregation in its schools, churches, and neighborhoods. Voter suppression remains an ongoing concern in the United States after the Supreme Court revoked the federal government's authority to enforce key provisions of the 1965 Voting Rights Act in southern US states. It is therefore not surprising that the United States' Freedom House democracy score has declined in recent years.

As I write these words in the aftermath of Donald Trump's presidency and the storming of the US Capitol in January 2021, the United States' Freedom House democracy score (83/100) trails that of several forced settlement colonies including Barbados (95), Cape Verde (92), Grenada (89) and Mauritius (87).[13] These disparities are both shocking and inexcusable, given the greater prosperity of the United States, and its longer history of democratic inclusion for white settlers and their descendants. Consequently, future research might explore the extent to which the racialized institutional development of southern US states may have hindered the well-being of African Americans relative to forced settlement colonies that implemented liberal institutional reforms following the abolition of slavery. Given the size and complexity of the United States, it might be helpful to compare district-level data on the expansion of education and voting rights for emancipated populations in the United States with similar data from one of the British forced settlement colonies or the French Antilles. This could help to place the unique experience of the southern United States in a broader historical perspective.

Overall, the comparative-historical evidence in this book suggests that liberal institutional reforms enabled many forced settlement colonies to expand educational access and voting rights following the abolition of slavery. As a result of these reforms, most forced settlement colonies have higher levels of educational attainment and postcolonial democracy than Global South countries that emerged from colonial occupation after 1945. The comparative-historical evidence in this book also demonstrates that liberal institutional reforms had a more powerful impact on the developmental trajectories of forced settlement colonies than the extent of plantation slavery prior to abolition. It is important to recognize that the postabolition reforms in British forced settlement colonies and the French Antilles were an extension of the British reform movement and the revolutionary upheavals that expanded parliamentary representation and citizenship rights in Britain and France during the middle decades of the nineteenth century. Local white planters vociferously opposed the partial implementation of democratic reforms in the forced settlement colonies. Nevertheless, reformist British and French colonial officials undermined the economic and political dominance of local white planters while strengthening the legal rights and political agency of emancipated slaves and their descendants. These institutional reforms also strengthened the legal-administrative capacity of colonial state officials to provide public goods such as state-funded education. By contrast, liberal institutional reforms were often watered down in postcolonial states where landowning elites maintained their economic and political dominance after independence.

The historical evidence from Brazil, Cuba, and the southern United States is particularly interesting because plantation slavery was far less extensive in these regions than in Jamaica or the French Antilles. This suggests that plantation slavery can have a very long afterlife in postcolonial states where landowning elites maintained their economic and political dominance following the abolition of slavery. Nevertheless, many forced settlement colonies ultimately promoted favorable developmental outcomes that resulted from the liberal institutional reforms that accompanied the abolition of slavery. These liberal institutional reforms undermined the economic and political dominance of local white planters and strengthened the political agency of emancipated slaves and their descendants. Over the *longue durée,* this enabled many forced settlement colonies—from Jamaica, Barbados, and Mauritius to Cape Verde and the French Antilles—to promote high levels of educational attainment and postcolonial democracy despite the legacy of plantation slavery.

Former Colonies in OLS Data Models

	Principal Colonizer (1)	Mode of Colonization (2)	Metropolitan Legal Institutions Prior to 1936 (Y/N)
92 Postcolonial States			
Algeria	France	Occupation	N (3)
Angola	Portugal	Occupation	N (4)
Antigua and Barbuda	Britain	Forced settlement	Y (5)
Bahamas	Britain	Forced settlement	Y (5)
Bahrain	Britain	Protected state	N (6)
Bangladesh	Britain	Occupation	N (5)
Barbados	Britain	Forced settlement	Y (5)
Belize	Britain	Mixed / forced settlement2	Y (5)
Benin	France	Occupation	N (3)
Botswana	Britain	Occupation	N (5)
Brunei Darussalam	Britain	Protected state	N (5)
Burkina Faso	France	Occupation	N (3)
Burundi	Belgium	Occupation	N (7)
Cambodia	France	Occupation	N (3)
Cameroon	France	Occupation	N (3)
Cape Verde	Portugal	Forced settlement	Y (4)
Central African Republic	France	Occupation	N (3)
Chad	France	Occupation	N (3)
Comoros	France	Occupation	N (3)
Congo	France	Occupation	N (3)
Congo, Democratic Republic	Belgium	Occupation	N (7)
Côte D'Ivoire	France	Occupation	N (3)
Djibouti	France	Occupation	N (3)
Dominica	Britain	Forced settlement	Y (5)
Equatorial Guinea	Spain	Occupation	N (8)
Fiji	Britain	Mixed	N (5)
Gabon	France	Occupation	N (3)
Gambia	Britain	Occupation	N (5)
Ghana	Britain	Occupation	N (5)
Grenada	Britain	Forced settlement	Y (5)

	Principal Colonizer (1)	Mode of Colonization (2)	Metropolitan Legal Institutions Prior to 1936 (Y/N)
Guinea	France	Occupation	N (3)
Guinea-Bissau	Portugal	Occupation	N (4)
Guyana	Britain	Forced settlement	Y (5)
India	Britain	Occupation	N (5)
Indonesia	Netherlands	Occupation	N (9)
Jamaica	Britain	Forced settlement	Y (5)
Jordan	Britain	Occupation	N (10)
Kenya	Britain	Occupation	N (5)
Kiribati	Britain	Occupation	N (5)
Kuwait	Britain	Protected state	N (6)
Laos	France	Occupation	N (3)
Lebanon	France	Occupation	N (3)
Lesotho	Britain	Occupation	N (3)
Libya	Italy	Occupation	N (11)
Madagascar	France	Occupation	N (3)
Malawi	Britain	Occupation	N (5)
Malaysia	Britain	Mixed	N (5)
Maldives	Britain	Protected state	N (6)
Mali	France	Occupation	N (3)
Mauritania	France	Occupation	N (3)
Mauritius	Britain	Forced settlement	Y (5)
Morocco	France	Occupation	N (3)
Mozambique	Portugal	Occupation	N (4)
Myanmar	Britain	Occupation	N (5)
Nauru	Australia	Occupation	Y (12)
Niger	France	Occupation	N (3)
Nigeria	Britain	Occupation	N (5)
Oman	Britain	Protected state	N (7)
Pakistan	Britain	Occupation	N (5)
Papua New Guinea	Australia	Occupation	N (12)
Philippines	United States	Occupation	N (13)
Qatar	Britain	Protected State	N (6)
Rwanda	Belgium	Occupation	N (5)
Saint Kitts and Nevis	Britain	Forced settlement	Y (5)
Saint Lucia	Britain	Forced settlement	Y (5)
Saint Vincent and the Grenadines	Britain	Forced settlement	Y (5)
Samoa	New Zealand	Occupation	N (15)
Sao Tomé and Príncipe	Portugal	Forced settlement	N (4)
Senegal	France	Occupation	N (3)
Seychelles	Britain	Forced settlement	Y (5)

	Principal Colonizer (1)	Mode of Colonization (2)	Metropolitan Legal Institutions Prior to 1936 (Y/N)
Sierra Leone	Britain	Occupation	N (5)
Singapore	Britain	City-state/mixed	Y (5)
Solomon Islands	Britain	Occupation	Y (5)
Somalia	Britain/Italy	Protected state	N (5) (11)
Sri Lanka	Britain	Occupation	Y (5)
Sudan	Britain	Occupation	N (5)
Suriname	Netherlands	Forced settlement	Y (9)
Swaziland	Britain	Occupation	N (5)
Syria	France	Occupation	N (3)
Tanzania	Britain	Occupation	N (5)
Togo	France	Occupation	N (3)
Tonga	Britain	Occupation	N (5)
Trinidad and Tobago	Britain	Forced settlement	Y (5)
Tunisia	France	Occupation	N (3)
Tuvalu	Britain	Occupation	N (5)
Uganda	Britain	Occupation	N (5)
United Arab Emirates	Britain	Protected state	N (6)
Vanuatu	Britain/France	Occupation	N (3) (5)
Vietnam	France	Occupation	N (3)
Yemen	Britain	Protected state	N (6)
Zambia	Britain	Occupation	N (5)
Zimbabwe	Britain	Occupation	N (5)

9 Dependent Territories

	Principal Colonizer (1)	Mode of Colonization (2)	Metropolitan Legal Institutions Prior to 1936 (Y/N)
French Guiana	France	Mixed / forced settlement2	Y (3)
French Polynesia	France	Mixed	N (3)
Guadeloupe	France	Forced Settlement	Y (3)
Hong Kong	Britain	City-state	Y (5)
Macau	Portugal	City-state	Y (4)
Martinique	France	Forced settlement	Y (3)
Netherlands Antilles	Netherlands	Forced settlement	Y (9)
Reunion	France	Forced settlement	Y (3)
US Virgin Islands	United States	Mixed / forced settlement2	Y (14)
Total observations	101	101	101

Notes:

(1) Principal colonizers based on country histories in the *Encyclopedia Britannica*.

(2) Mode of colonization is coded by the author, based on country histories in the *Encyclopedia Britannica* and 1975 ethnoracial data from Barrett 1982.

(3) French legal-administrative institutions were coded using citizenship data for 1936 from France 1944. French administration was based on legal distinctions between

French citizens and indigenous persons (*autochtones*), subject to a distinct legal code. The *indigénat* legal code was enforced in all French colonies with significant indigenous populations apart from Morocco and Tunisia, which had their own indigenous rulers (France 1944; Merle 2002). By contrast, French citizens made up the overwhelming majority in the forced settlement colonies, where local government administration was based on the French municipal law of 1884 (France 1944).

(4) Portuguese administration was also based on legal distinctions between metropolitan citizens (*civilisados*) and indigenous subjects (*indigenas*) until 1961. Portuguese colonies were coded based on 1950 citizenship data from Portugal 1960. Secondary sources note that these distinctions were formalized during the early twentieth century. See Duffy 1961; Coissoro 1984.

(5) The legal-administrative institutions of most former British colonies were coded based on Colonial Office Annual Reports for 1930–31 for the Bahamas; Barbados; Basutoland; Bechuanaland Protectorate; British Guiana; British Honduras; British Solomon Islands Protectorate; Brunei; Ceylon; Federated Malay States; Fiji; Gambia; Gilbert and Ellice Islands; Grenada; Hong Kong; Jamaica; Johore (Unfederated Malay State); Kedah and Perlis (Unfederated Malay State); Kelantan (Unfederated Malay State); Kenya Colony and Protectorate; Leeward Islands; Mauritius; New Hebrides; Nigeria; Nyasaland; Northern Rhodesia; St. Lucia; St. Vincent; Seychelles; Sierra Leone; Somaliland; Straits Settlement; Swaziland; Tongan Islands Protectorate; Trengganu (Unfederated Malay State); Trinidad and Tobago; and Uganda Protectorate (See Great Britain, Colonial Office, 1931). Matthew Lange's index of indirect rule also measures the percentage of legal cases heard in "native courts" presided over by traditional rulers in the following countries in 1955: Bahamas, Bangladesh, Barbados, Belize, Botswana, Fiji, Gambia, Ghana, Guyana, Hong Kong, India, Jamaica, Kenya, Lesotho, Malawi, Malaysia, Mauritius, Myanmar, Nigeria, Pakistan, Sierra Leone, Singapore, Sri Lanka, Sudan, Swaziland, Tanzania, Trinidad, Uganda, Zambia, and Zimbabwe (see Lange 2004, 2009). Only two countries, Brunei Darussalam and the Solomon Islands, seem to have adapted their legal institutions between 1930 and 1955. The Colonial Office's Annual Report for Brunei notes the existence of native courts in 1930 (Great Britain, Colonial Office 1931), whereas Matthew Lange codes Brunei as a directly ruled British colony in 1955 (see Lange 2009, 48). The shift to direct rule in Brunei likely reflects the bureaucratization of British rule in the Malay Peninsula following World War II (see Lange 2009, 184-86; Eck 2018). By contrast, there is no evidence of native courts in the Solomon Islands in the Colonial Office's Annual Report for 1932 (Great Britain, Colonial Office, 1933). The native courts in the Solomon Islands were established in 1942 (see Corrin and Paterson 2007, 3). The colonial administrations of Brunei and the Solomon Islands were coded based on British Colonial Office reports from the 1930s.

(6) These territories never came under the jurisdiction of the British Colonial Office. Instead, they retained their traditional Islamic rulers throughout the colonial era (see country histories in *Encyclopedia Britannica* online, http://www.britannica.com).

(7) In the Belgian Congo, native courts were established during the 1920s (Buell 1928, 488–91; Mamdani 1996, 86). Furthermore, Europeans and indigenous Africans were subjected to distinct legal codes until 1958 (see Young 1965, 100–102). In Rwanda and Burundi, Tutsi chiefs presided over a system of native tribunals that had legal jurisdiction over indigenous African subjects (Gelders 1954, 125–32).

(8) The Spanish system of "administrative chiefs" was similar to that of France and Portugal. As late as 1955, less than 1% of Africans enjoyed *emancipado* status, which provided for equality with colonial settlers under Spanish law. See Berman 1956, 359–60.

(9) Dutch administration in the postemancipation Caribbean resembled direct British rule. A uniform and inclusive legal-administrative structure protected individual civil liberties (i.e., metropolitan subject rights) but restricted political representation and voting rights (Ledgister 1998). In the Dutch East Indies (Indonesia), by contrast, native tribunals enforced customary (*adat*) law during the colonial era (see Jaspan 1965).

(10) Tribal courts were established in Trans-Jordan (present-day Jordan) during the 1920s. See Great Britain, Colonial Office 1938.

(11) In Italian-ruled Libya and Somalia, there were distinct legal systems for natives, Italians, and other Europeans (Malvezzi 1927, 235).

(12) In Nauru, native laws and customs were first permitted by the Germans, then disallowed by the Australians after 1923. Australian officials decided to recognize native laws and customs after 1936, provided that they were "not inconsistent with the written law and with the general principles of humanity" (see Corrin and Paterson 2007, 3–4). Nauru is coded as having had metropolitan legal rights during the 1930s. In previous work, I estimated alternative models that coded Nauru as having native laws, and the model results were substantively similar (see Owolabi 2015, Appendix V). In Papua New Guinea, native regulations were enforced by the Court of Native Affairs (see Weisbrot 1981).

(13) US administrators maintained distinct legal-administrative structures for non-Christian highland tribes and the Muslim regions of Mindanao and Sulu, despite attempting bureaucratic centralization in other parts of the Philippines (see Hutchcroft 2000).

(14) US citizenship and local self-government with universal suffrage were extended to the US Virgin Islands in 1932 and 1936 respectively (United States, Department of State 2009).

(15) In Samoa, native custom was recognized in colonial administration, and traditional chiefs had both advisory and judicial roles (Campbell 2005, 45).

Data Sources for Key Variables

Dependent Variable	Principal Source
Adult Literacy Rate, c. 1960	United Nations 1977[a]
Per Capita GDP, 1973	Maddison 2006
Years of "tutelary democracy" under colonial rule	Author's calculation based on electoral data from Przeworski et al. 2011, Political Institutions and Political Events dataset[b]
Mean Freedom House Imputed Polity Scores, 1972-2012	Quality of Government (2015) Standard Data, http://www.qog.pol.gu.se (fh_ipolity2 indicator)
Focal Independent Variables	
Mode of colonization variables	Author's coding, based on countries histories from *Encyclopedia Britannica,* ethnoracial data from Barrett 1982
Metropolitan legal rights, 1936	Various (see Appendix 1)
Key Control Variables	
British Colonization	*Encyclopedia Britannica*
% European Settlers	Lange 2004; France 1960; Barrett 1982; others[c]
% Asian Settlers (1975)	Barrett 1982
Ethnic Fractionalization (2000)	Alesina et al. 2003 (al_ethnic indicator), obtained from Quality of Government (2015) Standard Data, http://www.qog.pol.gu.sed
% Protestant (1900 and 1970)	Barrett, Kurian, and Johnson 2001[e]
% Muslim (1900 and 1970)	Barrett, Kurian, and Johnson 2001[e]
Protestant Missionary Variables	Woodberry 2012
Years Since Colonization (1960)	Olsson 2009
% Urban (1955)	United Nations, http://data.un.org
Logged per capita GDP, 1972-2004	Gleditsch (gle_rgdp indicator), obtained from Quality of Government (2015) standard data, http://www.qog.pol.gu.se
Oil Exporter	Woodberry 2012; Woodberry et al. 2010[f]
Small Island States	Island geography from Woodberry 2012; 1960 population data from http://data.un.org

Dependent Variable	Principal Source
Latitude	Quality of Government (2015) standard data, http://www.qog.pol.gu.se
Landlocked	Woodberry 2012; Woodberry et al. 2010

[a] Literacy data for Dominica, Saint Lucia, and Saint Kitts were obtained from Barrett 1982 for the year 1950 because UN literacy data are only available for 1946. For all other countries and territories, literacy data were obtained from the United Nations 1977.

[b] I also consulted a number of secondary sources, given that Przeworski et al. (2011) only include sovereign states, and this excellent source is not consistent about including elections that occurred prior to independence. Additional data sources are listed in note 5 of Chapter 4.

[c] European settlement data for most British colonies were obtained from Lange 2004, although Lange omits states with fewer than 100,000 inhabitants at independence. Consequently, I obtained European settler estimates for all microstates from Barrett 1982, which provides ethnoracial data for 1975. Data for French colonies in Africa and the Pacific were obtained from France 1960. Cambodia, Laos, and Vietnam were already independent by 1960, so I obtained their data from France 1949. There was a mass exodus of white settlers from Algeria, Morocco, the Dutch East Indies (Indonesia), Angola, and Mozambique prior to the independence of these countries. Consequently, I used country-specific monographs to obtain numbers of European settlers right before the mass exodus. Data for French North Africa are from 1954, prior to the mass exodus of European settlers from the region; see Christopher 1984. Data for Angola and Mozambique are from 1973, prior to the mass exodus of Portuguese settlers; see Enders 1997, 95. Data for Indonesia (c. 1930) were obtained from Ricklefs 2001, 217. For the remaining countries, data were obtained from Barrett 1982.

[d] Alesina et al.'s (2003) index is complete for all sovereign states except the Maldives and São Tomé and Príncipe. For these two countries, as well as all dependent territories, ethnic fractionalization was calculated based on 1975 ethnoracial data from Barrett 1982.

[e] Because Hong Kong and Macau are not listed in the Barrett, Kurian, and Johnson 2001, I obtained their 1970 religious data from Barrett 1982.

[f] See Woodberry 2012; Woodberry et al. 2010. I revised Woodberry's list of major oil producers to include Gabon, whose per capita oil production exceeds that of Algeria, Bahrain, and Nigeria after 1960.

Statistical Results Using Alternative Measures of Postcolonial Democracy

The OLS models in Table A3.1 demonstrate similar statistical results using alternative measures of postcolonial democratization. Cheibub, Gandhi, and Vreeland (2010) classify political regimes as democratic if their legislative officials are chosen by direct popular election, if their executive officials are chosen by an elected legislature or by direct popular election, and if they maintain competitive multiparty elections that generate electoral turnover (69). I used Cheibub, Gandhi, and Vreeland's (2010) data to calculate a new outcome variable that measures the percentage of democratic regime years in each postcolonial state from independence until 2008. This indicator ranges from 0% in countries with no democratic regime years after independence (such as Bahrain, Qatar, and Vietnam) to 100% in countries that have been continuously democratic since independence (such as Barbados, India, Jamaica, Mauritius, and Trinidad and Tobago). Forced settlement continues to predict statistically significant advantages for postcolonial democracy relative to colonial occupation in statistical models that estimate the percentage of democratic regime years after independence (Model 1, Table A3.1). I also estimated some data models that relax Cheibub, Gandhi, and Vreeland's (2010) requirement for electoral turnover. This qualification is important because it reclassifies countries like Botswana and Malaysia as democratic, based on the assumption that their political systems are sufficiently open to accept democratic alternation if their ruling parties were to lose an election (Cheibub, Gandhi, and Vreeland 2010, 70). Importantly, forced settlement continues to predict a higher percentage of democratic regime years after independence in statistical models that relax the requirement for electoral alternation (Model 2, Table A3.1).[1]

The statistical results are also consistent in data models that use the liberal democracy index from Coppedge et al.'s (2018) *Varieties of Democracy* (i.e., V-DEM) dataset (Models 3–5, Table A3.1). V-DEM'S liberal democracy index measures the extent of electoral contestation and participation (i.e., electoral democracy) as well as the protection of individual civil liberties and effective checks and balances that limit the use of executive power. These conditions are necessary for "protecting individual and minority rights against a potential 'tyranny of the majority'" (Coppedge et al. 2016, 5). This indicator is available from 1900 until 2012, which makes it possible to assess democratization outcomes before and after independence. Nevertheless, it is important to note that this data indicator is unavailable for 15 microstates in my primary dataset, including seven forced settlement colonies.[2] In other words, nearly half of the missing countries are forced settlement colonies with high Freedom House Imputed Polity scores after independence. Consequently, using V-DEM's liberal democracy index will reduce the likelihood that forced settlement will predict significantly higher liberal democracy scores than colonial occupation. Nevertheless, the OLS models in Table A3.1 reveal that forced settlement also predicts significantly higher liberal democracy scores than colonial occupation during the late colonial era (Model 3), and the magnitude of this effect is even greater after 1975 (Model 4).[3] Consequently, the statistical results from Table 3.4 are remarkably robust to alternative measurements of democracy. Regardless of which democracy indicator is used, forced settlement predicts greater postcolonial democratization relative to colonial occupation.

Table A3.1   OLS Results Using Alternative Measures of Postcolonial Democracy

Variable	% Dem. Years, Ind. to 2008	% Dem2 Years, Ind. to 2008	Lib. Dem. Score (V-DEM), 1946–74	Lib. Dem. Score (V-DEM), 1975–2012	Lib. Dem. Score (V-DEM), 1946–2012
	(1)	(2)	(3)	(4)	(5)
Forced settlement	36.94** (13.35)	26.42** (9.60)	9.09* (4.25)	17.59** (5.53)	14.01** (4.08)
Mixed colonization	−7.58 (27.75)	9.18 (14.72)	−9.85 (7.05)	−17.86 (9.80)	−14.03 (8.09)
British-protected state	−34.12* (16.17)	−42.24** (14.80)	−4.17 (4.50)	−10.65* (4.45)	−8.03* (3.71)
British colonization	10.69 (6.71)	18.08** (6.85)	5.84** (2.10)	5.92 (2.98)	6.00* (2.39)
Years since independence (2012)	−0.87 (0.52)	−0.66 (0.38)		0.11 (0.17)	0.22 (0.14)
Years since independence (1974)			0.46** (0.16)		
% European settlers	−2.04 (1.26)	−1.55 (1.20)	0.06 (0.39)	−0.19 (0.55)	−0.13 (0.40)
% Asian settlers	−0.38 (0.45)	0.10 (0.17)	0.20 (0.11)	0.23 (0.17)	0.21 (0.14)
Ethnic fractionalization	5.18 (13.08)	−5.83 (12.08)	−1.04 (3.31)	−0.22 (5.61)	−2.53 (4.51)
% Protestant (1970)	0.36 (0.25)	0.50* (0.20)	0.21 (0.12)	0.39* (0.19)	0.33* (0.15)
% Muslim (1970)	−0.06 (0.10)	−0.04 (0.10)	−0.01 (0.04)	0.03 (0.04)	0.01 (0.04)
Mean per capita GDP, 1972–2004 (logged)	−0.37 (4.62)	−1.74 (4.30)		3.16 (2.43)	
% Urban (1955)			0.09 (0.06)		0.12 (0.07)
Oil exporter	−7.80 (9.91)	−6.57 (8.37)	−3.36* (1.64)	−7.70 (4.22)	−4.52 (2.31)

Table A3.1 Continued

Variable	% Dem. Years, Ind. to 2008	% Dem2 Years, Ind. to 2008	Lib. Dem. Score (V-DEM), 1946–74	Lib. Dem. Score (V-DEM), 1975–2012	Lib. Dem. Score (V-DEM), 1946–2012
	(1)	(2)	(3)	(4)	(5)
Small island	−5.46	−5.16	0.80	6.88	4.18
	(11.43)	(7.63)	(3.24)	(5.03)	(3.68)
Landlocked	−10.51	−11.76	0.26	1.16	0.86
	(7.51)	(7.77)	(1.80)	(3.79)	(2.77)
Sub–Saharan Africa	−27.88*	−14.06	−1.63	1.96	0.15
	(11.65)	(8.17)	(2.87)	(4.72)	(3.43)
Constant	85.07	92.18*	3.14	−15.90	0.30
	(50.16)	(36.78)	(4.24)	(20.45)	(8.70)
Observations	92	92	77	77	77
R–squared	0.59	0.69	0.61	0.56	0.59

Note: Robust standard errors in parentheses, **p < 0.01, *p < 0.05. The dependent variable in Model 1 was calculated using Cheibub, Gandhi, and Vreeland's (2010) dichotomous indicator of democracy. Model 2 uses Cheibub, Gandhi, and Vreeland's (2010) "type2" indicator, which relaxes the requirement for electoral alternation in countries that uphold free, fair, and competitive elections. Models 3–5 use V-DEM'S liberal democracy index to measure the extent of democratization from 1946 to 1974 (Model 3), 1975 to 2012 (Model 4), and 1946 to 2012 (Model 5). The data sample is smaller because 15 microstates are excluded from the Varieties of Democracy database (see note 2).

APPENDIX 4

Statistical Models Using
an Expanded Sample of Postcolonial
States and Alternative Measurements
of Forced Settlement

The expanded data sample in this appendix includes 114–126 former colonies that gained independence after 1800. I also raised the cap on European settlement from 25% to 75% of the current population to include Latin American countries with extensive European settlement, like Cuba and Brazil. The full list of countries and territories in the expanded data sample can be found in Table A4.1. Haiti is classified as a forced settlement colony in the table because its population overwhelmingly comprised imported African slaves prior to the Haitian Revolution in 1791. Haiti was the only forced settlement colony to gain independence following a successful revolt against local white planters and French colonial domination. At the time of Haiti's independence in 1804, slavery remained legal and widespread in other forced settlement colonies. Consequently, the young Haitian republic was further marginalized and impoverished by French and US neocolonial exploitation after independence. Although Haiti is an extreme negative outlier as a result of its poor development outcomes, the data models in this appendix continue to show developmental advantages in forced settlement colonies relative to Global South countries that experienced colonial occupation (see Model 2 in Tables A4.2 and A4.3). In Tables A4.2 and A4.3, Model 3 provides an expanded measure of forced settlement that includes mixed plantation colonies like Brazil, Cuba, Belize, French Guiana, and the US Virgin Islands). These data models reveal that the expanded concept of forced settlement (i.e., forced settlement2) is also associated with favorable developmental outcomes relative to colonial occupation.

Table A4.1 Former Colonies in Expanded Dataset

Type of Colony	Countries in Primary Data Analysis	Additional countries included in expanded data set
Forced settlement (pop. descendants of imported African slaves, Asian indentured laborers)	Antigua and Barbuda, Bahamas, Barbados, Cape Verde, Dominica, Grenada, Guyana, Jamaica, Mauritius, Saint Kitts and Nevis, Saint Lucia, Saint Vincent and Grenadines, São Tomé and Príncipe, Seychelles, Suriname, Trinidad and Tobago, *Guadeloupe, Martinique, Netherlands Antilles, Réunion*	Haiti
Colonial occupation (indigenous pop. predates European colonization)	Algeria, Angola, Bangladesh, Benin, Botswana, Burkina Faso, Burundi, Cambodia, Cameroon, Central African Republic, Chad, Comoros, Congo (Democratic Republic), Congo (Republic), Cote d'Ivoire, Djibouti, Equatorial Guinea, Gabon, Gambia, Ghana, Guinea, Guinea- Bissau, India, Indonesia, Jordan, Kenya, Kiribati, Laos, Lebanon, Lesotho, Libya, Madagascar, Malawi, Mali, Mauritania, Morocco, Mozambique, Myanmar, Nauru, Niger, Nigeria, Pakistan, Papua New Guinea, Philippines, Rwanda, Samoa, Senegal, Sierra Leone, Solomon Islands, Sri Lanka, Sudan, Swaziland, Syria, Tanzania, Togo, Tonga, Tunisia, Tuvalu, Uganda, Vanuatu, Vietnam, Zambia, Zimbabwe	Egypt, Iraq, Liberia
Mixed colonization	Belize, Fiji, Malaysia, *French Guiana, French Polynesia, US Virgin Islands*	Bolivia, Brazil, Chile, Colombia, Cuba, Dominican Republic, Ecuador, El Salvador, Guatemala, Honduras, Israel, Mexico, Nicaragua, Panama, Paraguay, Peru, South Africa, Venezuela, *Guam, New Caledonia, Puerto Rico*
City-state	Singapore, *Hong Kong, Macau*	None
British-protected state	Bahrain, Brunei Darussalam, Kuwait, Maldives, Oman, Qatar, Somalia, United Arab Emirates, Yemen	None

Type of Colony	Countries in Primary Data Analysis	Additional countries included in expanded data set
Criteria for inclusion/ exclusion	Countries that experienced at least 25 years of Western overseas colonialism that ended between 1945 and 1985; excludes countries where European settlers exceed 25% of the population	Includes former colonies that gained independence after 1800; former colonies where European settlers comprised up to 75% of the population
N	92–101 (92 countries + 9 territories)	114–126 (114 countries + 12 territories)

Note: Dependent territories in italics.

Table A4.2 Adult Literacy Models (OLS) with Expanded Dataset and Alternative Measures of Forced Settlement

Adult Literacy Rate, 1960

VARIABLES	(1)	(2)	(3)
Forced settlement	18.10**	13.31**	
	(4.83)	(5.01)	
Forced settlement2			12.30**
			(4.32)
Mixed colonization	8.70	13.06*	16.47**
	(7.38)	(6.09)	(4.92)
City-states	−17.20	−19.62	−20.53*
	(11.79)	(10.04)	(9.68)
British-protected states	−4.06	−6.11	−6.04
	(7.40)	(6.28)	(6.20)
British colonization	4.56	4.46	4.45
	(2.69)	(2.50)	(2.49)
Years since independence (1960)	0.65	−0.08	−0.10*
	(0.55)	(0.05)	(0.05)
% European settlers	−0.29	0.22*	0.19*
	(0.57)	(0.10)	(0.08)
% Asian settlers	0.02	0.05	0.04
	(0.13)	(0.13)	(0.14)
Ethnic fractionalization	−23.59*	−21.50**	−22.79**
	(9.34)	(7.70)	(7.29)
% Protestant (1900)	0.42**	0.33**	0.32**
	(0.07)	(0.07)	(0.08)
% Muslim (1900)	−0.18*	−0.20**	−0.20**
	(0.08)	(0.07)	(0.07)
% Urban (1955)	0.43**	0.41**	0.42**
	(0.08)	(0.07)	(0.07)
Small island	0.19	1.38	1.06
	(5.16)	(4.70)	(4.53)
Landlocked	−2.61	−2.55	−2.95
	(3.67)	(3.51)	(3.48)
Latitude	−29.84	−19.38	−20.24
	(19.30)	(16.85)	(17.01)
Sub-Saharan Africa	−15.07**	−17.86**	−17.59**
	(5.12)	(4.40)	(4.23)
Constant	48.11**	49.03**	50.01**
	(6.72)	(5.84)	(5.94)
Observations	101	126	126
R-squared	0.85	0.83	0.83

Note: Robust standard errors in parentheses, **p < 0.01, *p < 0.05.

Table A4.3 Postcolonial Democratization Models (OLS) with Expanded Dataset and Alternative Measures of Forced Settlement

Mean Freedom House Imputed Polity Score, 1972–2012			
VARIABLES	(1)	(2)	(3)
Forced settlement	2.20**	2.51**	
	(0.65)	(0.65)	
Forced settlement2			2.36**
			(0.56)
Mixed colonization	0.82	3.14**	3.39**
	(1.35)	(0.92)	(0.92)
British-protected state	−2.66**	−1.88**	−1.93**
	(0.64)	(0.54)	(0.52)
British colonization	1.37**	1.11**	1.12**
	(0.38)	(0.35)	(0.35)
Years since independence (2012)	−0.05	−0.00	−0.00
	(0.02)	(0.01)	(0.01)
% European settlers	−0.05	−0.02	−0.02
	(0.06)	(0.04)	(0.03)
% Asian settlers	−0.01	−0.02	−0.01
	(0.02)	(0.02)	(0.02)
Ethnic fractionalization	−0.12	0.04	−0.08
	(0.80)	(0.77)	(0.76)
% Protestant (1970)	0.04**	0.04**	0.04**
	(0.01)	(0.01)	(0.01)
% Muslim (1970)	0.00	−0.00	−0.00
	(0.01)	(0.01)	(0.01)
Mean per capita GDP, 1972–2004 (logged)	0.13	0.21	0.23
	(0.31)	(0.29)	(0.28)
Oil exporter	−1.37*	−1.04	−1.14*
	(0.63)	(0.61)	(0.57)
Small island	0.35	0.90	0.84
	(0.56)	(0.54)	(0.56)
Landlocked	−0.38	−0.30	−0.33
	(0.51)	(0.46)	(0.46)
Sub–Saharan Africa	−0.72	−0.34	−0.34
	(0.65)	(0.63)	(0.62)
Constant	5.14	1.93	1.98
	(2.62)	(2.40)	(2.33)
Observations	92	114	114
R-squared	0.73	0.67	0.69

Note: Robust standard errors in parentheses, **p < 0.01, *p < 0.05.

Notes

Chapter 1

1. Enslaved Africans represented 95% of Tobago's population in the early 1800s (Clarke 2011, 286).
2. According to the CIA's World Factbook, Trinidad and Tobago's per capita GDP, at US$34,400, exceeded that of Portugal (US$29,100), Greece (US$27,300), and every country in Latin America in 2015. Trinidad and Tobago's per capita GDP also exceeds that of every country in sub-Saharan Africa.
3. Trinidad and Tobago's electoral competition is structured around two dominant political parties that represent and mobilize voters from the country's largest ethnic groups. The People's National Movement largely represents the Afro-Trinidadian population that held power after independence, whereas the United National Congress largely represents Trinidadians of South Asian ancestry who have gained political ascendancy since the 1990s. The political rivalry between these two groups has been managed without significant damage to the country's democratic and electoral institutions.
4. Historians estimate that approximately 400,000 African slaves were transported to the United States between 1619 and 1860. Data estimates by David Eltis and David Richardson (2010) show that 211,000 enslaved African slaves were transported to Georgia and the Carolinas, whereas Virginia planters imported 129,000 enslaved Africans to the Chesapeake region. The New England colonies and the Gulf Coast imported 50,000 enslaved Africans during this period. Consequently, the total number of slave shipments to the United States was significantly less than that of several Caribbean islands, including Jamaica (1.02 million), Haiti (792,000), Cuba (779,000) and Barbados (493,000) (Eltis and Richardson 2010, 18).
5. According to Freedom House, Barbados' democracy score in 2018 (96/100) exceeded that of its former colonizer, the United Kingdom (94) and its largest trading partner, the United States (86).
6. More than 90 Global South countries emerged from colonial domination between 1945 and 1985, and all of these countries have predominantly nonwhite populations that experienced significant labor coercion and political repression under colonial rule. Most countries that gained independence after World War II were led by indigenous nonwhite political leaders or the Creole descendants of enslaved African in the New World. In this way, their political origins differ significantly from the earlier wave of decolonization that was led by the descendants of local white settlers in the Americas. Despite these shared experiences, the newly independent countries that emerged after World War II have experienced varying levels of socioeconomic development and postcolonial democratization.

7. Brazil was the largest recipient of African slaves in the New World, with nearly five million slave imports between 1500 and 1860 (Eltis and Richardson 2010, 18). Although Brazil's colonial economy was largely established with imported slave labor, the country also attracted significant European settlement following its independence from Portugal in 1822. Consequently, the proportion of enslaved Africans in the Brazilian population declined from 46% in 1798 (Marx 1996, 49) to 16% in the 1880s (Beauvois 2017, 4). Racial miscegenation was also far more widespread in Brazil, and in many ways, this was actively encouraged by the Brazilian myth of racial democracy. In the last colonial census in 1818, 60% of Brazilians were classified as "black," whereas 41% of the population was classified as mulatto or mixed in the 1890 census (Marx 1996, 66).

8. Cuba imported more African slaves than any other Spanish American colony, but Cuba's enslaved Africans were always outnumbered by local white settlers and free people of color. The proportion of enslaved Africans in Cuba peaked around 40% of the population during the mid-nineteenth century, and it declined to less than 20% of the island's population by 1880. At the same time, decades of sustained European settlement increased the proportion of local whites to two-thirds of the island's population by the end of the nineteenth century (Engerman and Higman 1997, 50–54; Yelvington 2011, 327–33).

9. White settlers also outnumbered black slaves in British North American colonies. Black slaves comprised 18% of the United States' population in 1790, and 14% of the total population at the start of the Civil War in 1860 (O'Neill 2020). In the southern US states, where slavery was primarily concentrated, the proportion of black slaves ranged from 25% of the population in Tennessee to 57% in South Carolina in 1860 (Bertocchi and Dimico 2012, 13).

10. This scatterplot excludes city-state colonies like Singapore, mixed plantation colonies like Malaysia, and British-protected states like the Persian Gulf Arab kingdoms that gained independence after World War II. These patterns of colonization are briefly outlined in Chapter 4, and their developmental legacies are assessed in statistical data models.

11. The Freedom House Imputed Polity scores combine two widely used democracy indicators (i.e., Freedom House scores and Polity2 scores) on a 0–10 scale, in which higher scores denote favorable democratization outcomes. Hadenius and Teorell (2005) demonstrate that the Freedom House Imputed Polity scale performs better than its constituent parts in terms of validity and reliability. Freedom House Imputed Polity scores measure important aspects of political freedom, including legal protection for individual civil liberties, electoral participation, multiparty competition, and strong institutional constraints on executive authority (Dahlberg et al. 2018, 87).

12. Colonial occupation generated limited educational attainment and limited postcolonial democratization across the African continent from Angola (AGO) to Sudan (SDN), and from Guinea-Bissau (GNB) to Mozambique (MOZ). This pattern of poor literacy outcomes in 1960 and limited postcolonial democratization also extends to Arab countries like Algeria (ALG) and Asian countries like Bangladesh (BGD), Pakistan (PAK), Indonesia (IDN), and Cambodia (KHM). Only a small

number of countries in Figure 1.1, notably India (IND), Botswana (BWA), and Papua New Guinea (PNG), were able to promote high postcolonial democracy scores despite widespread illiteracy and general impoverishment at independence. India and Botswana also sustained several decades of rapid economic growth after independence.

13. The data in Table 1.1 also include overseas dependencies like the French and Dutch Caribbean territories that also experienced forced settlement colonization prior to World War II. This allows us to examine a wider range of forced settlement experiences outside of the British colonial empire.

14. The empirical analysis in this book examines the long-term developmental legacies of colonialism in dependent territories like Hong Kong, Martinique, and the Netherlands Antilles, as well as postcolonial states that gained independence between 1945 and 1985.

15. Fourteen of the 20 forced settlement colonies in Table 1.1 are island microstates with less than 500,000 inhabitants in 1960. By contrast, only eight colonies of occupation—i.e., the Comoros Islands, Kiribati, Nauru, Samoa, the Solomon Islands, Tonga, Tuvalu, and Vanuatu—are island microstates with less than 500,000 inhabitants in 1960. Nevertheless, even in this smaller sample of island microstates, the median HDI score for forced settlement colonies (0.761) is substantially higher than the median score for colonies of occupation (0.592).

16. Historians define the 1789 French Revolution as the founding political event of the long nineteenth century, which ended with the outbreak of World War I in 1914.

Chapter 2

1. The "Guinea Coast" refers to the West African coastline that stretches from Dakar in present-day Senegal to present-day Sierra Leone. This coastal region was explored by sixteenth century Portuguese slave traders and missionaries that intermarried with local African elites, and their descendants became part of the Luso-Creole African population whose language and culture persists in coastal regions of West Africa (Mark 1999).

2. Brazilian planters also imported large numbers of African slaves during the colonial era and after independence, but Brazil's colonial economy was more diverse, and less dependent on African slave labor than the forced settlement colonies in the West Indies. Brazil's southern regions were primarily colonized by white settlers, and local whites outnumbered Afro-descendants in the country by the middle of the twentieth century. Enslaved Africans were also outnumbered by European settlers and/or free people of color in Cuba, Puerto Rico, and Spanish Santo Domingo (see Engerman and Higman 1997, 49–52). For these reasons, Latin American countries like Brazil, Cuba, and Puerto Rico are classified as mixed plantation colonies. Their colonial and postcolonial development was also shaped by extensive European settlement. White settlers and/or indigenous peoples also outnumbered enslaved

Africans and free blacks in the mainland Spanish American colonies prior to 1800 (see Aguirre 2019, 79). The British North American colonies were also far less dependent on imported slave labor than the British forced settlement colonies in the West Indies. Black slaves comprised only 18% of the United States' population in 1790 (O'Neill 2020).

3. British forced settlement colonies in the West Indies accounted for a greater percentage of British imperial trade than the British North American colonies in 1773 (Williams 1994, 54). Yet the largest and most valuable forced settlement colony during this period was French-controlled Saint-Domingue (present-day Haiti).

4. The harsh living conditions of African slaves have been vividly portrayed in both historical and fictional works. Some of the best historical accounts include James 1989; Beckles 1997; Engerman and Higman 1997, 91–94. Fictional accounts of slave life are even more vivid. Isabel Allende's (2010) historical fiction describes the harsh realities of plantation life in Haiti, Cuba, and Louisiana at the time of the French and Haitian revolutions. Recent novels by Andrea Levy (2010) and Esi Edugyan (2018) provide equally harrowing tales of plantation slavery in colonial Jamaica and Barbados.

5. South Asian indentured labor migrants in Trinidad, Mauritius, or Guyana endured the same humiliating treatment and brutal working conditions as Indian convict laborers in Mauritius, Singapore, and Burma. Indeed, many Indians "volunteered" for indentured plantation labor to escape British colonial repression following the 1857 Sepoy Mutiny in India. Like the African slaves who preceded them, many indentured laborers died in transit to the New World, and most who survived the journey to the New World were never returned able to return home (Anderson 2016).

6. Knight (1997), Mentel (1984), Stewart (2007), and Seibert (2012) provide an excellent discussion of creolization in the West Indies and in Creole African islands.

7. This estimate of the current value of monetary compensation to British plantation owners is based on Nicholas Draper's (2010) analysis (100–107). Frédérique Beauvois (2017) estimated the value of French monetary compensation to plantation owners at one-quarter the value of British monetary compensation, based on the historic exchange rate of 25.23 French francs per British pound in 1848.

8. The electoral reforms that transformed the British political system from a competitive oligarchy to a full-fledged parliamentary democracy were primarily implemented between 1867 and 1918 (Colomer 2001, 41).

9. Europe's imperial powers significantly expanded their territorial control over the African continent between 1880 and 1914. The emergence of nationalism and the political integration of nation-states like Germany, France, and Italy generated an intense rivalry among European elites seeking to expand their power overseas. During 1884 and 1885, European statesmen gathered in Berlin to establish the rules that enabled European imperial powers to conquer indigenous African territories, and at the same time, respect each other's "spheres of influence" on the African continent (Herbst 2000, 71–73; Young 1994, 85–90). Nevertheless, existing studies have emphasized the arbitrary and violent way in which Europeans carved up the African continent, with devastating consequences for its long-term development and political stability (see Herbst 2000; Englebert 2000a; Young 1994; Davidson 1992).

10. South Africa's apartheid system went a step further, denying civil liberties and political rights to even the most highly educated black Africans after World War II (Mamdani 1996; Marx 1998).

11. Ceylon (present-day Sri Lanka) was the principal exception to the general pattern of bifurcated legal institutions in colonial states with significant indigenous populations. This reflects the conditions on Ceylon's agricultural plantations, which were primarily established using indentured Tamil laborers. Furthermore, Ceylon—like many forced settlement colonies in the Caribbean or Indian Ocean region—was successively colonized by Portugal, the Netherlands, and Britain over four centuries (Lange 2009, 190–91).

12. Lange (2009, 67–90, 187–88) designates the Bahamas, Barbados, Belize, Guyana, Jamaica, Mauritius, Trinidad, and Tobago as British-plantation colonies, rather than forced settlement colonies, and his research highlights their favorable development relative to indirectly-ruled British colonies. His research maintains a population threshold of 100,000 that excludes island microstates like Antigua and Barbuda, British Dominica, Grenada, and St. Lucia.

Chapter 3

1. Throughout the Americas, the descendants of European settlers enjoy a privileged position in economic and social matters because colonial institutions privileged European settlers at the expense of enslaved Africans and indigenous populations (see Sokoloff and Engerman 2000; Engerman, Mariscal, and Sokoloff 2009; Marx 1996, 1998). In other parts of the world, colonial institutions empowered specific ethnic and/or religious groups at the expense of others, generating ethnic and political grievances that persisted long after independence (see Bates 1974; Posner 2003; Lange 2012; King 2014; Mamdani 2002, 2012).

2. According to the United Nations Human Development Index (2019), the poorest Latin American countries (e.g., Bolivia, El Salvador, Guatemala, Nicaragua) have intermediate human development outcomes that resemble upper-middle-income African countries like Botswana, Cape Verde, Gabon, and South Africa. By contrast, the Southern Cone countries (i.e., Argentina, Chile, and Uruguay) have very high human development outcomes that resemble European countries like Greece, Portugal, and the Czech Republic.

3. Linz and Stepan (1996) define democratic consolidation as the point at which democratic institutions, norms, and practices are so strongly institutionalized that they can withstand significant economic, social, or political challenges without breaking down. In other words, all relevant political actors in the country recognize that democracy is "the only game in town" (25). Linz and Stepan's conceptual distinction between democratic transition and consolidation is important because most postcolonial states experienced authoritarian reversals that resulted from disputed elections, economic turmoil, ethnic conflict, or civil strife after independence.

4. Crawford Young briefly considers some important differences between the territorial expansion of British, French, German, and Belgian rule in continental Africa after 1880, and the earlier wave of Iberian colonization in Latin America (see Young 1994, 262–67). The Iberian colonization of Latin America lasted more than three centuries, and it was carried out with significant levels of European settlement, and the political dominance of Catholic Church officials who transplanted their language and culture into Latin America. Moreover, the widespread practice of racial miscegenation in Iberian-American colonies generated culturally integrated Creole societies, with racialized class differences. By contrast, Africa's indigenous populations were far more successful at maintaining their indigenous languages and cultures. This partly reflects the limited extent of European settlement in most tropical African colonies, but it also reflects the extent to which colonial African states maintained rigid legal and status distinctions between colonial settlers and indigenous colonial subjects (see Young 1994, 262–64; also see Mamdani 1996). Young (1994) also emphasizes some important differences between colonial-state building in Africa and the "plantation colonies" in the Caribbean Basin. He notes that Caribbean states fared significantly better than their African counterparts after independence, and he attributes this to the comparatively early elimination of the most oppressive features of colonial domination (i.e., slavery and indentured labor migration) in Caribbean societies. Consistent with the arguments presented here, Young argues that the lengthy duration of time between the abolition of slavery and independence allowed Caribbean "plantation colonies" to develop inclusive civil societies and less repressive state institutions than their African counterparts (264–66). Comparing colonial state-building in Africa to the Indian subcontinent, Young emphasizes the fact that the Indian subcontinent was far more consequential to British imperial trade and global prestige. Consequently, the British were far more willing to develop India's transportation and communications infrastructure and to establish a more professionalized civil service than anywhere in Africa (272–73). For these and other reasons, Young (1994) argues that African colonial states gained independence with significant political, cultural, and social deficits relative to postcolonial states in other developing regions. Jonathan Krieckhaus (2006) makes similar observations in acknowledging the pernicious effects of extractive institutions in Global South countries that were colonized following the scramble for Africa in the late 1880s (8–9).

5. Jeffrey Herbst (2000) emphasizes the importance of environmental and geographic constraints that have hindered effective state-building on the African continent from precolonial times until the present day. He argues that European colonial states, and the African kingdoms that preceded them, struggled to maintain effective political control over sparsely inhabited territories. The primary difference between them is that African colonial rulers were primarily concerned with controlling the populations that they governed, whereas the European concept of statehood also has a territorial dimension that requires the physical control over land as well as people. Moreover, the most advanced indigenous African states were located in the interior

of the continent, whereas Europeans tended to prioritize the political and economic development of coastal regions. This is why colonial African states tended to develop their coastal regions at the expense of interior regions. In general, colonial African states only developed the administrative capacity to control interior regions with significant mineral resources and/or European settler populations (such as the Kenyan highlands, or South Africa's gold and diamond mining belt).

6. Moreover, the statistical data results in Chapter 4 provide tentative support for the claims that geographic and environmental factors have contributed to underdevelopment in the Global South. The favorable developmental legacies of forced settlement relative to colonial occupation remain statistically significant after controlling for environmental and geographic factors.

7. Mamdani (1996) elaborates the relationship between chiefly authority and the repressive nature of colonial domination in continental Africa as follows: "It is the chief who has the right to make a bylaw governing his locality, who assesses the value of your petty property and therefore how much tax you pay, who comes to collect that tax, who fines you if you fail to pay that tax, who jails you if you fail to pay the tax and the fine, who decides where you labor when in jail, and who releases you upon termination of the sentence. The chief is the petty legislator, administrator, judge, and policeman all in one. Every moment of power—legislative, executive, judicial, and administrative—is combined in this one official. Here there is no question of any integral check and balance on the exercise of authority, let alone a check that is popular and democratic. The chief is answerable only to a higher administrative authority.... To the peasant, the person of the chief signifies power that is total and absolute, unchecked, and unrestrained" (54).

8. Protestant missionaries faced a more hostile environment outside of the British colonial empire. "Catholic" colonizers such as Spain, Portugal, and Belgium often granted the Catholic Church a state monopoly over indigenous education in their colonies, thereby shielding Catholic missionaries from Protestant competition. The secular French Republic actually banned state funding for religious schools in 1905, thereby restricting missionary activity in French colonies until after World War II (Woodberry 2012; Gallego and Woodberry 2010). Continental European powers were also far more hostile to indigenous language education (see Brown 2000; Albaugh 2007, 2009).

9. These arguments are pervasive in empirical literature on sub-Saharan Africa (see Englebert 2000; Herbst 2000; Davidson 1992), but colonial state policies also politicized ethnic differences in South Asia (Lange 2012; Vargehese 2016) and throughout the Caribbean region (Brerreton 1979; Munasinghe 2009; Lange 2009, 125–30).

10. Acemoglu, Johnson, and Robinson (2002) make a similar argument in their seminal paper "Reversal of Fortune." Sachs and Warner (1997) and Sachs (2005) also examine the impact of environmental factors that have hindered Africa's long-term development.

Chapter 4

1. This follows the precedent established by recent studies of colonial state-building and postcolonial development in the Global South (see Owolabi 2010, 2015; Ray 2018; Lee and Paine 2019a, 2019b).

2. The United Nations *Compendium of Social Statistics* provides 1960 literacy data for 92 of the 101 former colonies in my primary dataset (United Nations 1967). For the 10 remaining cases—i.e., Djibouti, Equatorial Guinea, Guam, Maldives, Qatar, São Tomé and Príncipe, the Solomon Islands, Tonga, Vanuatu, and the Solomon Islands— I obtained their 1975 adult literacy rates United Nations 1980 and multiplied these numbers by 0.82 to estimate adult literacy rates for 1960. This multiplier is based on the ratio of 1960 to 1975 literacy rates for postcolonial states with data for both years.

3. Maddison's (2006) dataset has wider geographic cover than other widely used sources like the Penn World Tables, and there are more data available for 1973 than for earlier years like 1960. Most island microstates and dependent territories in my dataset do not provide per capita GDP indicators for the 1960s (see Maddison 2006).

4. The HDI was first developed in the mid-1970s, but it was not widely available for many developing countries until the 1990s.

5. Przeworksi et al.'s (2011) database does not cover late colonial elections for small Pacific islands like Fiji and the Solomon Islands. Consequently, I obtained suffrage data for the small Pacific island states from Larmour 1994 and So'O and Fraenkel 2005. I also used secondary sources to obtain electoral data for dependent territories that are excluded from the PIPE database. I estimated the duration of tutelary democracy in the French and Dutch Antilles colonies using historical electoral data from Winnacker 1938, Murch 1971, and Sedoc-Dahlberg 1990, 71. I obtained electoral data for the US Virgin Islands was from Hill, Dixon, and Rodriguez 2011, 611. Last, I consulted secondary sources to obtain electoral data for Hong Kong (Langer 2007), Macau (Mendes 2013, 86), and Timor-Leste (Robbers 2006).

6. Hadenius and Teorell (2005) show that the Freedom House Imputed Polity scale performs better than its constituent parts—i.e., Freedom House scores and the Polity Index—in terms of validity and reliability (see Quality of Government 2013, 95). Freedom House Imputed Polity (FHIP) scores also provide a more nuanced assessment of postcolonial regimes than the dichotomous democracy indicators advanced by Przeworski et al. (2000) or Cheibub, Gandhi and Vreeland (2010).

7. I used ethnoracial data from 1975 (see Barrett 1982) to determine the countries where the combined total of emancipated Afro-descendants and indentured labor descendants exceeds three-quarters of the total population. This differentiates forced settlement colonies like Barbados and Jamaica from mixed plantation colonies like Brazil and Cuba, where the descendants of European settlers outnumber emancipated Afro-descendants.

8. Because traditional Islamic rulers controlled the domestic affairs of British-protected states, these countries are sometimes excluded from empirical analyses of the developmental legacies of colonialism (see Acemoglu, Johnson, and Robinson 2001, 2002; Lange 2004, 2009). At the same time, more recent studies with larger data samples

tend to classify these countries as former British colonies (see Lange and Dawson 2009; Owolabi 2015; Lee and Paine 2019a, 2019b). Consequently, I decided to include these British-protected states in my data analysis because British imperialism profoundly impacted the development their oil resources and it often strengthened the political dominance of their ruling families. At the same time, however, it is important to code these countries separately from other British colonies whose domestic political institutions were controlled by British colonial officials.

9. These data were mostly obtained from the Quality of Government 2013 standard dataset. Alesina et al.'s (2003) indicator is available for all sovereign states based on their ethnoracial composition at the end of the twentieth century. I estimated ethnic fractionalization indices for the dependent territories using ethnoracial data from the *World Christian Encyclopedia* (Barrett 1982). The extent of ethnic fractionalization in dependent territories ranges from 0.034 in Hong Kong to 0.745 in French Polynesia.

10. These data were obtained from the *World Christian Encyclopedia* (Barrett, Kurian, and Johnson 2001). The percentage of Protestants and Muslims in 1900 provides statistical controls for the impact of religion on human well-being and tutelary democracy prior to independence. Colonial rule advanced the spread of Christianity in coastal regions of West Africa, and throughout East, Central, and southern Africa during the first half of the twentieth century. But West Africa's Sahel region experienced a tremendous growth in Islam as an indigenous response to British and French colonial domination (Nunn 2010; Illife 2007, 229–37). To account for this religious change during the colonial era, I used the percentage of Protestants and Muslims in 1970 in the OLS models that examine postcolonial democratization trends from 1972 to 2012 and human well-being in 2015.

11. These regression models use Gleditsch's per capita GDP indicators from 1972 until 2004, measured in constant international dollars at base year 2000. I obtained these data from the Quality of Government 2015 database.

12. Apart from Models 5 and 6 in Table 4.8, the maximum VIF score in each model is less than 5.0. This suggests that these models do not suffer from high levels of collinearity among their independent variables (Allison 1999, 141–42).

13. Maddison's (2006) economic database has significantly wider geographic coverage in 1973 than in 1960, but there are no data available for Kiribati, Nauru, Samoa, the Solomon Islands, Tonga, Tuvalu, Vanuatu, French Polynesia, and the US Virgin Islands.

14. Many of the control variables in Table 4.4 have statistically significant effects on long-term economic development as outlined in previous studies. For example, European settlement is associated with higher per capita GDP in 1973 ($p < 0.05$), and major oil exporters have higher per capita GDP than non-oil exporters in 1973 ($p < 0.05$). The percentage of Protestants or Muslims in 1900 does affect long-term economic development, ceteris paribus, but distance from the equator (+) and landlocked geography (−) have statistically significant consequences for economic development outcomes in 1973. This likely reflects the fact that distance from the equator is associated with greater proximity to major export markets in the developed world, and that landlocked geography increases the cost of overseas trade with distant markets.

15. The statistical controls for ethnicity, religion, and geography are statistically insignificant in Table 4.6, suggesting that these factors did not determine the duration of mass electoral competition in colonial states prior to independence. The only control variables that are significantly associated with tutelary democracy are the extent of urbanization in 1955 and the year of independence. The positive association between urbanization and tutelary democracy is not surprising because urbanization—like other aspects of socioeconomic modernization—is generally associated with higher levels of political engagement and participation (Lipset 1959). The year of independence also matters because most colonial states did not introduce mass electoral competition until the 1950s. This means that colonial states that gained independence during the 1970s were more likely to hold several competitive elections prior to independence than those that emerged from colonial rule during the 1950s or 1960s. Forced settlement colonies were more urbanized than colonies of occupation by the mid-1950s, and many forced settlement colonies did not gain independence until the mid-1970s. Both of these factors contributed to the longer duration of tutelary democracy in forced settlement colonies relative to colonial occupation in Table 4.6.

16. In contrast to the positive and significant result for forced settlement, mixed colonization is not associated with favorable democratization outcomes after controlling for confounding factors. British-protected states also experienced limited postcolonial democratization, as many of these oil-rich countries established traditional Islamic monarchies that restricted political representation and electoral competition after independence.

17. The bivariate correlation between forced settlement and tutelary democracy is relatively high ($r = 0.63$) because most forced settlement colonies experienced a lengthy duration of tutelary democracy prior to independence.

18. The empirical relationship between European settlement and postcolonial democracy is insignificant in every model. This result is not shocking because European settler minorities often denied the political rights of nonwhite colonial subjects. This was particularly common in colonial states with large European settler minorities that violently resisted indigenous African demands for political rights and self-determination. This history of violent anticolonial resistance often had negative developmental consequences for postcolonial democratization in countries like Angola, Mozambique, and Zimbabwe (Paine 2019a, 2019b). By contrast, most forced settlement colonies experienced peaceful independence transitions following a lengthy period of tutelary democracy. Another lesson from Table 4.7 is that the postcolonial democratization of forced settlement colonies was not primarily driven by their superior economic development during the colonial era. The regression coefficient for logged per capita GDP is statistically insignificant in every model. This suggests that the economic dimensions of modernization theory are not supported by empirical evidence from developing countries that gained independence after 1945. Economic growth in forced settlement colonies has generally lagged behind city-states and the oil-rich British-protected states since the 1970s. Nevertheless, forced settlement colonies have been far more successful at maintaining highly democratic political regimes since their independence from colonial rule.

19. Many different sources were consulted to code the legal-administrative institutions of former colonies prior to World War II. British colonies were coded using Matthew Lange's (2009) measure of indirect rule, and Colonial Office annual reports from the 1930s. In cases of disagreement, I used the colonial reports from the 1930s, classifying the legal institutions of the Solomon Islands and Brunei as metropolitan and bifurcated, respectively. French and Portuguese colonies were respectively coded based on citizenship data from 1936 and 1950 respectively (see France 1944; Portugal 1960). The legal-administrative institutions of other colonial states were coded using secondary sources. For the full list of data sources, please see the notes to the data appendix of Owolabi 2015. The coding for most countries was relatively straightforward, but Nauru is an unusual case because its native laws and customs were first recognized by German colonial officials, but later disallowed by Australian officials from 1923 until 1936 (see Corrin and Paterson 2007, 3–4). Ultimately, I coded Nauru as having metropolitan legal rights prior to 1936, although the data results are substantively unchanged if this coding decision is reversed (see Owolabi 2015, Appendix V).

20. The collinearity between these variables ranges from $r = 0.75$ to $r = 0.80$, depending on whether dependent territories are included or excluded in the sample. This increases the variance inflation factor for metropolitan legal rights to 5.59 and 5.64 in Models 5 and 6, respectively.

21. Coppedge (1999) offers a good discussion of the distinction between "thick" and "thin" concepts, and the challenges involved in measuring "thick" concepts and theories in social science research.

Chapter 5

1. In 1770, for example, Jamaica was producing more than three times as much sugar as any other British Caribbean colony. In fact, Jamaica accounted for nearly half of the sugar production in the British Caribbean, and one-sixth of the total sugar production in the entire Caribbean (Eltis 1997, 113).

2. By the middle of the eighteenth century, most of Jamaica's cultivated land was concentrated on 467 sugar estates (Palmer 1997, 37).

3. Historians note that the early English settlements in the West Indies were founded not as slave societies but as mirror images of British society, with "independent" and "dependent" classes of European settlers, both of which were entitled to the same civil liberties or legal rights, but where dependents had no political rights or representation. Obviously, this dynamic was fundamentally altered by the large-scale introduction of African slaves, which generated a racial-caste hierarchy in which the overwhelming majority of colonial inhabitants had no rights whatsoever (see Greene 2016, 52; Dunn 1972).

4. In total, 128 British MPs received monetary compensation for slaves they owned in the West Indies (Draper 2010, 280–87). The wealthiest of these landowners was John

Gladstone, the father of the late nineteenth-century British prime minister William Gladstone. Gladstone received more than £100,000 (worth more than £80 million today) for the liberation of 2,508 slaves on nine agricultural plantations in Jamaica (Manning 2013).

5. In 1831, for example, sugar and coffee accounted for one-fifth of British commodity imports, and most of these imports were from British forced settlement colonies. By 1875, sugar and coffee only accounted for 6% of British imports, and these products were primarily imported from Brazil and Cuba. By this time, Britain was importing significantly larger quantities of grain, cotton, and wool, which were far more important for the country's industrialized economy (Knight 1997, 333).

6. The economic inefficiency of slave-based sugar production was already apparent by 1789, when one of Jamaica's leading planters estimated the total debt of British plantation owners at £70 million. West Indian planters assumed enormous debts to run their plantations because they could always use their slaves as collateral to secure loans. There was no need for planters to invest in more efficient means of production given the abundance of slave labor during the eighteenth century. Historians assume that the eighteenth-century debts of British planters likely increased in the decades leading up to the British abolition of slavery, but there are no estimates of British planter debts from the 1830s (Beauvois 2017, 129).

7. Many British forced settlement colonies curtailed political representation and voting rights following Jamaica's Morant Bay rebellion. Between 1865 and 1878, British colonial officials imposed direct crown colony rule in all of their Caribbean possessions apart from Barbados and the Bahamas. Barbados' white planter elites were sufficiently numerous and powerful to maintain their economic and political dominance following the abolition of slavery. The Bahamas islands also differed from other British forced settlement colonies that developed large-scale sugar plantations with African slave labor. Consequently, the Bahamas were the first British forced settlement colony to successfully reorient its economic structure toward commercial trade with the newly independent United States (Paine 2019b, 28–32).

8. As late as 1939, registered voters accounted for less than 6% of Jamaica's population (Hart 1998, 109).

9. Nova Scotia's black population also included many loyalists who had fought on the British side during the US War of Independence. They were later evacuated from New York and Boston to Nova Scotia during the 1780s, but continued to face discrimination in Canada, where they were neglected by the local colonial authorities. Consequently, Nova Scotian blacks were among the pioneers who settled the Sierra Leone colony at the end of the eighteenth century (Fyfe 1973, 39–40). This history is memorialized in Lawrence Hill's (2009) novel, *The Book of Negroes*.

10. Sierra Leone also attracted African American settlers, who later established their own colony in nearby Liberia, which became an independent country in 1847 (Fyfe 1967, 76).

11. West Indian settlers to Sierra Leone included Jamaican "Maroons" (the descendants of rebellious African slaves who escaped from sugar plantations to establish free and self-governing black communities in Jamaica's mountainous interior), freed slaves

from Barbados, and over 1,000 discharged soldiers from the Britain's West India regiments (Fyfe 1973, 40; Peterson 1969, 86).

12. This administrative strategy was the brainchild of Sir Frederick Cardew, who had used similar methods to quell indigenous resistance in South Africa during the 1880s (Kup 1975, 89).

13. These estimates are somewhat higher than those generated by Benavot and Riddle (1988), who standardize primary enrollment data based on the percentage of the population aged five to 14.

14. Prior to 1833, Jamaican planters had been overtly hostile to Protestant missionaries seeking to educate their slaves. In fact, Jamaica's meager education expenditures were primarily intended for poor whites who could not afford private school education for their children (Wesley 1933, 70).

15. The term "legitimate" commerce is widely used in British (and British-influenced) historiography on early colonization efforts in West Africa during the first half of the nineteenth century. It refers to British, Creole, and Americo-Liberian efforts to undermine slave trading by promoting alternative economic and commercial activities such as the production and retail of cash crops like rice, peanuts, cocoa, and palm oil.

16. In 1836, Portugal became the last European country to abolish the North Atlantic slave trade (Silva Cunha 1949, 126–27), which was almost entirely eradicated by 1850 (Fyfe 1973).

17. Jamaica's long history of partisan electoral violence dates back to its first democratic election, when Bustamante's JLP employed local gangs to harass and intimidate PNP supporters (Dawson 2016, 195–203). After Bustamante won the 1944 elections, Manley's PNP developed its own affiliated gang leaders to harass working-class JLP supporters. This enabled Manley's PNP to capture Kingston's municipal council in 1949 and to sweep the national elections of 1955 and 1959. This pattern of partisan electoral violence continued into the 1960s and 1970s, but Jamaica's political and legal institutions have been strong enough to maintain mass electoral competition despite relatively high levels of electoral polarization and partisan violence (Dawson 2016; Sives 2010).

18. The JLP-affiliated labor unions mostly represented Jamaica's agricultural and industrial workers, whereas the PNP's affiliated unions represented middle-class professionals like teachers, bureaucrats, and other state employees. Nevertheless, the PNP also attracted political support from Kingston's urban working classes that supported Manley's social-democratic and anticolonial rhetoric during the 1950s and 1960s (Rueschemeyer et al. 1992, 37–38; Ledgister 1998, 73–74, 86–87).

19. Interestingly, NCSL leaders based their demands on the historical argument that the British government had guaranteed Freetown to Krio settlers and their progeny, and that Freetown's existence as a separate Krio entity governed under British laws could not be compromised (Cole 2013, 146).

20. Sierra Leone's SLPP government maintained close ties with the old protectorate elites both before and after independence. On the eve of Sierra Leone's independence, the SLPP government reinstated most of the chiefs who had been suspended, deposed, or investigated for corruption following the antichief revolts of 1955–56. The SLPP

government even authorized monetary compensation of £400,000 to chiefs who had lost property during the peasant revolts (Cartwright 1970, 84; Lange 2009, 107). The close ties between African chiefs and the SLPP was mutually advantageous for both parties. In the words of political scientist John Cartwright,

> The chiefs' participation in the modern political procedures of elections helped make these new procedures comprehensible and legitimate for the bulk of the electorate. With its legitimacy in the eyes of the masses underpinned by the chiefs, the SLPP government could afford to devote less energy to ensuring its own acceptance than was the case with governments less securely rooted in tradition. In the short term, at least, it also appeared to benefit the SLPP leaders by sparing them the difficulty of building an autonomous party structure to organize the mass of the people. The chiefs, for their part, could rest assured that their interests would be safeguarded by an SLPP government. (Cartwright 1970, 89)

21. In fact, Jamaica became engulfed in the broader geopolitics of the Cold War after independence, when Michael Manley's PNP government embraced democratic socialism in response to the oil price shocks of the 1970s. Manley's PNP government also sought closer ties with Castro's Cuba and other leftist regimes in the Americas, provoking a conservative backlash from local business elites and US government officials who openly supported the conservative JLP and its US-born leader, Edward Seaga, who swept to power in 1980 (Rueschemeyer et al. 1992, 250–51; Edie 1991, 91–95; Stephens and Stephens 1986, 11, 32–33; Sives 2010, 98–102; Stone 1986, 144, 151–77).

22. See https://freedomhouse.org/country/jamaica/freedom-world/2017. Accessed November 26, 2022.

23. There is also a positive feedback loop between democratic consolidation and the provision of public goods like education, healthcare, and sanitation. Because democratic elections hold governments accountable to their citizens at regular intervals, democratically elected governments are more likely to implement policies that support overall human well-being, rather than catering to a narrow group of political elites or coethnics within the society. Authoritarian governments can also benefit from improving the well-being of their citizens (as in Singapore or China today), but these regimes are far less dependent on popular approval to remain in power. Indeed, many autocratic regimes have maintained power for decades by repressing their political opponents and providing selective benefits to a narrow group of political supporters (such as coethnic clients) or state elites like the military. This option is less viable available in democratic states, because electoral competition makes elected officials more responsive to voter preferences. Consequently, the accumulated stock of democracy over time has beneficial effects on public health outcomes like sanitation, immunization rates, and the provision of clean water, which are important for boosting life expectancy and decreasing infant mortality (Belsey and Kudamatsu 2006; Gerring, Thacker, and Alfaro 2012). This is part of the reason why a middle-income democracy like Jamaica can significantly boost its life expectancy, from 62.6 years in 1960 to 76.1 years in 2017. By 2017, several British forced settlement colonies—including

Barbados (76.1), the Bahamas (75.8), Jamaica (76.1 years) and Mauritius (74.9)—
have nearly reached the life expectancy of the United States (79.5), despite the fact
that their per capita incomes are significantly lower (United Nations HDI 2017).
Jamaica's life expectancy also exceeds that of several African countries with significantly higher per capita incomes, but less democratic experience, including Gabon
(66.5 years) and South Africa (63.5 year). Overall, Jamaica's social indicators outperform other developing countries with similar levels of economic development (Riley
2005). Thus, Jamaica provides a great example of how many forced settlement colonies have promoted significant human development and postcolonial democratization despite their modest economic development.

24. This was a common political trend in many African states after independence.
25. http://hdr.undp.org/en/composite/HDI.

Chapter 6

1. Most of Cape Verde's 550,000 inhabitants are concentrated on four lush and mountainous islands: Santiago, São Vicente, Santo Antão, and Fogo. The archipelago's outer
islands—i.e., Boa Vista, Brava, Maio, Sal, and São Nicolau, and Sta. Luzia—are barely
inhabited due to their harsh environmental conditions and arid climate. These outer
islands are basically an extension of the Sahara desert in the Atlantic Ocean.

2. Portugal once claimed sovereignty over the entire "Guinea Coast" of West Africa,
stretching from the Cassamance region in present-day Senegal to present-day Sierra
Leone. Guinean Creoles are the descendants of Cape Verdeans who settled on the
African mainland, intermarried with indigenous Africans and spread their Crioulo
language and folk Catholicism throughout West Africa's Guinea Coast (Mark 1999).

3. Portugal's per capita income never exceeded more than one-third of the United
Kingdom's between 1850 and 1950 (Maddison 2006).

4. Spain and Portugal were the only colonial powers that did not successfully democratize until after the independence of their colonial territories. The two Iberian countries did not consolidate their current democratic institutions until the "third wave
of democratization" in the late 1970s (see Huntington 1991; Linz and Stepan 1996,
esp. 88–129; Fishman 2018). Like its smaller Iberian neighbor, Spain also established
a short-lived democratic republic during the 1930s, but it was overthrown in a military coup that generated a violent civil war (1936–39) and a corporatist authoritarian
dictatorship that lasted into the 1970s. In contrast to Portugal, however, Spain was not
a major colonial power during the twentieth century, as most Spanish American colonies gained independence at the beginning of the nineteenth century, between 1810
and 1825. Spain lost most of its remaining colonies (i.e., the Philippines, Cuba, Guam,
and Puerto Rico) during the 1898 Spanish-American War. Consequently, the only
colonial territories that remained under Spanish rule during the first half of the twentieth century were Equatorial Guinea (formerly Spanish Guinea) and the Spanish colonial territories in Morocco.

5. The Colonial Act of 1930 established the principle that the Portuguese nation and empire were one and indivisible (Ribeiro Torres 1973, 47; Vale de Almeida 2008; Pombo Malta 2006, 113–14). Portugal's *Estado Novo* dictatorship maintained far higher levels of political repression in Portuguese African colonies relative to their British counterparts.

6. In 1836, Portugal became the last European colonial power to abolish the Atlantic slave trade, and Portuguese prime minister Sá de Bandeira argued that the slave trade was preventing the development of Portugal's African colonies. In a letter to the Portuguese royal court and imperial parliament, dated February 14, 1836, he wrote, "Without the abolition of the slave trade, . . . it would be impossible to promote the cultivation of [African] lands, because capital would continue to flow into the slave trade, which is more lucrative than any other industry" (quoted in Silva Cunha 1949, 126–27; my translation). Consequently, he proposed abolishing the slave trade as a way of strengthening Portuguese control in Africa and developing agricultural plantations in Angola, Mozambique, São Tomé and Príncipe, and Portuguese Timor using indigenous labor. Consequently, plantation slavery remained legal in Portuguese African colonies until 1869. Even after the formal abolition of slavery in 1869, Sá de Bandeira proposed significant labor and judicial reforms in the African colonies, including a Native Labor Code that would ensure that agricultural plantations in Angola, Mozambique, and elsewhere would survive the transition to "free" labor more effectively than in British forced settlement colonies such as Jamaica after 1838 (Silva Cunha 1949, 136–40).

7. Following the consolidation of Portuguese control in Angola and Mozambique, their indigenous African populations were subject to one of the most exploitative labor recruitment systems on the African continent (see Duffy 1959; Ferreira 1974; Newitt 1981, esp. chs. 5 and 6; Ball 2015). Angolan plantations laborers worked in slave-like conditions, and tens of thousands were sent to work as indentured laborers in São Tomé and Príncipe. Portuguese labor recruiters also "sold" indigenous African laborers to South African and British mining companies across East and Southern Africa. Official records suggest that more than 90,000 Mozambicans worked in South African mines in any given month between 1909 and 1916 (Newitt 1981, 113–14). Hundreds of thousands of Mozambicans were conscripted for plantation labor in present-day Tanzania and Malawi. Forced labor recruitment provided an important source of foreign exchange for Portuguese officials in Angola and Mozambique. Portuguese colonial officials also provided indigenous African "contract labor" for diamond mines in South Africa, copper mines in Zambia (Northern Rhodesia), and agricultural plantations in the French Congo in exchange for foreign exchange and reduced shipping rates on British and South African railways. South African and British investments also paid for most of the infrastructural development (i.e., roads, railways, ports, and bridges) in Mozambique and Angola (Newitt 1981, 34–39). As late as 1956, more than 500,000 Mozambicans were still working on cotton farms for as little as $11 per year. And in 1958, more than 120,000 Angolans were conscripted labor for forced labor in Portuguese-owned agricultural plantations and commercial mines (Ferreira 1974, 35).

8. Cape Verdean migrant laborers also suffered horrendous working conditions in Angola and São Tomé and Príncipe. Labor conditions were so bad that one-quarter of Cape Verdean workers died of disease, starvation, or overwork in São Tome and Príncipe's cocoa and coffee plantations (Bigman 1993, 86). Thus, despite their privileged legal status as metropolitan Portuguese citizens, Cape Verde's agricultural working class was also exploited by Portugal's labor-repressive economic policies.

9. During the nineteenth century, parishes were as much an administrative unit as they were a clerical unit, because voting often took place inside Catholic churches or on church property. Portugal's 1851 electoral law permitted polling stations to be set up in churches, if "no public buildings . . . [met] the necessary conditions in terms of capacity, safety, and convenient access" (Tavares de Almeida 2011, 74).

10. I use the French/Senegalese orthography here, because Abdoul N'Diaye was a Wolof mercenary from present-day Senegal. His name also appears as "Abdul Injai" or "Abdul Indjai" in scholarly literature on Guinea-Bissau (Forrest 1992, 18; Lyall 1938, 190).

11. Incidentally, N'Diaye insisted on his right to be tried under civil law in a Portuguese court, although this request was denied to him on account of his indigenous legal status (Bowman 1986, 477).

12. Creole populations and Portuguese Indians were classified as *civilisados*, given their greater assimilation of Portuguese language and culture.

13. Until 1951, African indentured laborers (and their descendants) in São Tomé and Príncipe were also legally classified as *indigenas*. This means that Cape Verde was the only Portuguese African colony to have universal citizenship rights throughout the twentieth century (Duffy 1961).

14. Benavot and Riddle's (1988) primary enrollment data suggest that the percentage of Portuguese children attending primary schools declined during World War I.

15. Catholic mission schools for indigenous African children were first established under the constitutional monarchy, although the First Portuguese republic restricted state funding for these schools following its separation of church and state in 1913. Three decades later, the Salazar dictatorship reinstated the Catholic Church's monopoly over "native education" under the Missionary Statute of 1941 (Ferreira 1974, 60).

16. Neither Cape Verde nor Guinea-Bissau experienced significant Protestant missionary evangelization prior to 1960 (see Woodberry 2012; Woodberry et al. 2010).

17. Under the First Portuguese Republic (1910–26), colonial deputies accounted for 11–14 of the 160 or so representatives in the national parliament. From 1934 to 1945, the national parliament had 100 deputies who were elected proportionally in a single national district. And from 1945 until 1961, the Portuguese colonies elected 13 out of 120 deputies in the national parliament (Tavares de Almeida 2010, 1536). Colonial representation in the national parliament increased significantly after 1961, although these gains primarily benefited the large number of white Portuguese who flooded into Angola and Mozambique after World War II.

18. Guinea-Bissau held its first multiparty elections in 1994, but these elections were rigged, and they returned the country's long-standing military strongman, Nuno

Vieira, to power as an elected president. Vieira was unable to complete his term, as the country collapsed in a civil war during the late 1990s. Vieira was ultimately deposed during the foreign military intervention that ended Guinea-Bissau's 1998–99 civil war. Kumba Yala was elected president in the aftermath of the civil war, but he too was deposed by military coup in 2003. Nuno Vieira was restored to the presidency by popular election in 2005, but he was brutally assassinated in 2009. The next elected president, Malam Bacai Sanhá, died in office in 2012. For a brief history of the regime instability that has plagued Guinea-Bissau since independence, see Forrest 2002, 2010; BBC News 2018.

19. In many ways, the ethnoracial frustrations that mobilized Guinea-Bissau's 1980 military coup were similar to the military coup that toppled Liberia's ruling party in April of the same year. Liberia had already been independent since the 1840s, but its economy, society, and governing institutions were dominated by a small minority of Americo-Liberians—i.e., the descendants of liberated slaves that returned to West Africa from the United States during the nineteenth century. The military coups in Liberia and Guinea-Bissau toppled the Creole minorities that had dominated their respective countries for generations. Both coups were initially celebrated by indigenous African groups that were frustrated by their marginalization at the hand of Creole neocolonial elites in their home countries. Nevertheless, neither country benefited from military rule during the 1980s. Both military coups initiated a prolonged period of political violence and economic instability that further eroded the living conditions of indigenous Africans.

Chapter 7

1. For example, France lost most of its vast North American possessions, and many of its South Asian trading posts, to Britain during the Seven Years War between 1756 and 1763. France's remaining North American foothold, the vast Louisiana Territory, was sold to the United States in 1803, to finance the Napoleonic wars in Europe. France also lost several forced settlement colonies, including Mauritius, St. Lucia, and the Seychelles, to British imperialist expansion during the Napoleonic wars. Consequently, French Guiana, Guadeloupe, Martinique, and Réunion were the colonial territories that remained under French control from the seventeenth century until their political incorporation as overseas departments of the Fourth Republic in 1946.

2. At the onset of the Haitian Revolution in 1791, enslaved Africans comprised 87% of the population in French-ruled Saint-Domingue, compared with only 12% of the population in Spanish-ruled Santo Domingo (Yelvington et al. 2011, 287).

3. These practices date back to 1793, when the French revolutionary general Léger-Felicité Sonthonax introduced a restrictive labor code that required Saint-Domingue's emancipated slaves to work as sharecroppers in exchange for one-third of the crop as salary. Skilled workers were to receive two (or even three) shares, but Haiti's labor

codes became increasingly restrictive and draconian over time. Haiti's postcolonial governments maintained draconian rural labor codes until the 1860s (Girard 2019).

4. The United States' diplomatic isolation of Haiti stands in contrast with its recognition of other Latin American republics following their independence from Spanish rule. Thomas Jefferson made a point of diplomatically isolating Haiti and imposing a trade embargo during the early 1800s. Haiti was also excluded from Pan-American conferences hosted in Washington, DC, in 1826, and from the first International Conference of American States in 1888 (Saye 2010, 80; Stinchcombe 1994).

5. Official US casualty reports claimed that 3,250 Haitians were killed for their resistance against the US military occupation, which claimed 14 or 16 American lives. Nevertheless, population statistics suggest that as many as 50,000 Haitian may have been killed during the insurgency against the US military occupation (Bellegarde-Smith 2004, 107).

6. The US high commissioner for Haiti, John Russell, argued that Haiti's French-language academic curriculum only reinforced the country's proclivities for revolution and political instability. The dominant opinion among top-ranking US officials in Haiti was that US vocational schools were better suited to Haiti's economic and social conditions (Pamphile 1985, 100–103). Consequently, US military officials did not expand access to primary schooling in Haiti, as they did in the Dominican Republic, Puerto Rico, and the Philippines during this period (Benavot and Riddle 1988).

7. In many ways, the brutality of the US military occupation reflected the prevailing racist views that shaped US government policies during the early twentieth century. The military occupation of Haiti was authorized by President Woodrow Wilson, a Virginia Democrat and committed segregationist, whose government extended Jim Crow segregation and racial discrimination into the US federal bureaucracy (González and King 2004, 207). Wilson's secretary of state, Williams Jennings Bryan, was also known for his racist views. When asked for his thoughts about the world's oldest black republic in 1912, he responded, "Dear me, think of it! Niggers speaking French!" (Angulo 2010, 2).

8. The main goals of the provisional republican government were to provide economic assistance to working-class Parisians and to expand parliamentary representation and voting rights with the introduction of universal male suffrage. These domestic political goals were a response to the working-class revolt that forced the abdication of the French king, Louis Phillipe, in February 1848. Nevertheless, the French abolitionist movement was strongly associated with republicanism, and abolitionist members of the provisional government demanded the immediate abolition of slavery in French colonies.

9. Schoelcher also championed important social reforms that were not implemented until the twentieth century—including female suffrage, medical insurance for the poor and elderly, the end of prison labor, and the abolition of the death penalty. Consequently, he is widely admired in France as a republican visionary and abolitionist hero (Wellborn 1969, 104; Girolet 2000).

10. Electoral participation was extremely high in Guadeloupe and Martinique, where 75% of registered voters participated in the Constituent Assembly elections

(Schmidt 2003, 312). Blacks and mulattos respectively accounted for 70% and 23% of Guadeloupe's registered voters in the 1848 elections for the National Constituent Assembly in France (France 1869a). The newly elected representatives included Victor Schoelcher (the lead author of the abolition decree), Auguste Bissette (a mulatto journalist, merchant, and abolitionist from Martinique), François Auguste Perrinon (a mulatto republican military officer and abolitionist from Martinique), Charles Dain (a Guadeloupean-born white lawyer, abolitionist, and socialist), Pierre Marie Pory-Papy (a mulatto republican lawyer and abolitionist), and Louisy Mathieu, the first freed slave elected to represent Guadeloupe in the 1848 Constituent Assembly (McCloy 1966, 161–62; Church 2017, 24). The 1848 elections brought republican abolitionists and nonwhite officials to power in Martinique, and this was the first time that nonwhite republicans held elected office in Guadeloupe since the revolutionary upheavals of the 1790s. Only Réunion's white planters were numerous and powerful enough to obstruct the 1848 elections. Consequently, Réunion's local whites maintained their political dominance until 1914 (Winnacker 1938, 270).

11. Guadeloupe's republican governors also supported modest land reforms to limit the political appeal of black socialist leaders during the 1890s (Heath 2011, 295–297).

12. To illustrate this point, Christopher Church notes that French and Antillean children learned from the same textbooks that emphasized the key political achievements of the Third Republic—i.e., universal male suffrage, the inclusion of colonial representatives in the National Assembly, free public education, and freedom of the press. French Antillean textbooks also praised the "the generous efforts" of republican visionaries "who fought and suffered to grant . . . liberty" to emancipated slaves "and raise [them] to the dignity of citizenship" (Church 2017, 40).

13. The World Bank's governance indicators are scored around a global mean of 0 and a standard deviation of 1, with 90% of countries receiving scores between +1 and −1. The World Bank provides governance scores for sovereign states and many overseas dependencies, including French Guiana, Martinique, and Réunion. Because the World Bank does not provide governance scores for Guadeloupe, the estimated scores for Guadeloupe are derived from the mean governance scores for French Guiana, Martinique, and Réunion. The four territories share the same political status as overseas French departments, so this should generate a reliable estimate for Guadeloupe's governmental performance.

14. Many political leaders from across French West Africa were educated in the elite lycées (i.e., French-language secondary schools) that were established in Dakar and other Senegalese towns during the first half of the twentieth century. Dakar's École William Ponty became the leading training college for Francophone African teachers after 1912. Dakar's École de Médecine was also established in 1918 to train African doctors and other medical personnel. European and African medical researchers were also trained at the Institute Pasteur, established in 1924 (Conklin 1997, 246).

15. Crawford Young's (1994) research highlights the brutal methods that were used to force indigenous African chiefs to comply with the labor and taxation demands of colonial district officials in French West Africa (see 128–33 and 150–51). Young notes that "revocations, imprisonment, and public whippings of chiefs, especially local,

were frequently in the early period for the derelict performance in fulfilling tax and labor demands of the administration. The chiefs were ordered to collect taxes; the means used were up to them, so long as the revenue was delivered" (129).

16. By 1910, 8.7% of Malagasy children were enrolled in primary schools, compared with 0.5% of indigenous black children in French West Africa, and 0.2% in French Equatorial Africa (Benavot and Riddle 1988, 206–7).

17. Because of this political repression, Madagascar was unable to sustain its early patterns of development that Christian missionaries promoted under indigenous political control. Recent research by Frank-Bore Wietzke (2014) demonstrates that Madagascar's early exposure to Christian missionary evangelization and Western education has not significantly impacted the island state's long-term economic and political development. Consequently, Madagascar's primary school enrollment rate—while higher than that of Algeria or Senegal—fell behind the French Antilles colonies during the first half of the twentieth century.

18. The World Bank's Voice and Accountability indicator is structured around a global mean of 0, with most countries falling between −1.0 and +1.0.

19. The *World Christian Encyclopedia* estimates that there were fewer than 500 white Europeans in Haiti during the mid-1970s, and mulatto Haitians of French and African origin comprised less than 5% of the country's population (Barrett 1982, 348). Even if 10% of Haitian mulattoes enjoyed dual nationality as Haitian and French citizens, this meant that French citizens comprised about 0.5% of Haiti's population after World War II.

Chapter 8

1. Most Spanish American colonies gained independence following anticolonial wars that began during Napoleon's occupation of the Iberian Peninsula (1808–14). Portuguese control over Brazil survived a bit longer because the Portuguese royal family relocated to Brazil during the Napoleonic wars. This is why Brazil gained independence without fighting or bloodshed. The Portuguese royal family simply transferred political control from the Portuguese Emperor, João VI, to his eldest son, Dom Pedro I, who became the first emperor of Brazil in 1822.

2. Cuba's colonial planters imported twice as many enslaved Africans as all of the mainland colonies in Spanish America. Cuba's colonial planters also imported more than twice as many enslaved Africans as the combined total of slave shipments to British North American colonies in the United States, and more than 30 times the number of enslaved Africans that were transported to Puerto Rico during the Spanish colonial era (Eltis and Richardson 2010, 18).

3. Cuba had the largest slave population in Spanish America, and slavery remained legal and widespread for longer than anywhere else in Spanish America. Nevertheless, the racial composition of Cuba's colonial population was similar to that of mid-Atlantic US states like Virginia and Maryland, as opposed to forced settlement colonies like

Jamaica, Barbados, or Haiti. Cuba's enslaved Africans were always outnumbered by local white settlers, and they comprised only 41% of Cuba's total population in 1830 (Engerman and Higman 1997, 52). By 1880, the proportion of enslaved Africans had declined to less than 15% of the Cuban population, and enslaved Africans were outnumbered by free people of color (Engerman and Higman 1997, 54). This suggests that Cuba's slaves benefited from Spanish manumission laws that were more generous and forgiving than in the southern United States or in British, French, or Dutch forced settlement colonies. Slavery was even less extensive in other Spanish Caribbean societies: enslaved Africans represented only 16% of the population of Spanish Santo Domingo and less than 12% of Puerto Rico's population during the 1830s (Engerman and Higman 1997, 52).

4. Gallego and Bruhn (2012) find similar results in an empirical analysis of colonial institutions and postcolonial development in 345 subnational districts in 17 Latin American countries.

5. Studies that explore district-level variations within a single country are particularly insightful because they minimize the cultural, geographic, and historical variations that differentiate countries in my global statistical analysis of forced settlement and colonial occupation. In this way, future research on the diverse developmental legacies of Spanish colonialism can build on existing studies that examine subnational developmental variations within postcolonial states like Nigeria (Okoye and Pongou 2014), South Africa (Fintel and Fourie 2019), India (Lankina and Getachew 2012, 2013; Mukherjee 2018; Lee 2019), and Indonesia (Dell and Olken 2020).

6. Both Cuba and Puerto Rico are excluded from James Mahoney's (2010) work on colonialism and postcolonial development in Latin America. The two countries are also excluded from recent studies of state-building and democratization in Latin America (e.g., Centeno 2003; Centeno and Ferraro 2014; Kurtz 2013; Mainwaring and Perez-Liñan 2013). This partly reflects the fact that Spanish colonial rule persisted in Cuba and Puerto Rico long after the independence of other Latin American countries, and that both countries were significantly exposed to US neocolonial intervention following the 1898 Spanish-American War. Puerto Rico became a US colony in 1898 and a US overseas dependency in 1946. Puerto Rico is excluded from many comparative studies because of its unique political status as a US overseas territory. Cuba was never formally colonized by the United States, but it became a de facto US protectorate following the US military intervention in the 1898 Spanish-American War (see Kohli 2020, 225–30). Following the Spanish-American War, US plantation colonies established large-scale sugar plantations that exacerbated Cuba's preexisting racial and class inequalities during the first half of the twentieth century. The US military presence, and the controversial terms of Cuba's independence constitution, which recognized the right of the US military to protect American lives and property in Cuba, enabled US investors and corporations, including the Rockefeller group and the Boston-based United Fruit Company, to purchase more than 75% of Cuba's plantation land during the first half of the twentieth century (Kohli 2020, 228). Rising discontent over Cuba's semi-sovereign development precipitated a violent social revolution that empowered Fidel Castro's Communist dictatorship after 1959. Cuba is

excluded from many comparative studies of democratization and development because its Communist dictatorship has prevented the type of political and economic reforms that were implemented in other Latin American countries during the "third wave" of democratization after 1975.

7. For a good comparative overview of colonialism and state-building in Brazil and South Africa, see Marx 1996, 1998.

8. South Africa's per capita GDP consistently exceeded Brazil's throughout the first half of the twentieth century (Maddison 2006), despite the larger share of white settlers in Brazil (Marx 1998). South Africa's primary school enrollment rate also exceeded Brazil's during the first half of the twentieth century (Benavot and Riddle 1988). This partly reflects the early efforts of Protestant missionary schools that were established following the British abolition of slavery in South Africa (Reed 2020, 114). South Africa's early political institutions were also more inclusive than Brazil's prior to the onset of apartheid in 1948. Przeworski et al. (2011) estimate that South Africa's electoral franchise increased from 5%–6% of the population in 1915 to 10%–11% after 1933, whereas only 4%–5% of Brazilians were eligible voters during the First Brazilian Republic, 1889–1930.

9. In 2003, the Brazilian government introduced a conditional cash transfer program that has been remarkably successful at reducing child poverty and infant mortality and boosting educational opportunities and living standards for the poorest Brazilian households (see Paiva 2016; Hunter, Patel, and Borges-Sugiyama 2020). Brazil also significantly increased its per capita spending on education, healthcare, and pensions during the PT government of Ignacio Lula da Silva, 2002–10. As a result of these policies, the percentage of Brazilian households living in poverty decreased from 27% in 1995 to 17% in 2007, while the percentage of Brazilian households in extreme poverty declined from 10% in 1995 to 6% in 2007 (Kingstone and Ponce 2010). South Africa's conditional cash transfer program, the Child Support Grant, is older than Brazil's Bolsa Familia program, but its results have been less impressive. Consequently, postapartheid South Africa continues to trail Brazil on most indicators of economic and social well-being. South Africa's per capita GDP, at purchasing power parity, only increased from $9,761 in 1996 to $12,202 in 2016, whereas Brazil's increased from $11,321 to $14,451 during the same period (Trading Economics 2021a, 2021b). South Africa also suffers from stubbornly high unemployment rates that reflect its long history of racially segregated neighborhoods. South Africa's unemployment rate has fluctuated between 22% and 31% of the labor force since the end of apartheid, whereas Brazil's unemployment fluctuated from 4.6% in 1995 to a peak of 14% in 2020 (Kingstone and Ponce 2010, 113; Trading Economics 2021c, 2021d). South Africa has also consistently lagged Brazil's performance on the United Nations' Human Development Index after 1990.

10. The details of military reconstruction are outlined in Richard Vallely's book *The Two Reconstructions: The Struggle for Black Enfranchisement*. See Valelly 2004, 30–45.

11. For example, Louisiana's notorious Angola prison was established on a plantation site that was leased to a former Confederate soldier, whose family controlled the largest prison facility in the United States with limited oversight from the state government

(Louisiana State Penitentiary 2019). Mississippi also established a brutal plantation prison whose labor conditions have been described as "worse than slavery" (Howard 2017, 152). Southern US states also profited from leasing prison laborers to work for private agricultural plantations, commercial mines, and public infrastructure projects (see Blackmon 2008; Howard 2017, 152–59).

12. Demographic data for African Americans are provided by the United States' Department of Health and Human Services (2015). The international comparisons are based on data from the United Nations' (2019) *World Population Prospects*.

13. https://freedomhouse.org/explore-the-map?type=fotnandyear=2021.

Appendix 3

1. Relaxing the requirement for electoral alternation reduces the magnitude of the forced settlement coefficient from +36.94 to +26.42. Nevertheless, both results are statistically significant at $p < 0.01$.

2. The following countries are not included in the Varieties of Democracy database: Antigua and Barbuda, Bahamas, Bahrain, Belize, Brunei Darussalam, Dominica, Grenada, Kiribati, Nauru, Saint Kitts and Nevis, Saint Lucia, Saint Vincent and the Grenadines, Samoa, Tonga, and Tuvalu. Many of the omitted countries are small Caribbean islands or Pacific island microstates that Cheibub, Gandhi, and Vreeland (2010) classify as "democratic."

3. For ease of interpretation, I multiplied the liberal democracy index by 100 to create a theoretical maximum democracy score of 100. Consequently, liberal democracy scores range from 2.29 in Mozambique to 49.0 in Sri Lanka between 1946 and 1974. From 1975 until 2012, liberal democracy scores range from 2.87 in Myanmar to 68.97 in Mauritius. On average, forced settlement colonies maintained a mean liberal democracy score of 49.76 between 1975 and 2012, whereas the mean liberal democracy score for colonies of occupation was only 19.95.

References

Abernethy, David. 2000. *The Dynamics of Global Dominance: European Overseas Empires, 1415–1980*. New Haven: Yale University Press.

Abou, Antoine. 1988. *L'école dans la Guadeloupe coloniale*. Paris: Editions Caribéens.

Abraham, Arthur. 1978. *Mende Government and Politics under Colonial Rule*. Freetown: Sierra Leone University Press.

Acemoglu, Daron, Francisco Gallego, and James A. Robinson. 2014. "Institutions, Human Capital, and Development." *Annual Review of Economics* 6: 875–912.

Acemoglu, Daron, Simon Johnson, and James A. Robinson. 2001. "The Colonial Origins of Comparative Development: An Empirical Investigation." *American Economic Review* 91(5): 1369–401.

Acemoglu, Daron, Simon Johnson, and James A. Robinson. 2002. "Reversal of Fortune: Geography and Institutions in the Making of the Modern World Income Distribution." *Quarterly Journal of Economics* 117(4): 1231–94.

Acemoglu, Daron, Simon Johnson, and James A. Robinson. 2005. "The Rise of Europe: Atlantic Trade, Institutional Change, and Economic Growth." *American Economic Review* 95(3): 546–79.

Acemoglu, Daron, Tristan Reed, and James A. Robinson. 2014. "Chiefs: Economic Development and Elite Control of Civil Society in Sierra Leone." *Journal of Political Economy* 122(2): 319–68.

Acemoglu, Daron, and James A. Robinson. 2010. "Why Is Africa Poor?" *Economic History of Developing Regions* 25(1): 21–50.

Acemoglu, Daron, and James A. Robinson. 2012. *Why Nations Fail: The Origins of Power, Prosperity, and Poverty*. New York: Crown Business.

Acemoglu, Daron, and James A. Robinson. 2019. *The Narrow Corridor: States, Societies, and the Fate of Liberty*. New York: Penguin.

Acharya, Avidit, Matthew Blackwell, and Maya Sen. 2018. *Deep Roots: How Slavery Still Shapes Southern Politics*. Princeton, NJ: Princeton University Press.

Adebajo, Adekeye. 2002. *Building Peace in West Africa: Liberia, Sierra Leone, and Guinea-Bissau*. Boulder, CO: Lynne Rienner Publishers.

Afigbo, A. E. 1966. *The Warrant Chiefs: Indirect Rule in Southeastern Nigeria, 1891–1929*. London: Longman.

Afigbo, A. E. 1973. "The Establishment of Colonial Rule, 1900–1918." In J. F. A. Ajayi and Michael Crowder (eds.), *History of West Africa*, vol. 2, 424-83. New York: Columbia University Press.

African Elections Database. 2016. "Elections in Cape Verde." http://africanelections.tripod.com/cv.html.

Aguirre, Alvaro. 2019. "Rebellions, Technical Change, and the Early Development of Political Institutions in Latin America." *Journal of Comparative Economics* 47(1): 65–89.

Ajayi, J. F. A., and Michael Crowder. 1973. "West Africa, 1919-1939: The Colonial Situation." In J. F. A. Ajayi and Michael Crowder (eds.), *History of West Africa*, vol. 2, 514-41. New York: Columbia University Press.

Albaugh, Ericka. 2007. "Language Choice in Education: A Politics of Persuasion." *Journal of Modern African Studies* 45(1): 1–32.

Albaugh, Ericka. 2009. "The Colonial Image Reversed: Language Preferences and Policy Outcomes in African Education." *International Studies Quarterly* 53(2): 389–420.

Albouy, David Y. 2012. "The Colonial Origins of Comparative Development: An Empirical Investigation. Comment." *American Economic Review* 102(6): 3059–76.

Alesina, Alberto, Arnaud Devleschauwer, William Easterly, Sergio Kurlat, and Romain Wacziarg. 2003. "Fractionalization." *Journal of Economic Growth*, 8(2): 155–94.

Allen, Richard B. 1999. *Slaves, Freedmen and Indentured Labourers in Colonial Mauritius*. Cambridge: Cambridge University Press.

Allen, Richard B. 2003. "The Mascarene Slave Trade and Labour Migration in the Indian Ocean during the Eighteenth and Nineteenth Centuries." *Slavery and Abolition* 24(2): 33–50.

Allende, Isabel. 2010. *Island Beneath the Sea*. New York: HarperCollins.

Allison, Paul. 1999. *Multiple Regression: A Primer*. Thousand Oaks, CA: Pine Forge Press.

Anckar, Carsten. 2008. "Size, Islandness and Democracy: A Global Comparison." *International Political Science Review / Revue internationale de science politique* 29(4): 433–59.

Anckar, Carsten. 2011. *Religion and Democracy: A Worldwide Comparison*. Abingdon, UK: Routledge.

Anckar, Dag. 2002. "Why Are Small Island States Democracies?" *Round Table* 9(365): 375–90.

Anckar, Dag. 2006. "Islandness or Smallness? A Comparative Look at Political Institutions in Small Island States." *Island Studies Journal* 1(1): 43–54.

Andersen, David, Jørgen Møller, Lasse Lykke Rørbæk, and Svend-Erik Skaaning. 2014. "State Capacity and Political Regime Stability." *Democratization* 21(7): 1305–25.

Anderson, Benedict. 1981. *Imagined Communities: Reflections on the Origins and Spread of Nationalism*. New York: Verso Books.

Anderson, Clare. 2016. "Convicts and Coolies: Rethinking Indentured Labour in the Nineteenth Century." *Slavery and Abolition* 30(1): 93–109.

Angell, Alan. 2010. "Democratic Governance in Chile." In Scott Mainwaring and Timothy Scully (eds.), *Democratic Governance in Latin America*, 269–306. Stanford, CA: Stanford University Press.

Angulo, A. J. 2010. "Education during the American Occupation of Haiti, 1915–1934." *Historical Studies in Education* 22(2): 1–17.

Avirgan, Tony. 2006. "South Africa's Economic Gap Grows Wider while Brazil's Narrows Slightly." *Economic Policy Institute* (April 19), See https://www.epi.org/publication/web features_snapshots_20060419/. Accessed March 2022.

Babou, Cheikh A. 2013. "The Senegalese 'Social Contract' Revisited: The Muridiyya Muslim Order and State Politics in Postcolonial Senegal." In Mamadou Diouf (ed.), *Tolerance, Democracy, and Sufis in Senegal*, 125–46. New York: Columbia University Press.

Bah, Abu Bakkar. 2010. "Democracy and Civil War: Citizenship and Peacemaking in Côte D'Ivoire." *African Affairs* 109(437): 597–615.

Baker, Bruce. 2006. "Cape Verde: The Most Democratic Nation in Africa?" *Journal of African Studies* 44(4): 493–511.

Baker, Bruce. 2009. "Comoros: The Search for Viability." *Civil Wars* 11(3): 215–33.

Ball, Jeremy. 2015. *Angola's Colossal Lie: Forced Labor on a Sugar Plantation, 1913–1977*. Leiden: Brill.

Barrett, David. 1982. *World Christian Encyclopedia: A Comparative Survey of Churches and Religions in the Modern World, AD 1900–2000*. New York: Oxford University Press.

Barrett, David, George Kurian, and Todd Johnson. 2001. *World Christian Encyclopedia: A Comparative Survey of Churches and Religions in the Modern World*. New York: Oxford University Press.

Barro, Robert J. 1991. "Economic Growth in a Cross Section of Countries." *Quarterly Journal of Economics* 106(2): 407–43.

Barrows, Paul Wayne. 1990. "The Historical Roots of Cape Verdean Dependency, 1460–1990." PhD dissertation, University of Minnesota. Ann Arbor, MI: UMI Dissertation Services.

Bates, Robert. 1974. "Ethnic Competition and Modernization in Contemporary Africa." *Comparative Political Studies* 6(4): 457–84.

Bates, Robert. 1981. *Markets and States in Tropical Africa: The Political Basis of Agricultural Policies*. Berkeley: University of California Press.

Bates, Robert. 2008. *When Things Fell Apart: State Failure in Late Twentieth Century Africa*. New York: Cambridge University Press.

BBC News. 2018. "Guinea-Bissau Profile: Timeline." Updated February 19, 2018. https://www.bbc.com/news/world-africa-13579838.

Beauvois, Frédérique. 2017. *Between Blood and Gold: The Debates over Compensation for Slavery in the Americas*. New York: Berghahn Books.

Beckford, George L. 1983. *Persistent Poverty: Underdevelopment in Plantation Economies of the Third World*. Abbreviated ed. Morant Bay, Jamaica: Maroon Publishing House; London: Zed Books.

Beckles, Hilary. 1997. "Social and Political Control in the Slave Society." In Franklin W. Knight (ed.), *General History of the Caribbean*, vol. 3, *The Slave Societies of the Caribbean*, 194–221. London: UNESCO Publishing / Macmillan Education.

Bellegarde-Smith, Patrick. 2004. *Haiti: The Breached Citadel*. 2nd ed. Toronto: Canadian Scholars' Press.

Belsey, Timothy, and Masayuki Kudamatsu. 2006. "Health and Democracy." *American Economic Association Papers and Proceedings* 96(2): 313–18.

Benavot, Aaron, and Phyllis Riddle. 1988. "The Expansion of Primary Education, 1870–1940: Trends and Issues." *Sociology of Education* 61(3): 191–210.

Bénot, Yves. 2003. "The Chain of Slave Insurrections in the Caribbean, 1789–1791." In Marcel Dorigny (ed.), *The Abolitions of Slavery: From Léger Félicité Sonthonax to Victor Schoelcher, 1793, 1794, 1848*, 147–54. New York: Berghahn Books.

Berman, Sanford. 1956. "Spanish Guinea: Enclave Empire." *Phylon* 17(4): 359–60.

Bermeo, Nancy. 2007. "War and Democratization: Lessons from the Portuguese Experience." *Democratization* 14(3): 388–406.

Bernhard, M., C. Reenock, and T. Nordstrom. 2004. "The Legacy of Western Overseas Colonialism on Democratic Survival." *International Studies Quarterly* 48(2): 225–50.

Bertocchi, Graziella, and Arcangelo Dimico. 2012. "The Racial Gap in Education and the Legacy of Slavery." *Journal of Comparative Economics* 40(4): 581–95.

Best, Lloyd. 1968. "Outline of a Pure Plantation Economy." *Social and Economic Studies* 17(3): 283–326.

Best, Lloyd, and Kari Polanyi Levitt. 2009. *Essays on the Theory of Plantation Economy: A Historical and Institutional Approach to Caribbean Economic Development*. Mona, Jamaica: University of the West Indies Press.

Betts, Raymond F. 1961. *Assimilation and Association in French Colonial Theory*. New York: Columbia University Press.

Betts, Raymond F. 1972. *The Scramble for Africa: Causes and Dimensions of Empire*. Lexington, MA: Heath Press.

Bigman, Laura. 1993. *History and Hunger in West Africa: Food Production and Entitlement in Guinea-Bissau and Cape Verde*. Westport, CT: Greenwood Press.

Black, Jeremy. 2015. *The British Empire: A History and a Debate*. Farnham, UK: Ashgate Publishing Limited.

Blackburn, Robin. 1988. *The Overthrow of Colonial Slavery, 1776–1848*. New York: Verso.

Blackmon, Douglas. 2008. *Slavery by Another Name: The Re-enslavement of Black Americans from the Civil War until World War II*. New York: Doubleday.

Bloom, John, and Jeffrey Sachs. 1998. "Geography, Demography and Economic Growth in Africa." *Brookings Papers in Economic Activity* 2: 207–95.

Bobonis, Gustavo J., and Peter M. Morrow. 2013. "Labor Coercion and the Accumulation of Human Capital." https://papers.ssrn.com/sol3/papers.cfm?abstract_id=2285632.

Bobonis, Gustavo J., and Harold J. Toro. 2007. "Modern Colonization and Its Consequences: The Effects of U.S. Educational Policy on Puerto Rico's Educational Stratification, 1899–1910." *Caribbean Studies* 35(2): 31–76.

Boix, Carles. 2003. *Democracy and Redistribution*. Cambridge: Cambridge University Press.

Bollen, Kenneth. 1979. "Political Democracy and the Timing of Development." *American Sociological Review* 44(4): 572–87.

Bollen, Kenneth, and Robert Jackman. 1985. "Political Democracy and the Size Distribution of Income." *American Sociological Review* 50(4): 438–57.

Bollen, Kenneth, and Robert Jackman. 1995. "Inequality and Democratization Revisited: Comment on Muller." *American Sociological Review* 60(6): 983–89.

Bowman, Joyce L. 1986. "Abdul Njai: Ally and Enemy of the Portuguese in Guinea-Bissau, 1895–1919." *Journal of African History* 27(3): 463–79.

Bowman, Larry W. 1991. *Mauritius: Democracy and Development in the Indian Ocean*. Boulder, CO: Westview Press.

Brady, Henry, and David Collier. 2004. *Rethinking Social Inquiry: Diverse Tools, Shared Standards*. New York: Rowman & Littlefield.

Bratton, Michael, and Eric C. Chang. 2006. "State Building and Democratization in Sub-Saharan Africa: Forwards, Backwards, or Together?" *Comparative Political Studies*, 39(9): 1059–83.

Bratton, Michael, and Nicolas van de Walle. 1997. *Democratic Experiments in Africa: Regime Transitions in Comparative Perspective*. Cambridge: Cambridge University Press.

Brerreton, Bridget. 1979. *Race Relations in Colonial Trinidad, 1870–1900*. Cambridge: Cambridge University Press.

Brown, David S. 2000. "Democracy, Colonization, and Human Capital in Sub-Saharan Africa." *Studies in Comparative International Development* 35(1): 20–40.

Brubaker, Rogers. 1992. *Citizenship and Nationhood in France and Germany*. Cambridge, MA: Harvard University Press.

Bruhn, Miriam, and Francisco A. Gallego. 2012. "Good, Bad, and Ugly Colonial Activities: Do They Matter for Economic Development?" *The Review of Economics and Statistics*, 94(2): 433–61.

Bryan, Patrick. 1991. *The Jamaican People, 1880–1902: Race, Class, and Social Control.* London: Macmillan Caribbean.

Bryan, Patrick. 1996. "The Black Middle Class in 19th Century Jamaica." In Hilary Beckles and Verene Shepherd (eds.), *Caribbean Freedom: Economy and Society from Emancipation to Present,* 284–96. Kingston, Jamaica: Ian Randle.

Buell, Raymond L. 1928. *The Native Problem in Africa.* New York: Macmillan.

Cabo Verde. 1915. "Cabo Verde: Estatísticas Gerais, 1911–1915." Lisbon: Arquivo Histórico Ultramarino, S/N/IL/SEMU/DGU/ex C_V/1911–1915.

Cabo Verde. 1949. "Processo respeitante à Assambleia de apuramento geral das Eleições para Deputados, Novembro 1949." Praia: Arquivo Histórico Nacional, RPSAC(A2), Cx. 496.

Cabo Verde. 1953. "Processo respeitante a Eleições para Deputados à Assembleia Nacional, em Diversas concelhos, Novembro 1953." Praia: Arquivo Histórico Nacional, RPSAC(A2), Cx. 496.

Cabo Verde. 1957. "Resultado das Eleições para Deputado à Assembleia Nacional pelo círculo de Cabo Verde, realizadas em 3 de Novembro de 1957." Praia: Arquivo Histórico Nacional, RPSAC(A2), Cx. 496.

Cabo Verde. 1961. "Resultado das Eleições para Deputado à Assembleia Nacional pelo círculo de Cabo Verde." Praia: Arquivo Histórico Nacional, RPSAC(A2), Cx. 496.

Cabo Verde. 1994. Secreteria-Geral do Governo, 1803–1927: Repertório Numérico Simples do Fundo Arquivistico. Praia: Arquivo Histórico Nacional.

Cabo Verde. 2004. Repartição Provincial dos Serviços de Administração Civil, 1907–1979. Praia: Instituto do Arquivo Histórico Nacional.

Cabo Verde, Boletim Oficial. 1858. "Boletim Oficial do Governo Geral da Provincia de Cabo Verde." Praia: Arquivo Histórico Nacional, No. 29, December 29.

Cabo Verde, Boletim Oficial. 1862. "Mandou-se considerer o governo da Guiné portuguesa em Guerra com os gentios Beafadas de Badora." Praia: Arquivo Histórico Nacional, Bol. No. 7, March 21.

Cabo Verde, Boletim Oficial. 1864. "O governador geral deve immediatamente participar ao governo às occorencias de Guerra aberta na provincial." Praia: Arquivo Histórico Nacional, Bol 43, 6 August.

Cabo Verde, Boletim Oficial. 1871. "Noticia Relativa á Expedição Militar Mandada á Guiné Portugueza para Pacificar Cacheu." Praia: Arquivo Histórico Nacional, Bols. No. 6 and 19.

Cabo Verde, Boletim Oficial. 1879. "Deannexado da provincial de Cabo Verde o districto da Guiné Portugueza, Formando o Territorio d'esta Posessão Uma Provincial Independente." Praia: Arquivo Histórico Nacional, Bol. No. 15, sup., March 18.

Cabo Verde, Boletim Oficial. 1894. "Boletim Oficial do Governo Geral da Provincia de Cabo Verde, No. 24. Sabbado 7 Abril 1894." Praia: Arquivo Histórico Nacional.

Cabo Verde, Secretería do Governo Geral. 1881. "Eleição de deputados às Cortes pelos Diversos circluos eleitorais das provincias de Cabo Verde e Guiné." Praia: Arquivo Histórico Nacional, SGG(A1), Cx.726.

Cabo Verde, Secretería do Governo Geral. 1890. "Eleição de deputados às Cortes pelos diversos circluos eleitorais das Provincias de Cabo Verde e Guiné." Praia: Arquivo Histórico Nacional, SGG(A1), Cx. 727.

Cabral, Amilcar. 1979. *Unity and Struggle: Speeches and Writings of Amilcar Cabral.* New York: Monthly Review Press.

Cabral, Amilcar. 2016. *Resistance and Decolonization*. Translated by Dan Wood. Lanham, MD: Rowman & Littlefield.

Cámara, Luís R. 2004. *The Phenomenon of Puerto Rican Voting*. Gainesville: University of Florida Press.

Campbell, Carl. 1996. "Social and Economic Obstacles to the Development of Popular Education in Post-emancipation Jamaica, 1834–1865." In Hilary Beckles and Verene Shepherd (eds.), *Caribbean Freedom: Economy and Society from Emancipation to the Present*, 262–68. Princeton, NJ: Markus Wiener.

Campbell, I. C. 2005. "Resistance and Colonial Government: A Comparative Study of Samoa." *Journal of Pacific History* 40(1): 45–69.

Campbell, Mavis Christine. 1976. *Dynamics of Change in a Slave Society: A Sociopolitical History of the Free Coloreds of Jamaica, 1800–1865*. Cranbury, NJ: Associated University Presses.

Caribbean Journal. 2012. "Trinidad & Tobago 50th independence celebrations: PM Kamla Persad-Bissessar's Independence Address, 31 August 2012." https://www.carib journal.com/2012/08/31/trinidad-at-50-prime-minister-kamla-persad-bissessars-independence-address/. Accessed October 25, 2022.

Carreira, António. 1982. *The People of the Cape Verde Islands: Exploitation and Emigration*. London: C. Hurst.

Carter, Marina. 1996. *Voices of Indenture: Experiences of Indian Migrants in the British Empire*. Leicester: Leicester University Press.

Cartwright, John. 1970. *Politics in Sierra Leone, 1947–1967*. Toronto: University of Toronto Press.

Carvalho, Maria Adriana. 2004. *A Construção Social do Discurso Educativo em Cabo Verde, 1911–1926*. Lisbon: Universidade de Lisboa, Faculdade de Psicologia e de Ciências da Educação, Mestrado em Ciências da Educação.

Centeno, Miguel A. 2003. *Blood and Debt: War and the Nation-State in Latin America*. University Park: Pennsylvania State University Press.

Centeno, Miguel A., and Agustin Ferraro. 2014. *State and Nation-Making in Latin America and Spain: Republics of the Possible*. New York: Cambridge University Press.

Chabal, Patrick. 1981. "The Social and Political Thought of Amílcar Cabral: A Reassessment." *Journal of Modern African Studies* 19(1): 31–56.

Chabal, Patrick. 2002. *A History of Postcolonial Lusophone Africa*. Bloomington: Indiana University Press.

Chabal, Patrick. 2003. *Amilcar Cabral: Revolutionary Leadership and People's War*. Trenton, NJ: Africa New World Press.

Chafer, Tony. 2002. *The End of Empire in French West Africa: France's Successful Decolonization?* Oxford: Berg.

Chamberlain, Mary. 2010. *Empire and Nation-Building in the Caribbean*. Manchester, UK: Manchester University Press.

Chatterjee, Aroop, Léo Czajka, and Amory Gethin. 2021. "Can Redistribution Keep Up with Inequality: Evidence from South Africa, 1993–2019." World Inequality Lab, Working Paper No. 2021/20.

Cheibub, José A., Jennifer Gandhi, and James M. Vreeland. 2010. "Democracy and Dictatorship Revisited." *Public Choice* 143(1–2): 67–101.

Chilcote, Ronald H. 1967. *Portuguese Africa*. Englewood Cliffs, NJ: Prentice-Hall.

Chilcote, Ronald H. 1968. "The Political Thought of Amilcar Cabral." *Journal of Modern African Studies* 6(3): 373–88.

Chivallon, Christine, and David Howard. 2017. "Colonial Violence and Civilising Utopias in the French and British empires: The Morant Bay Rebellion (1865) and the Insurrection of the South (1870)." *Slavery and Abolition* 38(3): 534–58.

Christopher, A. J. 1984. *Colonial Africa*. London: Croom Helm.

Christopher, A. J. 1988. *The British Empire at Its Zenith*. London: Croom Helm.

Church, Christopher. 2017. *Paradise Destroyed: Catastrophe and Citizenship in the French Caribbean*. Lincoln: University of Nebraska Press.

CIA. 2016. *The World Factbook*. https://www.cia.gov/library/publications/the-world-factbook/. Accessed March 3, 2018.

Clarke, Colin. 2011. "Demographic Change and Population Movement." In K. O. Laurence and Jorge Ibarra Cuesta (eds.), *General History of the Caribbean*, vol. 4, *The Long Nineteenth Century: Nineteenth Century Transformations*, 259–82. Paris: UNESCO.

Clemente-Kersten, Ana Catarina. 1999a. "Cape Verde." In Dieter Nohlen, Michael Krennerich, and Bernhard Thibaut (eds.), *Elections in Africa: A Data Handbook*, 189–204. Oxford: Oxford University Press.

Clemente-Kersten, Ana Catarina. 1999b. "Guinea-Bissau." In Dieter Nohlen, Michael Krennerich, and Bernhard Thibaut (eds.), *Elections in Africa: A Data Handbook*, 461–74. Oxford: Oxford University Press.

CNN. 2010. "Haiti Earthquake: Pat Robertson Says Haiti Paying for 'Pact to the Devil.'" January 13. http://www.cnn.com/2010/US/01/13/haiti.pat.robertson/index.html.

Coates, Ta-Nehisi. 2014. "The Case for Reparations." *The Atlantic*, June. https://www.theatlantic.com/magazine/archive/2014/06/the-case-for-reparations/361631/.

Cochin, Augustin. 1863. *The Results of Emancipation*. Boston: Walker, Wise.

Coissoro, Narana. 1984. "African Customary Law in the Former Portuguese Territories, 1954–1974." *Journal of African Law* 28(1–2): 72–79.

Cole, Gibril. 2013. *The Krio of West Africa: Islam, Culture, Creolization and Colonialism in the Nineteenth Century*. Athens: Ohio University Press.

Collier, David, and Steven Levitsky. 1997. "Democracy with Adjectives: Conceptual Innovation in Comparative Research." *World Politics* 49(3): 430–51.

Collier, David, and Ruth B. Collier. 1991. *Shaping the Political Arena: Critical Junctures, the Labor Movement, and Regime Dynamics in Latin America*. Princeton: Princeton University Press.

Collier, Paul J. 2000. "Economics, Politics, and Economic Performance." *Economics & Politics* 12(3): 225–45.

Collier, Paul J., and J. Willem Gunning. 1999. "Why Has Africa Grown Slowly?" *Journal of Economic Perspectives* 13(3): 3–22.

Collier, Ruth B. 1982. *Regimes in Tropical Africa: Changing Forms of Supremacy, 1945–75*. Berkeley: University of California Press.

Colomer, Josep. 2001. *Political Institutions: Democracy and Social Choice*. New York: Oxford University Press.

Conklin, Alice. 1997. *A Mission to Civilize: The Republican Idea of Empire in France and West Africa*. Stanford, CA: Stanford University Press.

Conklin, Alice. 1998. "Colonialism and Human Rights, a Contradiction in Terms? The Case of France and West Africa, 1895–1914." *American Historical Review* 103(2): 419–42.

Cooper, Frederick. 2000. "Conditions Analogous to Slavery: Imperialism and Free Labor Ideology in Africa." In Frederick Cooper, Thomas C. Holt, and Rebecca J. Scott (eds.),

Beyond Slavery: Explorations of Race, Labor and Citizenship in Postemancipation Societies, 107–49. Chapel Hill: University of North Carolina Press.

Cooper, Frederick. 2014. *Citizenship between Empire and Nation: Remaking France and French Africa, 1945–1960.* Princeton, NJ: Princeton University Press.

Coppedge, Michael. 1999. "Thickening Thin Concepts and Theories: Combining Large N and Small in Comparative Politics." *Comparative Politics* 31(4): 465–76.

Coppedge, Michael. 2012. *Democratization and Research Methods.* New York: Cambridge University Press.

Coppedge, Michael, John Gerring, Staffan Lindberg, and Svend-Erik Skaaning. 2016. *Varieties of Democracy, Version 5 Codebook.* University of Gothenburg, V-DEM Institute; University of Notre Dame, Kellogg Institute for International Studies.

Coppedge, Michael, John Gerring, Staffan Lindberg, and Svend-Erik Skaaning. 2018. *Varieties of Democracy, Version 8.* University of Gothenburg: V-DEM Institute. https://www.v-dem.net/data/dataset-archive/. Accessed December 2, 2022.

Corby, Richard. 1990. "Educating Africans for Inferiority under British Rule: Bo School in Sierra Leone." *Comparative Education Review* 34(3): 314–49.

Corrin, Jennifer, and Dan Paterson. 2007. *Introduction to South Pacific Law.* Abingdon, UK: Routledge.

Costa-Pinto, António. 2003. *Contemporary Portugal: Politics, Society and Culture.* Boulder, CO: Social Science Monographs, Distributed by Columbia University Press, New York.

Côté, Isabelle, and Matthew I. Mitchell. 2016. "Elections and 'Sons of Soil' Conflict Dynamics in Africa and Asia." *Democratization* 23(4): 657–77.

Crowder, Michael. 1964. "Indirect Rule—French and British Style." *Africa* 34(3): 197–205.

Crowder, Michael. 1968. *West Africa under Colonial Rule.* Evanston, IL: Northwestern University Press.

Curtin, Philip D. 1972. "The Atlantic Slave Trade 1600–1800." In J. F. A. Ajayi and Michael Crowder (eds.), *History of West Africa,* vol 1, 240–68. New York: Columbia University Press.

Cuzán, Alfred G. 1999. "Democratic Transitions: The Portuguese Case." In Marco Rimanelli (ed.), *Comparative Democratization and Peaceful Change in Single-Party Dominant Countries,* 119–38. New York: St. Martin's Press.

Da Silva Cunha, J. M. 1949. *O Trabalho Indígena: Estudo de Direito Colonial.* Lisbon: Agência Geral das Colónias.

Dahl, Robert. 1971. *Polyarchy: Participation and Opposition.* New Haven: Yale University Press.

Dahlberg, Stefan, Sören Holmberg, Bo Rothstein, Natalia Alvarado Pachon, and Richard Svensson. 2018. *The Quality of Government Basic Dataset 2018, Codebook.* University of Gothenburg: The Quality of Government Institute. http://www.qog.pol.qu.se.

Davidson, Basil. 1969. *The Liberation of Guiné: Aspects of an African Revolution.* Middlesex, UK: Penguin Books.

Davidson, Basil. 1989. *The Fortunate Isles: A Study in African Transformation.* London: Hutchinson.

Davidson, Basil. 1992. *The Black Man's Burden: Africa and the Curse of the Nation-State.* New York: Times Books.

Davidson, Basil. 2017. *No Fist Is Big Enough to Hide the Sky: The Liberation of Guinea-Bissau and Cape Verde, 1963–74.* New ed. London: Zed Books.

Davila, J. D. 1987. *Shelter, Poverty, and African Revolutionary Socialism: Human Settlements in Guinea Bissau.* Report. London: International Institute for Environment and Development.

Dawson, Andrew. 2016. "Political Violence in Consolidated Democracies: The Development and Institutionalization of Partisan Violence in Late Colonial Jamaica, 1938–62." *Social Science History* 40(2): 185–218.

Dell, Melissa. 2010. "The Persistent Effects of Peru's Mining 'Mita.'" *Econometrica* 78(6): 1863–903.

Dell, Melissa, and Benjamin A. Olken. 2020. "The Development Effects of the Extractive Colonial Economy: The Dutch Cultivation System in Java." *Review of Economic Studies* 87(1): 164–203.

Deschamps, Hubert. 1963. "Et Maintenant, Lord Lugard?" *Africa* 33(4): 293–306.

Diamond, Jared. 2005. *Collapse: How Societies Choose to Fail or Succeed.* New York: Penguin.

Dick, Devon. 2003. *Rebellion to Riot: The Jamaican Church in Nation Building.* Kingston, Jamaica: Ian Randle.

Diggs, Charles C. 1973. "Statement on the Proclamation of Independence of the Republic of Guinea-Bissau." *Issue: A Journal of Opinion* 3(3): 30–33.

Diouf, Mamadou. 2013. *Tolerance, Democracy, and Sufis in Senegal.* New York: Columbia University Press.

Domínguez, Jorge. 1993. "The Caribbean Question: Why Has Liberal Democracy (Surprisingly) Flourished?" in Domínguez, Jorge, Robert A. Pastor, and R. Delisle Worrell (eds.), *Democracy in the Caribbean: Political, Economic, and Social Perspectives,* 1–25. Baltimore: Johns Hopkins University Press.

Dos Reis, Dario D. 2007. "A Saúde em Cabo Verde: Trinta Anos Depois." In Jorge Carlos Fonseca (ed.), *Cabo Verde: Três Décadas Depois,* 439–68. Praia: Direito e Cidadania.

Dowd, Robert A. 2014. "Religious Diversity and Violent Conflict: Lessons from Nigeria." *The Flecther Forum of World Affairs* 38(1): 153–68.

Draper, Nicholas. 2010. *The Price of Emancipation: Slave-Ownership, Compensation and British Society at the End of Slavery.* Cambridge: Cambridge University Press.

Drescher, Seymour. 1987. *Capitalism and Anti-slavery.* New York: Oxford University Press.

Drescher, Seymour. 2009. *Abolition: A History of Slavery and Anti-slavery.* New York: Cambridge University Press.

Driscoll, Barry. 2018. "Why Political Competition Can Increase Patronage." *Studies in Comparative International Development* 53(4): 404–27.

Driessen, Michael D. 2014. *Religion and Democratization: Framing Religious and Political Identities in Muslim and Catholic Societies.* New York: Oxford University Press.

Dubois, Laurent. 2004a. *Avengers of the New World: The Story of the Haitian Revolution.* Cambridge, MA: Harvard University Press.

Dubois, Laurent. 2004b. *A Colony of Citizens: Revolution and Slave Emancipation in the French Caribbean, 1787–1804.* Chapel Hill: University of North Carolina Press.

Dubois, Laurent. 2012. *Haiti: The Aftershocks of History.* New York: Metropolitan Books.

Duffy, James. 1959. *Portuguese Africa.* Cambridge, MA: Harvard University Press.

Duffy, James. 1961. "Portuguese Africa (Angola and Mozambique): Some Crucial Problems and the Role of Education in Their Resolution." *Journal of Negro Education* 30(3): 294–301.

Duffy, James. 1967. *A Question of Slavery.* Cambridge, MA: Harvard University Press.

Duignan, Peter, and L. H. Gann. 1975. *Colonialism in Africa, 1870–1960*. Vol. 4, *The Economics of Colonialism*. Cambridge: Cambridge University Press.

Dunn, Leslie. 2011. "The Impact of Political Dependence on Small Island Jurisdictions." *World Development* 39(12): 2132–46.

Dunn, Richard S. 1972. *Sugar and Slaves: The Rise of the Planter Class in the English West Indies, 1624–1713*. Chapel Hill: University of North Carolina Press.

Dupuy, Alex. 1989. *Haiti in the World Economy: Class, Race and Underdevelopment since 1700*. Boulder, CO: Westview Press.

Dupuy, Alex. 2019. *Rethinking the Haitian Revolution: Slavery, Independence and the Struggle for Recognition*. London: Rowan & Littlefield.

Easterly, William, and Ross Levine. 1997. "Africa's Growth Tragedy: Policies and Ethnic Divisions." *Quarterly Journal of Economics* 112(4): 1203–50.

Easterly, William, and Ross Levine. 2016. "The European Origins of Economic Development." *Journal of Economic Growth* 21(3): 225–57.

Eck, Kristine. 2018. "The Origins of Policing Institutions: Legacy of Colonial Insurgency." *Journal of Peace Research* 55(2): 147–60.

Edie, Carlene. 1991. *Democracy by Default: Dependency and Clientelism in Jamaica*. Boulder, CO: Lynne Rienner.

Edie, Carlene. 1994. *Democracy in the Caribbean: Myths and Realities*. Westport, CT: Praeger.

Edugyan, Esi. 2018. *Washington Black*. Toronto: HarperCollins.

Edwards, Zophia. 2018. "No Colonial Working Class, No Post-colonial Development: A Comparative-Historical Analysis of Two Oil Rich Countries." *Studies in Comparative International Development* 53(4): 477–99.

Ekeh, Peter. 1975. "Colonialism and the Two Publics in Africa: A Theoretical Statement." *Comparative Studies in Society and History* 17(1): 91–112.

Eltis, David. 1997. "The Slave Economies of the Caribbean: Structure, Performance, Evolution and Significance." In Franklin Knight (ed.), *General History of the Caribbean*, vol. 3 *The Slave Societies of the Caribbean*, 105–37. London: UNESCO Publishing / Macmillan Education.

Eltis, David, and David Richardson. 2010. *Atlas of the Transatlantic Slave Trade*. New Haven: Yale University Press.

Enders, Armelle. 1997. *História da Africa Lusófona*. Lisbon: Mem. Martins, Editorial Inquérito.

Engerman, Stanley L. 2012. "Institutional Change." *Journal of Comparative Economics* 40(4): 596–603.

Engerman, Stanley L., and B. W. Higman. 1997. "The Slave Economies of the Caribbean: Structure, Performance, Evolution and Significance." In Franklin W. Knight (ed.), *General History of the Caribbean*, vol. 3, *The Slave Societies of the Caribbean*, 45–104. London: UNESCO Publishing / Macmillan Education.

Engerman, Stanley, Elisa V. Mariscal, and Kenneth L. Sokoloff. 2009. "The Evolution of Schooling in the Americas, 1800–1925." In David Eltis, Frank D. Lewis, and Kenneth L. Sokoloff (eds.), *Human Capital and Institutions: A Long-Run View*, 93–142. Cambridge: Cambridge University Press.

Engerman, Stanley, and Kenneth L. Sokoloff. 2011. *Economic Development in the Americas since 1500: Endowments and Institutions*. Cambridge: Cambridge University Press.

Englebert, Pierre. 2000. *State Legitimacy and Development in Africa*. Boulder, CO: Lynne Rienner.

Eriksen, Thomas H. 1998. *Common Denominators: Ethnicity, Nation-Building and Compromise in Mauritius*. Oxford: Berg.

Ertman, Thomas. 2010. "The Great Reform Act of 1832 and British Democratization." *Comparative Political Studies* 43(8/9): 1000–22.

Etherington, Norman. 2005. *Missions and Empire*. New York: Oxford University Press.

Evans, Peter. 1996. "Government Action, Social Capital and Development: Reviewing the Evidence on Synergy." *World Development* 24(6): 1119–32.

Evora, Roselma. 2004. *Cabo Verde: A abertura política e a transição para a democracia*. Cidade da Praia: Spleen Edições.

Eyre, Edward. 1865. "Letter of Governor Eyre to Secretary of State, Edward Cardwell." December 22. UK National Archives, CO 137/396.

Fails, Matthew, and Jonathan Krieckhaus. 2010. "Colonialism, Property Rights, and Modern World Income Distribution." *British Journal of Political Science* 40: 487–508.

Falola, Toyin. 1999. *The History of Nigeria*. Westport, CT: Greenwood Press.

Fanthorpe, Richard. 2001. "Neither Citizen nor Subject: 'Lumpen' Agency and the Legacy of Native Administration in Sierra Leone." *African Affairs* 100(400): 363–86.

Farmer, Paul. 1994. *The Uses of Haiti*. Monroe, ME: Common Courage Press.

Fearon, James, and David K. Laitin. 2006. "Jamaica: Random Narratives." Unpublished Manuscript.

Ferguson, Niall. 2003. *Empire: The Rise and Demise of the British World Order and the Lessons for Global Power*. London: Basic Books.

Fernandes, Tiago. 2015. "Rethinking Pathways to Democracy: Civil Society in Portugal and Spain, 1960s–2000s." *Democratization* 22(6): 1074–104.

Ferreira, Eduardo de Sousa. 1974. *Portuguese Colonialism in Africa: The End of an Era*. Paris: UNESCO.

Ferrer, Ada. 2014. *Freedom's Mirror: Cuba and Haiti in the Age of Revolutions*. New York: Cambridge University Press.

Feyrer, James, and Bruce Sacerdote. 2009. "Colonialism and Modern Income: Islands as Natural Experiments." *Review of Economics and Statistics* 91(2): 245–62.

Fintel, Dieter von, and Johan Fourie. 2019. "The Great Divergence in South Africa: Population and Wealth Dynamics over Two Centuries." *Journal of Comparative Economics* 47(4): 759–73.

Fish, Steven. 2002. "Islam and Authoritarianism." *World Politics* 55(1): 4–37.

Fish, Steven. 2011. *Are Muslims Distinctive? A Look at the Evidence*. Oxford: Oxford University Press.

Fishman, Robert. 2018. *Democratic Practice: Origins of the Iberian Divide in Political Inclusion*. Oxford: Oxford University Press.

Fonseca, Jorge C. 2007. *Cabo Verde: Três Décadas Depois*. Praia: Direito e Cidadania.

Forrest, Joshua. 1992. *Guinea-Bissau: Power, Conflict, and Renewal in a West African Nation*. Boulder, CO: Westview Press.

Forrest, Joshua. 2002. "Guinea-Bissau." In Patrick Chabal (ed.), *A History of Postcolonial Lusophone Africa*, 236–62. Bloomington: Indiana University Press.

Forrest, Joshua. 2003. *Lineages of State Fragility: Rural Civil Society in Guinea-Bissau*. Oxford: James Currey.

Forrest, Joshua. 2010. "Anatomy of State Fragility: The Case of Guinea-Bissau." In Neclâ Tschirgi, Michael S. Lund, and Francesco Mancini (eds.), *Security and Development: Searching for Critical Connections*, 171–210. Boulder, CO: Lynne Rienner.

Fortin, Jessica. 2012. "Is There a Necessary Condition for Democracy? The Role of State Capacity in Post-communist Communist Countries." *Comparative Political Studies* 45(7): 903–30.

France, Archives d'Outre-Mer. 1857. "Instruction Publique—Organisation de l'instruction primaire obligatoire. Correspondance, textes législatives, délibérations du Conseil privé, 1853–1857." FM/SG/Gua185/1131.

France, Archives d'Outre-Mer. 1869a. "Régime Politique des Colonies: Rapport au Ministre, 24 Mai 1869." FM/GEN/C224, d.1612.

France, Archives d'Outre-Mer. 1869b. "Régime Politique des Colonies: Note au Suffrage Universel, Paris, Décembre 1869." FM/GEN/C224, d.1612.

France, Archives d'Outre-Mer. 1870a. "Restoration de Droit Politiques aux Colonies." *Gazette Officiel de la Guadeloupe, 1 Octobre 1870.* BIB/AOM/50079/1870.

France, Archives d'Outre-Mer. 1870b. "Circulaire de M. Leon Gambetta, 11 Octobre 1870." *Gazette Officiel de la Guadeloupe.* BIB/AOM/50079/1870.

France, Archives d'Outre-Mer. 1870c. "Gouvernement de la Guadeloupe: Élections à la Constituante." *Gazette Officiel de la Guadeloupe, 5 Novembre 1870.* BIB/AOM/50079/1870.

France, Archives d'Outre-Mer. 1871. "Comité Colonial de Bordeaux: Pétition Envoyée à l'Assemblé Nationale, 21 Mars 1871." FM/GEN/C267/d.1844.

France, Archives d'Outre-Mer. 1880. "Application aux Colonies du Nouveau Plan d'étude adopté en Métropole, Septembre–Octobre 1880." FM/AFFPOL1/2519/1.

France, Archives d'Outre-Mer. 1885. "Guadeloupe, Naturalisation des Immigrants Africains." FM/SG/Gua107/754.

France, Archives d'Outre-Mer. 1898. "Décret du 24 mai, 1898." FM/AFFPOL1/2519/3.

France, Assemblé Nationale. 2019. "Basse de Données des Députés Français depuis 1789." http://www2.assemblee-nationale.fr/sycomore/recherche. Accessed November 15, 2019.

France, Ministère de la France Outre-Mer. 1949. *Annuaire Statistique de l'Union Française Outre-Mer, 1939–46.* Paris: Imprimerie Nationale de France.

France, Ministère des Colonies. 1944. *Annuaire Statistique des Possessions Françaises: Années Antérieures à la Guerre.* Paris: Imprimerie Nationale Française.

France, Services des Statistiques d'Outre-Mer. 1960. *Outre-Mer, 1958: Tableau Économique et Social des États et Territoires d'Outre-mer à la veille de la mise en place des nouvelles institutions.* Paris: Presses Universitaires de France.

Frankema, Ewout. 2012. "The Origins of Formal Education in Sub-Saharan Africa: Was British Rule More Benign?" *European Review of Economic History* 16(4): 335–55.

Frymer, Paul. 1999. *Uneasy Alliances: Race and Party Alliances in America.* Princeton, NJ: Princeton University Press.

Frynas, Jedrzej and Geoffry Wood. 2001. "Oil and War in Angola." *Review of African Political Economy* 28(90): 587–606.

Fujiwara, Thomas, Humberto Laudares, and Felipe C. Valencia. 2019. "Tordesillas, Slavery and the Origins of Brazilian Inequality." UC-Davis Economics Working Paper, https://economics.ucdavis.eu/events/papers/copy_of_416Valencia.pdf.

Fyfe, Christopher. 1967. *A Short History of Sierra Leone.* London: Longman Press.

Fyfe, Christopher. 1973. "Reform in West Africa: The Abolition of the Slave Trade." In J. F. A. Ajayi and Michael Crowder (eds.), *History of West Africa*, vol. 2, 30–56. New York: Columbia University Press.

Gaffield, Julia. 2015. *Haitian Connections in the Atlantic World: Recognition after Revolution*. Chapel Hill: North Carolina University Press.

Gallego, Francisco, and Miriam Bruhn. 2012. "Good, the Bad and Ugly Colonial Activities: Do They Matter for Economic Development?" *Review of Economics and Statistics* 94(2): 433–61.

Gallego, Francisco, and Robert D. Woodberry. 2010. "Christian Missionaries and Education in Former African Colonies: How Competition Mattered." *Journal of African Economies* 19(3): 294–329.

García-Ponce, Omar, and Leonard Wantchekon. n.d. (Forthcoming). "Critical Junctures: Independence Movements and Democracy in Africa." *American Journal of Political Science*.

Gardín, Carlos. 2010. "Race and Income Distribution: Evidence from the US, Brazil, and South Africa." Society for the Study of Economic Inequality, Working Paper 2010-179.

Geertz, Clifford. 1973. *The Interpretation of Cultures: Selected Essays*. New York: Basic Books.

Gelders, V. 1954. "Native Political Organization in Ruanda-Urundi." *Civilisations* 4(1): 125–32.

Gellar, Sheldon. 2005. *Democracy in Senegal: Tocquevilian Analytics in Senegal*. New York: Palgrave Macmillan.

George, Alexander L., and Andrew Bennett. 2005. *Case Studies and Theory Development in the Social Sciences*. Cambridge, MA: MIT Press.

Gerring, John, Daniel Ziblatt, Johan Van Gorp, and Julián Arévalo. 2011. "An Institutional Theory of Direct and Indirect Rule." *World Politics* 63(3): 377–433.

Gerring, John, Strom Thacker and Rodrigo Alfaro. 2012. "Democracy and Human Development." *Journal of Politics* 74(1): 1–17.

Gerring, John. 2016. *Case Study Research: Principles and Practices*. New York: Cambridge University Press.

Geschiere, Peter. 1993. "Chiefs and Colonial Rule in Cameroon: Inventing Chieftaincy, French and British Style." *Africa* 63(2): 151–75.

Getachew, Adom. 2019. *Worldmaking after Empire: The Rise and Fall of Self-Determination*. Princeton, NJ: Princeton University Press.

Gibson, Edward L. 2012. *Boundary Control: Subnational Authoritarianism in Federal Democracies*. New York: Cambridge University Press.

Girard, Philippe. 2019. "Making Freedom Work: The Long Transition from Slavery to Freedom during the Haitian Revolution." *Slavery & Abolition* 40(1): 87–108.

Girolet, Anne. 2000. *Victor Schoelcher, Abolitioniste et Républicain: Approche Juridique et Politique de l'ouevre d'un Fondateur de la République*. Paris: Éditions Karthala.

Girolet, Anne. 2001. "The Insufficiencies of Legal Assimilation for Economic and Social Integration in the French Colonies in the 19th Century." Paper presented at "The Legacy of Colonization and Decolonization in Europe and the Americas," Center of Social History of the 20th Century, University of Paris, Pantheon-Sorbonne, June 22–23.

Glaeser, Edward L, Giacomo Ponzetto, and Andrei Schleifer. 2007. "Why Does Democracy Need Education?" *Journal of Economic Growth* 12(2): 1–24.

Goldsmith, Arthur. 1999. "Africa's Overgrown State Reconsidered: Bureaucracy and Economic Growth." *World Politics* 51(4): 520–46.

González, Francisco E., and Desmond King. 2004. "The State and Democratization: The United States in Comparative Perspective." *British Journal of Political Science* 34(2): 193–210.

Grantham, Dewey W. 1988. *The Life and Death of the Solid South: A Political History.* Lexington, KY: The University Press of Kentucky.

Great Britain, Colonial Office. 1931. *Colonial Reports, Annual, 1930–31.* London: His Majesty's Stationery Office.

Great Britain, Colonial Office. 1933. *Annual Report for the Solomon Islands, 1932.* London: His Majesty's Stationery Office.

Great Britain, Colonial Office. 1938. *Report by His Majesty's Government in the United Kingdom of Great Britain and Northern Ireland to the Council of the League of Nations on the Administration of Palestine and Trans-Jordan for the Year 1937.* London: His Majesty's Stationery Office.

Greene, Jack. 2016. "The Transfer of British Liberty to the West Indies, 1627–1865." In Jack Greene (ed.), *Exclusionary Empire: English Liberty Overseas, 1600–1900,* 50–76. Cambridge: Cambridge University Press.

Grier, Robin. 1997. "The Effect of Religion on Economic Development: A Cross-National Study of 63 Former Colonies." *Kyklos* 50(1): 47–62.

Grier, Robin. 1999. "Colonial Legacies and Economic Growth." *Public Choice* 98(3–4): 317–35.

Griffin, Clifford E. 1997. *Democracy and Neoliberalism in the Developing World: Lessons from the Anglophone Caribbean.* Aldershot, UK: Ashgate.

Guiné. 1910. Estatísticas Gerais, 1907–1910. Lisbon: Arquivo Histórico Ultramarino, AHU/ACL/SEMU/DGU/3R/Cx.8.

Guiné, Provincia da. 1972. *Mapa Resumo do Apuramento dos Resultados do Acto Eleitoral de 16 de Janeiro 1972, Para a Eleição do Deputado à Assembeia Nacional.* Lisbon: Assembleia Nacional de Portugal.

Habyarimana, James, Marcartan Humphreys, Daniel Posner, and Jeremy M. Weinstein. 2007. "Why Does Ethnic Diversity Undermine Public Goods Provision." *American Political Science Review* 101(4): 709–25.

Hadenius, Axel and Jon Teorrell. 2005. "Cultural and Economic Prerequisites of Democracy: Reassessing Recent Evidence." *Studies in Comparative International Development* 39(4): 87–106.

Hadenius, Axel. 1992. *Democracy and Development.* Cambridge: Cambridge University Press.

Hailey, William M., Lord. 1950. *Native Administration in the British African Territories.* London: His Majesty's Stationary Office.

Hailey, William M., Lord. 1957. *An African Survey.* New York: Oxford University Press.

Hall, Catherine. 1994. "Rethinking Imperial Histories: The Reform Act of 1867." *New Left Review* 1(208): 3–29.

Hall, Catherine. 2002. *Civilising Subjects: Metropole and Colony in the English Imagination, 1830–1867.* Chicago: University of Chicago Press.

Hall, Douglas. 1969/1959. *Free Jamaica, 1838–1865: An Economic History.* New Haven: Yale University Press.

Hall, Douglas. 1978. "The Flight from the Estates Reconsidered: The British West Indies, 1838–42." *Journal of Caribbean History* 10–11: 7–24.

Hall, Peter. 2010. "Historical Institutionalism in Rationalist and Sociological Perspective." In James Mahoney and Kathleen Thelen (eds.), *Explaining Institutional Change: Ambiguity, Agency and Power,* 204–23. New York: Cambridge University Press.

Hanson, Steven. 2010. "The Founding of the French Third Republic." *Comparative Political Studies* 43(8–9): 1023–58.

Harris, David. 2014. *Sierra Leone: A Political History*. New York: Oxford University Press.

Harrison, Lawrence E. 2006. *The Central Liberal Truth: How Politics Can Change a Culture and Save It from Itself*. New York: Oxford University Press.

Hart, Richard. 1998. *From Occupation to Independence: A Short History of the Peoples of the English-Speaking Caribbean Region*. London: Pluto Press.

Hassan, Hamdy A. 2009. "The Comoros and the Crisis of Building a National State." *Contemporary Arab Affairs* 2(2): 229–39.

Heath, Elizabeth. 2011. "Creating Rural Citizens in Guadeloupe in the Early Third French Republic." *Slavery and Abolition* 32(2): 289–307.

Herbst, Jeffrey. 2000. *States and Power in Africa: Comparative Lessons in Authority and Control*. Princeton, NJ: Princeton University Press.

Hill, Richard, John Dixon, and Mariela Rodriguez. 2011. *The Marcus Garvey and Universal Negro Improvement Association Papers*. Vol. 11, *The Caribbean Diaspora, 1910–20*. Durham, NC: Duke University Press.

Hochschild, Adam. 1998. *King Leopold's Ghost: A Story of Greed, Terror, and Heroism in Colonial Africa*. Boston: Mariner Books.

Hodges, Tony. 1977. "Cape Verde under the PAIGC." *Africa Report* 22(3): 43–47.

Hoefte, Rosemarijn. 1998. *In Place of Slavery: A Social History of British Indian and Javanese Laborers in Suriname*. Gainesville: University Press of Florida.

Holt, Thomas C. 1992. *The Problem of Freedom: Race, Labor, and Politics in Jamaica and Britain, 1832–1938*. Baltimore: Johns Hopkins University Press.

Horowitz, Donald. 2000. *Ethnic Groups in Conflict*. Berkeley: University of California Press.

Horowitz, Michael M. 1960. "Metropolitan Influences in the Caribbean: The French Antilles." *Annals of the New York Academy of Sciences* 83: 802–8.

Howard, Christopher. 2017. *Thinking Like a Political Scientist: A Practical Guide to Research Methods*. Chicago: University of Chicago Press.

Howard, Marc M. 2009. *The Politics of Citizenship in Europe*. Cambridge: Cambridge University Press.

Howard, Marc M. 2017. *Unusually Cruel: Prisons, Punishment, and the Real American Exceptionalism*. Oxford: Oxford University Press.

Hsin-Chi, Kuan and Lau Siu-Kai. 2002. "Between Liberal Autocracy and Democracy: Democratic Legitimacy in Hong Kong." *Democratization* 9(4): 58–76.

Hunter, Wendy, Leila Patel, and Natasha Borges-Sugiyama. 2020. "How Family and Child Cash Transfers Can Empower Women: Comparative Lessons from Brazil and South Africa." *Global Social Policy* 21(2): 1–20.

Huntington, Samuel J. 1984. "Will More Countries Become Democratic?" *Political Science Quarterly* 99(2): 193–218.

Huntington, Samuel J. 1991. *The Third Wave: Democratization in the Late Twentieth Century*. Norman: University of Oklahoma Press.

Huntington, Samuel J. 1993. "The Clash of Civilizations?" *Foreign Affairs* 72(3): 22–49.

Hurwitz, Samuel J., and Edith F. Hurwitz. 1971. *Jamaica: A Historical Portrait*. New York: Praeger.

Hutchcroft, Paul D. 2000. "Colonial Masters, National Politicos, and Provincial Lords: Central Authority and Local Autonomy in the American Philippines, 1900–1913." *Journal of Asian Studies* 59(2): 277–306.

Ibekwe, Chinweizu. 1975. *The West and the Rest of Us: White Predators, Black Slavers, and the African Elite*. New York: Random House.

Idowu, H. O. 1968. "The Establishment of Elective Institutions in Senegal 1869–1880." *Journal of African History* 9(2): 261–77.

Iliffe, John. 2007. *Africans: The History of a Continent.* 2nd ed. Cambridge: Cambridge University Press.

Jamaica [Colony of]. 1838. Jamaica Blue Book, 1838. UK National Archives, CO 142/52.

Jamaica [Colony of]. 1858. Jamaica Blue Book, 1851. UK National Archives, CO 142/65.

Jamaica [Colony of]. 1865. Jamaica Blue Book, 1865. UK National Archives, CO 142/79.

Jamaica [Colony of]. 1885. Jamaica Blue Book, 1884. UK National Archives, CO 142/98.

Jamaica [Colony of]. 1901. Jamaica Blue Book, 1900–01. UK National Archives, CO 142/114.

Jamaica [Colony of]. 1914. Jamaica Blue Book, 1913–1914. UK National Archives, CO 142/127.

Jamaica [Colony of]. 1929. Jamaica Blue Book, 1928. UK National Archives, CO 142/142.

Jamaica. 1948a. *Colonial Office Annual Report on Jamaica for the Year 1946.* London: Her Majesty's Stationery Office.

Jamaica [Colony of]. 1948b. Jamaica Blue Book, 1945. UK National Archives, CO 142/142.

Jamaica. 1956. *Colonial Office Report on Jamaica for the Year 1955.* London: Her Majesty's Stationery Office.

Jamaica. 1965. *Report for the Year 1961.* London: Her Majesty's Stationery Office.

Jamaica Royal Gazette. 1834. UK National Archives, CO 141/29.

Jamaica Royal Gazette and Times. 1838. UK National Archives, CO 141/32.

James, C. L. R. 1989. *The Black Jacobins: Toussaint L'Ouverture and the San Domingo Revolution.* 2nd ed. New York: Vintage Books.

Janoski, Thomas. 2010. *The Ironies of Citizenship: Naturalization and Integration in Industrialized Countries.* Cambridge: Cambridge University Press.

Jaspan, M. A. 1965. "In Quest of New Law: The Perplexity of Legal Syncretism in Indonesia." *Comparative Studies in Society and History* 7(3): 252–66.

Jennings, Eric. 2001. *Vichy in the Tropics: Pétain's National Revolution in Madagascar, Guadeloupe and Indochina.* Stanford, CA: Stanford University Press.

Jennings, Eric. 2015. *Free French Africa in World War Two: The African Resistance.* New York: Cambridge University Press.

Jennings, Laurence. 2000. *French Anti-slavery: The Movement for the Abolition of Slavery in France, 1802–1848.* New York: Cambridge University Press.

Joshi, Sharmila. 2005. "Theories of Development: Modernization vs. Dependency." http://infochangeindia.org/defining-developments/theories-of-development-modernisation-vs-dependency.html. Accessed November 30, 2016.

Johnson, G. W. 1971. *The Emergence of Black Politics in Senegal: The Struggle for Power in the Four Communes, 1900–20.* Stanford: Stanford University Press.

Kale, Madhavi. 1998. *Fragments of Empire: Capital, Slavery, and Indian Indentured Labour Migration in the British Caribbean.* Philadelphia: University of Pennsylvania Press.

Kantrowitz, Rachel. 2018. "Catholic Schools as 'a Nation in Miniature': Catholic Civism in Senegal and Benin." *Journal of African History* 59(2): 221–39.

Karp, Matthew. 2016. *This Vast Southern Empire: Slaveholders at the Helm of American Foreign Policy.* Cambridge, MA: Harvard University Press.

Key, V. O. 1949. *Southern Politics in State and Nation.* New York: A. A. Knopf.

Khan, Wasiq N. 2010. "Economic Growth and Decline in Comparative Perspective: Haiti and the Dominican Republic." *Journal of Haitian Studies* 16(1): 112–25.

Khan, Wasiq N. 2010. "Economic Growth and Decline in Comparative Perspective: Haiti and the Dominican Republic, 1930–86." *Journal of Haitian Studies* 16(1): 112–25.

Kilson, Martin. 1969. *Political Change in a West African State: A Study of the Modernization Process in Sierra Leone.* Cambridge, MA: Harvard University Press.

King, Elisabeth. 2014. *From Classrooms to Conflict in Rwanda.* New York: Cambridge University Press.

Kingstone, Peter R., and Aldo F. Ponce. 2010. "From Cardoso to Lula: The Triumph of Pragmatism in Brazil." In Kurt Weyland, Raúl Madrid, and Wendy Hunter (eds.), *Leftist Governments in Latin America: Successes and Shortcomings*, 98-123. New York: Cambridge University Press.

Kirk-Greene, Anthony. 1995. "Le Roi est mort! Vive le roi: The Comparative Legacy of Chiefs after the Transfer of Power in British and French West Africa." In Anthony Kirk-Green and Daniel Bach (eds.), *State and Society in Francophone Africa since Independence,* 16-33. New York: St. Martin's Press.

Klingberg, Frank J. 1939. "The Lady Mico Charity Schools in the British West Indies." *Journal of Negro History* 24(3): 291–344.

Knight, Franklin W. 1997. "The Disintegration of the Caribbean Slave Systems." In Franklin W. Knight (ed.), *General History of the Caribbean*, vol. 3, *The Slave Societies of the Caribbean,* 322-45. London: UNESCO Publishing / Macmillan Education.

Kohli, Atul. 2004. *State-Directed Development: Political Power and Industrialization in the Global Periphery.* Cambridge: Cambridge University Press.

Kohli, Atul. 2020. *Imperialism and the Developing World: How Britain and the United States Shaped the Global Periphery.* New York: Oxford University Press.

Koudawo, Fafali. 2001. *Cabo Verde e Guiné-Bissau: Democracia Revolucionária à Democracia Liberal.* Bissau: Instituto Nacional de Estudos e Pesquisa.

Krieckhaus, Jonathan. 2006. *Dictating Development: How Europe Shaped the Global Periphery.* Pittsburgh: University of Pittsburgh Press.

Kup, Alexander P. 1975. *A Concise History of Sierra Leone.* New York: St. Martin's Press.

Kuran, Timur. 2012. *The Long Divergence: How Islamic Law Held the Middle East Back.* Princeton, NJ: Princeton University Press.

Kurtz, Marcus J. 2009. "The Social Foundations of Institutional Order: Reconsidering War and the 'Resource Curse' in Third World State Building." *Politics and Society* 37(4): 479–520.

Kurtz, Marcus J. 2013. *Latin American State-Building in Comparative Perspective: Social Foundations of Institutional Order.* New York: Cambridge University Press.

La Porta, Rafael, Florencio Shleifer, Andrei Shleifer, and Robert W. Vishny. 1998. "Law and Finance." *Journal of Political Economy* 106(6): 1113–55.

La Porta, Rafael, Florencio Shleifer, Andrei Shleifer, and Robert W. Vishny. 1999. "The Quality of Government." *Journal of Law, Economics and Organization* 15(1): 222–79.

Laitin, David, and Rajesh Ramachandran. 2016. "Language Policy and Human Development." *American Political Science Review* 110(3): 457–80.

Laitin, David. 1986. *Hegemony and Culture: Politics and Religious Change among the Yoruba.* Chicago: University of Chicago Press.

Landes, David S. 1998. *The Wealth and Poverty of Nations: Why Some Nations are so Rich and Some So Poor.* New York: Norton.

Lange, Matthew K. 2003. "Structural Holes and Structural Synergies: A Comparative-Historical Analysis of State-Society Relations and Development in Colonial Sierra Leone and Mauritius." *International Journal of Comparative Sociology* 44(4): 372–407.

Lange, Matthew K. 2004. "British Colonial Legacies and Political Development." *World Development* 32(6): 905–22.

Lange, Matthew K. 2005. "British Colonial State Legacies and Developmental Trajectories: A Statistical Analysis of Direct and Indirect Rule." In Matthew K. Lange and Dietrich Rueschemeyer (eds.), *States and Development: Historical Antecedents of Stagnation and Advance*, 117–39. London: Palgrave Macmillan.

Lange, Matthew K. 2009. *Lineages of Despotism and Development: British Colonialism and State Power*. Chicago: University of Chicago Press.

Lange, Matthew K. 2012. *Educations in Ethnic Violence: Identity, Educational Bubbles and Resource Mobilization*. New York: Cambridge University Press.

Lange, Matthew K. 2013. *Comparative-Historical Methods*. London: Sage.

Lange, Matthew K,, and Andrew Dawson. 2009. "Dividing and Ruling the World: A Statistical Test of the Effects of Colonialism on Postcolonial Civil Violence." *Social Forces* 88(2): 785–817.

Lange, Matthew K., James Mahoney, and Matthias Vom Hau. 2006. "Colonialism and Development: A Comparative Analysis of Spanish and British Colonies." *American Journal of Sociology* 111(5): 1412–62.

Langer, Lorenz. 2007. "The Elusive Aim of Universal Suffrage: Constitutional Developments in Hong Kong." *International Journal of Constitutional Law* 5(3): 419–52.

Lankina, Tomila, and Lullit Getachew. 2012. "Mission or Empire, Word or Sword? The Human Capital Legacy in Postcolonial Democratic Development." *American Journal of Political Science* 56(2): 465–83.

Lankina, Tomila, and Lullit Getachew. 2013. "Competitive Religious Entrepreneurs: Christian Missionaries and Female Education in Colonial and Postcolonial India." *British Journal of Political Science* 43(1): 103–31.

Larcher, Silyane. 2014. *l'autre citoyen: L'idéal republican et les Antilles après l'esclavage*. Paris: Armand Colin.

Larmour, Peter. 1994. "A Foreign Flower? Democracy in the South Pacific." *Pacific Studies* 17(1): 45–77.

Latimer, James. 1964. "The Apprenticeship System in the British West Indies." *Journal of Negro Education* 32(4): 52–57.

Latimer, James. 1965. "The Foundations of Religious Education in the British West Indies." *Journal of Negro Education* 34(4): 453–42.

Lawrence, Adria K. 2013. *Imperial Rule and the Politics of Nationalism: Anti-colonial Protest in the French Empire*. New Yor: Cambridge University Press.

Lawrence, Adria K. 2020. "Colonial State Formation: Direct Rule, Indirect Rule, and State Violence in Algeria." Paper presented at "Sixty Years after Independence: Rethinking France's Colonial Legacy," Villanova University.

Ledgister, F. S. J. 1998. *Class Alliances and the Liberal-Authoritarian State: The Roots of Post-colonial Democracy in Jamaica, Trinidad & Tobago, and Suriname*. Trenton, NJ: Africa World Press.

Lee, Alexander. 2019. "Land, State Capacity and Colonialism: Evidence from India." *Comparative Political Studies* 52(3): 412–44.

Lee, Alexander, and Jack Paine. 2019a. "British Colonialism and Democracy: Divergent Inheritances and Diminishing Legacies." *Journal of Comparative Economics* 47(3): 487–503.

Lee, Alexander, and Jack Paine. 2019b. "What Were the Consequences of Decolonization?" *International Studies Quarterly* 63(2): 406–16.

Lemière, Sophie. 2018. "The Downfall of Malaysia's Ruling Party." *Journal of Democracy* 29(4): 114–28.

Levy, Andrea. 2010. *The Long Song*. New York: Farrar, Straus and Giroux.

Lewis, Martin D. 1962. "One Hundred Million Frenchmen: The 'Assimilation' Theory in French Colonial Policy." *Comparative Studies in Society and History* 4(2): 129–53.

Lieberman, Evan. 2005. "Nested Analysis as a Mixed-Method Strategy for Comparative Research." *American Political Science Review* 99(3): 435–52.

Lieberman, Evan, and Prerna Singh. 2012. "The Institutional Origins of Ethnic Violence." *Comparative Politics* 45(1): 1–23.

Lindberg, Staffan. 2003. "It's Our Time to 'Chop': Do Elections in Africa Feed Neo-Patrimonialism Rather than Counter-Act It? *Democratization* 10(2): 121–40.

Lindberg, Staffan. 2006. *Democracy and Elections in Africa*. Baltimore: Johns Hopkins University Press.

Lindberg, Staffan. 2009. *Democratization by Elections: A New Mode of Transition*. Baltimore: Johns Hopkins University Press.

Linz, Juan J., and Alfred Stepan. 1996. *Problems of Democratic Transition and Consolidation: Southern Europe, South America and Post-communist Europe*. Baltimore: Johns Hopkins University Press.

Lipset, Seymour M. 1959. "Some Social Requisites of Democracy: Economic Development and Political Legitimacy." *American Political Science Review* 53(1): 69–105.

Lipset, Seymour M., Kyoung-Ryung Seong, and John C. Torres. 1993. "A Comparative Analysis of the Social Requisites of Democracy." *International Social Science Journal* 45: 155–75.

Livramento, José Luis. 2007. "Cabo Verde: 30 Anos de Educação." In Jorge Carlos Fonseca (ed.), *Cabo Verde: Três Décadas Depois*, 391–412. Praia: Direito e Cidadania.

Logan, Rayford W. 1930. "Education in Haiti." *Journal of Negro History* 15(4): 401–60.

Louisiana State Penitentiary. 2019. *Angola Museum at the Louisiana State Penitentiary*. https://www.angolamuseum.org/history-of-angola. Accessed November 30, 2022.

Lowenthal, David. 1995. "The Wayward Leewards." In Karen F. Olwig (ed.), *Small Islands, Large Questions: Society, Culture and Resistance in the Post-Emancipation Caribbean*, 179–87. London: Frank Cass.

Lowry, Richard. 2019. "Five Things They Don't Tell You about Slavery." *National Review* (April 4, 2019). https://www.nationalreview.com/2019/09/five-things-they-dont-tell-you-about-slavery/. Accessed November 30, 2022.

Lugard, Frederick. 1922. *The Dual Mandate in British Tropical Africa*. London: W. Blackwood and Sons.

Lyall, Archibald. 1938. *Black and White Make Brown: An Account of a Journey to the Cape Verde Islands and Portuguese Guinea*. London: William Heinemann.

Macqueen, Norrie. 1999. "Portugal's First Domino: 'Pluricontinentalism' and Colonial War in Guiné-Bissau, 1963–74." *Contemporary European History* 8(2): 209–30.

Maddison, Angus. 2006. *The World Economy*. Paris: Development Center for the Organization of Economic Cooperation and Development.

Mahoney, James. 2001. *The Legacies of Liberalism: Path Dependence and Political Regimes in Central America*. Baltimore: Johns Hopkins University Press.

Mahoney, James. 2010. *Colonialism and Postcolonial Development: Spanish America in Comparative Perspective*. Cambridge: Cambridge University Press.

Mainwaring, Scott, and Aníbal Pérez-Liñan. 2013. *Democracies and Dictatorships in Latin America: Emergence, Survival, and Fall*. New York: Cambridge University Press.

Mair, Lucy. 1969. *Native Policies in Africa*. New York: Negro Universities Press.

Malvezzi, Aldobrandino. 1927. "Italian Colonies and Colonial Policy." *Journal of the Royal Institute of International Affairs* 6(4): 233–45.

Mamdani, Mahmood. 1996. *Citizen and Subject: Contemporary Africa and the Legacy of Late Colonialism*. Princeton, NJ: Princeton University Press.

Mamdani, Mahmood. 2001. "Beyond Settler and Native as Political Identities: Overcoming the Political Legacy of Colonialism." *Comparative Studies of Society and History* 43(4): 651–64.

Mamdani, Mahmood. 2002. *When Victims Become Killers: Colonialism, Nativism and the Genocide in Rwanda*. Princeton, NJ: Princeton University Press.

Mamdani, Mahmood. 2012. *Define and Rule: Native as Political Identity*. Cambridge, MA: Harvard University Press.

Mann, Gregory. 2009. "What Was the *Indigénat*? The 'Empire of Law' in French West Africa." *Journal of African History* 50(3): 331–53.

Manning, Sanchez. 2013. "Britain's Colonial Shame: Slave Owners Given Huge Payouts after Abolition." *Independent*, June 24. https://www.independent.co.uk/news/uk/home-news/britains-colonial-shame-slave-owners-given-huge-payouts-after-abolit ion-8508358.html.

Mark, Peter. 1999. "The Evolution of 'Portuguese' Identity: Luso-Africans on the Upper Guinea Coast from the Sixteenth to the Early Nineteenth Century." *Journal of African History* 40(2): 173–91.

Mark-Thiesen, Cassandra, and Moritz A. Milhatsch. 2019. "Liberia an(d) Empire? Sovereignty, 'Civilisation' and Commerce in Nineteenth-Century West Africa." *Journal of Imperial and Commonwealth History* 47(5): 884–911.

Marx, Anthony D. 1996. "Race-Making and the Nation-State." *World Politics* 48(2): 180–208.

Marx, Anthony D. 1998. *Making Race and Nation: A Comparison of the United States, South Africa, and Brazil*. Cambridge: Cambridge University Press.

Mazrui, Ali. 1983. "Francophone Nations and English-Speaking States: Imperial Ethnicity and African Political Formation." In Donald Rotchild and Victor A. Olorunsola (eds.), *State versus Ethnic Claims: African Policy Dilemma*, 25–43. Boulder, CO: Westview Press.

McCloy, Shelby T. 1966. *The Negro in the French West Indies*. Lexington: University of Kentucky Press.

McDougall, James. 2017. *A History of Algeria*. New York: Cambridge University Press.

Mendes, Carmen Amado. 2013. *Portugal, China and the Macau Negotiations, 1986–99*. Hong Kong: University of Hong Kong Press, 2013.

Mentel, Diedre. 1984. *Race, Culture and Portuguese Colonialism in Cabo Verde*. Syracuse, NY: Maxwell School of Citizenship and Public Affairs.

Mendez, Juan E., Guillermo O'Donnell, and Paulo Sergio Pinheiro. 1999. *The (Un)Rule of Law and the Underprivileged in Latin America*. Notre Dame, IN: University of Notre Dame Press.

Meredith, Martin. 2005. *The Fate of Africa: From the Hopes of Freedom to the Heart of Despair. A History of Fifty Years of Independence*. New York: Public Affairs.

Merle, Isabelle. 2002. "Retour sur le regime de l'indigénat: Genèse et contradictions des principes repressifs dans l'empire français." *French Politics, Culture, and Society* 20(2): 77–97.

Metz, Helen C. 1995. *Indian Ocean: Five Island Countries*. Lanham, MD: Bernan.

Meyer, John W., Francisco O. Ramírez, and Yasemin N. Soysal. 1992. "World Expansion of Mass Education." *Sociology of Education* 65(2): 128–49.

Meyns, Peter. 2002. "Cape Verde: An African Exception." *Journal of Democracy* 13(3): 153–65.

Migdal, Joel S. 1988. *Strong States and Weak Societies*. New York: Cambridge University Press.

Miles, William F. 1985. *Elections and Ethnicity in French Martinique: A Paradox in Paradise*. New York: Praeger.

Mukherjee, Shivaji. 2018. "Historical Legacies of Colonial Indirect Rule: Princely States and Maoist Insurgency in Central India." *World Development* 111(1): 113–29.

Muller, Siegfried H. 1964. *The World's Living Languages: Basic Facts of Their Structure, Kinship, Location and Number of Speakers*. New York: Ungar.

Munasinghe, Viranjini. 2009. "Foretelling Ethnicity in Trinidad: The Post-emancipation Labor Problem." In Andrew Willford and Eric Tagliacozzo (eds.), *CLIO/ Anthropos: Exploring the Boundaries between History and Anthropology*, 139–82. Stanford, CA: Stanford University Press.

Munroe, Trevor, and Arnold Bertram. 2006. *Adult Suffrage and Political Administrations in Jamaica, 1944–2002*. Kingston, Jamaica: Ian Randle.

Munslow, Barry. 1981. "The 1980 Coup in Guinea-Bissau." *Review of African Political Economy* 21: 109–13.

Murch, Arvin. 1968. "Political Integration as an Alternative to Independence in the French Antilles." *American Sociological Review* 33(4): 544–62.

Murch, Arvin. 1971. *Black Frenchmen: The Political Integration of the French Antilles*. Cambridge, MA: Schenkman.

Naseemullah, Adnan, and Paul Staniland. 2016. "Indirect Rule and Varieties of Governance." *Governance* 29(1): 13–30.

Needell, Jeffrey D. 2014. "The State and Development under the Brazilian Monarchy." In Miguel A. Centeno and Augustin E. Ferraro (eds.)., *State and Nation Making in Latin America and the Caribbean: Republics of the Possible*, 79–99. Princeton: Princeton University Press.

Newitt, Malyn D. 1981. *Portugal in Africa: The Last Hundred Years*. Harlow, UK: Longman.

Nogueira da Silva, Cristina. 2011. "Political Representation and Citizenship under the Empire." In Fernando Cartoga and Pedro Tavares de Almeida (eds.), *Res Publica: Citizenship and Political Representation in Portugal, 1820–1926*, 90–111. Lisbon: Assembleia da República; Biblioteca Nacional de Portugal.

Noland, Marcus. 2005. "Religion and Economic Performance." *World Development* 33(8): 1215–32.

Northrup, David. 2000. "Indentured Indians in the French Antilles." *Revue Française d'Histoire d'Outre-mer* 87(326–27): 245–71.

Nunn, Nathan. 2008. "The Long-Term Effects of Africa's Slave Trades." *Quarterly Journal of Economics* 123(1): 139–76.

Nunn, Nathan. 2010. "Religious Conversion in Colonial Africa." *American Economic Review Papers & Proceedings* 100(2): 147–52.

Nunn, Nathan, and Leonard Wantchekon. 2011. "The Slave Trade and the Origins of Mistrust in Africa." *American Economic Review* 101(7): 3221–52.

O'Donnell, Guillermo. 1993. "On the State, Democratization, and Some Conceptual Problems: A Latin American View with Glances at Some Post-communist Countries." *World Development* 21(8): 1355–69.

O'Donnell, Guillermo. 2004. "Why the Rule of Law Matters." *Journal of Democracy* 15(4): 32–46.

O'Donnell, Guillermo. 2010. *Democracy, Agency, and the State: Theory with Comparative Intent.* Oxford: Oxford University Press.

O'Donnell, Guillermo, and Philippe Schmitter. 1986. *Transitions from Authoritarian Rule.* Vol. 4, *Tentative Conclusions about Uncertain Democracies.* Baltimore: Johns Hopkins University Press.

O'Laughlin, Bridgitte. 2000. "Class and the Customary: The Ambiguous Legacy of the *Indigenato* in Mozambique." *African Affairs* 99(394): 5–42.

O'Neill, Aaron. 2020. "Black and Slave Population in the United States, 1790–1880." *Statistica.* https://www.statista.com/statistics/1010169/black-and-slave-population-us-1790-1880/#:~:text=Of%20the%204.4%20million%20African,that%20they%20lived%20in%20slavery. Accessed October 25, 2022.

Okoye, Dozie, and Roland Pongou. 2014. "Historical Missionary Activity, Schooling and the Reversal of Fortunes: Evidence from Nigeria." MPRA Paper. https://mpra.ub.uni-muenchen.de/58052/.

Olsson, Ola. 2009. "On the Democratic Legacy of Colonialism." *Journal of Comparative Economics* 37(4): 534–51.

Ortmann, Stephan and Mark Thompson. 2016. "China and the Singapore Model." *Journal of Democracy* 27(1): 39–48.

Owolabi, Olukunle P. 2007. "Politics, Institutions and Ethnic Voting in Plural Democracies: Comparative Lessons from Trinidad & Tobago, Guyana and Mauritius." Paper presented at the Midwest Political Science Annual Meeting, Chicago, IL, April 12–15.

Owolabi, Olukunle P. 2010. "Forced Settlement, Colonial Occupation and Divergent Political Outcomes in the Developing World, 1946–2004." Paper presented at the American Political Science Association Annual Meeting, Washington, DC, September 2–5.

Owolabi, Olukunle P. 2014. "Colonialism, Development and Democratization: Beyond National Colonial Legacies." *APSA-Comparative Democratization Newsletter* 12(1): 2, 12–15.

Owolabi, Olukunle P. 2015. "Literacy and Democracy Despite Slavery: Forced Settlement and Postcolonial Outcomes in the Developing World." *Comparative Politics* 48(1): 43–66.

Owolabi, Olukunle P. 2017. "The Developmental Legacies of the Bifurcated Colonial State: Statistical Evidence from 67 Former British, French, and Portuguese Colonies." Kellogg Institute Working Paper No. 419.

Owolabi, Olukunle P., and Christopher G. Klosko. 2017. "Racial Threat, Electoral Alliances, and the Institutional Dynamics of Suffrage Expansion in the French Antilles, Jamaica, and the Southern United States." Paper presented at the American Political Science Association Annual Meeting, San Francisco, CA, August 31–September 3.

Packenham, Thomas. 1992. *The Scramble for Africa: The White Man's Quest for the Dark Continent from 1876 to 1912.* New York: Avon Books.

Padmore, George. 1969. *How Britain Rules Africa.* New York: Negro Universities Press.

Paine, Jack. 2019a. "Redistributive Political Transitions: Minority Rule and Liberation Wars in Colonial Africa." *Journal of Politics* 81(2): 505–23.

Paine, Jack. 2019b. "Democratic Contradictions in European Settler Colonies." *World Politics* 71(3): 542–85.

Paiva, Luis. 2016. "Poverty and Inequality Reduction in Brazil: A Parenthesis in History or the Road Ahead?" *Ibero-Americana* 45(1): 37–50.

Palagashvili, Liya. 2018. "African Chiefs: Comparative Governance under Colonial Rule." *Public Choice* 174: 277–300.

Palmer, Colin A. 1997. "The Slave Trade, African Slavers and the Demography of the Caribbean to 1740." In Franklin W. Knight (ed.), *General History of the Caribbean*, vol. 3, *The Slave Societies of the Caribbean*, 9–44. London: UNESCO Publishing / Macmillan Education.

Pamphile, Leon D. 1985. "America's Policy-Making in Haitian Education, 1915–1934." *Journal of Negro Education* 54(1): 99–108.

Papaioannou, Ellias, and Gregorious Siourounis. 2008. "Economic and Social Factors Driving the Third Wave of Democratization." *Journal of Comparative Economics* 36(3): 365–87.

Paracka, Danial J. 2002. "The Athens of West Africa: International Education at Fourah Bay College, 1814–2002." Paper presented at the Southeastern Regional Seminar in African Studies Conference, Georgia State University, March 22–23.

Paschel, Tianna S. 2018. *Becoming Black Political Subjects: Movements and Ethno-racial Rights in Colombia and Brazil*. Princeton, NJ: Princeton University Press.

Patinha, María da Piedade. 1999. *O Sistema Educativo na Republica da Guiné-Bissau: Contribuição para o Estudo da Política Educativa*. Lisbon: Universidade Técnica da Lisboa, Instituto Superior de Ciências Sociais e Politicas, Mestrado em Estudos Africanos.

Perham, Margery. 1937. *Native Administration in Nigeria*. London: Oxford University Press.

Peterson, John. 1969. *Province of Freedom: A History of Sierra Leone, 1787–1870*. Evanston, IL: Northwestern University Press.

Phillips, Anthony. 2008. "Haiti, France, and the Independence Debt of 1825." Institute for Justice and Democracy in Haiti. https://canada-haiti.ca/sites/default/files/Haiti,%20 France%20and%20the%20Independence%20Debt%20of%201825_0.pdf. Accessed October 6, 2017.

Pombo-Malta, António J. 2006. *História da Educação na Guiné Portuguesa, 1879–1974*. Lisbon: Universidade Técnica de Lisboa, Instituto Superior de Ciências Sociais e Politicas, Mestrado em Estudos Africanos.

Porter, Andrew. 2004. *Religion versus Empire*. Manchester: Manchester University Press.

Portugal, Assemleia de Apuramento Geral. 1953. "Assembleia de Apuramento Geral, Círculo No. 25: Guiné." Lisbon: Assembleia Nacional de Portugal.

Portugal, Assemleia de Apuramento Geral. 1957. "Assembleia de Apuramento Geral, Círculo No. 25: Guiné." Lisbon: Assembleia Nacional de Portugal.

Portugal, Assemleia de Apuramento Geral. 1961. "Mapa Resumo dos Resultados das Assembleias Eleitorais e Secções de Voto do Círculo da Guiné." Lisbon: Assembleia Nacional de Portugal.

Portugal, Assemleia de Apuramento Geral. 1965. "Mapa Resumo dos Resultados das Assembleias e Secções de voto do Círculo Eleitoral da Guiné." Lisbon: Assembleia Nacional de Portugal.

Portugal, Assemleia de Apuramento Geral. 1969. "Mapa Resumo dos Resultados das Assembleias e Secções de voto do Círculo da Guiné." Lisbon: Assembleia Nacional de Portugal.

Portugal, Instituto Nacional de Estatística. 1950. *Anuário Estatístico do Imperio Colonial, 1947 e 1948*. Lisbon: Tipografia Portuguesa, Lda.

Portugal, Instituto Nacional de Estatística. 1959. *Anuario Estatístico do Ultramar.* Lisbon: Bertrand Irmãos.

Portugal, Instituto Nacional de Estatística. 1960. *Anuário Estatístico do Ultramar, 1959.* Lisbon: Bertrand Irmãos.

Portugal, Instituto Nacional de Estatística. 1968. *Anuário Estatístico do Ultramar, 1958.* Lisbon: Bertrand Irmãos.

Portugal, Ministerio dos Negocios da Marinha e Ultramar. 1905. *Annuario Estatistico dos Dominios Ultramarinos Portugueses, 1899 e 1900.* Lisbon: Imprensa Nacional.

Posner, Daniel. 2003. "The Colonial Origins of Ethnic Cleavages: The Case of Linguistic Divisions in Zambia." *Comparative Politics* 35(2): 127–46.

Posner, Daniel. 2004. "The Political Salience of Cultural Difference: Why Chewas and Tumbukas Are Allies in Zambia and Adversaries in Malawi." *American Political Science Review* 98(4): 529–45.

Posner, Daniel. 2005. *Institutions and Ethnic Politics in Africa.* Cambridge: Cambridge University Press.

Premdas, Ralph. 2007. *Trinidad and Tobago: Ethnic Conflict, Inequality and Public Sector Governance.* Basingstoke: Palgrave Macmillan.

Przeworski, Adam, Michael A. Alvarez, José Antonio Cheibub, and Fernando Limongi. 2000. *Democracy and Development: Political Institutions and Well-Being in the World, 1950–1990.* Cambridge: Cambridge University Press.

Przeworski, Adam, et al. 2011. *Political Institutions and Political Events (PIPE) Dataset.* New York: New York University, Department of Politics.

Quality of Government. 2015. *Quality of Government Standard Dataset, Version Jan15,* University of Gothenburg: The Quality of Government Institute. http://www.qog.pol. gu.se.

Ramirez, Francisco, and John O. Boli. 1987. "The Political Construction of Mass Schooling: European Origins and Worldwide Institutionalization." *Sociology of Education* 60(1): 2–17.

Ray, Subhasish. 2018. "Beyond Divide and Rule: Explaining the Link between British Colonialism and Ethnic Violence." *Nationalism and Ethnic Politics* 24(4): 367–88.

Reed, Amber R. 2020. *Nostalgia after Apartheid: Disillusionment, Youth, and Democracy in South Africa.* Notre Dame, IN: University of Notre Dame Press.

Reed, Michael C. 1987. "Gabon: A Neo-colonial Enclave of Enduring French Interest." *Journal of Modern African Studies* 25(2): 283–320.

Reinsch, Paul S. 1901. "French Experience with Representative Government in the West Indies." *American Historical Review* 6: 475–97.

Reno, William. 1995. *Corruption and State Politics in Sierra Leone.* New York: Cambridge University Press.

Reynolds, Andrew. 1999. "Sierra Leone." In Dieter Nohlen, Michael Krennerich, and Berhard Thibaud (eds.), *Elections in Africa: A Data Handbook,* 789–802. Oxford: Oxford University Press.

Ribeiro Torres, J. L. 1973. "Race Relations in Moçambique." *Zambezia* 3(1): 39–52.

Richards, Paul. 2005. "To Fight or to Farm? Agrarian Dimensions of the Mano River Conflicts, Liberia and Sierra Leone." *African Affairs* 104(417): 571–90.

Ricklefs, Merle. 2001. *A History of Modern Indonesia since c. 1200.* Stanford, CA: Stanford University Press.

Riley, James C. 2005. *Poverty and Life Expectancy: The Jamaican Paradox.* Cambridge: Cambridge University Press.

Robbers, Gerhard. 2006. *Encyclopedia of World Constitutions*. New York: Fact on File.

Robinson, David. 1988. "French 'Islamic' Policy and Practice in Late Nineteenth-Century Senegal." *Journal of African History* 29(3): 415–35.

Robinson, David. 1999. "The Murids: Surveillance and Collaboration." *Journal of African History* 40(2): 193–213.

Rodney, Walter. 1981. *How Europe Underdeveloped Africa*. Rev. ed. Washington, DC: Howard University Press.

Ross, Michael. 2001. "Does Oil Hinder Democracy?" *World Politics* 53(3): 325–61.

Rudebeck, Lars. 1972. "Political Mobilization for Development in Guinea-Bissau." *Journal of Modern African Studies* 10(1): 1–18.

Rudebeck, Lars. 1974. *Guinea-Bissau: A Study of Political Mobilization*. Uppsala: Scandinavian Institute of African Studies.

Rueschemeyer, Dietrich, John D. Stephens, and Evelyn H. Stephens. 1992. *Capitalist Development and Democracy*. Chicago: University of Chicago Press.

Sablé, Victor. 1955. *La transformation des Isles d'Amérique en departements français*. Paris: Editions Larose.

Sachs, Jeffrey. 2005. *The End of Poverty: Economic Possibilities for Our Time*. New York: Penguin.

Sachs, Jeffrey, and Mark Warner. 1997. "Sources of Slow Growth in Africa Economies." *Journal of African Economies* 6(3): 335–76.

Safford, Frank. 2014. "The Construction of National States in Latin America, 1820–1980." In Miguel A. Centeno and Augstin E. Ferraro (eds.), *State and Nation Making in Latin America and Spain: Republics of the Possible*, 25–55. Princeton: Princeton University Press.

Samaroo, Brinsley. 2011. "The Immigrant Communities." In K. O. Lawrence (ed.), *General History of the Caribbean*, vol. 4, *The Long Nineteenth Century,* 223–58. Paris: UNESCO Publishing.

Sanborn, Howard, and Clayton Thyne. 2013. "Learning Democracy: Education and the Fall of Authoritarian Regimes." *British Journal of Political Science* 44(4): 773–97.

Sartori, Giovanni. 1970. "Concept Misformation in Comparative Politics." *American Political Science Review* 64(4): 1033–53.

Satchell, Veront M. 1990. *From Plots to Plantations: Land Transactions in Jamaica, 1866–1900*. Mona, Jamaica: Institute of Social and Economic Research, University of the West Indies.

Sawyer, Edward. 2008. "Remove or Reform: A Case for (Restructuring) Chiefdom Governance in Post-conflict Sierra Leone." *African Affairs* 107(428): 387–403.

Saye, Lisa Macha. 2010. "The Haitian State: Something Alien." *Journal of Third World Studies* 27(2): 71–88.

Schmidt, Nelly. 2003. "The Drafting of the 1848 Decrees: Immediate Application and Long-Term Consequences." In Marcel Dorigny (ed.), *The Abolitions of Slavery: From L.F. Sonthonax to Victor Schoelcher, 1793, 1794, 1848,* 305–13. New York: Berghahn Books.

Schoelcher, Victor. 1998. *Des colonies françaises: Abolition immediate de l'esclavage*. 1842; reprint Paris: Éditions du C.T.H.S.

Sedoc-Dahlberg. 1990. *The Dutch Caribbean: Prospects for Democracy*. New York: Gordon & Breach.

Seibert, Gerhard. 2006. *Clients, Comrades, and Cousins: Colonialism, Socialism, and Democratization in São Tomé & Principe*. Leiden: Brill.

Seibert, Gerhard. 2012. "Creolization and Creole Communities in the Portuguese Atlanic: São Tomé, Cape Verde, the Rivers of Guinea and Central Africa in Comparison." In Toby Green (ed.), *Brokers of Change: Atlantic Commerce and Cultures in Pre-Colonial Western Africa*, 29–51. Oxford: Oxford University Press.

Seibert, Gerhard. 2014. "Crioulização em Cabo Verde e São Tomé e Principe: Divergências Históricas e Identitárias." *Afro-Asia* 49: 41–70.

Sen, Amartya. 1999. *Development as Freedom*. New York: Anchor Books.

Sheller, Mimi. 2000. *Democracy after Slavery: Black Publics and Peasant Radicalism in Haiti and Jamaica*. Gainesville: University of Florida Press.

Sherlock, Philip, and Hazel Bennett. 1998. *The Story of the Jamaican People*. Kingston, Jamaica: Ian Randle; Princeton, NJ: Markus Wiener.

Sierra Leone [Colony of]. 1838. *Sierra Leone Blue Book, 1838*. UK National Archives, CO 272/15.

Sierra Leone [Colony of]. 1851. *Sierra Leone Blue Book, 1851*. UK National Archives, CO 272/28.

Sierra Leone [Colony of]. 1865. *Sierra Leone Blue Book, 1865*. UK National Archives, CO 272/42.

Sierra Leone [Colony of]. 1884. *Sierra Leone Blue Book, 1884*. UK National Archives, CO 272/61.

Sierra Leone [Colony of]. 1901. *Sierra Leone Blue Book, 1901*. UK National Archives, CO 272/78.

Sierra Leone [Colony of]. 1914. *Sierra Leone Blue Book, 1913*. UK National Archives, CO 272/90.

Sierra Leone [Colony of]. 1928. *Sierra Leone Blue Book, 1928*. UK National Archives, CO 272/105.

Sierra Leone [Colony of]. 1939. *Annual Report of the Provincial Administration for the Year 1936(-38)*. Freetown: Government Printer.

Sierra Leone [Colony of]. 1943. *Sierra Leone Blue Book, 1943*. UK National Archives, CO 272/120.

Sierra Leone [Colony of]. 1947. *Annual Report for Sierra Leone, 1946*. London: Her Majesty's Stationery Office.

Sierra Leone [Colony of]. 1953. *Colonial Office Report on Sierra Leone for the Year 1952*. London: Her Majesty's Stationery Office.

Sierra Leone [Colony of]. 1955. *Annual Report for Sierra Leone, 1954*. London: Her Majesty's Stationery Office.

Sierra Leone. 1960. *Colonial Office Report on Sierra Leone for the Year 1958*. London: Her Majesty's Stationery Office.

Silva Andrade, Elisa. 2002. "Cape Verde." In Patrick Chabal (ed.), *A History of Postcolonial Lusophone Africa*, 264–90. Bloomington: Indiana University Press.

Silva Cunha, J. M. da. 1949. *O Trabalho Indígena: Estudo de Direito Colonial*. Lisbon: Agência Geral das Colónias.

Sires, Ronald V. 1942. "The Jamaica Slave Insurrection Loan." *Journal of Negro History* 27(3): 295–319.

Sives, Amanda. 2010. *Elections, Violence and the Democratic Process in Jamaica, 1944–2007*. Kingston, Jamaica: Ian Randle.

Smith, Andrea. 2006. *Colonial Memory and Post-colonial Europe: Maltese Settlers in Algeria and France*. Bloomington: Indiana University Press.

Smith, James P. 1994. "The Liberals, Race, and Political Reform in the British West Indies." *Journal of Negro History* 79(2): 131–46.

Smith, Matthew G. 2014. *Liberty, Fraternity, Exile: Haiti and Jamaica after Emancipation*. Chapel Hill: University of North Carolina Press.

Smith, Michael G. 1965. *The Plural Society in the British West Indies*. Berkeley: University of California Press.

Smith, Tony. 1974. "Muslim Impoverishment in Colonial Algeria." *Revue de l'Occident Musulman et de la Méditerranée* 17: 139–62.

Smith, Tony. 1975. "The French Economic Stake in Colonial Algeria." *French Historical Studies* 9(1): 184–89.

So'O, Asofou, and Jon Fraenkel. 2005. "The Role of Ballot Chiefs (Matai Pälota) and Political Parties in Samoa's Shift to Universal Suffrage." *Commonwealth and Comparative Politics* 43(3): 333–61.

Soares, Rodrigo, Juliano Assunção, and Tomás Goulart. 2012. "A Note on Slavery and the Roots of Inequality." *Journal of Comparative Economics* 40(4): 565–80.

Sokoloff, Kenneth L., and Stanley L. Engerman. 2000. "History Lessons: Institutions, Factor Endowments, and Paths of Development in the New World." *Journal of Economic Perspectives* 14(3): 217–32.

Sokoloff, Kenneth L., and Stanley L. Engerman. 2006. "Colonialism, Inequality, and Long-Run Paths of Development." In Abhijit Vinayak Banerjee, Roland Bénabou, and Dilip Mookherjee (eds.), *Understanding Poverty*, 37–62. Oxford: Oxford University Press.

Sperling, Dan. 2017. "In 1825, Haiti Paid France $21 Billion to Preserve its Independence— Time for France to Pay It Back." *Forbes,* December 6, https://www.forbes.com/sites/realspin/2017/12/06/in-1825-haiti-gained-independence-from-france-for-21-billion-its-time-for-france-to-pay-it-back/?sh=5add20f6312b. Accessed December 1, 2022.

Spitzer, Leo. 1974. *The Creoles of Sierra Leone: Responses to Colonialism, 1870–1945*. Madison: University of Wisconsin Press.

Stamatov, Peter. 2010. "Activist Religion, Empire, and the Emergence of Modern Long-Distance Advocacy Networks." *American Sociological Review* 75(4): 607–28.

Stepan, Alfred. 2000. "Religion, Democracy, and the 'Twin Tolerations.'" *Journal of Democracy* 11(4): 37–57.

Stepan, Alfred. 2012. "Rituals of Respect: Sufis and Secularists in Senegal in Comparative Perspective." *Comparative Politics* 44(4): 379–401.

Stepan, Alfred, Juan Linz, and Yogendra Yadav. 2011. *Crafting State-Nations: India and Other Multinational Democracies*. Baltimore: The Johns Hopkins University Press.

Stephens, John D., and Evelyn Huber Stephens. 1986. *Democratic Socialism in Jamaica: The Political Movement and Social Transformation in Dependent Capitalism*. Princeton, NJ: Princeton University Press.

Stewart, Charles. 2007. "Creolization: History, Ethnography, Theory." In Charles Stewart (ed.), *Creolization: History, Ethnography, Theory*, 1–25. Walnut Creek, CA: Left Coast Press.

Stinchcombe, Arthur L. 1994. "Class, Conflict and Diplomacy: Haitian Isolation in the Nineteenth Century World System." *Sociological Perspectives* 37(1): 1–23.

Stinchcombe, Arthur L. 1995. *Sugar Island Slavery in the Age of Enlightenment: The Political Economy of the Caribbean World*. Princeton, NJ: Princeton University Press.

Stone, Carl. 1986. *Class, State, and Democracy in Jamaica*. New York: Praeger.

Sumner, D. L. 1963. *Education in Sierra Leone*. Freetown: Government of Sierra Leone.

Tavares de Almeida, Pedro. 2010. "Elections in Portugal." In Dieter Nohlen and Philip Stover (eds.), *Elections in Europe: A Data Handbook*, 1525–77. Baden-Baden, Germany: Nomos.

Tavares de Almeida, Pedro. 2011. "Elections, Voting, and Representatives." In Fernando Cartoga and Pedro Tavares de Almeida (eds.), *Res Publica: Citizenship and Political Representation in Portugal, 1820–1926*, 60–89. Lisbon: Assambleia da República; Biblioteca Nacional de Portugal.

Teichman, Judith. 2011. "Mexico: From Perfect Dictatorship to Imperfect Democracy." In Katherine Isbester (ed.), *The Paradox of Democracy in Latin America: Ten Country Studies of Division and Resilience*, 105–29. Toronto: University of Toronto Press.

Teixeira da Mota, A. 1954. *Guiné Portuguesa*. Lisbon: Agencia Geral do Ultramar.

Teorrell, Jan, and Axel Hadenius. 2009. "Elections as Levers of Democratization." In Staffan Lindberg (ed.), *Democratization by Elections: A New Mode of Transition*, 77–100. Baltimore: Johns Hopkins University Press.

Tibendenara, Peter K. 1983. "The Emirs and the Spread of Western Education in Northern Nigeria, 1910–1946." *Journal of African History* 24(4): 517–34.

Tilly, Charles. 1975. "Reflections on the History of European Statemaking." In Charles Tilly (ed.), *The Formation of National States in Western Europe*, 3–83. Princeton, NJ: Princeton University Press.

Tinker, Hugh. 1974. *A New System of Slavery: The Export of Indian Labour Overseas, 1830–1920*. London: Institute of Race Relations, Oxford University.

Trading Economics. 2021a. Brazil GDP per capita PPP. https://tradingeconomics.com/brazil/gdp-per-capita-ppp. Accessed November 30, 2021.

Trading Economics. 2021b. South Africa GDP per capita PPP. https://tradingeconomics.com/south-africa/gdp-per-capita-ppp. Accessed November 30, 2021.

Trading Economics. 2021c. Brazil Unemployment Rate. https://tradingeconomics.com/brazil/unemployment-rate. Accessed November 30, 2021.

Trading Economics. 2021d. South Africa Unemployment Rate. https://tradingeconomics.com/south-africa/unemployment-rate. Accessed November 30, 2021.

Tusalem, Rollin F. 2009. "The Role of Protestantism in Democratic Consolidation among Transitional States." *Comparative Political Studies* 42(7): 882–915.

Ulsaner, Eric, and Bo Rothstein. 2016. "The Historical Roots of Corruption: State-Building, Economic Inequality and Mass Education." *Comparative Politics* 48(2): 227–48.

United Nations. 1963. *Compendium of Social Statistics*. New York: United Nations.

United Nations. 1967. *Compendium of Social Statistics*. New York: United Nations.

United Nations. 1980. *Compendium of Social Statistics, 1977*. New York: United Nations.

United Nations. 2016. *UN Data: A World of Information*. New York: United Nations. http://data.un.org/.

United Nations. 2017. *World Population Prospects*. New York: United Nations. http://data.un.org/Explorer.aspx. Accessed March 15, 2017.

United Nations. 2019. *World Population Prospects: The 2019 Revision*. New York: United Nations. http://data.un.org/Explorer.aspx. Accessed June 3, 2020.

United Nations Development Program. 2016. *Human Development Index and its Components, 2015*. http://hdr.undp.org/en/composite/HDI. Accessed February 10, 2017.

United Nations Development Program. 2019. *Human Development Index Trends, 1990–2017*, http://hdr.undp.org/en/composite/trends. Accessed June 16, 2020.

United States, Department of Health and Human Services. 2015. *National Vital Statistics Report*, 63(6): 1–120.

United States, Department of State. 2009. *Purchase of the Virgin Islands, 1917.* https://2001-2009.state.gov/r/pa/ho/time/wwi/107293.htm#:~:text=Formal%20transfer%20of%20the%20islands,U.S.%20citizenship%20were%20not%20conferred. Accessed December 2, 2022.

Vale de Almeida, Miguel. 2008. "Portugal's Colonial Complex: From Colonial Lusotropicalism to Postcolonial Lusophony." Paper presented at the Queen's Postcolonial Research Forum, Queen's University, Belfast, April 28.

Valelly, Richard. 2004. *The Two Reconstructions: The Struggle for Black Enfranchisement.* Chicago: University of Chicago Press.

Valeris, Rebb. 2013. "The Great Leap Backward: Exploring the Differences in Developmental Paths between the Dominican Republic and Haiti." Honor's thesis, University of Central Florida. http://stars.library.ucf.edu/honorstheses1990-2015/1512.

Varghese, Ajay (2016). *The Colonial Origins of Ethnic Violence in India.* Stanford, CA: Stanford University Press.

Varshney, Ashutosh. 1997. "Postmodernism, Civic Engagement, and Ethnic Conflict: A Passage to India." *Comparative Politics* 30(1): 1–20.

Veiga, Carlos. 2007. "Estado de Direito e Democracia em Cabo Verde Trinta Anos Depois." In Jorge Carlos Fonseca (ed.), *Cabo Verde: Três Décadas Depois,* 31–54. Praia: Direito e Cidadania.

Walker, Iain. 2019. *Islands in a Cosmopolitan Sea: A History of the Comoros.* New York: Oxford University Press.

Wallace, Elisabeth. 1977. *The British Caribbean: From the Decline of Colonialism to the End of the Federation.* Toronto: University of Toronto Press.

Wantchekon, Leonard, Natalija Notva and Marko Klansja. 2015. "Education and Human Capital Externalities: Evidence from Colonial Benin." *Quarterly Journal of Economics* 130(2): 703–57.

Watson, Hilbourne A. 2013. "Transnational Capitalist Globalization and the Limits of Sovereignty: State, Security, Order, Violence, and the Caribbean." In Linden Lewis (ed.), *Caribbean Sovereignty, Development, and Democracy in an Age of Globalization,* 33–67. New York: Routledge.

Weber, Eugene. 1976. *Peasants into Frenchmen: The Modernization of Rural France, 1870–1914.* Stanford, CA: Stanford University Press.

Weber, Max. 1978. *Economy and Society: An Outline of Interpretive Sociology.* Edited by Guenther Roth and Claus Wittich. Berkeley: University of California Press.

Weber, Max. 2001. *The Protestant Ethic and the Spirit of Capitalism.* Translated by Stephen Kalberg. Chicago: Fitzroy Dearborn.

Weiner, Myron. 1987. "Empirical Democratic Theory." In Myron Weiner and Ergun Ozbudun (eds.), *Competitive Elections in Developing Countries,* 3–34. Durham, N.C.: Duke University Press.

Weisbrot, David. 1981. "Customizing the Common Law: The True Papua New Guinea Experience." *American Bar Association Journal* 67(6): 727–31.

Welborn, Max. 1969. "Victor Schoelcher: A Superior Breed of Abolitionist." *The Journal of Negro History* 54(2): 93–108.

Wesley, Charles H. 1932. "The Rise of Negro Education in the British Empire—I." *Journal of Negro Education* 1(3–4): 354–66.

Wesley, Charles H. 1933. "The Rise of Negro Education in the British Empire—II." *Journal of Negro Education* 2(1): 68–82.

Wesley, Charles H. 1934. "The Emancipation of the Free Colored Population in the British Empire." *Journal of Negro History* 19(2): 137–70.

Wesley, Charles H. 1938. "The Abolition of Negro Apprenticeship in the British Empire." *Journal of Negro History* 23(2): 155–99.

Whitaker, Paul M. 1970. "The Revolutions of 'Portuguese' Africa." *Journal of Modern African Studies* 8(1): 15–35.

White, Carmen M. 2003. "Historicizing Educational Disparity: Colonial Policy and Fijian Educational Attainment." *History of Education* 32(4): 345–65.

Whyte, Christine H. 2008. "School's Out: Strategies of Resistance in Colonial Sierra Leone." *Resistance Studies Magazine* 2: 81–91.

Wietzke, Frank-Borge. 2014. "Long-Term Consequences of Colonial Institutions and Human Capital Investments: Sub-national Evidence from Madagascar." *World Development* 66(2): 293–307.

Wikipedia. 2016. "List of Countries by Human Development Index." https://en.wikipedia.org/wiki/List_of_countries_by_Human_Development_Index. Accessed July 5, 2017.

Williams, Eric. 1941. "The Impact of the International Crisis upon the Negro in the Caribbean." *Journal of Negro Education* 10(3): 536–44.

Williams, Eric. 1994. *Capitalism & Slavery*. Chapel Hill: University of North Carolina Press.

Wimmer, Andreas. 2018. *Nation-Building: Why Some Countries Come Together While Others Fall Apart*. Princeton, NJ: Princeton University Press.

Winnacker, Rudolph. 1938. "Elections in Algeria and the French Colonies under the Third Republic." *American Political Science Review* 32(2), 261–77.

Wood, Peter H. 1974. *Black Majority: Negroes in Colonial South Carolina from 1670 through the Stono Rebellion*. New York: Norton.

Woodberry, Robert D. 2004. "The Shadow of Empire: Christian Missions, Colonial Policy and Democracy in Postcolonial Societies." PhD dissertation, University of North Carolina.

Woodberry, Robert D. 2012. "The Missionary Roots of Liberal Democracy." *American Political Science Review* 106(2): 244–74.

Woodberry, Robert D., Juan Carlos Esparza Ochoa, Reid Porter, and Xiaoyun Lu. 2010. "Conceptual Framework and Technical Innovations for Creating the Project on Religion and Economic Change Geo-spatial Database." Project on Religion and Economic Change Working Paper No. 004.

Woodward, J. David. 2013. *The New Southern Politics*. Boulder, CO: Lynne Rienner.

World Bank. 2016. *World Wide Governance Indicators*. Washington, DC: The World Bank. https://info.worldbank.org/governance/wgi/. Accessed June 1, 2017.

Wright, Ernest. 1976. *French Politics in the West Indies: A Study of the Assimilation Policy in the History of Martinique and Guadeloupe, 1789–1900*. PhD dissertation, Howard University.

Wrong, Hume. 1923. *Government of the West Indies*. Oxford: Oxford University Press.

Wucherpfenning, Julian, Philipp Hunziker and Lars-Erik Cederman. 2016. "Who Inherits the State? Colonial Rule and Postcolonial Conflict." *American Journal of Political Science* 60(4): 882–98.

Wyse, Akintola. 1991. *The Krio of Sierra Leone: An Interpretive History*. Washington, DC: Howard University Press.

Yelvington, Kelvin, Jean-Pierre Sainton, Michel Hector, and Jean Casimir. 2011. "Caribbean Social Structure in the Nineteenth Century." In K. O. Lawrence (ed.),

General History of the Caribbean, vol. 4, *The Long Nineteenth Century*, 283-333. Paris: UNESCO Publishing.

Young, Crawford. 1965. *Politics in the Congo: Decolonization and Independence*. Princeton, NJ: Princeton University Press.

Young, Crawford. 1994. *The African Colonial State in Comparative Perspective*. New Haven: Yale University Press.

Index